AN INTRODUCTION TO
THE PHILOSOPHY OF RELIGION

For Peter Geach and James Sadowsky

And in memory of Elizabeth Anscombe (1919–2001)
and Gareth Moore (1948–2002)

AN INTRODUCTION TO
THE PHILOSOPHY
OF RELIGION

Third Edition

BRIAN DAVIES

OXFORD
UNIVERSITY PRESS

OXFORD

UNIVERSITY PRESS

Great Clarendon Street, Oxford ox2 6dp

Oxford University Press is a department of the University of Oxford.
It furthers the University's objective of excellence in research, scholarship,
and education by publishing worldwide in

Oxford New York

Auckland Cape Town Dar es Salaam Hong Kong Karachi
Kuala Lumpur Madrid Melbourne Mexico City Nairobi
New Delhi Shanghai Taipei Toronto

With offices in

Argentina Austria Brazil Chile Czech Republic France Greece
Guatemala Hungary Italy Japan Poland Portugal Singapore
South Korea Switzerland Thailand Turkey Ukraine Vietnam

Oxford is a registered trade mark of Oxford University Press
in the UK and in certain other countries

Published in the United States
by Oxford University Press Inc., New York

First published 1982 as an Oxford University Press paperback
and simultaneously in a hardback edition
Second edition first published 1993 as an Oxford University Press paperback
and simultaneously published in a hardback edition
This new edition first published 2004 as an Oxford University Press paperback

British Library Cataloguing in Publication Data
Data available

Library of Congress Cataloging in Publication Data
Data available

ISBN 978–0–19–926347–9

16

Typeset in Meridien
by RefineCatch Limited, Bungay, Suffolk
Printed in Great Britain
by Ashford Colour Press Ltd, Gosport, Hants

CONTENTS

ACKNOWLEDGEMENTS

A number of people have been kind enough to comment on material which has found its way into this book. In particular, I must thank Christopher Arroyo, Sarah Dancy (who did an expert copy-editing job on my text), Antony Flew, Peter Geach, W. Matthews Grant, John Greco, Peter Groves, Paul Helm, Brian Leftow, Anthony Lisska, David McNaughton, Hugo Meynell, Howard Mounce, Sara Penella, David Reed, Alan Ryan, James Sadowsky, Stephen Salter, Richard Swinburne, Charles Taliaferro, Simon Tugwell, Margaret Walker, Kathy Wilkes, Timothy Wright, Charles Wrightington, and Mark Wynn. None of these individuals should be taken as agreeing with the content of the book as it stands. But I think that they have helped to make it a better text than it would have been without their advice. And I must say the same with respect to five recently deceased friends who also assisted at various times: Elizabeth Anscombe, Herbert McCabe, Gareth Moore, H. P. Owen, and C. J. F. Williams. I shall always be grateful for their intelligence and for their great generosity to me.

Brian Davies
Fordham University
New York

INTRODUCTION

It is difficult to say what the philosophy of religion is. One might define it as 'philosophizing about religion'. But people disagree when it comes to what philosophy is. They also disagree about the meaning of the word 'religion'. Philosophy of religion is a recognized branch of philosophy. Yet it would be rash to conclude that we can quickly explain its nature.

In this book, I do not attempt the perilous task of defining 'philosophy of religion'. Instead, my intention is to offer an introductory look at some of the topics traditionally thought to fall within its scope. The most prominent of these is the existence of God. So much of what follows is devoted to that issue and to matters related to it. I also focus on morality and religion, the concept of miracle, and the notion of life after death. It is hard to discuss any philosophical issue without taking sides. But I have tried to write so as to help you to adopt some positions of your own. I have also tried to write on the assumption that you have no philosophical background. This book is aimed at people approaching philosophy of religion for the first time. Its advice on further reading, and its suggested questions for discussion, will, I hope, allow you to take matters further for yourselves.

A great deal more than I discuss could be brought in under the heading of philosophy of religion. There are, for example, matters arising from the comparative study of religions, from various beliefs peculiar to specific religions, and from recent developments in postmodernist and feminist thinking. But a complete treatise on the philosophy of religion would be long and complicated, and space is limited in an introduction. In any case, one has to start somewhere, and the purpose of this introduction is to do just that.

What follows is the third edition of a text published by Oxford University Press in 1982 and substantially revised in 1993. When asked to provide a new version of the 1993 text, I originally thought that I could do so by making only a few changes. But I have effectively ended up writing a new book. The present work contains chapters on topics largely ignored in the 1993 edition (Chapters 1, 8, and 9). And those chapters which deal with topics discussed in the earlier volume all have significantly different texts. As was not the case with the 1993 book, each chapter in the present one also comes with detailed advice on further reading and with questions for discussion. Those who wish to read the present work together with some important primary sources might care to consult my *Philosophy of Religion: A Guide and Anthology* (Oxford University Press, 2000), a volume to which the present one serves as a suitable companion, and vice versa.

I am grateful to Angela Griffin, Ruth Anderson, and Oxford University Press for inviting me to provide this new edition and for their patience in waiting for the finished product. In what follows, I have tried to avoid gender-specific reference to God. In some instances, however, I have used 'he'/'his' simply to avoid awkwardness in wording. I should add that all biblical quotations come from the Revised Standard Version of the Bible.

1
CONCEPTS OF GOD

Much philosophy of religion focuses on the topic of God. All through the centuries philosophers have asked whether there is reason to believe that God exists. They have also considered what, if anything, can be known of God's nature. But what should we take the word 'God' to mean? You might find this question puzzling. You might say: 'We all know what "God" means. What we need to ask is "Does God exist?" and "What can we know about him?".' Yet are matters as simple as that?

Unfortunately, they are not. And anyone starting work on philosophy of religion should be aware of this fact at the outset. For those who say that they believe in God often disagree in their respective accounts of God. The word 'God' has been understood in different ways even by those who subscribe to belief in what the *Oxford English Dictionary* calls its 'specific Christian and monotheistic sense'.

'Monotheistic' is the adjectival form of the noun 'monotheism', which means 'belief that there is only one God'. And the *Oxford English Dictionary* is clearly thinking of belief in God as professed by Jews, Muslims, and Christians, all of whom declare that there is but one, true God. Yet there is substantial disagreement about what God is even among Jewish, Islamic, and Christian monotheists. So, when you hear Jews, Muslims, and Christians using the word 'God', you should not assume that they all understand it in the same sense. You should not even assume this when confining your attention to one of these groups.

Among philosophers of religion, God is typically taken to be the God of monotheism (or theism, for short). And I shall now fall in with this line of thinking. From this point on I take 'God' to mean 'the God of Judaism, Islam, and Christianity'. As I have said, however, this still leaves us with a problem of understanding. So now I shall try to explain why. It is not easy to do so, but to simplify matters, I shall begin by saying that monotheism or theism can be divided into at least two approaches to God. For reasons which should soon be obvious, I shall call them 'classical theism' and 'theistic personalism'.

Classical Theism

Classical theism is what you can find endorsed in the writings of people like the Jewish author Moses Maimonides (1135–1204), the Islamic author Avicenna (980–1037), and the Christian author Thomas Aquinas (1224/6–74).[1] Classical theism is what all Jews, Christians, and Muslims believed in for many centuries (officially, at least). And numerous philosophers have taken it for granted that God is as defenders of classical theism take him to be. From the time of St Augustine of Hippo (354–430)[2] to that of G. W. Leibniz (1646–1716),[3] philosophers almost always worked on the assumption that belief in God is belief in classical theism. And their understanding has been shared by many theologians. The major tenets of classical theism are part of the official teaching of the Roman Catholic Church. They were also taught by most of the major sixteenth-century Protestant reformers and by heirs of theirs, such as Jonathan Edwards, the famous eighteenth-century American Puritan divine.

But what does classical theism amount to? Central to it is a particular approach to the doctrine of creation, according to which everything other than God somehow depends on God causally. All theists accept this doctrine in some form. For classical theism, however, it has a particular meaning.

(a) Classical theism and the doctrine of Creation

According to classical theism, God is primarily the Creator. God is what accounts for there being any world at all. He is causally responsible for the existence of everything other than himself. More specifically, God, for classical theism, is the one (and the only one) who creates 'from nothing' (*ex nihilo* in the traditional Latin phrase). The idea here is not that God works on something called 'Nothing' in order to create. Classical theism's claim is that God makes things to be without there being anything prior to his creative act save himself. He makes to be, but not *out of* anything.

According to classical theism, for God to create is for God to make it to be that something simply exists. Artists make it to be that there is a work of art. Surgeons make it to be that someone's insides get modified. Nuclear explosions make it to be that landscapes are rearranged. According to classical theism, however, God makes it to be that things are just *there* regardless of what they are *like* (although he is also responsible for that). He accounts for there being something rather than *nothing*. Many people think that to say that God has created is just to say that God brought it about that the universe *began* to exist. Although classical theists typically agree that the universe began to exist, and although they hold that it was God who brought this about, they also typically say that belief in God as Creator is not just belief in God's past activity. For classical theists, God's creative work is just as much present in the continued existence of you and me as it was in the origin of the universe.

In the thirteenth century there was a great debate about 'the eternity of the world'. Some philosophers and theologians said that it can be proved that the world had a beginning. Others denied this. Thomas Aquinas, although he believed that the world had a beginning, conceded that this belief of his could not be shown to be true by philosophical reasoning. But he also argued that whether or not the world had a beginning is irrelevant to the doctrine of creation. He said that to believe that the world is created is chiefly to believe that its being there at all and at any time is God's doing. And this conclusion is very characteristic of classical theism. According to this, all creatures depend on God for their sheer existence. And God is as much the creator of things which *continue* to exist as he is of those which *begin* to exist, regardless of when they happen to do so. In terms of classical theism, God is both the initiating and the constantly sustaining cause of the universe and all it contains.

If this account is true, then everything other than God is totally dependent on God for its existing and for its being as it is. Not surprisingly, therefore, classical theists commonly stress God's intimate presence to creatures. For them, God is everywhere since he is making everything that exists to be what it is for as long as it exists.[4] For classical theists, God is not everywhere by being physically located in all places. But he is everywhere as causing the existence of all places. According to classical theism, God is always everywhere, always present to creatures. And this, among other things, means that God cannot, strictly speaking, intervene in his created order. For to intervene is to step into a place or situation where one was not present to start with. According to the *Oxford English Dictionary*, it is to 'come in as something extraneous'. Yet classical theists hold that God is always present and never comes in as something extraneous. Some people would say that God can intervene so as to bring it about that changes occur in the world. On the classical theist's account, however, such changes cannot be literally thought of as divine interventions since they and what preceded them are equally the creative work of God.[5] As one classical theist puts it:

> It is clear that God cannot *interfere* in the universe, not because he has not the power but because, so to speak, he has too much. To interfere you have to be an alternative to, or alongside, what you are interfering with. If God is the cause of everything, there is nothing that he is alongside. Obviously, God makes no difference to the universe. I mean by this that we do not appeal specifically to God to explain why the universe is this way rather than that. For this we need only appeal to explanations within the universe ... What God accounts for is that the universe is there instead of nothing.[6]

You cannot intervene in what you are doing yourself. And, say classical theists, God cannot literally intervene in his own created order. Sometimes they make this point by claiming that for God to create is not for him to effect any change. Something can be changed only if it pre-exists the activity of a changer. But, asks the classical theist, what can pre-exist the activity of God the Creator?

(b) Classical theism and the nature of God

The classical theist's answer to that last question is, as you might now suspect, 'Nothing'. Or, as Aquinas writes:

> We must consider not only the emanation of a particular being from a particular agent, but also the emanation of all being from the universal cause, which is God; and this emanation we designate by the name of creation. Now what proceeds by particular emanation is not presupposed to that emanation; as when a man is generated, he was not before, but man is made

from *not-man*, and white from *not-white*. Hence, if the emanation of the whole universal being from the first principle be considered, it is impossible that any being should be presupposed before this emanation. For nothing is the same as no being. Therefore, as the generation of a man is from the *not-being* which is *not-man*, so creation, which is the emanation of all being, is from the *not-being* which is *nothing*.[7]

And this answer has further implications for those who subscribe to classical theism. One is that nothing created can cause God to change or be modified in any way. In terms of classical theism, there is no causality from creatures to God since creatures are wholly God's effects. Parents can act causally on their children. And children can act causally on their parents. But that is so because they belong to the same world as each other and because neither parents nor children owe all that they are to each other. According to classical theism, however, creatures constantly owe all that they are to God, and any causal activity of theirs is, first and foremost, God's causal activity in them. Many classical theists make this point by insisting that God is impassible.

In this context 'impassible' does not mean 'callous', 'heartless', or 'indifferent'. It means 'not able to be causally modified by an external agent'. And for most classical theists the claim that God is impassible goes hand in hand with the teaching that God is immutable. The idea here is twofold: (1) God cannot be altered by anything a creature does, and (2) God is intrinsically unchangeable. Why intrinsically unchangeable? For classical theists, the answer lies in their understanding of what is involved in God creating. On their account, all change is the coming to be of something new. And yet, so they reason, all coming to be of something new is God's doing, which means that God himself cannot change without being a creature, something whose way of being at a given time is derived from another.

For many classical theists, this idea also suggests that God is outside time. Many philosophers have thought that change and time go together, since (a) anything undergoing change is also temporal, and (b) anything wholly changeless and unchangeable is distinct from time. Classical theists frequently share this view and often, therefore, speak of God being timeless (or eternal). According, for instance, to St Anselm of Canterbury (1033–1109):

All that is enclosed in any way by place or time is less than that which no law of place or time constrains. Since, then, nothing is greater that You [sc. God], no place or time confines You but You exist everywhere and always . . . You were not, therefore, yesterday, nor will You be tomorrow, but yesterday and today and tomorrow You *are*. Indeed You exist neither yesterday nor today nor tomorrow but are absolutely outside all time. For yesterday and today and tomorrow are completely in time; however, You, though nothing can be without You, are nevertheless not in place or time but all things are in You. For nothing contains You, but You contain all things.[8]

The Bible tells us that God delivered (past tense) the Israelites from Egypt. And it says that God will come (future tense) to judge the living and the dead. One might instinctively read such assertions as mapping God's progress through time. For classical theists, however, God exists at no particular time (and therefore neither existed at some instant in the past nor will exist at some instant of time in the future). In their view, tenses applied to God's activity should be understood as helping us to date created events (like the escape of the Israelites from Egypt or the state of those judged by God in the future). They should not be construed as locating God in time. The idea here is that God can act so as to bring about dateable events without himself being part of any temporal process. Or, as Aquinas observes:

Since God is altogether outside the order of creatures, since they are ordered to him but not he to them, it is clear that being related to God is a reality in creatures, but being related to creatures is not a reality in God. We say it about him because of the real relation in creatures. So it is that, when we speak of his relation to creatures, we can apply words implying temporal sequence and change, not because of any change in him but because of a change in the creatures; just as we can say that a pillar has changed from being on my left to being on my right, not through any alteration in the pillar but simply because I have turned round.[9]

If all that is so, however, God must be vastly different from anything with which we are acquainted. Yet classical theists embrace that implication. For them, we must sharply distinguish between God and everything else. Things in the world are subject to the causal activity of other things in the world. But, says the classical theist, God is not so subject. Things in the world are either changing or able to undergo change. According to classical theism, however, God is unchangeable. Everything in the world exists at some time. According to classical theism, however, God transcends time.

For classical theism, we get things badly wrong if we take God to be something we can picture or get our minds around. 'I would be surprised', says Anselm, 'if we could find anything from among the nouns and verbs which we apply to things created from nothing that could worthily be said of the substance that created all.'[10] Classical theists happily agree that God may be compared to things that we know. They also agree that he can be truly described using words which we employ when speaking of what is not divine. They hold, for example, that God truly acts, causes, moves, knows, wills, and loves. Yet classical theists also typically insist that none of this means that we therefore have a grasp of God or a concept which allows us to say that we understand what God is.

This fact partly emerges from the way in which classical theists often characterize God in negative terms (as *not* created, *not* passive, *not* changeable, or *not* temporal). But it also comes out in the fact that classical theists tend to deny that words used to characterize God mean what they do when applied to what is not divine. Hence, for example, although they agree that God acts, causes, and moves, classical theists do not think that he does so as part of a world in which other things act, cause, and move. For them, God's action, causation, and movement of things are in a class of their own. And, they hold, the same is true of God's knowing, willing, and loving.

When we think of knowledge, will, and love, we are normally thinking of people. It is people we look to in the first place when trying to explain what 'knowledge', 'will', and 'love' mean. According to classical theism, however, knowledge, will, and love are different in God from what they are in people. People, for instance, know because they have learned. But, says the classical theist, to learn is to change and God cannot learn since he is changeless. People come to know because of being taught or because of what they have observed by means of their senses or discovered by means of empirical investigation. But, says the classical theist, God has no body and, therefore, no senses.

Classical theists would also normally add that God's willing and loving must further differ from ours, since, unlike ours, it cannot involve him in reacting to anything. I sometimes choose (will) to catch a train for some reason or other. But, according to the classical theist, God does not choose (will) in the light of a scenario which he confronts and which disposes him to act thus and so for reasons he has as part of that scenario. A wife may love her husband. Yet, notes the classical theist, love, in people, is an emotion. So it is rooted in bodily contact and bodily reactions. And the classical theist holds that God has no body, since, making the difference between there being something and nothing, he creates all bodies. In people, love can show itself in their attempts to do good to the objects of their love. Yet God, says the classical theist, cannot *try* to do good to things. In terms of classical theism, the unchangeable (and, therefore, the untrying) God is effortlessly responsible for anything that we find to be good in the world. Or, as St Augustine writes:

> The truest beginning of piety is to think as highly of God as possible; and doing so means that one must believe that he is omnipotent, and not changeable in the smallest respect; that he is the creator of all good things, but is himself more excellent than all of them; that he is the supremely just ruler of everything that he created; and that he was not aided in creating by any other being, as if he were not sufficiently powerful by himself. It follows that he created all things from nothing.[11]

(c) God as an individual

We can put all this by saying that, according to classical theism, God is not a person. When we speak of persons, we are normally referring to human beings. For classical theists, however, God should be sharply distinguished from these. Human beings have bodies and are parts of a changing and changeable universe. According to classical theism, however, God is incorporeal, unchanging, and not part of the universe. As we shall see later in this chapter, and also in Chapter 13, some philosophers have thought that human persons are really non-material. But even these philosophers take persons to be distinct individuals belonging to a kind so that one person added to another makes two things of the same sort. For classical theism, however, God is not an individual belonging to any kind. You and I are both human beings. Neptune and Mars are both planets. According to classical theism, however, there is nothing of the same kind that God is.

Classical theists have sometimes expressed this point by saying that God is entirely simple. They do not, of course, mean that he is stupid or unintelligent (one sense of 'simple'). What, then, do they mean? We shall be turning in some detail to the notion of divine simplicity in Chapter 8. For the present, though, the point to grasp is that classical theists who say that God is simple mean in part that God is not a member of any genus or species. They are claiming that God is not what we would ordinarily call an individual.

To call something an individual is usually to imply that there could be another such thing distinct from it though just like it. In this sense, different people are individuals. But in this sense, says the classical theist, God is not an individual. He belongs to no kind or sort. According to the teaching that God is simple, God also lacks attributes or properties distinguishable from himself. You can differentiate between me and, say, my weight, height, or colouring at some particular time. Today I might weigh one hundred and forty pounds. And I might be six feet tall and pale. But in ten years time my weight and height could be different. So my weight, height, and colouring are not simply identical with me. To have weight, height, and colouring is not to *be* weight, height, and colouring. According to the teaching that God is simple, however, attributes or properties of God are, in fact, the same as God himself. On this account, God does not, strictly speaking, *have* attributes or properties. He is identical with them. As St Anselm puts it: 'The supreme nature is simple: thus all the things which can be said of its essence are simply one and the same thing in it.'[12]

Theistic Personalism

Turning, however, to what I am calling theistic personalism, we get a very different picture. Take, for instance, the contemporary Christian author Alvin Plantinga.[13] According to him, the teaching that God is simple is false since God possesses different properties and is a person, not 'a mere abstract object'.[14] Then again, according to Richard Swinburne (also a Christian),[15] a theist is 'a man who believes that there is a God', and by 'God' the theist 'understands something like a "person without a body"'.[16] 'That God is a person, yet one without a body, seems', says Swinburne, 'the most elementary claim of theism.'[17] Both Plantinga and Swinburne count as theistic personalists on my understanding of the expression. And one reason for saying so is that, unlike classical theists, they think it important to stress that God is a person.

(a) Persons and bodies

What do Plantinga and Swinburne mean by 'person'? Their writings, and the writings of those who share their view of God, proceed from the assumption that, if we want to understand what persons are, we must begin with human beings. Yet Plantinga and Swinburne, and those who broadly agree with them about God, do not want to suggest that God is just like a human being. So they also think that there can somehow be a person who, while being like human beings, is also decidedly different from what people are. In particular, and as Swinburne's phrase 'person without a body' indicates, they think that there can be a disembodied person. Yet, what are we to understand by expressions like 'person without a body' and 'disembodied person'?

Many philosophers hold that such expressions make little sense.[18] They argue that persons are essentially embodied because human beings are such. On their account, the word 'person' has 'embodied' built into its meaning so that phrases like 'person without a body' and 'disembodied person' have an air of self-contradiction about them. Hence, for example, Aristotle (384–322 BC)[19] holds that the persons we call people are essentially corporeal. For him, persons are as necessarily bodily as cats are necessarily mammalian. This line of thinking can also be found in writers such as Bertrand Russell (1872–1970)[20] and Ludwig Wittgenstein (1889–1951).[21] But other philosophers take a different view. Consider, for instance, John Locke (1632–1704).[22] According to him, persons might swap bodies with each other. A person, says Locke, is 'a thinking intelligent Being, that has reason and reflection, and can consider itself as itself, the same thinking thing in different times and places'.[23] And, so Locke goes on to say, the person of a prince could come to occupy the body of a cobbler. The prince's person, now in the cobbler's body, would not, Locke suggests, be the same *man* as the prince. But it would, he argues, be the same *person*.[24] Locke is asserting that persons can be distinguished from particular bodies and are not, therefore, identical with them. And if he is right to do so, then persons are not essentially corporeal.

The view that persons are not essentially corporeal is most often associated with René Descartes (1596–1650).[25] In his *Meditations on First Philosophy*, Descartes looks for a truth which cannot be doubted. He hits on 'I exist' as what he is searching for. One cannot doubt that one exists, he argues, since one cannot even doubt if one does not exist. It is, says Descartes, absurd to doubt one's existence as long as one is thinking. And he goes on to suggest that being a person (being able to refer to oneself as 'I') is inseparable from thinking. 'What am I?', Descartes asks. His answer is 'I am a thing that thinks: that is, a thing that doubts, affirms, denies, understands a few things, is ignorant of many things, is willing, is unwilling, and which also imagines and has sensory perceptions.'[26] And this thinking thing, Descartes adds, is not anything bodily.[27]

So the history of philosophy contains examples of authors who take persons to be distinguishable from what is essentially corporeal. And it is their approach, or something very like it, which seems to surface in theistic personalism. Generally, theistic personalists take God to be strikingly similar to what Descartes describes himself as being when explaining what he thinks he is.

(b) Theistic personalism and the rejection of classical theism

Not surprisingly, therefore, theistic personalists frequently reject almost all the tenets of classical theism as introduced above. Take, for example, their approach to the topic of creation. All theistic personalists agree that God is the Creator. They believe that God causes things to exist. But they also tend to regard God as standing to the created order as an onlooker who is able to step in and modify how things are. While classical theists typically hold that all history is God's doing, theistic personalists more commonly see it only as partly this. Some events, they often say, are not so much caused by God as *permitted* by him. Hence, for example, when explaining what he means by the assertion that God is the Creator, Swinburne writes: 'The main claim is that God either himself brings about or makes or permits some other being to bring about (or permits to exist uncaused) the existence of all things that exist . . . that those things exist only because of God's action or permission.'[28] It would, Swinburne adds, 'hardly seem to matter for theism if God on occasion permitted some other being to create matter'. Speaking in a similar vein, John Lucas declares:

> Not everything that happens can be attributed directly to the detailed decision of God. Although He knows how many hairs I have on my head, He has not decided how many there shall be. He distances Himself from the detailed control of the course of events in order, among other things, to give us the freedom of manoeuvre we need both to be moral agents and to go beyond morality into the realm of personal relations.[29]

According to Lucas: 'Even if God did not know the secrets of men's hearts, but only what they explicitly told Him or implied in their importunate petitions, He would still be better informed than most of us.'[30]

Swinburne and Lucas are here causally distancing God from the world in ways that most classical theists would not. And the difference between theistic personalism and classical theism often shows itself in a tendency among theistic personalists to echo Swinburne and Lucas in this respect. Hence, for example, while classical theists typically say that God knows all history by being its maker, theistic personalists are more likely to assert that God's knowledge of history may partly be acquired by him as history unfolds. On their picture, God's knowledge of the world, especially the world of human affairs, is capable of increase. It is also much derived from a process comparable with taking a look at an object or event which confronts one from outside. In the Middle Ages some classical theists summarized their teaching on God's knowledge by saying that the knowledge of God is the cause of things (*scientia dei causa rerum*). Theistic personalists, by contrast, often conceive of God's knowledge as caused by things other than himself. Hence, for example, Richard Creel writes: 'God must be affirmed as a privileged observer.' Why? Because, says Creel, if God cannot observe things as we do, he must be in error.[31]

Thinking along Creel's lines, theistic personalists often deny that God is impassible and unchangeable. Indeed, many of them make a point of doing so. Why? Largely because they think that, if God is impassible and unchangeable, then he cannot be taken seriously as a person. The persons we call people are changed by what they encounter and discover. They are modified by other things. And, says the theistic personalist, this is how it must be with God. An impassible and unchanging God would, they argue, be lifeless. Such a God, they often add, would also not be admirable. We admire people who can be moved by tragic events. We admire people who can become elated when good things happen. And, theistic personalists sometimes say, we can admire God only if he, like admirable people, is suitably affected by the good and the bad which occurs in the world. A notable defender of this view is Charles Hartshorne (1897–2000), according to whom God undergoes joy as we flourish and grieves as we suffer. For Hartshorne, this means that God undergoes development. God improves as time goes on.[32] Hartshorne's understanding of God is, of course, utterly at odds with the suggestion that God is outside time. And God's timelessness is rejected, whether explicitly or implicitly, by all theistic personalists. The same goes for the teaching that God is simple. As we shall later see, some theistic personalists reject this teaching on purely philosophical grounds. Some, for example, argue that it is logically indefensible or in some way incoherent. But, as we shall also later see, others reject it on theological grounds. Why? The reasons they give are usually based on the way they read the Bible. In their view, the biblical picture of God is just flatly at odds with what those who believe in divine simplicity take God to be. The Old and New Testaments speak of God as though he were a distinct individual with distinct attributes or properties. And this, say many theistic personalists, is reason enough for dismissing the notion of divine simplicity.

Many of them would add that it is also reason for rejecting classical theism's emphasis on the difficulty of understanding what God is. St Augustine of Hippo, like classical theists in general, expresses himself baffled when it comes to the divine nature. 'Who then are you, my God?', he asks. He answers his own question by stressing that God is supremely mysterious. God, says Augustine, is 'most high, utterly good, utterly powerful, most omnipotent, most merciful and most just, deeply hidden yet most intimately present, perfection of both beauty and strength, stable and incomprehensible, immutable and yet changing all things, never new, never old ... always active, always in repose.'[33] According to theistic personalists, however, God is nothing like as extraordinary as Augustine's account suggests.

Augustine's account is inseparable from his commitment to the teaching that God is simple. But what if we reject that teaching? And what if we think of God as being how Descartes thought he was, albeit much less limited? Then we might think that God is not so hard to fathom after all. Descartes says: 'I can achieve an easier and more evident perception of my own mind than of anything else.'[34] If Descartes is right here, and if he is also correct in his view of what it is to be a human person, might we not claim a fair comprehension of God by reflecting on what we are as thinking things?

Theistic personalists often suggest that we can do just this. They always concede that God is something of a mystery. But they frequently imply that we can have some sense of what it is to be God since we know from our own case what it is to be a person. They also sometimes suggest that words (especially adjectives) used by believers when speaking of God are most naturally to be construed in the same way as when they are applied to people. Theists say that God is, for example, knowing, loving, and good. But we know what it means to say that people are knowing, loving, and good. So, reasons many a theistic personalist, we know something of what it means to say that God is knowing, loving, and good. Some theistic personalists (Swinburne is a notable example) add that our knowledge of people and God allows us (with no reference to divine revelation) to form conjectures and expectations concerning how God is likely to act. Others suggest that God, like us, could be subject to lapses of memory. Hence, for example, Steven T. Davis asks: 'Suppose God knows the answer to any question that can be asked except this: What colour shoes did Martha Washington wear on the day of her wedding to George? Suppose God has somehow forgotten this fact and has forgotten how to deduce it from other facts he knows. Is it so clear he would then no longer be God?' Davis answers: 'I believe that God is in fact omniscient—he does know the answer to this question. But I am not prepared to grant that if he didn't he would no longer be divine.'[35]

Why These Differences?

What accounts for the different approaches to theism noted above? Classical theists take theirs to be a natural way of expressing what the Bible teaches concerning God's nature. But classical theism also derives from reading the Bible in the light of various philosophical positions. In this sense, it is also the product of philosophical reasoning and argument. You can clearly see how this is so by turning, for instance, to the first part of Aquinas's *Summa Theologiae*. Here we find Aquinas defending all the tenets of classical theism as I have sketched them. And we find him seeking to ground them in texts from the Old and New Testaments (he spent many years lecturing on the Bible). But Aquinas also tries to argue for them philosophically and without appeal to Scripture. The same is true when it comes to some other notable classical theists. For example, Augustine (who wrote commentaries on biblical texts) and Anselm (who did not) each seek to defend their approach to God on both biblical and philosophical grounds.

Yet grounds such as these are also appealed to by theistic personalists. They commonly insist that their approach to God is what best reflects biblical talk about God.[36] And they frequently maintain that their position makes the best philosophical sense of belief in God. Why the best philosophical sense? Because, say some theistic personalists, philosophical reasoning shows that we should believe in the existence of God as construed along the lines of theistic personalism. Many theistic personalists also hold that there are flaws in the philosophical arguments offered by classical theists in favour of their understanding of God.

So the divisions between classical and theistic personalists derive both from their reading of theological texts and from ways in which they differ philosophically. And this, of course, means that the divisions are both complex and far-reaching. So, if you want to take sides, you are going to have to do a lot of work. You are going to have to adjudicate between classical and theistic personalists with an eye on biblical texts and how they should best be understood. You will also have to study the various philosophical arguments which both classical and theistic personalists give as they attempt to tell us what God should be taken to be.

Moving On

In distinguishing between classical theism and theistic personalism, I have been trying to paint a picture using rather broad strokes. My aim has been to give you an impression of some substantial differences to be found among theists. But you should not assume that those who side with some of the tenets of classical theism as I have outlined them also agree with all of them. Nor should you suppose that there is an easily identifiable body of classical theists who all believe the same when it comes to the question 'What is God?' You should also not suppose that there is a solid body of thinkers calling themselves 'theistic personalists' and all saying exactly the same thing when it comes to God's nature. 'Classical theism' and 'theistic personalism' are just labels I have used in order to draw your attention to some significant diversity which often goes unnoticed. But the diversity is notable. And those approaching the philosophy of religion for the first time should be aware of it. As I have said, much philosophy of religion centres on questions about God. So it is important at the start to realize that 'God' is a word which has been understood differently.

But it is also important to realize that philosophers have turned to philosophy of religion not just with different understandings of God but also with different approaches to the general relationship between philosophy and religion. Should philosophy necessarily be viewed as religion's foe? Should it be thought of as a necessary ally? Do religious beliefs need philosophical support? Is it the job of philosophy to pronounce on their truth or falsity? Answers to these questions can be found in the writings of many philosophers, and in the next chapter we shall see something of what the questions amount to and how they have been dealt with.

NOTES

1. Moses Maimonides was born at Cordova and finally settled in Cairo. The author of numerous works on Jewish theology, he is best known today for his *Guide for the Perplexed* (1190), which is devoted to the relation between reason and religious faith. Avicenna, sometimes called Ibn Sina, was an Islamic philosopher who also had a strong influence on medieval Christian thinkers. Thomas Aquinas lived and worked in France and Italy and became one of the most respected Roman Catholic philosophers and theologians. He wrote voluminously, but is best known for his *Summa Theologiae* and *Summa contra Gentiles*.

2. Augustine of Hippo lived most of his life in North Africa. His impact on Christian thinking is second to none. His many writings include the *Confessions*

(a kind of theological autobiography) and a variety of works on both philosophical and theological topics.

3. Leibniz was born in Leipzig, where he later studied. Generally regarded as one of the greatest seventeenth-century 'rationalist' philosophers, he wrote on physics, mathematics, metaphysics, and theology.

4. Cf. Thomas Aquinas, *Summa Theologiae*, Ia, 8.

5. Cf. Chapter 11 below.

6. Herbert McCabe, 'Creation', *New Blackfriars* 61 (1980). I quote from this article as reprinted in Brian Davies (ed.), *Philosophy of Religion: A Guide and Anthology* (Oxford, 2000), p. 199.

7. Thomas Aquinas, *Summa Theologiae*, Ia, 45, 1. I quote from the translation of the English Dominican Fathers (London, 1911).

8. Anselm, *Proslogion*, chs. 13 and 19. I quote from Brian Davies and G. R. Evans (eds.), *Anselm of Canterbury: The Major Works* (Oxford, 1998). Anselm was at one time abbot of Bec, in Normandy. He died as Archbishop of Canterbury. His best-known writings include his *Monologion*, *Proslogion*, and *Cur Deus Homo*.

9. Thomas Aquinas, *Summa Theologiae*, Ia, 13, 7. I quote from volume 3 of the Blackfriars edition of the *Summa Theologiae* (London and New York, 1964).

10. Anselm, *Monologion*, ch. 15. I quote from Brian Davies and G. R. Evans (eds.), *Anselm of Canterbury: The Major Works* (Oxford, 1998), p. 26.

11. St Augustine of Hippo, *De Libero Arbitrio*, I, 2. I quote from Thomas Williams (ed.), *Augustine: On Free Choice of the Will* (Indianapolis, IN, 1993), pp. 3 f.

12. Anselm of Canterbury, *Monologion*, ch. 17. I quote from Brian Davies and G. R. Evans (eds.), *Anselm of Canterbury: The Major Works* (Oxford, 1998), p. 30.

13. Plantinga teaches at the University of Notre Dame, Indiana. His publications include *God and Other Minds* (1967), *The Nature of Necessity* (1974), and *Warranted Christian Belief* (1999).

14. Alvin Plantinga, *Does God Have A Nature* (Milwaukee, WI, 1980), p. 47.

15. Richard Swinburne retired as Nolloth Professor of the Philosophy of the Christian Religion at Oxford University in 2002. He has written widely in the areas of probability theory, philosophy of mind, and philosophy of religion. His books include *The Existence of God* (2nd edn., 1991), *The Evolution of the Soul* (1986), *Is There A God?* (1996), and *Providence and the Problem of Evil* (1998).

16. Richard Swinburne, *The Coherence of Theism* (rev. edn., Oxford, 1993), p. 1.

17. Ibid., p. 101.

18. For more on all this, see Chapter 13.

19. Aristotle, generally thought to be one of the greatest of ancient Greek

thinkers, wrote treatises on science, metaphysics, and ethics. He more or less invented the discipline of logic. He acted as tutor to Alexander the Great. He also studied under Plato.

20. Bertrand Russell taught at Cambridge University. He is best known for his work on logic and mathematics. But he also wrote on other matters, including religion. His major writings include *The Principles of Mathematics* (1903/1937), *The Problems of Philosophy* (1912), *The Philosophy of Logical Atomism* (1918), *A History of Western Philosophy* (1945), and *Human Knowledge: Its Scope and Limits* (1948).

21. Wittgenstein studied under Russell but came to disagree with him philosophically on a number of issues. He taught at Cambridge University, but also worked in non-academic contexts. Widely regarded as one of the greatest twentieth-century philosophers, his works (almost all published posthumously) include *Tractatus Logico-Philosophicus* (1922), *Philosophical Investigations* (1953), *The Blue and Brown Books* (1958), and *On Certainty* (1969).

22. John Locke is best known for his work in epistemology (theory of knowledge) and political philosophy. His *Essay Concerning Human Understanding* was published in 1690.

23. John Locke, *An Essay Concerning Human Understanding*, edited with an introduction by Peter H. Nidditch (Oxford, 1975), Book II, ch. XXVII, p. 335.

24. Cf. ibid., p. 340.

25. Often called 'the father of modern philosophy', Descartes is especially famous for his philosophy of mind. His major works include the *Discourse on Method* (1637) and the *Meditations on First Philosophy* (1641).

26. I quote from *The Philosophical Writings of Descartes*, vol. II, trans. John Cottingham, Robert Stoothoff, and Dugald Murdoch (Cambridge, 1984), p. 24.

27. See Chapter 13.

28. Swinburne, *The Coherence of Theism*, p. 131.

29. John Lucas, *The Future* (Oxford, 1989), p. 229.

30. Ibid., p. 221.

31. Richard Creel, *Divine Impassibility* (Cambridge, 1986), p. 96.

32. Cf. Charles Hartshorne, *Omnipotence and Other Theological Mistakes* (New York, 1983).

33. I quote from *Saint Augustine: Confessions*, trans. Henry Chadwick (Oxford, 1991), pp. 4f.

34. *The Philosophical Writings of Descartes*, vol. II, trans. John Cottingham, Robert Stoothoff, and Dugald Murdoch, p. 23.

35. Steven T. Davis, *Logic and the Nature of God* (London, 1983), pp. 4f.

36. Cf. John Lucas as quoted in Chapter 8 below.

FURTHER READING

For helpful accounts of some different understandings of the word 'God', see H. P. Owen, *Concepts of Deity* (London, 1971) and Ronald H. Nash, *The Concept of God* (Grand Rapids, MI, 1983). For a concise survey of different accounts of God given by Jews, Christians, and others, see the article on 'God' in E. A. Livingstone and F. L. Cross (eds.), *The Oxford Dictionary of the Christian Church* (Oxford, 1997). See also the entry on 'God' in volume VI of *The New Catholic Encyclopedia* (New York, 1967). For statements of Roman Catholic approaches to God, see Karl Rahner *et al.* (eds.), *Sacramentum Mundi*, vol. 2 (New York, 1968), pp. 381–401, and the *Catechism of the Catholic Church* (2nd edn., Vatican City, 2000), pp. 13–18, and 54–61.

For brief introductions to biblical teachings concerning God, see Raymond E. Brown, Joseph A. Fitzmyer, and Ronald E. Murphy (eds.), *The Jerome Biblical Commentary* (Englewood Cliffs, NJ, 1968), pp. 737–46. See also J. B. Baur (ed.), *Encyclopedia of Biblical Theology* (New York, 1981), pp. 298–316; Alan Richardson (ed.), *A Theological Word Book of the Bible* (London, 1950), pp. 89–99; and *The Interpreters Dictionary of the Bible*, vol. 2 (Nashville and New York, 1962), pp. 417–36.

For an account of Christian teaching about God in the period immediately following that of New Testament authors, see J. N. D. Kelly, *Early Christian Creeds* (3rd edn., Harlow and New York, 1972). See also J. N. D. Kelly, *Early Christian Doctrines* (5th edn., London, 1977) and G. L. Prestige, *God in Patristic Thought* (2nd edn., London, 1952).

Aquinas is often regarded as a paradigm classical theist. For introductions to him, see Brian Davies, *The Thought of Thomas Aquinas* (Oxford, 1992) and id., *Aquinas* (London, 2002). For a clear statement of what I am calling 'theistic personalism', see Richard Swinburne, *The Coherence of Theism* (rev. ed., Oxford, 1993). For a wholly different approach, written with authors like Swinburne in mind, see Gareth Moore, *Believing in God* (Edinburgh, 1988). For a discussion of the formula 'God is a person', see Keith Ward, 'Is God a Person?', in Gijsbert van den Brink, Luco van den Brom, and Marcel Sarot (eds.), *Christian Faith and Philosophical Theology* (Kampen, Netherlands, 1992). For a critical exposition of what I am calling theistic personalism (he calls it 'neotheism'), see Norman L. Geisler, *Creating God in the Image of Man?* (Minneapolis, MN, 1997).

QUESTIONS FOR DISCUSSION

1 Jane asks Paul 'Do you believe in God?' Paul says 'No'. Jane asks John 'Do you believe in God?' John says 'Yes'. Should we automatically suppose that Paul and John are contradicting each other? If so, why? If not, why not?

2 What should we take the word 'God' to mean?

3 Can we draw a serious distinction between 'classical theism' and 'theistic personalism'? If so, why? If not, why not?

4 Philosophers sometimes refer to 'the concept of God'. What might they have in mind when doing so? Is there any such thing as 'the concept of God'?

5 How do biblical authors conceive of God? To what extent can their teachings be invoked in favour of classical theism? To what extent can they be appealed to in support of theistic personalism?

6 How might one decide whether or not different people share an understanding as to what 'God' means?

7 People sometimes say 'We all worship the same God'. Is that true? If so, why? If not, why not? How might one decide that two people worship the same God?

8 If I am a person and if God is a person, does anything make God different from me?

9 Artists are sometimes said to create their works of art. How do they do this? Are they doing what theists seem to mean when they speak of God as Creator?

10 'God is a mystery.' What might be meant by this statement? Are there any reasons for endorsing it?

2

PHILOSOPHY AND RELIGIOUS BELIEF

....

Students of philosophy often dread being asked what it is that they study. For, as soon as they reply 'Philosophy', they are likely to be asked what that is. And it is not easy to say. Philosophy is not easily defined. The *Oxford English Dictionary* says that in 'the original and widest sense' philosophy is 'the love, study, or pursuit of wisdom, or of knowledge of things and their causes whether theoretical or practical'. The *Dictionary* adds that the currently 'most usual' sense of 'philosophy' is 'that department of knowledge or study which deals with ultimate reality, or with the most general causes and principles of things'. But even these definitions are none too illuminating.

A problem of definition also faces us when we turn to the word 'religion'. In Henry Fielding's novel *Tom Jones*, Mr Thwakum declares: 'When I mention religion, I mean the Christian religion; and not only the Christian religion, but the Protestant religion; and not only the Protestant religion, but the Church of England.'[1] But Mr Thwakum is not to be taken seriously. Christians may not believe in, for example, Buddhism, Hinduism, or Islam. Yet it would be odd to deny that these are religions. And although members of the Church of England might not care for the beliefs of, say, Calvinists, Baptists, and Roman Catholics, there is no good reason to deny that people such as these count as religious believers.

Yet philosophers and others have sometimes approached particular religious beliefs, or religious belief as a whole, while advocating wide-ranging views about philosophy and religion. In this chapter we shall briefly look at four such views:

- according to the first, philosophy can show that religious beliefs are unintelligible since they are empirically unverifiable or unfalsifiable;
- according to the second, religious beliefs should be rejected unless they can be defended by means of philosophical argument;
- according to the third, the job of philosophy is not to comment on the truth or falsity of religious beliefs but to seek to understand them;
- according to the fourth, it can be reasonable to accept some religious beliefs without any evidence at all.

Verification and Falsification

(a) The arguments

If I say that Fred is a brilliant physicist, you will rightly doubt my assertion unless I can point to something about his talk or behaviour that would provide evidence for its veracity. And you would be justly and similarly sceptical if (i) I say on Tuesday that it will rain on Wednesday, (ii) by Thursday it has not rained, and (iii) on Thursday I insist that I was right on Tuesday.

But why is all this so? Because 'Fred is a brilliant physicist' and 'It will rain on Thursday' look like factual assertions, and factual assertions normally tell us what we can and cannot expect to discover empirically (i.e. by means of sensory experience). If sensory experience cannot confirm that Fred is a brilliant physicist, then the claim that he is so is empty of content. If the non-observance of rain by Thursday does not count against 'It will rain on Wednesday', then 'It will rain on Wednesday' is saying nothing of significance.

In that case, therefore, how should we think of religious assertions? How, for example, does 'God exists' fare? According to some philosophers, the answer is 'Very badly'. On their account, genuine factual claims must be either verifiable or falsifiable (at least in principle) by sensory experience. And, these philosophers add, since religious believers commonly take 'God exists' to be neither empirically verifiable (not verifiable by sensory experience) nor empirically falsifiable (not disprovable by sensory experience), it really says nothing. People often say that seeing is believing. And the philosophers I am now alluding to are basically offering a sophisticated statement of the same conclusion.

In the twentieth century an important version of it emerged in the work of a group of thinkers who gathered in Vienna in association with Moritz Schlick (1882–1936). The group became known as the Vienna Circle, and it included Otto Neurath (1882–1945), Friedrich Waismann (1896–1959), and Rudolf Carnap (1891–1970). Claiming to be influenced by Ludwig Wittgenstein, these thinkers propounded a theory of meaning called 'the verification principle', a theory from which they drew drastic and far-reaching conclusions.

They held that meaningful statements fall into two groups. First, there are mathematical statements (e.g. $2 + 2 = 4$), tautologies (e.g. 'All cats are cats'), and logically necessary statements (e.g. 'P and not-P cannot both be true'). Second, there are factual statements which can be confirmed by means of the senses, especially through methods used in sciences like physics, chemistry, and biology. In this way the Vienna Circle linked factual meaningfulness with sense experience. And in doing so, it stood in a well-known philosophical tradition. In effect, it was agreeing with the Scottish philosopher David Hume (1711–76).[2] 'If', says Hume, 'we take in our hand any volume; of divinity or school metaphysics, for instance, let us ask, *Does it contain any abstract reasoning concerning quantity or number? No. Does it contain any experimental reasoning concerning matter of fact and existence?* No. Commit it then to the flames: for it can contain nothing but sophistry and illusion.'[3]

The verification principle became the most distinctive doctrine of Logical Positivism, as the school of thinking represented and influenced by the Vienna Circle came to be called. But the principle was not always stated in the same way. For instance, some logical positivists distinguished between what have been called the 'weak' and the 'strong' versions of the verification principle. The weak version became the most popular. It held that (forgetting about mathematical statements, tautologies, and truths of logic) a statement is factual and meaningful only if sense experience can confirm it in *some way*. Yet, in the early days of Logical Positivism, it was the strong version of the verification principle that was in vogue. Waismann stated it thus: 'Anyone uttering a sentence must know under what conditions he calls it true and under what conditions he calls it false. If he is unable to state these conditions, he does not know what he has said. A statement which cannot be conclusively verified cannot be verified at all. It is simply devoid of any meaning.'[4]

The history of the verification principle is too complicated to follow in detail here. But we can note that all its proponents held that its implications are devastating for belief in God. Take, for example, Carnap. 'In its metaphysical use,' he observes, 'the word "God" refers to something beyond experience. The word is deliberately divested of its reference to a physical being or to a spiritual being that is immanent in the physical. And as it is not given a new meaning, it becomes meaningless.'[5] Another illustration of logical positivist methods for dealing with God's existence can be found in A. J. Ayer's book *Language, Truth and Logic*. 'The term "god" ', says Ayer,

> is a metaphysical term. And if 'god' is a metaphysical term, then it cannot even be probable that a god exists. For to say that 'God exists' is to make a metaphysical utterance which cannot be either true or false. And by the same criterion, no sentence which purports to describe the nature of a transcendent god can possess any literal significance.[6]

Note that here Ayer is not just denying the existence of God; he is dismissing the question of God's existence altogether. His position is: (i) if we cannot verify the existence of God empirically, it is meaningless to say that there is a God; (ii) we cannot verify the existence of God empirically; (iii) so it is meaningless to say that there is a God.

What, though, of empirical falsification? Here one can introduce the name of Antony Flew, with whom the emphasis changes from verification to falsification.[7] According to the verification principle, religious statements, including 'There is a God', are meaningless simply because it is not possible to verify them. Flew does not support the principle in this form, but in 'Theology and Falsification' he asks whether certain religious statements might not be viewed with suspicion because no sense experience could count *against* them.[8]

Flew begins by offering what he calls a 'parable'.[9] Two explorers come upon a clearing in the jungle. The first explorer maintains that there is an invisible gardener who looks after it. The second disagrees. Various physical tests (such as keeping watch, using bloodhounds and electric fences) are applied to check whether there is a gardener. All the tests fail to show the gardener's presence, but the first explorer continues to believe in the gardener's existence. He says, 'But there is a gardener who has no scent and makes no sound, a gardener who comes secretly to look after the garden which he loves.' The second explorer rejects this move and suggests that there is no difference between the first explorer's 'gardener' and no gardener at all.

At this point Flew applies his parable to religious statements. Religious believers make claims. They say, for instance, that there is a God who loves human beings. But they are apparently unwilling to allow anything to count against these claims. The claims seem unfalsifiable. Are they, then, genuine claims?

Flew does not dogmatically say that they cannot be. But he clearly has doubts. 'Sophisticated religious people', he observes, 'tend to refuse to allow, not merely that anything actually does occur, but that anything conceivably could occur, which would count against their theological assertions and explanations. But in so far as they do this their supposed explanations are actually bogus, and their seeming assertions are really vacuous.'[10] In this passage Flew does not talk about falsification by sense experience, but this is clearly what he has in mind. And, from his parable of the gardener, it is clear that, in raising the issue of falsification, he is thinking very much about the question of God's existence. He is suggesting that those who believe in God are unwilling to allow any sense experience to count against their belief. And he is implying that this renders it unintelligible.

(b) Comments

One reason for sympathizing with the authors noted above lies in the way in which we come to make sense of ordinary factual statements (as distinct from statements of logic or mathematics).[11] For we do so insofar as we can picture or imagine empirical states of affairs which would obtain if they were true. And we take ordinary factual statements not to be compatible with just *any* empirical state of affairs. Ordinary factual statements are always open to empirical verification or falsification.

Another point which might be made in favour of what writers like Carnap, Ayer, and Flew say could be put in the form of the dictum 'God-talk often seems puzzling'. Many things said about God just do strike some people as obscure or even unintelligible. Nobody with a basic command of English will have problems in understanding sentences like 'There are elephants in Africa'. But many people are puzzled by what theists say about God. It is, of course, true that there are intelligible statements which few people can understand, as is the case with various statements accepted by scientific specialists. But talk about God is not just employed by a band of experts. And it is usually presented as something important to everyone. Yet many who listen to it simply find themselves at sea. They cannot make sense of it. We might say that they lack imagination. But to imagine something is to be able to form a picture of it. And God is not supposed to be picturable.

Yet there are also points to be made against authors like Carnap, Ayer, and Flew. One concerns the way in which they read statements like 'God exists'. Their attack clearly presupposes that such statements should be viewed as empirical hypotheses. But why should we grant that assumption? It is certainly very implausible when it comes to 'God exists'. Theists do not think of God as detectable by the senses or as disprovable by what our senses might tell us. And this suggests that it is wrong to attack them with reference to empirical verification and falsification. Perhaps some things said by religious believers can be challenged along these lines. But religious believers do not normally make common or garden empirical observations when stating the teachings which they think of as central to their religion. And 'God exists' is a case in point. It is not normally offered as a scientific assertion. And it is not about anything subject to sensory inspection. Given what theists have said about God as Creator, it is, if anything, a statement about what accounts for there being any true empirical descriptions. In that case, however, to observe that such is the case is hardly to offer a serious objection to 'God exists'. To suggest otherwise seems like condemning a tennis player for not scoring goals. Tennis players are not in the business of scoring goals. By the same token, so we might argue, religious believers are not in the business of asking us to believe in what is open to empirical inspection or refutation.

Sometimes, however, they do say that what can be empirically inspected provides grounds for believing that God exists. And this brings us to a second possible criticism of authors such as Carnap and Ayer. For what of the claim that belief in God is a justified (and, therefore, meaningful) inference from some empirically verifiable feature of the world, or from the existence of the world as a whole? Many philosophers have defended this claim. Are they right to do so? It seems fair to reply that whether or not they are can be decided only by considering the strength of their arguments. Yet the philosophers I am now discussing do not, for the most part, do this. Defenders of the weak version of the verification principle simply assume that empirical investigation just cannot support belief in God. And Flew (though no logical positivist) says nothing (in the paper from which I have quoted) about reasons we might have for thinking that God exists as believers take him to be. For this reason, we may suggest that their conclusions concerning the meaningfulness of belief in God are arrived at prematurely.

We might also wonder whether they are sound in their approach to the notions of the meaningful and the factual. Is it, for instance, right to say that a statement is meaningful and factual only if it is conclusively verifiable or falsifiable by means of sense experience? Arguably not. For it seems possible to make intelligible and factual universal statements like 'All people spend part of their lives asleep' or 'All cats are mortal'. The first statement here is, so far as we know, true. And it is surely not meaningless even if it is false. Yet there is no way in which anyone could conclusively show that it is true by means of sense experience. For it is always possible that we will one day come across someone who needs no sleep at all. As for the second statement, that too seems true and meaningful. But it cannot be conclusively falsified. For whatever the age of the cats we know, they may sometime die.

One might reply that there still remains the weak verification principle and that this serves to establish the nonsensicality of 'God exists' and comparable statements. But this reply is open to the objection that the weak verification principle does not even satisfy its own criterion of meaningfulness. If we accept it, then we have to say that a statement is only factual and meaningful if some sense experience or observation statement makes it probable or counts in its favour. But what sense experience or observation statement can count in favour of the claim that a statement is only factual and meaningful if some sense experience or observation statement makes it probable or counts in its favour? Presumably, none.

It has been urged that the verification principle is acceptable because it draws on the ordinary understanding of words like 'factual' and 'meaningful'. Schlick, for example, said that it is 'nothing but a simple statement of the way in which meaning is actually assigned to propositions in everyday life and in science. There never has been any other way, and it would be a grave error to suppose that we have discovered a new conception of meaning which is contrary to common opinion and which we want to introduce into philosophy.'[12] But consider the following statement given as an example by Richard Swinburne: 'Some of the toys which to all appearances stay in the toy cupboard *while people are asleep and no one is watching* [my emphasis] actually get up and dance in the middle of the night and then go back to the cupboard leaving no traces of their activity.'[13] If someone were to say this, talking, let us suppose, about a particular cupboard, we might be utterly incredulous. But it would be stretching things to say that the statement that Swinburne asks us to consider is meaningless.

You might say that we cannot understand a statement unless we know how it can be shown to be true or false. You might also suggest that knowing how to show a statement to be true or false means knowing what sense experience would make it probable or improbable. But people can understand statements without being able to say what sense experience shows them to be likely or unlikely to be true. To take another example of Swinburne's:

> A man can understand the statement 'once upon a time, before there were men or any other rational creatures, the earth was covered by sea', without his having any idea of what geological evidence would count for or against this proposition, or any idea of how to establish what geological evidence would count for or against the proposition.[14]

The truth of this observation is just what someone could well refer to if it were said that Flew's comments about falsifiability successfully indicate that statements about God are meaningless. People who hold that there is a God may not be able to specify what would count against the truth of their assertion. But it does not follow from this that the assertion is meaningless.

So the verification principle in the forms in which we have considered it does not discredit belief in God. Nor does it seem that such belief is called into question because it cannot be falsified. Significantly, even Ayer finally came to admit as much. In response to an argument originating from Alonzo Church, he agreed that the verification principle cannot be formulated in any satisfactory way. He also conceded that the same applies to criteria of meaning stated in terms of falsification.[15]

Religious Belief and Evidence

(a) The arguments

Our second general view about philosophy and religion can be simply summarized. It holds that religious beliefs stand or fall depending on whether or not they can be defended on the basis of evidence. Suppose I am convinced that Hitler has been raised from the dead or that aliens have landed in New Mexico. You will probably tell me that I should abandon my conviction unless I can point to the facts supporting it. And that is what many philosophers have said when it comes to the convictions of religious believers. Their suggestion has been that we have no business accepting religious beliefs if they cannot be backed up by evidence.

A much quoted example of someone taking this line is Antony Flew. Focusing on belief that God exists, Flew defends what he calls 'the presumption of atheism'. In law courts, defendants are presumed innocent until the prosecution establishes their guilt by bringing forth evidence for it. And Flew thinks that this procedure is right and proper. But he also thinks that it has theological implications. For, he argues, it implies that those who believe that God exists should equally be required to marshal their evidence. In law courts, it is the prosecution who is proposing a conclusion—that so and so committed a crime. And it is up to the prosecution to show that this conclusion is true. When it comes to belief in God, says Flew, it is believers who are proposing a conclusion—that God exists. And it is up to them to show that their conclusion is true. 'If it is to be established that there is a God,' Flew reasons, 'then we have to have good grounds for believing that this is indeed so. Until and unless some such grounds are produced, we have literally no reason at all for believing; and in that situation the only reasonable posture must be that of either the negative atheist or the agnostic.'[16]

What does Flew mean by 'good grounds'? He does not specify. He clearly does not mean something as definitive as proof or demonstration. He is not, for instance, suggesting that we should not believe in God unless 'God does not exist' can be shown to be self-contradictory. Instead, he appeals to what he calls 'sufficient reason' and probability. His view is that we should only believe in God if we can appeal to something which shows that it is more likely than not that God exists. And he is implying that the same is true when it comes to any other religious belief.

In this respect, Flew may be compared with the British mathematician and philosopher W. K. Clifford (1845–79). Clifford reminds us that people can sometimes die because we act without checking to see that all is well. Are we to be held responsible in such instances? Clifford argues that we are. We would, he suggests, be morally culpable if, for example, we send people off in a ship which we have reason to believe to be less than thoroughly seaworthy or which we have not checked to see whether or not it is such. According to Clifford, there are beliefs that we have a right to, and beliefs that we are not entitled to hold and to act on. He sums up this conclusion by saying that 'it is wrong, everywhere, and for anyone, to believe anything upon insufficient evidence'.[17] Clifford does not directly apply this conclusion to religious beliefs such as the belief in the existence of God. But he would obviously have been prepared to do so. Originally a Roman Catholic, Clifford ended up an agnostic. Perhaps he came to feel that the teachings of Roman Catholicism lack sufficient evidence.

(b) Comments

'Evidence' is a tricky word. The same can be said of 'sufficient' (as in 'sufficient reason') and of 'insufficient' (as in 'insufficient reason'). Evidence in favour of one belief need not be evidence for the truth of another. And 'sufficient', which means 'enough', and 'insufficient', which means 'not enough', are vague terms which, taken as they stand, give us little to get our teeth into. Yet few of us would be happy should people make claims while adding that they are based on no evidence or reasons at all, or that they are based on insufficient evidence or reason. When doctors tell us that smoking causes cancer, we ask for the evidence. If a detective tells a husband that his wife is cheating on him, the husband will seek reasons to believe that she is doing so.

Hume once said that 'wise' people 'proportion their belief to the evidence'.[18] And that seems a plausible verdict if only because it sounds odd to say that wise people make no attempt to proportion their belief to the evidence. Do we not learn how to use the word 'wise' with reference to people acting and talking just as Hume thinks that wise people should? And do we not learn to use 'reasonable' with reference to people who not only tell us that such and such is the case but who also explain why we should believe them? We obviously do. And, if that is so, then authors like Flew and Clifford have a point.

There is, however, a problem with their position. We can draw attention to it by noting how we commonly come to determine whether or not something counts as evidence or reason for believing that such and such is the case. I might reasonably conclude that John's fingerprints on a gun are evidence for him having used it. But why? Presumably, because I have been taught about fingerprints. But how do I know that what I was taught is true?

Was it by personal investigation and the weighing of evidence and reasons? If not, then by Flew and Clifford's standards I am not entitled to believe that John used the gun. But if so, and if Flew and Clifford are right, then I am still subject to criticism. For on what basis did I conduct my original investigations concerning fingerprints? Was it by checking to see that all my beliefs relevant to the matter at hand were themselves based on evidence and reasons? But how could I have done this without effectively inventing the science of fingerprinting for myself? Can anyone seriously suppose that it is unreasonable for people to believe that such and such is the case if they cannot cite evidence and reasons for all that they presuppose when appealing to what they take to be evidence or reason for such and such being the case? If Flew and Clifford are right, then they ought to. But the conclusion is preposterous. In *On Certainty*, Wittgenstein writes:

> The child learns by believing the adult. Doubt comes after belief. I learned an enormous amount and accepted it on human authority, and then I found some things confirmed or disconfirmed by my own experience. In general I take as true what is found in text-books, of geography for example. Why? I say: All these facts have been confirmed a hundred times over. But how do

I know that? What is my evidence for it? I have a world picture. Is it true or false? Above all it is the substratum of all my inquiring and asserting ... Doesn't testing come to an end? ... The difficulty is to realize the ground-lessness of our believing ... Think of chemical investigations. Lavoisier makes experiments with substances in his laboratory and now he concludes that this and that take place when there is burning. He does not say that it might happen otherwise another time. He has got hold of a definite world-picture—not of course one that he invented: he learned it as a child. I say world-picture and not hypothesis, because it is the matter-of-course foundation for his research and as such also goes unmentioned.[19]

Here Wittgenstein is saying that demands for evidence, grounds, or reasons make sense only in the light of ways of thinking which do not themselves rest on evidence, grounds, or reasons. And his point is correct. In that case, however, it is wrong to suggest that believers in general, and religious believers in particular, are not entitled to believe as they do unless their beliefs can be supported by evidence or grounds. It is implausible to hold that *all* believing must be supported by evidence or grounds before we can take it seriously. As Norman Malcolm puts it: 'Grounds come to an end. Answers to How-do-we-know? questions come to an end. Evidence comes to an end. We must speak, act, live, without evidence.'[20]

Yet, might we not accept this conclusion and still require religious believers to provide what, for example, Flew has in mind when looking for a defence of 'God exists'? Even if much of our reasoning inevitably rests on beliefs for which we do not or cannot provide evidence, grounds, or reasons, it surely does not follow that we are always entitled to believe as we do without such things. What if I say that Jones committed the crime? Or what if I say that dinosaurs still exist? Can I legitimately ward off your request to be shown why this is so just by referring to my example concerning fingerprints or to what we have just seen Wittgenstein saying? Surely not. Maybe not all beliefs stand in need of evidence, grounds, or reasons. But some do.

Yet how are we to decide which do and which do not? And are religious beliefs examples of those that do? Your answer to this question will be much affected by what you take religious beliefs to be. If you think of them as logically akin to empirical hypotheses or to scientific theories, then you will presumably think of them as requiring empirical evidence, grounds, and reasons. But if your approach to the meaning of religious beliefs sharply contrasts them with empirical hypotheses or scientific theories, then you will presumably take a different view. And this brings us to yet another general approach to philosophy and religion, one especially associated with D. Z. Phillips, who claims to be especially influenced by Wittgenstein.[21]

Grammar and Religious Belief

(a) The arguments

Authors like Flew are saying that religious believers need to justify their beliefs at the bar of reason. According to Phillips, however, the project of rationally justifying religious belief is misguided both because it springs from a mistaken view of the nature of philosophy and because it does not engage with the true nature of religious belief. Take, for example, belief in God. In Phillips's view, belief in God is intelligible and acceptable on its own terms. It does not stand in need of the support of rational or philosophical argument.[22]

With respect to belief in God and the nature of philosophy, Phillips appeals to what Wittgenstein says in his *Philosophical Investigations*. In particular, he sets much store by the following comments:

> A philosophical problem has the form: 'I don't know my way about'. Philosophy may in no way interfere with the actual use of language; it can in the end only describe it. For it cannot give it any foundation either. It leaves everything as it is.[23]

Phillips also invokes a distinction made by Wittgenstein between 'surface grammar' and 'depth grammar'.[24] Roughly speaking, this is a distinction between what utterances or sentences *appear* to mean and what they *really* mean. Consider the sentence 'I have a pain in my foot'. Grammatically, this resembles 'I have a key in my pocket'. But we would be wrong to think of a pain as a material object with a precise physical location. Here, then, we can distinguish between what the first sentence seems to mean and what it really means. It might seem to mean that, if surgeons cut my leg open, they will find a pain-shaped thing. But it actually means something quite different.

Now, says Phillips, the role of philosophy with respect to belief in God is not to ground it in something called 'reason'. Rather, philosophy should simply analyse or describe what belief in God amounts to. Or, as Phillips himself writes:

> If the philosopher wants to give an account of religion, he must pay attention to what religious believers do and say ... The whole conception of religion standing in need of justification is confused ... Philosophy is neither for nor against religion: 'it leaves everything as it is' ... It is not the task of the philosopher to decide whether there is a God or not, but to ask what it means to affirm or deny the existence of God.[25]

And, Phillips goes on to suggest, when philosophers have done this, they will see that, contrary to what surface indications may lead us to suppose, belief in God does not require 'rational' support or justification. If I say 'I have a pain in my foot', it would be wrong for me to try to defend what I say by urging you to bring in the surgeons and by telling them to look in my foot for a pain. By the same token, says Phillips, 'There is a God' is not an utterance which needs to be defended by 'rational' arguments of the sort for which people like Antony Flew are looking.

For example, Phillips argues, belief in God is not a hypothesis based on grounds. It is not open to falsification, and it is not held tentatively:

> The believer's hope is not hope *for* anything, moral improvement, for example ... It is simply hope, hope in the sense of the ability to live with himself ... To see the world as God's creation is to see meaning in life. This meaningfulness remains untouched by the evil in the world because it is not arrived at by inference from it.[26]

Nor is it true, adds Phillips, that belief in God is based on empirical evidence. God is not an empirical object which might or might not exist.

> One will never understand what is meant by belief in God if one thinks of God as a being who may or may not exist ... [L]et us assume, for a moment, that the reality of God is akin to the reality of a physical object. It will then make sense to assume that one day we will be able to check whether our belief is true. Let us assume, further, that such a day comes, and that we find that there is a God and that He is as we had always thought Him to be. What kind of a God would we have discovered? Clearly, a God of whom it would still make sense to say that He might not exist. Such a God may, as a matter

of fact, never cease to exist . . . A God who is an existent among existents is not the God of religious belief.[27]

According to Phillips, 'God exists' is not an indicative statement. 'Talk of God's existence or reality', he explains, 'cannot be considered as talk about the existence of an object.'[28] Following up on this he writes:

> To ask whether God exists is not to ask a theoretical question. If it is to mean anything at all, it is to wonder about praising and praying; it is to wonder whether there is anything in all that. This is why philosophy cannot answer the question 'Does God exist?' with either an affirmative or a negative reply . . . 'There is a God', though it appears to be in the indicative mood, is an expression of faith.[29]

(b) Comments

As the pain/key example indicates, Wittgenstein's distinction between surface grammar and depth grammar is a proper one to draw. And one can hardly object to the suggestion that philosophers need to clarify the meaning of what people say (philosophers have been acting on this suggestion for centuries). So our assessment of Phillips on the topic of philosophy and religion must presumably hinge on our reaction to the way in which he elucidates the nature of religious belief. He takes it to be intrinsically different from what people have in mind when they think of beliefs which stand in need of evidence, grounds, or reason. But is he right?

One point in Phillips's favour is that those who believe in God often do not do so just because of philosophical arguments. Some of them offer philosophical arguments for the claim that God exists. But many of them do not believe as they do because of such arguments. Then again, Phillips is right to suggest that there are differences between believing in God and believing in a hypothesis, or in something for which we have evidence. Hypotheses are entertained tentatively. But those who believe in God do not normally speak as though it might, after all, turn out that there is no God.

One might object to Phillips by saying that those who believe in God take him to be a person like you and me, something we should only believe in because we have reason for doing so. As we saw in Chapter 1, however, many theists do not think of God as a person. And some of the things that these theists say might be noted in defence of what Phillips asserts when it comes to belief in God. Take, for example, Phillips's claim that God 'is not an existent among existents'. Theistic personalists are likely to reject this claim considered as an account of what they take God to be. But classical theists might very well recognize it as a neat way of summarizing their belief in God's simplicity. According to Aquinas, God is 'outside the realm of existents, as a cause from which pours forth everything that exists in all its variant forms'.[30] Here we have a notable classical theist who seems to be saying something very like what Phillips proclaims to be part and parcel of belief in God.

When it comes to the difference between belief in persons and belief in God, we can also defend Phillips with an eye on biblical texts. These texts (in standard English translations) speak of God as 'he', and they tell us that God does what many of us do. He talks, he gets angry, he loves his children, he 'goes forth', he stamps his foot, and so on. But the Bible also tells us that God has no body, that nothing can thwart him, that he tends to all things, and that he lives in no place from which he can go forth. Readers of the Bible may be forgiven for thinking that the biblical God is different from anything we normally think of as a person.[31] And Phillips could appeal to this fact when defending his claim that belief in God is not subject to defence or refutation in the way that belief in other things is.

Yet even classical theists take some of the things they say about God to be true without supposing that the words they use to describe God lack a common meaning with these words as used to talk about what is not divine. Hence, for example, although Aquinas holds that God is 'outside the realm of existents', he also asserts that God is causal, alive, knowing, active, good, and powerful. And, he says, to speak of God as being such is not to use words in a sense which differs entirely from the sense we have in mind when we use them in non-theistic discourse. Like Phillips, Aquinas is keen to stress the difference between God and items in the spatio-temporal universe. And one can imagine him agreeing that Phillips's account of belief in God captures much that is essential to it. But one cannot imagine him saying, as Phillips does, that 'God exists' is an expression of faith and *not* a statement in the indicative mood. Nor can one imagine any theistic personalist saying that. So we might wonder whether Phillips has really got it right when it comes to philosophy and religion in general. Claiming to elucidate only what religious beliefs amount to, Phillips speaks as though these are utterly different from all other beliefs. And he insists that belief in God cannot be compared to belief in the existence of what is not divine. Given the ways in which religious believers speak, however, perhaps he is wrong to do so.

In that case, however, should we conclude that religious believers really do need to produce evidence, grounds, or reasons before being entitled to hold their beliefs? Phillips denies that they do. For him, there is no rational perspective outside religion from which it can be judged to be reasonable or unreasonable. Without buying into Phillips's way of talking, however, might we reasonably maintain that at least some religious beliefs need no evidence, grounds, or reasons to support them? With no reference to Wittgenstein, might we cogently claim that it is proper to believe in God without any evidence at all?

Belief Without Evidence

(a) The arguments

According to some philosophers, the answer to these questions is 'Yes'. Take, for example, Alvin Plantinga, according to whom 'it is entirely right, rational, reasonable, and proper to believe in God without any evidence or argument at all'.[32] Why so? Because, says Plantinga, there is no reason to suppose that people are being unreasonable if they start by believing in God and make no attempt to ground it with reference to some other belief. People, says Plantinga, are rationally entitled to take 'God exists' as a foundation for their thinking and arguing.

Some philosophers have taught or implied that a belief is reasonable only if it is self-evidently true, evident to the senses, or rationally derivable from what is self-evident or evident to the senses. And some of these philosophers have rejected belief in God since they do not think it meets their standards for reasonable belief. According to Plantinga, however, all these philosophers are mistaken. Plantinga calls them 'classical foundationalists', and he refers to their position as 'classical foundationalism'. And, he argues, classical foundationalism is wrong.

For one thing, he suggests, it is not always unreasonable to believe without evidence. Second, he argues, we do not arrive at all of our day-to-day beliefs in ways sanctioned by classical foundationalism. And finally, says Plantinga, classical foundationalism is just self-referentially incoherent. Why? Because it does not satisfy its own criteria for reasonable belief. Why not? Because, notes Plantinga, it is not self-evidently true. Nor is its truth evident to the senses or derivable from what is self-evidently true or evident to the senses.

This conclusion, in turn, leaves Plantinga siding with what he calls 'the reformed objection to natural theology'. Here he is thinking of certain Protestant theologians who deny that theism needs to be based on arguments for God's existence, theologians such as Herman Bavinck (1854–1921). According to Bavinck:

> There is not a single object the existence of which we hesitate to accept until definite proofs are furnished. Of the existence of self, of the world round about us, of logical and moral laws, etc., we are so deeply convinced because of the indelible impressions which all these things make upon our consciousness that we need no arguments or demonstration. Spontaneously, altogether involuntarily, without any constraint or coercion, we accept that existence. Now the same is true in regard to the existence of God.[33]

Here Bavinck is characterizing theism as something which does not depend on philosophical reasoning. And he is saying that those who believe in God can rationally start with belief that God exists. On Bavinck's account, there is no need for me to justify my belief in God with reference to other beliefs. And this is Plantinga's position. He is not denying that there are good philosophical arguments for the truth of 'God exists'. But he does not think that those who believe in God need such arguments in order to be believing reasonably. In this sense, he holds, belief in God's existence is 'properly basic'.

(b) Comments

But is it? Those who suspect that it cannot be are likely to do so because they subscribe to something like what Plantinga calls classical foundationalism. Yet Plantinga's case against classical foundationalism is a strong one. Classical foundationalism does not, indeed, satisfy its own standards for rational belief. It is not self-evident that we believe reasonably only if the truth of our belief is self-evident, evident to the senses, or derivable from what is self-evident or evident to the senses. Nor is it evident to the senses, or derivable from what is self-evident or evident to the senses, that we believe reasonably only if the truth of our belief is self-evident, evident to the senses, or derivable from what is self-evident or evident to the senses.

And, as Plantinga notes, much that passes for reasonable belief is not arrived at by people reasoning as classical foundationalists say that we should reason. Someone's belief that such and such is the case is not to be dismissed as 'unreasonable' just because the person cannot produce evidence for the truth of the belief. Children may not be able to produce evidence for the belief that such and such people are their parents. But they need not be believing unreasonably in believing that certain people actually are their parents. In fact, and as Elizabeth Anscombe notes, 'the greater part of our knowledge of reality rests upon the belief that we repose in things we have been taught and told'.[34] And, as Anscombe goes on to say:

> Nor is what testimony gives us entirely a detachable part, like the thick fringe of fat on a chunk of steak. It is more like the flecks and streaks of fat that are often distributed through good meat; though there are lumps of pure fat as well. Examples could be multiplied indefinitely. You have received letters; how did you ever learn what a letter was and how it came to you? You will take up a book and look in a certain place and see 'New York, Dodd Mead and Company, 1910'. So do you know from personal observation that that book was published by that company, and then, and in New York? Well, hardly. But you do know it *purports* to have been so. How? Well, you know that is where the publisher's name is always put, and the name of the place where his office belongs. How do you know that? You were taught it . . . You may think you know that New York is in North America. What is New York, what is North America? You may say you have been to these places. But how much does that fact contribute to your knowledge? Nothing, in comparison with testimony. How did you know you were there? Even if you inhabit New York and you have simply learned its name as the name of the place you inhabit, there is the question: How extensive a region is this place you are calling 'New York'? And what has New York got to do with this bit of a map? Here is a complicated network of received information.[35]

One might reply that Plantinga has no way of ruling out even the wildest of beliefs. If those who believe in God are rationally entitled to do so without supporting reason, why should the same not be true of everyone, regardless of what they believe? Yet Plantinga need not be especially embarrassed by this question. He is not denying that people can make mistakes and believe what is false. He is not committed to saying that anything goes. Nor is he denying that we can reasonably reject a whole range of beliefs. Rather, he is simply insisting that certain beliefs are properly basic. An objector might say that any belief, no matter how odd, must be deemed to be rational unless we have a criterion to determine what can properly be believed without further evidence or grounds. And, the objector might add, Plantinga supplies us with no such criterion. Yet Plantinga can reply that we need not have any such criterion in order to be entitled to say that certain beliefs are irrational—just as we need have no grand, philosophical criterion of meaningfulness to be entitled to reject as meaningless some such utterance as 'T'was brillig; and the slithy toves did gyre and gymble in the wabe'.[36]

Yet, might we not argue that Plantinga is going too far in claiming that 'it is entirely right, rational, reasonable, and proper to believe in God without any evidence or argument at all'? That conclusion could be taken to mean that it is fine to believe in God for no reason at all. Yet, why should we agree that this is so? Does even Plantinga believe that it is so? He denies that reasonable belief in God has to be arrived at by inference from beliefs which are supposedly better grounded than is belief in God. But he also refers to people coming to believe in God because of circumstances that give rise to their belief. Although he says that belief in God is properly basic, he insists that it is not 'groundless'. Why? Because he thinks that it can be compared to other beliefs which we form, not on the basis of inference or argument, but just because of the way things seem to us as we go about our lives. Yet forming beliefs just because of the way things seem to us is to form beliefs on the basis of evidence. Forming beliefs in this way is not to do so with no evidence at all.

In other words, we can sympathize with some of the points made by Plantinga while also denying that they show that belief in God can be rationally held without any evidence. Those who think that theists need evidence for their position do not generally state what sort of evidence is needed. In general, they are only suggesting that it is irrational to believe that God exists without any evidence or reason at all. And

Plantinga has not proved that suggestion to be misguided.[37] If anything, his account of basic belief in God coheres with it. To say that belief in God is basic is not, he explains, to say 'that there are no justifying circumstances for it'.[38] There are, says Plantinga, 'many conditions and circumstances that call forth belief in God'.[39] In that case, however, Plantinga is effectively conceding that properly basic belief in God can, indeed, spring from evidence, from sufficient support or backing of some sort. And if he is right to do so, it is fair to ask what sort of support or backing there could be for this belief and for others like it.

Moving On Yet Again

In this chapter we have looked at a variety of views. None of them lacks merit. And all of them have had an influence in the (admittedly small) world inhabited by philosophers. But do they suggest a direction in which we might now turn as we continue to explore the philosophy of religion?

All of the views in question have a bearing on belief in the existence of God. And all of them are, in one way or another, concerned with the question 'Is it reasonable to believe that God exists?' As we have seen, some philosophers think that belief in God is untenable, while others disagree, albeit for different reasons. As I have so far presented them, however, none of these thinkers has anything detailed to say about arguments in defence of 'God exists'. At this point, therefore, maybe we can turn to some of these. Or, as some philosophers would say, perhaps we might turn to some arguments of natural theology.

We met the phrase 'natural theology' above. What does it mean? Definitions vary, but we can think of it as the attempt to ground beliefs about God on purely rational reflection. We can think of it as the attempt to show that belief in God's existence can be (even if it does not *have* to be) defended by reason or argument which ought to be acceptable to anyone, not simply to those who already believe in God. But is there any good natural theology available? Can belief in God be defended without presupposing it? Many philosophers (even Alvin Plantinga) have argued that it can.[40] In the next few chapters, therefore, we shall look at some of their reasons for doing so.

NOTES

1. Henry Fielding, *Tom Jones*, Book III, ch. 3.

2. David Hume lived most of his life in Edinburgh. He is especially well known among philosophers for defending an empiricist approach to knowledge (an approach stressing the importance of sensory experience as a source of knowledge). His most important works are *A Treatise of Human Nature* (1739/1740), *An Enquiry concerning Human Understanding* (1748), *An Enquiry concerning the Principles of Morals* (1751), and *Dialogues concerning Natural Religion* (1778).

3. David Hume, *An Enquiry concerning Human Understanding*, ed. L. A. Selby-Bigge (3rd edn., Oxford, 1975), p. 165.

4. Friedrich Waismann, 'Logische Analyse des Wahrscheinlichkeitsbegriffs', *Erkenntnis* 1 (1930–1).

5. In A. J. Ayer (ed.), *Logical Positivism* (Glencoe, IL, 1959), p. 63.

6. A. J. Ayer, *Language, Truth and Logic* (2nd edn., London, 1946), p. 115. Ayer (1910–89) taught philosophy at Oxford University prior to his retirement.

7. Antony Flew is Emeritus Professor of Philosophy at Reading University, England. He is well known for his work on Hume, but he has also published a lot on philosophy of religion, including *God and Philosophy* (1966), *The Presumption of Atheism* (1976), and *Atheistic Humanism* (1993). The notion of empirical falsification is important in philosophy of science especially in the light of the work of Karl Popper (1902–94).

8. Antony Flew, 'Theology and Falsification', reprinted in Basil Mitchell (ed.), *The Philosophy of Religion* (Oxford, 1971). As Flew himself likes to point out, 'Theology and Falsification', though very short, is probably the most reprinted twentieth-century essay in philosophy of religion.

9. Flew's 'parable' derives from John Wisdom's 'Gods', to be found in John Wisdom, *Philosophy and Psychoanalysis* (Oxford, 1953).

10. Flew, 'Theology and Falsification', p. 13.

11. Note that the writers we have been looking at did not believe that logical or mathematical statements stand in need of empirical verification. Nor did they think of them as empirically falsifiable. But they also held that such statements are not factual.

12. Moritz Schlick, 'Meaning and Verification', reprinted in Herbert Feigl and Wilfrid Sellars (eds.), *Readings in Philosophical Analysis* (New York, 1949).

13. Richard Swinburne, *The Coherence of Theism* (rev. edn., Oxford, 1993), p. 28.

14. Ibid. pp. 28f.

15. For Church's discussion, see Alonzo Church's review of Ayer's *Language, Truth and Logic* (2nd edn.) in *Journal of Symbolic Logic* 14 (1949), pp. 52ff. For Ayer's admission, see his *The Central Questions of Philosophy* (London, 1973).

16. Antony Flew, *The Presumption of Atheism and Other Essays* (London, 1976), p. 22.

17. Clifford's position can be found in 'The Ethics of Belief', in W. K. Clifford, *Lectures and Essays*, ed. Leslie Stephen and Frederick Pollock (2nd edn., London, 1886). This essay has been frequently reprinted in whole or in part. I quote from the reprint in Brian Davies (ed.), *Philosophy of Religion: A Guide and Anthology* (Oxford, 2000), p. 35.

18. Hume, *An Enquiry concerning Human Understanding*, p. 110. See also Chapter 11 below.

19. Ludwig Wittgenstein, *On Certainty*, trans. D. Paul and G. E. M. Anscombe (Oxford, 1974), §§160–7.

20. Norman Malcolm, 'The Groundlessness of Belief', in Stuart C. Brown (ed.), *Reason and Religion* (Ithaca, NY, and London, 1977), p. 151. Norman Malcolm (1911–90) was one of the most distinguished of Wittgenstein's pupils and the main conveyor of his ideas to the USA, where Malcolm taught for many years at Cornell University.

21. D. Z. Phillips is Danforth Professor of Philosophy of Religion at Claremont Graduate University, California, and Rush Rhees Research Professor at the University of Wales, Swansea.

22. For the statement of a view similar to that of Phillips, see D. C. Barrett, 'Faith and Rationality', in A. Phillips Griffiths (ed.), *Key Themes in Philosophy* (Cambridge, 1989).

23. Ludwig Wittgenstein, *Philosophical Investigations*, trans. G. E. M. Anscombe (Oxford, 1968), §§123–4.

24. Ibid., §664.

25. D. Z. Phillips, *The Concept of Prayer* (London, 1965), pp.1ff.

26. Ibid., pp. 67f.

27. Ibid., p. 81.

28. D. Z. Phillips, *Religion Without Explanation* (Oxford, 1976), p. 174.

29. Ibid., p. 181.

30. Thomas Aquinas, *In Peri Hermeneias*, Lec. XIV.

31. For a sophisticated development of this point, see Gareth Moore, *Believing in God* (Edinburgh, 1988).

32. Alvin Plantinga, 'Reason and Belief in God', in Alvin Plantinga and Nicholas Wolterstorff (eds.), *Faith and Rationality* (Notre Dame, IN, 1983), p. 17.

33. Herman Bavinck, *The Doctrine of God*, trans. William Hendricksen (Grand Rapids, MI, 1951), quoted by Plantinga in 'Reason and Belief in God'.

34. G. E. M. Anscombe, 'What Is It to Believe Someone?' in C. F. Delaney (ed.), *Rationality and Religious Belief* (Notre Dame, IN, and London, 1979), p. 143. See also Norman Malcolm, 'The Groundlessness of Belief', in Stuart C. Brown (ed.), *Reason and Religion* (London, 1977).

35. Anscombe, 'What Is It to Believe Someone?', pp. 143f.

36. Here, of course, I am quoting the opening line of the poem 'Jabberwocky', to be found in chapter 1 of Lewis Carroll's *Through the Looking Glass and What Alice Found There* (first published in 1871).

37. For a detailed defence of this conclusion, see Norman Kretzmann, 'Evidence Against Anti-Evidentialism', in K. J. Clark, *Our Knowledge of God* (Dortrecht, 1992). This essay is reprinted in a slightly abridged form in (see n.17) Davies, *Philosophy of Religion: A Guide and Anthology*, pp. 95–107.

38. Plantinga and Wolterstorff (eds.), *Faith and Rationality*, p. 80.

39. Ibid., p. 81.

40. For Plantinga being positive with respect to natural theology, see Chapter 5 below.

FURTHER READING

For more on the topics covered in this chapter, you should consult some general works on philosophy and religion. Particularly worth turning to are: Robert Audi and William Wainwright (eds.), *Rationality, Religious Belief, and Moral Commitment* (Ithaca, NY, 1986); Jack A. Bonsor, *Athens and Jerusalem: The Role of Philosophy in Theology* (New York, 1993); Stuart Brown (ed.), *Reason and Religion* (Ithaca, NY, and London, 1977); Vincent Brümmer, *Theology and Philosophical Inquiry* (London and Basingstoke, 1981); Anthony Kenny, *What is Faith?* (Oxford and New York, 1992); Terence Penelhum, *Reason and Religious Faith* (Oxford, 1995); John E. Smith, *Reason and God: Encounters of Philosophy with Religion* (New Haven, CT, and London 1961); Richard Swinburne, *Faith and Reason* (Oxford, 1981); Timothy Tessin and Mario von der Ruhr (eds.), *Philosophy and the Grammar of Religious Belief* (New York, 1995); and Roger Trigg, *Rationality and Religion* (Oxford, 1998).

For an introductory discussion of verificationism, falsificationism, and religious belief, see Frederick Ferré, *Language, Logic and God* (London and Glasgow,

1970). For a more technical discussion, see R. S. Heimbeck, *Theology and Meaning* (London, 1969). For an introduction to logical positivism, see Oswald Hanfling, *Logical Positivism* (Oxford, 1981) and id. (ed.), *Essential Readings in Logical Positivism* (Oxford, 1981). For a trenchant defence of an empirical critique of belief in God, see Kai Nielsen, *Scepticism* (London, 1973) and *An Introduction to the Philosophy of Religion* (London, 1982). For subtle criticism of certain verificationist assumptions, see W. V. O. Quine, 'Two Dogmas of Empiricism', in W. V. O. Quine, *From a Logical Point of View* (Cambridge, MA, and London, 1953). For a reader on verificationism and religious belief, see Malcolm I. Diamond and Thomas V. Litzenburg, Jr. (eds.), *The Logic of God: Theology and Verification* (Indianapolis, IN, 1975). For general discussion on the nature of talk about God, see William P. Alston, *Divine Nature and Human Language* (Ithaca, NY, and London, 1989); Janet Martin Soskice, *Metaphor and Religious Language* (Oxford, 1985); and David Tracy, *The Analogical Imagination* (London, 1981).

Authors such as Clifford and Flew argue in ways reminiscent of John Locke, who is a significant author when it comes to the topic of philosophy and religion in general. Locke deals with faith and reason in Part IV of his *Essay Concerning Human Understanding* and in *The Reasonableness of Christianity*. For editions of these texts, see Peter H. Nidditch (ed.), *An Essay Concerning Human Understanding* (Oxford, 1975) and I. T. Ramsey (ed.), *The Reasonableness of Christianity* (Stanford, CA, 1958). For discussions of Locke on faith and reason, see Paul Helm, 'Locke on Faith and Knowledge', *The Philosophical Quarterly* 90 (1973); Alan P. F. Sell, *John Locke and the Eighteenth-Century Divines* (Cardiff, 1997); and Nicholas Wolterstorff, *John Locke and the Ethics of Belief* (Cambridge, 1996).

D. Z. Phillips has published many books. To get a proper sense of his position, you should consult at least a few of them. They include: *The Concept of Prayer* (London, 1965); *Faith and Philosophical Enquiry* (London, 1970); *Religion Without Explanation* (Oxford, 1976); *Belief, Change and Forms of Life* (Atlantic Highlands, NJ, 1986); *Faith after Foundationalism* (London and New York, 1988); *Wittgenstein and Religion* (London, 1993); *Recovering Religious Concepts: Closing Epistemic Divides* (London and New York, 2000).

If you are interested in exploring what might be said about religion with an eye on Wittgenstein's philosophy, there are several authors worth reading apart from Phillips. In *Religion, Truth and Language-Games* (London, 1977), Patrick Sherry provides a sober and insightful discussion on the importance of Wittgenstein to philosophy of religion, which takes a stance somewhat different from that of Phillips. In *Does God's Existence Need Proof?* (Oxford, 1993), Richard Meser offers a balanced discussion of the question contained in his book's title, a discussion which deals with Plantinga, Phillips, and a number of other authors. For a critical evaluation of Wittgensteinan trends in philosophy of religion, see Roger Trigg, *Reason and Commitment* (Cambridge, 1973). For a fine account of Wittgenstein's thinking on religious matters, see Cyril Barrett, *Wittgenstein on Ethics and Religious Belief* (Oxford, 1991). Also see Brian R. Clack, *An Introduction to Wittgenstein's Philosophy of Religion* (Edinburgh, 1999). This contains some good expositions of Wittgenstein and some helpful introductions to, and discussions of, authors such as Phillips.

Plantinga has written about belief in God and proper basicality in a number of works. See in particular: 'Is Belief in God Rational?', in C. F. Delaney (ed.), *Rationality and Religious Belief* (Notre Dame, IN, 1979); 'The Reformed Objection to Natural Theology', *Christian Scholar's Review* 11 (1982); 'The Reformed Objection Revisited', *Christian Scholar's Review* 12 (1983); 'Advice to Christian Philosophers', *Faith and Philosophy* 1 (1984); and *Warrant and Proper Function* (Oxford, 1993). Someone who agrees in many ways with Plantinga on the topic of religious belief and reason is Nicholas Wolterstorff. See his 'The Migration of the Theistic Arguments: From Natural Theology to Evidentialist Apologetics', in Audi and Wainwright, *Rationality, Religious Belief, and Moral Commitment*. See also his 'Can Belief in God Be Rational If It Has No Foundations?' in Alvin Plantinga and Nicholas Wolterstorff (eds.), *Faith and Rationality* (Notre Dame, IN, 1983). For some discussion of Plantinga on proper basicality and belief in God, see Philip Quinn, 'In Search of the Foundations of Theism', *Faith and Philosophy* 2 (1985); D. Z. Phillips, *Faith After Foundationalism*; Gary Gutting, 'Plantinga and the Rationality of Religious Belief', in Tessin and von der Ruhr (eds.), *Philosophy and the Grammar of Religious Belief*; and Linda Zagzebski (ed.), *Rational Faith: Catholic Responses to Reformed Epistemology* (Notre Dame, IN, 1983). Plantinga has replied to Quinn in 'The Foundations of Theism: A Reply', *Faith and Philosophy* 3 (1986). For a general study of 'reformed epistemology', see Dewey Hoitenga, *Faith and Reason from Plato to Plantinga: An Introduction to Reformed Epistemology* (Albany, NY, 1991).

QUESTIONS FOR DISCUSSION

1 How would you explain what philosophy is? How would you explain what religion is? Does your understanding of 'philosophy' and 'religion' allow you to say what philosophy of religion is?

2 To what extent does knowledge depend on sensory experience?

3 Suppose that X is wholly immaterial. Does it follow that 'X exists' is nonsensical? If so, why? If not, why not?

4 'I don't care what you say. I know that my husband loves me.' Might a wife

reasonably assert that? If so, why? If not, why not? Answer these questions with an eye on what Antony Flew says about belief in God and falsification.

5 What do you take the word 'evidence' to mean? On the basis of your answer, consider the claim that one should never hold beliefs without evidence.

6 How can we know that what we take to be evidence really is evidence?

7 Is there a clear distinction to be made between religious beliefs and other ones?

8 Can God be thought of as an item in any world? If so, why? If not, why not?

9 'Santa Claus exists.' 'Everyone is out to harm me.' 'There are fairies at the bottom of my garden.' If Plantinga is right to say that belief in God can be properly basic, does it follow that any of these beliefs can also be properly basic?

10 Do you think that anyone believes in God without any reason for doing so?

3

COSMOLOGICAL ARGUMENTS

Advocates of natural theology hold that there are reasons for believing in God which do not presuppose that God, in fact, exists. As William Alston puts it, natural theologians commonly begin 'from the mere existence of the world, or the teleological order of the world, or the concept of God'. And they try 'to show that when we think through the implications of our starting point we are led to recognize the existence of a being that possesses attributes sufficient to identify him as God'.[1] Alston goes on to say that the credentials of natural theology 'have often been challenged in the modern era'. As he also observes, however, 'like the phoenix it keeps rising from its ashes in ever new guises'.[2]

One form in which natural theology keeps rising is sometimes referred to as 'the cosmological argument'. When people who believe in God are asked why they do so, they often say, 'The world cannot come from nothing'. The idea here is that the existence of the universe demands a cause, reason, or explanation. And that is the basic idea of the cosmological argument. But it is better to speak of 'cosmological arguments' rather than of 'the cosmological argument'. For, as we shall now see, the history of philosophy has witnessed a variety of arguments for God's existence all of which can fairly be referred to as 'cosmological'.[3]

God and the Beginning of the Universe

There are many things which we know to have come into being. And they raise a perfectly natural question. What brought them into being? What got them started? When we are dealing with things that have begun to exist, we do not assume that they 'just happened'. We suppose that something produced them.

This familiar way of reasoning brings us to one major cosmological argument. It is particularly associated with a group of writers in the Middle Ages and earlier, a group which belonged to the Islamic kalām tradition of philosophy. So we can call it 'the kalām cosmological argument' ('kalām' is Arabic for 'speech'). But, although the name may sound unfamiliar, the argument is not, for it is commonly advanced at a popular level. Whether they know it or not, it is the kalām argument that people are basically offering when they say, as they often do, that 'things cannot have got going by themselves'.

The fundamental idea here is that God exists because the universe must have had a beginning and because only God could have brought this about. Together with this idea goes the belief that everything that begins to exist must have a cause. In the words of William Lane Craig, one of the kalām's argument's most recent defenders:

> Since everything that begins to exist has a cause of its existence, and since the universe began to exist, we conclude, therefore, the universe has a cause of its existence . . . Transcending the entire universe there exists a cause which brought the universe into being . . . But even more: we may plausibly argue that the cause of the universe is a personal being . . . If the universe began to exist, and if the universe is caused, then the cause of the universe must be a personal being who freely chooses to create the world . . . The kalām cosmological argument leads to a personal Creator of the universe.[4]

You may wonder why it should be thought that, if the beginning of the universe was caused to be, 'the cause of the universe must be a personal being'. Defenders of the kalām argument would, however, say that only free, intelligent choice can account for the emergence of what, like the beginning of the universe, cannot be explained in terms of unfree, non-intelligent, physical processes. The occurrence of such processes depends on the universe being there in the first place. So the cause of the beginning of the universe, if there is one, cannot be an unfree, non-intelligent, physical process. According to defenders of the kalām argument, that leaves only one other kind of cause to be responsible for the universe coming into being. The cause, so they argue, must be a personal being.

(a) Beginnings and causes

But must whatever has a beginning of existence have a cause? Some philosophers have said that it evidently must. An example is Thomas Reid (1710–96). According to him: '*That neither existence, nor any mode of existence, can begin without an efficient cause*, is a principle that appears very early in the mind of man; and it is so universal, and so firmly rooted in human nature, that the most determined scepticism cannot eradicate it.'[5]

But some philosophers have argued that there is no way of proving that whatever has a beginning of existence has a cause. A famous example is David Hume. According to him:

> As all distinct ideas are separable from each other, and as the ideas of cause and effect are evidently distinct, 'twill be easy for us to conceive any object to be non-existent this moment, and existent the next, without conjoining to it the distinct idea of a cause or productive principle. The separation, therefore, of the idea of a cause from that of a beginning of existence is plainly possible for the imagination, and consequently the actual separation of these objects is so far possible that it implies no contradiction or absurdity.[6]

Yet this argument is open to question. Hume is saying that, since we can imagine a beginning of existence without any cause, it follows that there can be a beginning of existence without any cause. But that is false. As F. C. Copleston observes, 'even if one can imagine first a blank, as it were, and then X existing, it by no means follows necessarily that X can begin to exist without an extrinsic cause'.[7] The same point has been made by Elizabeth Anscombe. In her words:

> If I say I can imagine a rabbit coming into being without a parent rabbit, well and good: I imagine a rabbit coming into being, and our observing that there is no parent rabbit about. But what am I to imagine if I imagine a rabbit coming into being without a cause? Well, I just imagine a rabbit coming into being. That this *is* the imagination of a rabbit coming into being without a cause is nothing but, as it were, the *title* of the picture. Indeed I can form an image and give my picture that title. But from my being able to do *that*, nothing whatever follows about what it is possible to suppose 'without contradiction or absurdity' as holding in reality.[8]

In reply to Anscombe, you might say that you can imagine something coming into existence at some time and place and there being no cause of this. But how do you know that the thing in question has come into existence at the time and place you picture it as beginning to exist? You have to exclude the possibility that it previously existed elsewhere and, by some means or other, came to be where you picture it as beginning to exist. Yet, how are you to do that without supposing a cause which justifies you in judging that the thing really came into existence, rather than just reappeared? As Anscombe writes: 'We can observe beginnings of new items because we know how they were produced and out of what . . . We know the times and places of their beginnings without cavil because we understand their origins.'[9]

In other words, to know that something began to exist is already to know that it has been caused. So it is odd to suppose that there could be a beginning of existence without a cause. Even Hume seems to have thought this, in spite of what he argues about cause and effect. In a letter written in 1754, he says: 'But allow me to tell you that I never asserted so absurd a Proposition as *that anything might arise without a cause*: I only maintain'd that, our Certainty of the Falsehood of that Proposition proceeded neither from Intuition nor Demonstration; but from another Source.'[10] In a similar vein, C. D. Broad (1887–1971) explains that, 'whatever I may *say* when I am trying to give Hume a run for his money, I cannot really *believe* in anything beginning to exist without being *caused* (in the old-fashioned sense of *produced* or *generated*) by something else'.[11]

(b) The beginning of the universe

So the kalām argument is evidently on to something. We might reasonably suppose that beginnings of existence arise from causal activity. And if the universe began to exist, perhaps we should conclude that the same is true of it. But this, of course, brings us to another question. Did the universe have a beginning?

Some have maintained that scientific evidence suggests that the universe began to exist a finite time ago. According to Richard Swinburne, for instance:

> There is no doubt that the models best substantiated today are ones which show the Universe expanding from a 'big bang' some 14,000 million years ago. These models successfully predict not merely the density and rate of

recession of the galaxies, but the ratios of the various chemical elements to each other and to radiation in the universe, and above all the background radiation.[12]

We may wonder, however, whether the scientific evidence for this conclusion truly shows that the universe actually had a beginning. Should we not regard it as evidence only of our ability somehow to date a 'big bang'? And might we not ask whether the universe could not have existed in some sense before that event, or before any limit to which science can reach at the moment? Our scientific research may take us just so far back and no further. But does it follow that there is no 'further back' to which our science, at present, does not reach?

At this point, however, certain philosophers will argue that there are non-scientific considerations that should lead us to conclude that the universe had a beginning.[13] Such philosophers will, for example, say that, if the universe had no beginning, then an infinity of years or generations has actually elapsed before now, and that this is impossible. Why? Because, so the argument goes, an infinity of actual past years or generations cannot be thought of as now over. Suppose I turn up looking all hot and bothered. I then gasp, 'Four, three, two, one. Finished!' You ask me what is going on. I say that I have just finished counting backwards from infinity. Would you believe me? Probably not. According to some philosophers, however, you ought to have no problem with what I say if you also believe that an infinity of years or generations has elapsed before now.

Another philosophical argument in favour of the claim that the universe must have had a beginning holds that, if the universe never began, infinity is being constantly added to as time goes on, which is impossible. For, how can infinity admit of addition? Yet another argument hinges on the notion of infinity and the possibility of removing a past event. If the universe had no beginning, then the number of past events is infinite. But, so our third argument runs, the number of members of an infinite set is unaffected by the addition or subtraction of one. There are as many odd numbers as even numbers. And there are as many odd numbers not counting the number 1 as counting it. So, the argument concludes, if the universe had no beginning, a past event could be removed and we would still be left with the same number of events—which is surely unbelievable.

Not all philosophers have accepted such arguments, however. Some, for instance, have said that, if the universe never had a beginning, there was no definite number of elapsed past events prior to today. It has also been suggested that, if the universe never had a beginning, then there is no reason to suppose that infinity is being added to in any objectionable sense. Why not? Because, the argument goes, if the universe had no beginning, there is no definite number of past moments or events being added to as time goes on. Why not? Because there is no definite number to which addition is thereby made.

The chief issue at stake in the philosophical arguments for the thesis that the universe began to exist is whether or not there can be an infinite set of actual things (e.g. past events). Can there be such a thing? This is a question which I shall now have to leave you to consider for yourself. Note, however, that you would be saying something odd if you end up concluding that there could be an infinite set of actual things since it is possible that every event has a predecessor (which is one way of expressing the claim that the universe never had a beginning). 'It is possible that every event has a predecessor' could mean either (a) there might have been more past events than there have been, or (b) it might have been the case both that a certain set comprised all the events that occurred, and also that an additional event occurred. Although (a) is arguably true, it does not entail that the universe never began. And (b) is simply self-contradictory.[14]

(c) A personal being?

But even if we grant that the beginning of the universe was caused, should we also agree that we therefore have good reason to believe in the existence of God? Could not a cause of the beginning of the universe be something other than God? Must it be 'a personal being' as the kalām argument holds?

One reason for saying that it need not be 'a personal being' lies in the suggestion that personal beings are all material objects.[15] If the beginning of the universe had a cause, then it cannot have been a material one. For material objects are part of the universe and cannot, therefore, account for the universe beginning to exist. But what if all personal beings are material objects? If that is the case, then we ought to conclude that the beginning of the universe (assuming that the universe began to exist) cannot have been effected by a personal being.

It would, however, be widely accepted that, to account for what happens, there are only two alternatives available. On the one hand, we can invoke an explanation of a scientific kind, thereby appealing to ways in which physical effects are brought about by physical causes operating involuntarily. On the other hand, we can appeal to personal explanation in terms of the free choice or choices of a rational agent—these not being rightly thought of as merely physical processes. And, if that way of looking at things is correct, then the kalām argument can be, at least partly, defended. For, if that way of looking at things is correct, and if we agree that the universe was caused to begin, it is only personal (i.e. non-material) explanation to which we can appeal as we look for a cause in this context.

Even if we find the kalām argument persuasive, however, we may still wonder whether it counts as a good argument for the existence of God. For to believe in God is not just to believe that something brought it about that the universe *began* to be. Those who believe in God normally assert that he is responsible for the fact that the universe *continues* to exist. As we have seen, Aquinas, for example, found no difficulty in holding that, as far as philosophy can show, the universe might never have had a beginning.[16]

So, can it be argued that the universe's continued existence should lead us to conclude that God exists? With this question, we come to some other notable cosmological arguments, starting with what we may call 'the argument from sufficient reason'.

God and Sufficient Reason

Consider the fact that you have a book in your hands. Would you say that this fact calls for no explanation? Presumably not. You would probably say that there are reasons which account for the book being where it now is. But why would you say this? Suppose I said that there are no reasons accounting for the book being in your hand. What could you say to show me wrong?

Well, in jargon used by some philosophers, you might observe that your now holding a book is a *contingent* matter—something which, though *in fact* the case, does not, absolutely speaking, *have* to be the case. And with that thought in mind you might then go on to suggest that reasons are called for when something that does not have to be the case (a contingent fact) actually turns out to be the case. Some statements look as though they tell us something that could not possibly be false. Take, for example, 'Any triangle has three sides' or 'Any bachelor is unmarried'. These statements do not report truths for which external reasons need to be invoked. As philosophers would commonly say, they are *necessarily* true. But is your holding this book now true of necessity? If not, you might suppose that there are reasons which account for why you are doing so. You might argue that, when it comes to contingent truths or facts, reasons outside them should always be sought.

And that, we may say, is the 'big idea' informing the cosmological argument from sufficient reason. Is 'The world exists' contingently true? Or is it true of necessity? A characteristic of statements that are necessarily true is that to deny them is to contradict oneself. Hence, for example, 'Some bachelors are married' is not just 'false as a matter of fact'. It could not be true. Because of the meaning of 'bachelor' and 'unmarried', the statement, so to speak self-destructs. But is this the case with 'There is no world'? Is the negation of 'The world exists' contradictory? If it is not, then 'The world exists' would seem to report a contingent matter— something which is the case without having, absolutely speaking, to be so. Yet, if that is true, should we not suppose that there are reasons, or that there is at least one reason, for there being a world? According to the cosmological argument from sufficient reason, the answer is a resounding 'Yes'.

But what sort of reason? Proponents of the argument I am now referring to hold that the existence of the world must ultimately lie in something the existence of which is not contingent but necessary. Given the contingently existing world, they say, there has to be something (a reason for it, or an ultimate reason for it) which exists of necessity— something which, logically speaking, could not fail to be. And, they add, this necessary being is God. In their view, if there is no God, then the existence of the world lacks a reason. But the existence of the world must, they say, have a reason. So God exists.

Take, for example, G. W. Leibniz. According to him, God is 'the

has to be
a necessary being =
God.

ultimate reason for things'.[17] If we consider the world as a whole, says Leibniz, it is evident that 'neither in any one single thing, nor in the whole aggregate and series of things, can there be found the sufficient reason of existence'.[18] One might suspect that the world we now inhabit owes its nature and character to a beginningless series of past causes. And yet, Leibniz argues, 'however far back you go to earlier states, you will never find in those states a full reason why there should be any world at all rather than none, and why it should be such as it is'.[19] 'Even by supposing the world to be eternal', says Leibniz, 'we cannot escape the ultimate, extra-mundane reason of things, or God.'[20] We must, he adds, 'pass from physical or hypothetical necessity, which determines the subsequent things of the world by the earlier, to something which is of absolute or metaphysical necessity, for which no reason can be given'.[21]

(a) In defence of this argument

But must we? Not if the existence of the world does not need not be accounted for. Leibniz is asking: 'Why is there any world or universe?' But do we need to raise that question? Some philosophers would say 'No'. According, for instance, to Bertrand Russell, 'the universe is just there, and that's all'.[22] Following a similar line of thought, John Hick writes: 'How do we know that the universe is not "a mere unintelligible brute fact"? Apart from the emotional colouring suggested by the phrase, this is precisely what the sceptic believes it to be; and to exclude this possibility at the outset is merely to beg the question at issue.'[23]

Yet, may we not reply that our understanding of the universe does not include an understanding that it *has* to be? We know what cats are. But our knowledge of cats does not entail that cats cannot but exist. And if we find it reasonable to ask why cats exist, why should we not think the same when it comes to anything else in the world? And why should we not think the same when it comes to the world as a whole? Russell and Hick are saying that there being a world is a fact that might be taken as basic. And some suppositions certainly have to be taken as basic by various people. Chemists would be seriously hampered by doubts about the existence of chemicals. Geographers would make little progress if they started to doubt the existence of the Earth. But should the

existence of the world be taken simply for granted? Does it really not call
for explanation?

One might say that it does not, since there is no intelligible alternative
to there being a world. Thinkers like Leibniz are asking why there is a
world as opposed to there being absolutely nothing. Yet, can we take
nothing to be a genuine possibility to be set beside *something*? We may
speak of there being nothing in the room, or of there being nothing
between Australia and New Zealand. But here we mean something like
'There is no furniture in the room' or 'There is no land between
Australia and New Zealand'. In other words, the notion of there being
absolutely nothing lacks positive content. So why suppose that there not
being nothing (that there is *something* rather than *nothing*) is a fact to get
worked up about?

But is the notion of nothing really so problematic even in this context? Suppose that we are hunting for a corkscrew in my kitchen. I open
one of the drawers there and say 'Well, there is nothing in this one'. You
will understand what I am saying. I am saying that there is no corkscrew
in the drawer. In that case, however, could you not equally well understand me if I were to claim that there is nothing at all? I would obviously
be speaking falsely. But would you not be able to understand why that is
so? Would you not take me wrongly to be insisting that there are no
nameable and describable individuals?

We do not have a concept of nothing as we have a concept of longev-
ity or tallness or liquidation. But might it not be thought that we do have
a concept of nothing insofar as we have a knowledge of things that there
are and insofar as we can think of them just not being there? And might
it not also be thought that there being nothing at all is a genuine possibility insofar as the 'all' we are concerned with is what we take to make up
the world or universe? Some have suggested that the world or universe
cannot but exist. But why should we think that? Triangles cannot but be
three-sided. 'There are four-sided triangles' is clearly contradictory. But
do we contradict ourselves by saying that the world or universe might
never have existed?

So perhaps it is not absurd to hold that there might have been nothing
at all. In that case, however, maybe we should side with those who ask
why there is something rather than nothing. This question is certainly
an unusual one. But that fact is no good reason for dismissing it. The

asking of unusual questions often leads people to expand their intellectual horizons and to make serious intellectual progress. We might suggest that the question 'Why is there anything at all?' is intrinsically silly or ill-formed. But is it? Questions like 'How thick is the equator?' or 'How much money does algebra earn?' certainly make no sense. But is this the case with 'Why is there anything at all?'

Echoing Russell, we might reply that things are just there. Yet Russell would never have said that cats, for example, are *just there*. He would have asked how cats came to be and continue to be. So, why should we not ask why there is anything at all or why there is something rather than nothing? It might be said that we have not familiarized ourselves with the answer to this question and that this is a reason for fighting shy of it. But not understanding what the answer to a question is does not justify refusing to ask it or refusing to suppose that it must have an answer. The earliest scientists were not acquainted with what we now take to be accurate scientific answers. They were venturing into the unknown. Yet we commend them for their efforts and are seriously indebted to them. They could have said that X, Y, or Z was 'just there' and left it at that. Fortunately, however, they did not.

(b) Problems

Yet, as many have pointed out, there are problems with the cosmological argument from sufficient reason. For example, should we accept its claim about reason? According to Leibniz, every fact and every true statement has an explanation. Leibniz calls this the 'principle of sufficient reason'.[24] And if that principle is true, then there is an explanation for there being a world and for it being as it is. But can we know that Leibniz's principle of sufficient reason is true?

Well, the truth of the principle clearly cannot be settled on empirical grounds. No amount of sensory experience will confirm it. For it is not an empirical principle. Nor does it seem to be a logical truth (one which cannot consistently be denied). And it does not seem to follow from any obvious non-empirical truth such as 'No proposition can be simultaneously both true and false'. Some philosophers have said that the principle of sufficient reason is something that we can know innately or a priori (that we can, without argument or evidence, just 'see' that it is true). But other philosophers have thought otherwise. Hence, for example, J. L. Mackie writes: 'The principle of sufficient reason expresses a demand that things should be intelligible *through and through*. The simple reply to the argument which relies on it is that there is nothing that justifies this demand, and nothing that supports the belief that it is satisfiable even in principle.'[25] Mackie's point is that defenders of the principle of sufficient reason are merely expressing a conviction they have. And he is saying, surely rightly, that one's conviction that such and such is the case does not guarantee that it is, in fact, the case. We might respond to him by suggesting that someone who believes in the principle of sufficient reason has what Alvin Plantinga calls a 'properly basic' belief.[26] We might say that we are entitled to believe in it even though we cannot do anything to ground it in beliefs more basic than it. And this line of thinking is surely worth exploring. But not if there is a reason for thinking that the principle of sufficient reason could not possibly be true.

Is there such a reason? Perhaps there is. As Leibniz presents it, and as it is understood by those who broadly agree with him, the principle of sufficient reason holds that all contingent facts have an explanation. It also holds that a sufficient reason ensures the truth of that to which it stands as a sufficient reason. But now consider the sum total of contingent facts. According to the principle of sufficient reason, this has a sufficient reason. So let us now consider this reason (call it R), and let us ask whether it is contingent or necessary. It is, presumably, either contingent or necessary. But R cannot be contingent since it is not part of the sum total of contingent facts. Yet R cannot be necessary either. For, if a sufficient reason entails that to which it stands as a sufficient reason, then R entails the sum total of contingent facts, which means that they are not contingent after all. They are entailed by what is necessary so that, if R exists, there are no contingent facts.[27]

The First Cause Argument

If the argument in the last paragraph is sound, then the principle of sufficient reason is untenable and cosmological arguments based on it are flawed. But there are cosmological arguments which do not invoke the principle. For, without appealing to a general 'principle of sufficient reason', some of them focus on the notion of causality so as to suggest that the world ought to be viewed as brought about, effected, or made. The basic idea here is that the world must derive from something which is able to bring it into being, something not produced by anything, something which can be sensibly referred to as 'the first cause'.

Perhaps the most famous exponent of this line of thinking is Thomas Aquinas, according to whom 'we are bound to conclude that everything that is at all real is from God. For when we encounter a subject which shares in a reality then this reality must needs be caused there by a thing which possesses it of its nature.'[28] Why does Aquinas think this? For two main reasons.

First, he believes that something which does not exist by nature can only exist because something else causes it to do so. Second, he thinks that there being things which owe their existence to another implies that there is something which does not—something whose nature it is to be. As well as asking what in the world causes what, we need, says Aquinas, also to consider the notion of 'being as being' and to ask about the cause of things 'inasmuch as they are beings, not merely as things of such a kind or quality'.[29] According to Aquinas, God is the 'all-embracing cause of beings'. God is 'sheer existence subsisting of his very nature'.[30] And, according to Aquinas, God must exist since there are things which do not exist by nature. Aquinas also thinks that the world contains effects of causes and that there being effects of causes ultimately implies the existence of a first, uncaused cause. As Aquinas puts it in a much quoted passage:

> In the observable world causes are found to be ordered in series; we never observe, nor ever could, something causing itself, for this would mean it preceded itself, and this is not possible. Such a series of causes must however stop somewhere; for in it an earlier member causes an intermediate and the intermediate a last (whether the intermediate be one or many). Now if you eliminate a cause you also eliminate its effects, so that you cannot have a last cause, nor an intermediate one, unless you have a first. Given therefore no stop in the series of causes, and hence no first cause, there would be no intermediate causes either, and no last effect . . . One is therefore forced to suppose some first cause, to which everyone gives the name 'God'.[31]

(a) Comments on this argument

Aquinas's 'first cause' approach to God depends partly on the assumption that there is a causal question prompted by the mere or sheer existence of some things. Rather like Leibniz, Aquinas is clearly thinking that we can look around us and wonder why we and everything else are there at all. In this connection, Aquinas, unlike Leibniz, does not talk about 'sufficient reasons'. But, like Leibniz, he evidently thinks that we ought to ask: 'Why is there something rather than nothing?' Hence his talk about enquiring into 'being as being'. Yet, does existence *as such* raise any serious questions? Is there, indeed, any such thing as existence *as such*?

My cat Smokey is grey, slinky, energetic, and inquisitive. But does it make sense to say that he is also 'existent'? And does it make sense to suggest that his being such is a fact about him which ought to prompt us to further questions? Does 'existent' serve to characterize him in any way? Does it signify something about him which needs to be accounted for? Arguably not. A non-existing cat would not be *different* from Smokey. And, just by existing, Smokey is neither descriptively *unlike* nor descriptively *like* anything you care to mention.

'Existent' (like the phrase 'is numerous') does not tell us what any object or individual is like. If I say that there are no unicorns, I am asserting that unicorns do not exist. But 'Unicorns do not exist' does not describe any unicorn, from which it would seem to follow that 'Unicorns exist' also fails to describe any object or individual. Yet, if that is so, why should we take existence (*mere, sheer,* or *as such*) as in any way problematic? We might sensibly wonder how Smokey comes to be grey, slinky, energetic, and inquisitive. But does it make sense to ask how it comes about that he simply *exists*? You might reply to this question by noting that Smokey is real enough. He is a living breathing cat. But now you would be describing Smokey without making 'exists' part of your account of him. It is true that Smokey is living and breathing. And it is true that he is a cat. But is it, in a similar way, true of him that he *exists*?

That is one question that philosophers who are suspicious of Aquinas on God as first cause are likely to raise.[32] Yet it is not at all clear that the thinking behind it is damaging to Aquinas's account of God as the cause of the existence of things. For this account does not depend on the assumption that existence can enter into a description of anything. Aquinas would agree that we cannot, for example, characterize a particular cat by saying that, as well as being feline, agile, and so on, it *also* exists. According to Aquinas, there is no such class of things as things which simply *are*.[33] Aquinas says that things made by God 'have being'. But he does not thereby mean that they have a property or quality that needs explaining.

In that case, however, what does Aquinas mean when he speaks of things other than God as existing or being? And what does he mean when he says that existence or being has to be caused by God? In one place he writes:

> There are two proper uses of the term 'being': firstly, generally for whatever falls into one of Aristotle's ten basic categories of thing, and secondly, for whatever makes a proposition true. These differ: in the second sense, anything we can express in an affirmative proposition, however unreal, is said to be: in this sense, lacks and absences are, since we say that absences are opposed to presences, and blindness exists in an eye. But, in the first sense, only what is real is, so that in this sense blindness and such are not beings.[34]

Aquinas is here distinguishing between (a) talk about distinct individuals (e.g. some human being, or some particular cat) and (b) attributes which can only be said to exist because of what is true of some distinct individual existing in its own right. According to Aquinas, it makes sense to say, for example, that John (who is blind) exists. But it is, he thinks, wrong to say that John's blindness exists as John does. For Aquinas, John's blindness exists only in the sense that it is true to say that John is blind.

So, on Aquinas's account, to say that something exists is chiefly to say that it is a genuine individual corresponding to a certain description. We can describe fictional objects or characters, but we would not thereby be truly saying what anything actually is. We would only be pretending to do so. On the other hand, however, we can single out genuine individuals and speak truly about them. And this is what Aquinas has in mind when saying that things exist or 'have being'. And, in his view, this is a fact which needs to be accounted for causally.

But is Aquinas right to say that? Some philosophers would suggest that his position commits us to a false view concerning existence and necessity. According to Aquinas, God accounts for the being of the world. But what accounts for the being of God? Aquinas's answer is that it is God's nature to exist. For him, there is nothing which causes God to be. In that case, however, it would seem that Aquinas is saying that God exists of necessity. And, many have argued, that must be false since nothing exists of necessity. Why not? Because, so the argument runs, we can always consistently deny a statement asserting that something exists. As Hume writes:

> Whatever we conceive as existent, we can also conceive as non-existent. There is no Being, therefore, whose non-existence implies a contradiction . . . It will still be possible for us, at any time, to conceive the non-existence of what we formerly conceived to exist; nor can the mind ever lie under a necessity of supposing any object to remain always in being; in the same manner as we lie under a necessity of always conceiving twice two to be four. The words, therefore, *necessary existence* have no meaning.[35]

Yet Aquinas does not seem to be vulnerable to this criticism. For he does not believe that the statement 'God does not exist' can be proved to be self-contradictory.[36] Rather, his claim is that the existence of the world needs a cause which cannot (even if we cannot understand why) be thought of as depending for its existence on something else.

But is that so? Not if Russell was right to say that the world is 'just there'. If that is all we can say, then the world is, indeed, a brute fact. Indeed, it would seem to be a necessary being. But what of Hume's claim as noted above? Is it true that whatever we conceive as existent can also be conceived as non-existent? If we take 'whatever we conceive as existent' to include the world as a whole, then, if Hume is right, we can conceive of the world as non-existent. Yet there is a world. So why is this so? Aquinas replies that it is so because God, as the uncaused cause, makes it to be so. And that is not an absurd suggestion. We could say that it is mistaken, since the existence of the world could be explicable in terms of its nature. We might say that it exists because it is in its nature to do so. But the world cannot have the nature it has unless it exists. So its existing cannot be explicable in terms of its nature. As David Braine writes:

> The continuance of the very stuff of the Universe, the fact that it goes on existing, is not self-explanatory. It is incoherent to say that the very stuff of

the Universe continues to exist by its very nature since it has to continue to exist in order for this nature to exist or to be operative. Hence, nature presupposes existence.[37]

At the end of his *Tractatus Logico-Philosophicus*, Wittgenstein writes: 'Not *how* the world is, is the mystical, but *that* it is.'[38] For Wittgenstein, *how the world is* is a scientific matter with scientific answers (even if we do not have all the answers as yet). But, he insists, even when the scientific answers are in, we are still left with the *thatness* of the world, the fact *that* it is. So, as he says in his *Lecture on Ethics*: 'I wonder at the existence of the world. And I am then inclined to use such phrases as "how extraordinary that anything should exist" or "how extraordinary that the world should exist".'[39] According to Wittgenstein: 'We feel that even if *all possible* scientific questions be answered, the problems of life have still not been touched at all.'[40] By 'scientific questions', Wittgenstein seems to have in mind what we might call 'ordinary causal questions'. He seems to be thinking of questions like 'Why did John fall sick?' or 'Why is it hot today?' And when he speaks of answers to scientific questions, he seems to be thinking of reference to what in the world produces what. But when we have asked and (hopefully) answered such questions, are we not still left with a question about the world as a whole? Should we not wonder what brings about its existence? And should we not suppose that there is an answer to this question?

Some philosophers would say that we should not, since our reason breaks down when confronted with the notion of something which causes or produces absolutely everything in the world. And, as Herbert McCabe says, 'there is indeed a difficulty about having a concept of "everything", for we ordinarily conceive of something with, so to say, a boundary around it: this is a sheep and not a giraffe. But *everything* is bounded by *nothing*, which is just to say that it is not bounded by anything.'[41] But the fact that we cannot understand what causally accounts for the world as a whole is no reason for concluding that nothing does. I may not understand what is causing me to cough. But should I therefore conclude that nothing is causing me to do so? I may not be able to understand the nature of what causally accounts for the world as a whole. But should I therefore conclude that nothing causally accounts for this?

Yet should I conclude that there is, as Aquinas puts it, a 'first cause'?

Why should I not suppose that there is an infinity of causes lying behind anything you care to mention? Referring to a version of the first cause argument, Simon Blackburn concedes that it 'speaks to worries that are natural'.[42] When we ask causal questions, he says, 'we are not happy with the answer "no reason"; the drive to explanation grips us'.[43] And yet Blackburn adds:

> The drive now threatens to go on forever. If we have cited God at this point, we either have to ask what caused God, or cut off the regress by arbitrary fiat. But if we exercise an arbitrary right to stop the regress at this point, we might as well have stopped it with the physical cosmos. In other words, we are in the position of the Indian philosopher who when asked what the world rested on, replied 'an elephant', and when asked what the elephant rested on, replied 'a tortoise', and when asked what the tortoise rested on, begged to change the subject.[44]

Essentially the same point is made by Kai Nielsen, who writes:

> Why could there not be an infinite series of caused causes? An infinite series is not a long or even a very, very long *finite* series. The person arguing for an infinite series is not arguing for something that came from nothing, nor need he be *denying* that *every* event has a cause. He is asserting that we need not assume that there is a *first* cause that started everything. Only if the series were finite would it be impossible for there to be something if there were no first cause or uncaused cause. But if the series were literally infinite, there would be no need for there to be a first cause to get the causal order started, for there would always be a causal order since an infinite series can have no first member.[45]

The idea here is that, if each member in a series is supported by another member, the series will somehow be able to stand on its own.

But there are reasons for resisting this idea. For, as James Sadowsky puts it:

> It is just as difficult for any supporting member to exist as the member it supports. This brings back the question of how any member can do any causing unless it first exists. B cannot cause A until D brings it into existence. What is true of D is equally true of E and F without end. Since each condition for the existence of A requires the fulfilment of a prior condition, it follows that none of them can ever be fulfilled. In each case what is offered as part of the solution turns out instead to be part of the problem.[46]

As Sadowsky also observes, to suggest otherwise is a bit like saying 'No one may do anything (including asking for permission) without asking for permission'. And something like that is what a defender of the first cause argument can say if the possibility of infinite regress were claimed to refute it. Philosophers such as Blackburn might reply that thinkers like Aquinas are being arbitrary in holding that the cause of the existence of the world is uncaused. But are they? If it is right to say that the existence of the world must be caused, then why may we not appeal to Sadowsky's line of reasoning so as to suggest that only what is not caused to exist can account for there being anything which is? (Sadowsky's example about asking for permission reminds me of a story I read in a newspaper. An English farmer who kept ferrets found that all of them had vanished. He concluded that they must have eaten each other.)

Cosmological Arguments and God

Suppose we accept that the arguments introduced in this chapter are all good ones. We might still wonder whether they have significant religious implications. In particular, we might wonder whether they manage to give us reason for believing in the existence of God. Take, for example, the first cause argument. Many thinkers would observe that it is hardly a good argument for God's existence even if its reasoning is basically sound. Why? Because it does not show us that God exists with the nature or attributes commonly ascribed to him by theists. Perhaps the argument gives us reason to believe in a first uncaused cause, say the thinkers I am now referring to. But, they ask, why should we suppose that a first uncaused cause is, for instance, good or knowing (as God is regularly said to be)?

This, of course, is a perfectly sensible question to ask. And we can adapt it so as to challenge both the kalām argument and the argument from sufficient reason. But does the question undermine the cosmological arguments we have noted? In one sense, it does. For none of these arguments shows that what they conclude to is all that believers in God typically take him to be. On the other hand, however, they do not purport to do this. Their aim is more modest. Defenders of the kalām argument claim only that it gives us reason to believe that something freely brought it about that the world began to be. Supporters of the argument from sufficient reason claim only to show that there is a necessary being. Those who favour the first cause argument maintain only that it supports belief in the existence of something causing the world to be at any time. And all of these people have normally gone on to provide additional arguments for supposing that what they call 'God' corresponds to what theists have taken God to be. Aquinas, for instance, argues that God is good and knowing in texts quite distinct from those in which he develops his version of the first cause argument.

So cosmological arguments should not be read as their defenders' last word on God. They are, in a sense, best viewed as attempts to set the ball rolling—as efforts designed to show that people who believe in God somehow have reason on their side. We might complain that they should not, therefore, employ the word 'God' when referring to the conclusion to which they come. But to do so would surely be unfair. I could have reason to claim that Fred is in my house even if I have no grounds for claiming that the person in my house is everything that those who know him well recognize him to be. So, why may I not claim that I have reason to believe that God exists—reason which does not, by itself, show that God is all that theists take God to be?

And is there not a case to be made for using the word 'God' when thinking of the conclusion at which cosmological arguments arrive? Defenders of the kalām argument might, perhaps, content themselves with saying that they have successfully argued for the existence of a Cobu (the word we might invent to signify a cause of the beginning of the universe). Supporters of the argument from sufficient reason might happily say that they have shown why we should believe in a Neb (a necessary being). Aquinas might rephrase his way of putting things and hold that we have reason to believe that Cet (a cause of the existence of things) exists. But do defenders of cosmological arguments really need to be pressed to such extremes?

Surely not. For suppose we try to produce a very quick account of what theists take God, and *only God*, to be. Would it be false to say that God is why there is any world at all? Obviously not. So much is evident from even a cursory glance at, for example, the Jewish and Christian tradition. For this speaks of God as the source of all things other than himself. According to the book of Genesis: 'In the beginning God created the heavens and the earth.'[47] According to the letter to the Hebrews, 'the world was created by the word of God, so that what is seen was made out of things which do not appear'.[48] When reflecting on the cosmos, defenders of cosmological arguments have a convenient, familiar, and obvious word to employ. And, so we might add, the same is true of those who defend another way of doing natural theology—one to which we can now turn.

NOTES

1. William Alston, *Perceiving God: The Epistemology of Religious Experience* (Ithaca, NY, and London, 1991), p. 289.

2. Ibid.

3. The phrase 'the cosmological argument' was introduced into philosophy by Immanuel Kant (1724–1804). See his *Critique of Pure Reason*, A591/B619. Kant is commonly taken to be one of the greatest of western philosophers. Influenced by the thought of authors such as Leibniz and Hume, he came to defend an original position synthesizing some of their key ideas. His main works include *Critique of Pure Reason* (1st edn., 1781), *Prolegomena to any Future Metaphysic* (1783), *Groundwork to the Metaphysics of Morals* (1785), and *Critique of Practical Reason* (1788).

4. William Lane Craig, *The Kalām Cosmological Argument* (London, 1979), pp. 149ff.

5. *Thomas Reid's Inquiry and Essays*, ed. Ronald E. Beanblossom and Keith Lehrer (Indianapolis, IN, 1983), p. 330. A contemporary of Hume, Reid has been much neglected by philosophers. But he is now undergoing something of a revival among them. For an introduction to Reid, see John Haldane (ed.), *Thomas Reid* (special issue of *American Catholic Philosophical Quarterly* LXXIV, Issue 3, 2000).

6. David Hume, *A Treatise of Human Nature*, ed. L. A. Selby-Bigge (Oxford, 1965), pp. 79f.

7. Frederick Copleston, *A History of Philosophy*, vol. 5 (London, 1959), p. 287.

8. G. E. M. Anscombe, ' "Whatever Has a Beginning of Existence Must Have a Cause": Hume's Argument Exposed', *Analysis* 34 (1974), p. 150. This paper is reprinted in G. E. M. Anscombe, *Collected Philosophical Papers* (Oxford, 1981), vol. I.

9. Anscombe, *Collected Philosophical Papers*, vol. II, p. 162. For criticism of

Anscombe's argument, see David Gordon, 'Anscombe on Coming into Existence and Causation', *Analysis* 44 (1984).

10. *The Letters of David Hume*, ed. J. Y. T. Greig (Oxford, 1932), vol. I, p. 187.

11. C. D. Broad, 'Kant's Mathematical Antinomies', *Proceedings of the Aristotelian Society*, LV, p. 10.

12. Richard Swinburne, *Space and Time* (2nd edn., London, 1981), p. 258. Cf. J. L. Mackie, *The Miracle of Theism* (Oxford, 1982), p. 93.

13. The list of classical authors famous for maintaining that there are good philosophical arguments for the view that the universe had a beginning includes Al-Ghazali (b.1058/59), the sixth-century writer John Philoponus, and St Bonaventure (c.1217–74). A lively discussion of ancient and medieval authors on the beginning of the world can be found in Richard Sorabji, *Time, Creation and the Continuum* (London, 1983), chs. 13–17.

14. For an expression of this argument, see William Charlton, *Philosophy and Christian Belief* (London, 1988), ch. 2. For recent defence of the argument, see William Lane Craig, 'Time and Infinity', *International Philosophical Quarterly* XXXI (1991).

15. I alluded to this view in Chapter 1. For more on it, see Chapter 13 below.

16. See *Summa Theologiae*, Ia, 46, 1, and *De Aeternitate Mundi*.

17. G. W. Leibniz, 'On the Ultimate Origination of Things'. I quote from G. H. R. Parkinson (ed.), *Leibniz: Philosophical Writings* (London and Toronto, 1973), p. 136.

18. Parkinson (ed.), *Leibniz: Philosophical Writings*, p. 136.

19. Ibid.

20. Ibid., p. 137.

21. Ibid.

22. Russell famously took this line in a radio debate with Frederick Copleston. See 'A Debate on the Existence of God', reprinted in John Hick (ed.), *The Existence of God* (London and New York, 1964), pp. 167–91.

23. John Hick, *Philosophy of Religion* (4th edn., Englewood Cliffs, NJ, 1990), p. 21.

24. Cf. Leibniz, *Monadology*, §32. For the text, see Parkinson (ed.), *Leibniz: Philosophical Writings*, p. 184. Unfortunately, Leibniz does not always state what he calls 'the principle of sufficient reason' in the same way. Sometimes his view of it seems more inclusive than it does at other times. For some discussion of this, see William Lane Craig, *The Cosmological Argument from Plato to Leibniz* (London, 1980), pp. 259ff. See also Benson Mates, *The Philosophy of Leibniz* (New York and Oxford, 1986), pp. 154ff.

25. J. L. Mackie, *The Miracle of Theism* (Oxford, 1982), p. 85. Cf. G. J. Warnock, 'Every Event has a Cause', in A. G. N. Flew, *Logic and Language* (2nd series, New York, 1953).

26. See Chapter 2 above.

27. For philosophers arguing along these lines, see Peter Van Inwagen, *An Essay on Free Will* (Oxford, 1983), pp. 202 ff. and William L. Rowe, 'Cosmological Arguments', in Philip L. Quinn and Charles Taliaferro (eds.), *A Companion to Philosophy of Religion* (Oxford, 1997).

28. Thomas Aquinas, *Summa Theologiae*, Ia, 44, 1. I quote from volume 8 of the Blackfriars edition of the *Summa Theologiae* (London and New York, 1967), p. 7.

29. Ibid., Ia, 44, 2.

30. Ibid., Ia, 44, 1.

31. Ibid., Ia, 2, 3. I quote from volume 2 of the Blackfriars edition of the *Summa Theologiae* (London and New York, 1964).

32. Their line of thinking would be echoing ideas set forth by Immanuel Kant, according to whom *'Being* is obviously not a real predicate', and by Gottlob Frege (1848–1925), according to whom existence is not a property of objects or individuals. We shall be seeing more of Kant and Frege on existence in Chapter 5 below. For a critique of Aquinas that appeals to their teachings, see C. J. F. Williams, 'Being', in Quinn and Taliaferro (eds.), *A Companion to Philosophy of Religion*, pp. 223–8.

33. Cf. Thomas Aquinas, *Summa contra Gentiles*, I, 24–6, and *Summa Theologiae*, 3a, 77, 1.

34. Thomas Aquinas, *De Ente et Essentia* (*On Being and Essence*), 1.

35. David Hume, *Dialogues concerning Natural Religion*, ed. Norman Kemp Smith (Indianapolis, IN, 1977), p. 189.

36. Cf. Aquinas, *Summa Theologiae*, Ia, 2, 1.

37. David Braine, *The Reality of Time and the Existence of God* (Oxford, 1988), p. 10.

38. Ludwig Wittgenstein, *Tractatus Logico-Philosophicus*, trans. C. K. Ogden (London, 1922), 6.44.

39. Ludwig Wittgenstein, 'A Lecture on Ethics', reprinted in James Klagge and Alfred Nordmann (eds.), *Ludwig Wittgenstein: Philosophical Occasions 1912–1951* (Indianapolis, IN, 1993).

40. Wittgenstein, *Tractatus Logico-Philosophicus*, 6.52.

41. Herbert McCabe, 'Creation', *New Blackfriars* 61 (1980). I quote from this

article as reprinted in Brian Davies (ed.), *Philosophy of Religion: A Guide and Anthology* (Oxford, 2000), p. 199.

42. Simon Blackburn, *Think* (Oxford, 1999), p. 162.

43. Ibid.

44. Ibid.

45. Kai Nielsen, *Reason and Practice* (New York, 1971), p. 171. Cf. Paul Edwards, 'The Cosmological Argument', in Paul Angeles (ed.), *Critiques of God* (Buffalo, 1976), pp. 48ff.

46. James Sadowsky, 'The Cosmological Argument and the Endless Regress', *International Philosophical Quarterly* 20 (1980), pp. 465f. For a classical philosopher who makes the same point neatly, see Leibniz, *On the Ultimate Origination of Things*.

47. Genesis 1: 1.

48. Hebrews 11: 3.

FURTHER READING

If you are looking for book-length treatments of one or more cosmological arguments, the following can all be recommended: David Braine, *The Reality of Time and the Existence of God* (Oxford, 1988); Hugo Meynell, *The Intelligible Universe: A Cosmological Argument* (London, 1982); Barry Miller, *From Existence to God* (London and New York, 1992); Bruce R. Reichenbach, *The Cosmological Argument: A Reassessment* (Springfield, IL, 1972); William Rowe, *The Cosmological Argument* (Princeton, NJ, and London, 1975); and John J. Shepherd, *Experience, Inference and God* (London, 1975). For valuable but shorter discussions, see David Braine, 'Cosmological Arguments', in Brian Davies (ed.), *Philosophy of Religion: A Guide to the Subject* (London, 1998); Stephen T. Davis, *God, Reason and Theistic Proofs* (Grand Rapids, MI, 1997), ch. 4; Peter Van Inwagen, *Metaphysics* (Boulder, CO, and San Francisco, CA, 1993), ch. 6; William L. Rowe, 'Cosmological Arguments', in Philip L. Quinn and Charles Taliaferro (eds.), *A Companion to Philosophy of Religion* (Oxford, 1997); Richard Taylor, *Metaphysics* (Englewood Cliffs, NJ, 1992), pp. 99 ff.; and Richard Swinburne, *The Existence of God* (rev. edn., Oxford, 1991), ch. 7. For a now somewhat dated but still useful research bibliography on cosmological arguments, see Clement Dore, *Theism* (Dordrecht, 1984).

For a good account of some major cosmological arguments, see William Lane Craig, *The Cosmological Argument from Plato to Leibniz* (London, 1980). For a scholarly survey of cosmological arguments in ancient thinking, see L. P. Gerson, *God and Greek Philosophy: Studies in the History of Natural Theology*

(London and New York, 1990). For an expert guide through medieval Islamic and Jewish thinking on cosmological arguments, see Herbert A. Davidson, *Proofs for Eternity, Creation, and the Existence of God in Medieval Islamic and Jewish Philosophy* (Oxford, 1987).

For a contemporary exposition and defence of kalām cosmological arguments, see William Lane Craig, *The Kalām Cosmological Argument* (London, 1979). For a critique of Craig (and of cosmological arguments defended by other authors), see J. L. Mackie, *The Miracle of Theism* (Oxford, 1982), ch. 5. Craig replies to Mackie's discussion of him in 'Professor Mackie and the *Kalām* Cosmological Argument', *Religious Studies* 20 (1985). For other criticism of kalām cosmological arguments, see Quentin Smith, 'A Big Bang Cosmological Argument for God's Nonexistence', *Faith and Philosophy* 9 (1992); Graham Oppy, 'Professor William Craig's Criticisms of Critiques of Kalām Cosmological Arguments by Paul Davies, Stephen Hawking, and Adolf Grünbaum', *Faith and Philosophy* 12 (1995); and Graham Oppy, 'Kalām Cosmological Arguments: Reply to Professor Craig', *Sophia* 34 (1995). For an erudite and lively discussion of historical and philosophical issues bearing on kalām cosmological arguments, see Richard Sorabji, *Time, Creation and the Continuum* (London, 1983).

For more on Leibniz and cosmological arguments, see Nicholas Jolley (ed.), *The Cambridge Companion to Leibniz* (Cambridge, 1995), chs. 4, 5, and 10; G. H. R. Parkinson, *Logic and Reality in Leibniz's Metaphysics* (Oxford, 1965), ch. 4; and Nicholas Rescher, *Leibniz: An Introduction to his Philosophy* (Oxford, 1979), chs. 2 and 14.

For more on Aquinas and cosmological arguments, see Brian Davies, *The Thought of Thomas Aquinas* (Oxford, 1992), ch. 2, and Brian Davies, *Aquinas* (London and New York, 2002), chs. 4–6. For lively, modern statements of Aquinas's approach, see Herbert McCabe, *God Matters* (London, 1987), ch. 1, and Herbert McCabe, 'The Logic of Mysticism', in Martin Warner (ed.), *Religion and Philosophy* (Cambridge, 1992).

QUESTIONS FOR DISCUSSION

1 How can one determine that something began to exist?

2 Does the fact that something began to exist require a cause? If so, why? If not, why not?

3 'You investigate to find the cause of a thing—or to find, say, whether heat or impact is the cause. But you never investigate to find out whether it has a cause or not. You look for the cause of it, but you don't look to see whether it has a cause. And you would never speak either of finding out

that it has a cause or of finding out that it hasn't' (Ludwig Wittgenstein, quoted by Rush Rhees in 'Five Topics in Conversations with Wittgenstein', *Philosophical Investigations* 25 (2002), p. 19). What would you say in response to these comments?

4 'Every event has a predecessor'. Is that claim reasonable? Is so, why? If not, why not?

5 'If the world does not end, there will never be a time when all the future events will have occurred, whereas at any given time it will be true that all the past events have occurred.' Is that statement true? If so, consider what it implies with respect to the kalām cosmological argument.

6 'Why is there something rather than nothing?' Does this question make any sense at all? How might one attempt to answer it?

7 If God is the sufficient reason needed to account for the existence of contingent things, what accounts for God's choosing which contingent things there should be? Consider this question with an eye on Leibniz's version of the cosmological argument. Does this version of the argument ultimately imply that the contingent things that exist are also, somehow, necessary?

8 'The universe is just there.' Comment on this suggestion.

9 'The universe exists.' Is this an intelligible assertion? If so, what might it be taken to mean? Also, consider whether 'exists' can be thought of as meaning the same in 'The universe exists' as in 'God exists'.

10 Can there be a decent argument for God's existence which does not establish the existence of all that theists mean when they use the word 'God'? If so, why? If not, why not?

4

DESIGN ARGUMENTS

....

The focus of cosmological arguments is the existence of the world or universe. But some natural theologians have tried to develop a case for God's existence based not on the fact that there is a world, but on the fact that the world displays certain features. What sort of features? Ones which suggest that the world is somehow designed. But are there such features? And can they be appealed to as evidence for God's existence? Does the world work so as to suggest that it is governed, planned, or ordered, although not by any mind or intelligence within it.

Versions of Design Arguments

What is it that convinces people that, in noting the way the world goes, we ought to invoke the notion of design? Here we need to distinguish two different, though related, concepts of design.

First, there is design in the sense of purpose. We are working with this sense of 'design' if we talk about something being designed because it has parts put together for some end or other, as in the case of a telephone or a television.

On the other hand, however, there is design in the sense of regularity. Instances of this are a succession of regular marks on paper, a musical score, the orderly arrangement of flowers in a garden, or the repeated and predictable operations of an artefact (e.g. a clock which chimes every hour).

With this distinction in mind, we can now note two lines of argument offered by people who find evidence in the universe of divine design: the first states that the universe displays design in the sense of purpose; the second holds that it displays design in the sense of regularity.

(a) Design as purpose

The most famous argument from design as purpose is that defended by William Paley (1743–1805) in *Natural Theology; or Evidences of the Existence and Attributes of the Deity, Collected from the Appearances of Nature.*[1] 'In crossing a heath', says Paley,

> suppose I pitched my foot against a *stone*, and were asked how the stone came to be there, I might possibly answer, that, for anything I knew to the contrary, it had lain there for ever; nor would it perhaps be very easy to show the absurdity of this answer. But suppose I found a *watch* upon the ground, and it should be inquired how the watch happened to be in the place, I should hardly think of the answer which I had before given, that, for anything I knew, the watch might have always been there. Yet why should not this answer serve for the watch, as well as for the stone?[2]

Paley's reply is that the parts of a watch are obviously put together to achieve a definite result: 'When we come to inspect the watch, we perceive (what we could not discover in the stone) that its several parts are framed and put together for a purpose, e.g. that they are so formed and adjusted as to produce motion, and that motion so regulated as to point out the hour of the day.'[3] And, Paley goes on to suggest, the universe resembles a watch and must therefore be accounted for in terms of intelligent and purposive agency.

Suppose we use the phrase 'teleological system' to refer to anything which has parts which operate so as to achieve one or more goals.[4] In that case, Paley's view is that watches imply purpose because they are teleological systems. And his argument is that nature contains systems of this kind which are not ascribable to people but which are ascribable to purpose of the kind displayed by them. You can find a similar argument in the writings of Aquinas. Are there things in the world, other than people, that can reasonably be thought of as seeking to achieve ends or goals? Aquinas suggests that there are. 'For we see', he says, 'that certain things that lack knowledge, namely, natural material substances, act for the sake of an end. And this is evident because they always or more frequently act in the same way in order to achieve what is best, and hence it is evident that they reach their goal by striving, not by chance.'[5]

Aquinas believes in chance events. As he sees it, you and I would meet by chance if we happened to bump into each other on a crowded street. But is it by chance that, for example, acorns regularly grow into oak trees? Nobody would say that it is. It is in the nature of acorns to grow into oaks. Or, as Aquinas would say, acorns have a tendency (*appetitus*) to become oak trees. Yet, to refer to a tendency is to draw attention to what something is moving towards, or inclined to, and it brings to mind the notion of an end or a goal or a striving towards. And the notion of an end, a goal, or a striving naturally brings to mind the notion of purpose or intention. Goal-directed activity is something which it makes sense to think of as *meant*.

And yet, of course, things such as acorns lack minds. They cannot reflectively direct themselves to the ends to which they naturally incline. So, what accounts for them doing so? We cannot just say that it is their nature to do so because it is this very nature which is now in question. So, might we suggest that they aim as they do because their nature and activity is, indeed, meant? Aquinas, at any rate, thinks that we can. 'Things that lack knowledge', he argues, 'do not strive for goals unless a being with knowledge and intelligence directs them, as, for example, an archer aims an arrow.'[6] Aquinas thinks that goal-directed phenomena in nature imply the activity of a director beyond nature. Or, as he puts it: 'There is a being with intelligence who orders all the things of nature to their ends, and we call this being God.'[7]

(b) Design as regularity

[handwritten margin note: an intelligent being (God) has to order all things.]

Perhaps the most significant design as regularity argument is that defended by Richard Swinburne, who calls it a 'teleological argument from the temporal order of the world'. That there is temporal order is, says Swinburne, very evident. Why so? Because:

> Regularities of succession are all pervasive. For simple laws govern almost all successions of events. In books of physics, chemistry, and biology we can learn how almost everything in the world behaves. The laws of their behaviour can be set out by relatively simple formulae which men can understand and by means of which they can successfully predict the future. The orderliness of nature to which I draw attention here is its conformity to formula, to simple, formulable, scientific laws. The orderliness of the universe in this respect is a very striking fact about it. The universe might so naturally have been chaotic, but it is not—it is very orderly.[8]

From all of this, Swinburne concludes that some explanation is needed. And his suggestion is that the temporal order of the universe is explicable in terms of something analogous to human intelligence.

In Swinburne's view, there are only two kinds of explanation: scientific explanation (in terms of scientific laws) and personal explanation (in terms of the free, conscious choices of a person).[9] According to Swinburne, there can be no scientific explanation of the universe's temporal order, since

> in scientific explanation we explain particular phenomena as brought about by prior phenomena in accord with scientific laws; or we explain the operation of scientific laws (and perhaps also particular phenomena) ... [yet] from the very nature of science it cannot explain the highest level laws of all; for they are that by which it explains all other phenomena.[10]

So as Swinburne sees it, if we are to account for the fact that there are such laws, we must appeal to personal explanation. Someone (i.e. God) has brought it about that the universe exhibits a high degree of temporal order. And, Swinburne adds, the likelihood of this supposition is increased by the fact that God has reason to produce an orderly world. For example, says Swinburne, order is a necessary condition of beauty, and it is good that the world is beautiful rather than ugly.

Hume and the Argument from Design

At this point, however, many philosophers would appeal to Hume as someone who has shown that there is no good design argument for the existence of God. In his *Dialogues concerning Natural Religion* and *An Enquiry concerning Human Understanding*, Hume makes eight basic points against the idea that the world displays the work of an extra-mundane designer rightly referred to as God. So let us now turn to these.

(a) Hume's arguments

Hume's first point concerns what we can deduce from an effect. 'When we infer any particular cause for an effect', he says, 'we must proportion the one to the other, and can never be allowed to ascribe to any cause any qualities, but what are exactly sufficient to produce the effect.'[11]

Now, Hume adds, if design needs to be explained, then explain it, but only by appealing to a design-producing being. To say that this being is God is to go beyond the evidence presented by design.

Hume's second point hinges on the fact that the universe is unique. 'When two *species* of objects have always been observed to be conjoined together', he writes, 'I can *infer*, by custom, the existence of one wherever I *see* the existence of the other. And this I call an argument from experience.'[12] But, Hume continues, this notion of inference cannot be invoked by supporters of theistic design arguments. Why not? Because, he says, the universe is unique, and we therefore have no basis for inferring that there is anything like a human designer behind it. 'Will any man tell me with a serious countenance', he asks, 'that an orderly universe must arise from some thought and art, like the human; because we have some experience of it?' He adds: 'To ascertain this reasoning, it were requisite, that we had experience of the origin of worlds; and it is not sufficient surely, that we have seen ships and cities arise from human art and contrivance.'[13]

But suppose we agree that there is an extra-mundane designer. Would not such a designer also call for explanation? Hume's next argument is that the answer to this question is 'Yes'. 'If *Reason* be not alike mute with regard to all questions concerning cause and effect', he urges, 'this sentence at least it will venture to pronounce, That a mental world, or universe of ideas requires a cause as much as does a material world or universe of objects.'[14] In fact, says Hume, positing a designer of the world leads to an infinite regression: 'If the material world rests upon a similar ideal world, this ideal world must rest upon some other; and so on, without end.'[15]

Hume makes his fourth point in the form of a question: 'And why not become a perfect anthropomorphite? Why not assert the Deity or Deities to be corporeal, and to have eyes, a nose, mouth, ears, &c.?'[16] Some people argue from human artefacts to the existence of a designer supposed to account for the universe considered as one great artefact, or as a collection of different artefacts none of which are explicable in mundane terms. They do not, however, suppose that this designer is exactly like the people responsible for human artefacts. For example, they normally deny that this designer has a body. But, Hume argues, they ought not to do that if they want to be consistent. They should regard the cause of the universe's design as something in every respect like human artificers. Following a similar line of argument, Hume goes on to suggest (his fifth point) that defenders of design arguments have no reason to disbelieve that there may not be a whole gang of gods working together to produce design in the universe. 'A great number of men', he says, 'join together in building a house or ship, in rearing a city, in framing a commonwealth: Why may not several Deities combine in contriving and framing a world?'[17]

Finally, says Hume, there remain three other objections to design arguments (his last three points). The first is that the universe can easily be regarded as a living organism such as a plant, in which case design arguments fail because they depend on comparing the universe to a machine or artefact. The second is that the order in the universe could easily be the result of chance. The third is that design arguments are suspect because the universe shows many signs of disorder. *another 3 objections to design argument*

(b) Has Hume refuted design arguments?

Hume is surely right to say that we should not postulate more than is necessary to account for a given effect. If I know that X is made by a human being, I may reasonably suppose that its maker has two legs. But I could be wrong. The maker may have only one leg. We might therefore wonder why, if order in the universe needs explaining, it follows that what explains it has to be all that God is commonly said to be.

Hume's point about the uniqueness of the universe also has something to recommend it. For, in reasoning from effect to cause, we often depend on knowledge of previous instances. If you received a postcard from Paris saying 'Weather here, wish you were nice, Love, Us', you would probably be puzzled. But if I received such a card, I would know that it came from some friends of mine who always write that on their holiday postcards to me. What is it that enables me to conclude as I do, while you would be merely baffled? It is that I have past experience of my friends and their curious ways, while you (probably) do not. Yet, even though we have experience of human designers and what they produce, nobody supposes that anyone has experience of the origin of universes and of causes which bring them about. And since that is so, we might wonder how we can reason from the universe we inhabit to a designing cause.

What of Hume's other arguments? These, too, have merit. It is true, for example, that designers of our acquaintance are bodily. It is also true that products which are designed frequently derive from groups of people working together. Design arguments are arguments from analogy. They all somehow hold that the universe resembles designed things within it and must therefore have a cause like theirs. So we might wonder how they could justify our ruling out the idea that design in the universe is evidence for what is bodily, or evidence for the existence of several cooperating designers. And if designers exhibit order, why should we suppose that God, considered as a designer, explains the order we find in the universe? If God is an instance of something orderly, how can he possibly account for the order of orderly things?

Yet this is not to say that Hume has indeed succeeded in refuting design arguments. And we now need to note that defenders of such arguments have a number of replies which they can make in response to his various criticisms of them.

Take first his point about not ascribing to a cause anything other than what is exactly sufficient to produce its effect. Hume thinks that, even if we may causally account for order in the universe by inferring the existence of something distinct from it, the most we can conclude is that the order is produced by a design-producing being. He does not think that we are entitled to say that we have evidence of God's existence. Yet reason to suppose that order in the universe has a cause outside the universe is reason to suppose that the cause of the order in the universe is powerful, purposive, and incorporeal. It needs to be powerful to achieve its effect. It has to be incorporeal since it lies outside the universe. Since it is not a material thing, and since what it produces is order, we may suppose that it is able to act with intention. For order is naturally explained with reference to intention unless we have reason to suppose that it has been brought about by something material, i.e. something the effects of which are not the result of choice or planning on its part.

So we are entitled to infer more than an order-producing being if, as design arguments claim, we are right to ascribe order in the universe to a cause outside it. And if it should be said that more is supposed to be true

[handwritten margin notes: response against Hume saying order produced by a design-producing Being and supporting the evidence of God through the design arg.]

of God than that he is powerful, incorporeal, and purposive, defenders of design arguments can reply that God is normally said to be at least this, and that design arguments, therefore, provide at least some support for God's existence.

But what of Hume's suggestion that design arguments fail because the universe is unique? Although, as I have said, it has something to recommend it, this suggestion is also open to question. For it is wrong to assume that we cannot reasonably raise and answer questions concerning the origin of what is unique. Scientists try to account for various things which are unique. The human race is a good example. Are scientists being unreasonable here? Surely not.

In any case, we may deny that the universe is unique. To say that the universe is unique is not to ascribe to it a property which cannot be ascribed to anything else. It is to say that there is only one universe. And even if there is only one universe, it does not follow that the universe is unique in its properties, that it shares no properties with lesser systems. If you were the only girl in the world, and I were the only boy, there would still be two human beings. And there are lots of things like the universe even if there is only one universe. For the universe shares with its parts properties which can be ascribed both to it and to its parts. The universe, for example, is in process of change, like many of its parts. And it is composed of material elements, as people and machines are. According to arguments from design which emphasize the notion of regularity, the universe also exhibits regularity, as, once again, do people and machines.

This brings us to Hume's third argument: that arguing for a designer confronts us with the prospect of an infinite regress. Does that line of reasoning serve to rule out design arguments? Arguably not. It assumes that if we can explain A in terms of B, but do not (or cannot) explain B in terms of something else, then we have not accounted for A. Yet as one of the characters in Hume's *Dialogues* says, 'Even in common life, if I assign a cause for any event; is it any objection . . . that I cannot assign the cause of that cause, and answer every new question, which may incessantly be started?'[18] Even scientific explanations operate within a framework where certain ultimate laws are just claimed to hold. And there is another response to be made to Hume at this point. For, why should we suppose that what is responsible for order must exhibit an order which stands in need of a cause distinct from itself? Sources of order are sometimes things whose order is caused by other things. A factory machine devised to regulate the flow of bottles would be a case in point. But thoughts are sources of order exhibiting order. And we do not need to seek independent causes to account for the fact that they exhibit order. For they would not be thoughts if they did not.

Hume maintained that thoughts are a series of ideas which succeed one another in an orderly way. So he holds that they have temporal order, which requires a cause if any order does. But thoughts are not just ordered by virtue of temporal succession. Each thought is intrinsically ordered, for thoughts have a logical structure which philosophers can analyse and try to explicate. Confronted by Hume's third objection, therefore, defenders of design arguments can reply that design in the universe derives from the mind of God conceiving it. They may then suggest that it therefore derives from an order which does not, considered simply as orderly, stand in need of an ordering cause. Like a human designer's thoughts which lead to something designed, so they may argue, the thoughts of a divine designer could be essentially ordered.

But defenders of design arguments will not want to say that God is exactly like human designers, which brings us to Hume's 'Why not become a perfect anthropomorphite?' and 'Why not many gods?' arguments. Yet, although one can see their force, they do not succeed in ruling out design arguments. For there are a number of possible replies to them.

First, it could be said that the designer of the universe cannot be corporeal without being part of the system of things for which design arguments propose to account. Design arguments are normally concerned to account for material order in the universe. But they cannot do this by appealing to yet another instance of such order.

Second, it might be pointed out that design arguments do not have to conclude that the designer of the universe shares all the attributes of the causes whose operations provide the justification for inferring it in the first place. This is so because arguments from analogy do not have to assert that, since A accounts for B and since C resembles B, something *exactly* like A must also account for C.

Suppose that my office is cleaned by Mrs Mopp. She is Irish and cheerful, and she has a limp. I observe her cleaning my office week after week. She always comes in at 10.30 a.m., just before I leave for my coffee-break.

Now suppose that I am told one Monday afternoon that Mrs Mopp has resigned. Nobody comes to clean my office at 10.30 on the following Tuesday. Yet (how nice!) when I return from my coffee-break, I find that my room has been cleaned in the usual way.

What can I infer? That a cleaner has been around, of course. But I do not need to infer that the cleaner was a cheerful Irish woman with a limp. For all I know, my office could have been cleaned by a thin, depressed, Australian man with two strong legs.

The point which this example illustrates is applicable both to Hume's 'anthropomorphite' argument and to his question 'Why not many gods?' Human beings imposing order certainly have bodies. But this does not bind us to ascribing a body to everything that can be thought of as responsible for order. And, although order is often imposed by groups of human beings, it does not follow that every instance of order must be produced by a collection of individuals.

In other words, and as Richard Swinburne observes, the argument from design may be thought of as employing a common pattern of scientific reasoning which can be stated as follows:

> A's are caused by B's. A*s are similar to A's. Therefore—given that there is no more satisfactory explanation of the existence of A*s—they are produced by B*s similar to B's. B*s are postulated to be similar in all respects to B's except in so far as shown otherwise, viz. except in so far as the dissimilarities between A's and A*s force us to postulate a difference.[19]

On the basis of this principle, Swinburne proceeds to defend his design argument against Hume's fourth point. He writes:

> For the activity of a god to account for the regularities, he must be free, rational, and very powerful. But it is not necessary that he, like men, should only be able to act on a limited part of the universe, a body, and by acting on that control the rest of the universe. And there is good reason to suppose that the god does not operate in this way. For, if his direct control was confined to a part of the universe, scientific laws outside his control must operate to ensure that his actions have effects in the rest of the universe. Hence the postulation of the existence of the god would not explain the operations of those laws: yet to explain the operation of all scientific laws

was the point of postulating the existence of the god. The hypothesis that the god is not embodied thus explains more and explains more coherently than the hypothesis that he is embodied.[20]

As a reply to Hume, this seems correct. And with respect to the suggestion that there might be many divine designers, it can be supplemented by appeal to the principle commonly called 'Ockham's razor'.[21] According to this, 'Entities are not to be multiplied beyond necessity'. So defenders of design arguments could argue that, although there is reason to believe in one designer god, there is no reason to believe in more than one, even though there might possibly be more than one. It is worth noting that even Hume accepts a version of Ockham's razor. 'To multiply causes, without necessity', he says, 'is indeed contrary to true philosophy.'[22]

Let us now pass quickly to Hume's last three objections to design arguments: that the universe can be thought of as a living organism, that chance might account for order in the universe, and that the universe contains much disorder. Are these objections decisive? We may well doubt that they are.

Even if we press the analogy between the universe and a living organism, we are still faced by regularity in the universe. I have said little about this so far, but it is true that the universe behaves in regular and predictable ways, as Swinburne stresses. Defenders of design arguments could therefore reasonably draw attention to what Swinburne is talking about, and they might emphasize the similarity between the universe and machines. For it is characteristic of machines that they behave in regular and predictable ways and obey scientific laws. Defenders of design arguments might add that, in accounting for the order in the universe, their appeal to a designer explains more than does appeal to the generative power of living organisms (contrary to Hume's suggestion that the analogy between the universe and an organism is a problem for the argument from design). For living organisms reproduce regularity as objects displaying regularity themselves. Living organisms cannot explain all the regularity in the universe.

Hume's point about chance is that, over the course of time, there will be periods of order and periods of chaos. So, he says, the universe may once have been in chaos, and from this state the present ordered universe may have derived from this state. But Hume is here noting a logical possibility which does not affect the fact that the universe is not now in chaos, which still calls for explanation. And an explanation of order in the universe which does not refer to chance becomes more credible as time goes by. As Swinburne suggests: 'If we say that it is chance that in 1960 matter is behaving in a regular way, our claim becomes less and less plausible as we find that in 1961 and 1962 and so on it continues to behave in a regular way.'[23] In any case, why should it be thought that, if something comes about by chance, there is no causality or planning afoot? Suppose that the Pope sneezes in Rome at exactly the time that the US President sneezes in Washington. Must we suppose there is a cause of this coincidence of sneezes? Surely not. It is a matter of chance. But this is not to suppose that the Pope's sneezing and the President's sneezing lack causal explanations.

What of Hume's final point? In one sense it is clearly right: the universe contains disorder since there are, for example, pain-producing events of a natural kind (the sort of disorder which Hume actually has in mind). But this fact need not deter defenders of design arguments since they do not typically hold that every particular thing works to the advantage of other particular things. They only say that there is order in need of explanation; and disorder, in the sense of pain-producing natural events, is an illustration of order.

The Reasonableness of Design Arguments

So Hume's objections to design arguments admit of reply if they are taken individually. Yet a supporter of Hume might concede this and still urge that Hume has knocked a massive hole in them. For consider the following imaginary dialogue:

A. Brown has stabbed Jones to death.

B. Prove that.

A. Brown had a motive.

B. That does not prove that Brown stabbed Jones. Many people had a motive for killing Jones.

A. Brown was found at the scene of the crime.

B. That fact is compatible with his innocence.

A. Brown was found standing over Jones holding a blood-stained knife.

B. He may have picked it up after the murder was committed.

A. Brown says he stabbed Jones.

B. He may be trying to cover up for somebody.

Now B's comments here could all be quite justified. But, although A may be wrong about Brown, a reasonable person would surely conclude that, when A's points are taken together, they put a question-mark over Brown's innocence. Suppose, then, it were said that Hume's arguments, if not all decisive individually, make it reasonable to reject design arguments. Evidently, a great deal turns here on the initial strength of design arguments. So let us now consider this by turning to the two forms of argument distinguished at the outset of this chapter.

The Argument from Purpose

— argument from analogy

The argument from purpose in nature (which I shall henceforth call 'Paley's argument') is an argument from analogy. It rests on the premise that natural things resemble human artefacts. So, if it is to convince, there must be more than a passing resemblance between human artefacts and things in nature. The trouble, however, is that there are notable dissimilarities between them.

For example, human artefacts directly result from intentional actions. But this is not so in the case of things in nature. Our eyes, for instance, when we were developing in the womb, originated from genetically controlled processes that themselves had natural causes, and so on, back as far as we can determine. These processes may have been the result of design. But, if this is the case, the design seems to have been woven into the fabric of nature, so to speak.[24] Defenders of Paley sometimes say that it is reasonable to think of certain things in nature as machines. They sometimes claim that it is reasonable to think of the whole universe as a machine. But nothing in nature comes about as machines do. And we have no reason to think that the origins of the universe resemble the conditions under which machines are produced. We might also ponder on what it makes sense to ask of a machine and what it makes sense to ask of natural things or of the universe as a whole. Confronted by a machine, we can always ask what it is for. But does it make sense to ask this when confronted by natural phenomena or the universe as a whole? Does it, for instance, make sense to ask what dogs are for? Does it make sense to ask what the universe is for? We might say that dogs have a role in a structure which contains them, that they serve a purpose when viewed against their background. But even if that is so, it is hard to see how the same could be said of the universe. Against what background could the universe be thought of as serving a purpose?

On the other hand, Paley is surely right about one thing. We would think of a watch as displaying purpose. Might we not therefore argue thus: 'Given that there are things in nature which, like watches, display purpose, we should conclude to something outside nature lying behind them'?

A common reply is: 'No. We know about watches, and we know that they are designed by watchmakers. But we have no comparable knowledge about watch-like things in the universe which are not produced by people. We know about the origins of watches, so from any given watch we can safely infer a watchmaker. But we cannot make any such inference concerning the origins of watch-like things which arise in nature. Since our universe is the only one we know, we have nothing on which to base an inference concerning the things it produces.'

Yet this line of reasoning does not really engage with what Paley actually says. He does not presume that we are entitled to ascribe purpose to a watch only on the basis of our knowledge of watches and watchmakers. Paley thinks that our ascription would be justified even if we had never before seen a watch. In his view, watches suggest watchmakers because their workings are purposive or functional. He thinks that watches bespeak purpose because they are teleological systems in the sense defined above. And his argument is that there are systems of this kind in nature which, though not ascribable to people, are ascribable to purposes of the kind displayed by people.

In support of this view, perhaps the first thing to say is that few people know about the processes of watchmaking through personal knowledge. Our assumption that watches have watchmakers is not, in general, based on what we know of watchmakers and the way they turn out their products. We can, however, say that there are natural teleological systems the origin of which cannot be ascribed to human beings. For there are various things in nature which are not made or planned by people but which do have parts that function so as to result in something specifiable.

The obvious examples are biological. Kidneys, for instance, perform to secrete urine. Eyes exist for sight. And hearts pump so that blood may circulate. With respect to things like these, we naturally talk about the jobs they do. And we presume that the characteristic result of their performance comes about because they perform their functions properly and not by virtue of chance or external and random constraint. It makes sense to say that kidneys are for the secretion of urine, that eyes are for sight, and that hearts are for the circulation of the blood. In cases like these there is a terminus which is more than accidentally connected with the conditions under which it is realized. In such cases we naturally speak about one thing working thus and so in order that such and such should occur. In this sense there are teleological systems in nature which are not the product of human beings. The question, of course, is whether this has any theistic significance. Does it, for instance, allow us to infer the existence of anything analogous to human intention or purpose?

A common reply is that it does not, since teleological systems in nature can be accounted for in terms of natural selection as explained by Charles Darwin (1809–82) and his successors (not to mention his predecessors).[25] The argument here is that teleological systems in the natural world exist because of conditions favouring the development of species which arise due to chance factors at a genetic level. Natural selection is supposed to rule out design, since, according to the theory, the living organisms we find are those which survive the struggle for existence due to useful variations. What accounts for the appearance of design is the disappearance of the unfit. There are no hostile witnesses to testify against design. They have all been killed off.

Even if this theory is true, however, it does not undermine the drift of Paley's argument. Suppose I am a 'creationist'. That is to say, suppose I believe that every member of a given species is directly created by God or is a descendant of a member of that species. If I come to believe in the evolution of species by natural selection, must I conclude that the species that exist cannot be designed? By no means. For I can consistently assert that something may arise by mechanical means while also being designed. As Anthony Kenny observes:

> If the argument from design ever had any value, it has not been substantially affected by the scientific investigation of living organisms from Descartes through Darwin to the present day. If Descartes is correct in regarding the activities of animals as mechanistically explicable, then a system may operate teleologically while being mechanistic in structure. If Darwin is correct in ascribing the origin of species to natural selection, then the production of a teleological structure may be due in the first instance to factors which are purely mechanistic. But both may be right and yet the ultimate explanation of the phenomena be finalistic.[26]

And to Kenny's point we might add another: that, although natural selection might give us some true account of the emergence of teleological systems, it is logically debarred from giving us a full account. As Peter Geach writes:

> There can be no origin of species, as opposed to an Empedoclean chaos of varied monstrosities, unless creatures reproduce pretty much after their kind; the elaborate and ostensibly teleological mechanism of this reproduction logically cannot be explained as a product of evolution by natural selection from among chance variations, for unless the mechanism is presupposed there cannot be any evolution.[27]

Geach is saying that the development of living things cannot be fully explained by the theory of evolution. And he is right in this. Natural selection can occur only if creatures bear offspring which closely resemble their parents but without resembling them too closely. If offspring are exactly like their parents, natural selection cannot lead to the development of new characteristics. If offspring do not closely resemble their parents, then even if parents have highly adaptive characteristics and bear many more offspring than others, their offspring will not be likely to inherit their characteristics, and the process will stop. So there can be no origin of species unless creatures reproduce pretty much after their kind. And the mechanism of this reproduction is complex and ostensibly teleological.

Yet even if this is so, it still does not follow that nature implies a non-human purposer. Some would say that it does since any teleological system must be accounted for by intelligence. But why should we believe that view? It has a certain plausibility if we take it to mean that, wherever there is irreducible purpose, there is a designer. For, as Kenny also says:

> It is essential to teleological explanation that it should be in terms of a good to be achieved; yet the good which features in the explanation, at the time of the event to be explained, does not yet exist and indeed may never exist. This is difficult to understand except in the case where the good pre-exists in the conception of the designer: the mind of the designer exists at the appropriate time, even if the good designed does not.[28]

But the point of a process need not be its final stage. And must we suppose that teleological systems in nature are examples of irreducible purpose? Or can they be explained as due to some naturalistic, non-purposive factor?

Those who say they cannot sometimes reply that, unless we agree with them, we must ascribe the existence of teleological systems in nature to chance. But this assumes that, if they are not due to chance, then they must be planned. And that is not obviously true. We may presume that a thing must be planned if it does not emerge by chance. But do we contradict ourselves in supposing that something might arise in a perfectly predictable way without anything analogous to fore-thought? This question leads us straight into the design argument which focuses on the notion of regularity. So let us now turn to that.

The Argument from Regularity

To begin with, the argument starts with a premise which few people would dispute. The universe does contain a high degree of order in that scientific laws can be framed and expectations reasonably made about the behaviour of things over a very wide span of space and time. Even when we cannot formulate a law to account for some phenomenon, we tend to assume that there is one. This is not to say that there is a rigid causal nexus such that the state of the universe at any given time neces-sitates its state at a later time. Nor is it to say that, given certain condi-tions, such and such effects must follow. It is not even to say that there is temporal order to be discerned everywhere in the universe. But it is to say what we certainly believe: that there are many objects making up the universe and behaving in a uniform way.[29]

Now should we seek to account for this fact? Design arguments based on regularity hold that we should do so with reference to an intelligent cause distinct from the universe. This suggestion is open to the reply that, while we may think that order requires explanation in terms of intelligence, there might be no such explanation. But it is not always reasonable to speculate on this basis. When confronted with orderly arrangements of things, and unless we have positive reason to account for this order without reference to intelligence, we rightly seek to account for it with reference to intelligence. Numbers on a set of fifty pages could be set down in a totally random way; but once we discover that they can be regularly translated into something resembling a language, we rightly presume that we are dealing with a code. Bits of machinery could be piled up in a formless and inert heap; but when we come across bits which operate together so as to do something repeatedly and predictably, we rightly presume that they form an artefact. Unless we have a reason for ruling out explanation with reference to intelligent agency, it is reasonable to postulate such agency when confronted by order which is not logically necessary. But if this is so, and unless we have a reason for ruling out explanation with reference to intelligent agency, then it is reasonable to postulate such agency when confronted by the order in the universe. For that might never have been there at all, and yet it is there to a high degree. Someone may always observe that the order in the universe is 'just there', that order in the universe is a brute fact needing no explanation. But, granted that we normally attempt to account for order in terms of intelligence when we lack a reason for doing otherwise, such a reply seems arbitrary.

Some philosophers would say that there is nothing surprising and in need of explanation in the fact that we observe a universe displaying temporal regularity. For, if it did not display such regularity, we would not be there to observe it. Yet, although we could be aware of the universe as orderly only if there were quite a degree of order in the universe, this does not dispose of the fact that there is order, and it does not show that this is not something puzzling and in need of explanation. The point is well brought out by Swinburne. With the present objection in mind, he introduces a very suggestive analogy.

Suppose that a madman kidnaps a victim and shuts him in a room with a card shuffling machine. The machine shuffles ten packs of cards simultaneously and then draws a card from each pack and exhibits simultaneously the ten cards. The kidnapper tells the victim that he will shortly set the machine to work and it will exhibit the first draw, but that unless the draw consists of an ace of hearts from each pack, the machine will simultaneously set off an explosion which will kill the victim, in consequence of which we will not see which cards the machine drew. The machine is then set to work, and to the amazement and relief of the victim the machine exhibits an ace of hearts drawn from each pack. The victim thinks that this extraordinary fact needs an explanation in terms of the machine having been rigged in some way. But the kidnapper, who now reappears, casts doubt on this suggestion. 'It is hardly surprising', he says, 'that the machine drew only aces of hearts. You could not possibly see anything else. For you would not be here to see anything at all, if any other cards had been drawn.' But of course the victim is right and the kidnapper is wrong. There is something extraordinary in need of explanation in ten aces being drawn. The fact that this peculiar order is a necessary condition of the draw being perceived at all makes what is perceived no less extraordinary and in need of explanation.[30]

In response to what Swinburne says here, we might reply that, if we are to see at all, then there must be order. For seeing depends on there being order to see. But it still remains that there is order to see in the universe.

Still, one can always refuse to ask why the universe exhibits the order it does. And those who refuse to ask this question are unlikely to be swayed by arguments to the contrary. But the position of those who want to ask it is still a plausible one. And this conclusion is strengthened by the fact that, if we accept it, we can appeal to what is less in need of explanation than the fact of there being vast temporal regularity. For, if we allowed that this regularity is not explicable scientifically, we could account for it in terms of something analogous to decision. And the attempt to account for regularity or order in terms of decision is intrinsically more satisfying than the attempt to avoid accounting for it by saying that it is simply there.

The point I have in mind here is usefully brought out by Peter Geach, who refers to a story which tells of a Tsar who sought to account for the fact that a soldier always stood on guard in the middle of a lawn in the palace grounds. The Tsar was told that it had always been so, that there was a standing order for it. This explanation did not satisfy him. Finally he discovered that a sentimental Tsaritsa had once put a man on guard to prevent a snowdrop from being trampled on, and the order was never countermanded. As Geach observes, 'The Tsaritsa's capricious will was a satisfying explanation beyond which we need not look.'[31]

With respect to the design argument from regularity, it is also significant that what its advocates think of as explicable in terms of God is something which resembles what we would otherwise seek to explain in terms of intention. To employ an example used by Swinburne, suppose we have many packs of cards some of which prove to be arranged in suits and by seniority. We could reasonably infer that the unexamined packs are similarly arranged, and we would account for the grouping observed and inferred not in terms of chance, but in terms of intention. By the same token, we might plausibly argue, we have reason for inferring that, given the temporal order of the universe, an order on the basis of which we infer further unobserved order, we again have something for which intentional explanation is legitimate.

Conclusion

I have been suggesting in this chapter that design arguments have some life in them. You might disagree. If so, however, I have at least given you something with which to disagree. And, whatever you and I think, there can be little doubt that discussion of design arguments will continue for a long time to come. This, however, is not the place to try to take matters further. Instead we must turn to a wholly different approach to God's existence from those mentioned so far. Unlike defenders of cosmological arguments and design arguments, its supporters hold that there are grounds for believing that God exists simply by reflecting on the concept of God.

NOTES

1. *Natural Theology* is volume IV of *The Works of William Paley* (Oxford, 1838). Paley was an English theologian and moral philosopher. His writings include *The Principles of Moral and Political Philosophy* (1785) and *A View of the Evidences of Christianity* (1794).

2. William Paley, *Natural Theology* (Oxford, 1838), p. 1.

3. Ibid., p. 2.

4. The word 'teleology' derives from the Greek word *telos*, meaning 'end' or 'result'.

5. Thomas Aquinas, *Summa Theologiae*, Ia, 2, 3. Here, and in the next two notes, I quote from Richard J. Regan's translation in *St. Thomas Aquinas: God and Creation* (Scranton, PA, 1994), p. 43.

6. Ibid.

7. Ibid.

8. Richard Swinburne, *The Existence of God* (Oxford, 1979, rev. edn., 1991), p. 136.

9. We met this view above when looking at the kalām cosmological argument and its case for thinking of the cause of the beginning of the universe as personal.

10. Swinburne, *The Existence of God*, pp. 138ff.

11. David Hume, *An Enquiry concerning Human Understanding*, ed. Tom L. Beauchamp (Oxford, 2000), p. 102.

12. *Hume's Dialogues concerning Natural Religion*, ed. Norman Kemp Smith (Indianapolis, IN, 1947), p. 149.

13. Ibid., pp. 149f.

14. Ibid., p. 160.

15. Ibid., pp. 161ff.

16. Ibid., p. 168.

17. Ibid., p. 167.

18. Ibid., p. 163.

19. Richard Swinburne, 'The Argument from Design', *Philosophy* 43 (1968), p. 205.

20. Ibid., p. 209.

21. This principle is named after William of Ockham (1285–1347), whose philosophical writings favour simplicity when it comes to explanation.

22. *Hume's Dialogues concerning Natural Religion*, p. 168.

23. Swinburne, 'The Argument from Design', p. 211.

24. Cf. Robert Hambourger, 'The Argument from Design', in Cora Diamond and Jenny Teichman (eds.), *Intention and Intentionality* (Brighton, 1979), p. 112.

25. For a neat anticipation of Darwin's theory of natural selection, see Aquinas's commentary on Book II of Aristotle's *Physics*, #243.

26. Anthony Kenny, *The Five Ways* (London, 1969), p. 118.

27. P. T. Geach, 'An Irrelevance of Omnipotence', *Philosophy* 48 (1973), p. 330.

28. Anthony Kenny, *Reason and Religion* (Oxford, 1987), p. 82.

29. Not everyone has believed this, of course. The Aztecs thought that every so often a crisis came and that thereafter the unexpected was to be expected. Hence the impact on them of the arrival of the Spaniards with their weapons.

30. Swinburne, *The Existence of God*, p. 138.

31. P. T. Geach, *Providence and Evil* (Cambridge, 1977), p. 74.

FURTHER READING

For two book-length treatments of design arguments, see Robert H. Hurlbutt III, *Hume, Newton, and the Design Argument* (Lincoln, NB, 1965), and Thomas McPherson, *The Argument from Design* (London, 1972). For a defence of an argument from design which concentrates on beauty and goodness in the world, see Mark Wynn, *God and Goodness* (London and New York, 1999). For an impressive defence of a design argument not mentioned above, see F. R. Tennant, *Philosophical Theology*, vol. 2 (New York and Cambridge, 1930). Also see Richard Taylor, *Metaphysics* (3rd edn., Englewood Cliffs, NJ, 1983), ch. 10. Two significant essays on design arguments are: Robert Hambourger, 'The Argument from Design', in Cora Diamond and Jenny Teichmann (eds.), *Intention and Intentionality* (Brighton, 1979), and Anthony Kenny, 'The Argument from Design', reprinted in id., *Reason and Religion* (Oxford, 1987).

A good source book to consult with reference to Paley and Darwin is Tess Cosslett (ed.), *Science and Religion in the Nineteenth Century* (Cambridge, 1984). Did Darwin undermine design arguments? For helpful discussions of this question, see Peter Geach, *Providence and Evil* (Cambridge, 1977), ch. 4, and James A. Sadowsky, 'Did Darwin Destroy the Design Argument?', *International Philosophical Quarterly* XXVIII (1988). See also Kenny's 'The Argument from Design', cited above. For Aquinas on God and design, see Leo J. Elders, *The Philosophical Theology of St. Thomas Aquinas* (Leiden, 1990), ch. 3; Anthony Kenny, *The Five Ways* (London, 1969), ch. 6; and John F. Wippel, *The Metaphysical Thought of Thomas Aquinas* (Washington, DC, 2000), ch. 12.

For introductions to Hume on design arguments, see J. C. A. Gaskin, 'Hume on Religion', in David Fate Norton (ed.), *The Cambridge Companion to Hume* (Cambridge, 1993), and J. C. A. Gaskin, *Hume's Philosophy of Religion* (2nd edn., London, 1988), chs. 2 and 7. For an introduction to and discussion of Hume's *Dialogues* as a whole, see Stanley Tweyman (ed.), David Hume *Dialogues Concerning Natural Religion* in Focus (London and New York, 1991). For a collection of discussions on Hume on religion (including discussions of Hume on design arguments), see Stanley Tweyman (ed.), *David Hume: Critical Assessments*, vol. 5 (London and New York, 1995).

Richard Swinburne has written extensively on design arguments. See, for example: 'The Argument from Design—A Defence', *Religious Studies* 8 (1972); *Evidence for God* (Oxford, 1986); and *Is There a God?* (Oxford and New York, 1986), ch. 4.

In recent years there has been much discussion of contemporary scientific findings which indicate that the origin and evolution of intelligent life on earth depend on the fact that the universe is 'fine-tuned' for its production. This discussion is relevant for those with interests in design arguments. Its relevance is considered by Swinburne in Appendix B to the revised edition of *The Existence of God*. For scientific matters, see John D. Barrow and Frank J. Tipler, *The Anthropic Cosmological Principle* (Oxford, 1986). For more on their relevance to design arguments, see William Lane Craig, 'The Teleological Argument and the Anthropic Principle', in William Lane Craig and M. McLeod (eds.), *The Logic of Rational Theism* (Lewiston, NY, 1990), and (for a different approach) R. Dawkins, *The Blind Watchmaker* (Harlow, 1986). See also John Leslie, *Universes* (London and New York, 1989).

QUESTIONS FOR DISCUSSION

1 People might be able to tell you about the purposes they have as they do what they do. But does it make sense to say that non-animate things in nature act with purposes?

2 'It happened by chance.' What does this mean?

3 When would you say that something happened by chance? How would you back up your claim that it did so?

4 Is Richard Swinburne right to say that there is vast temporal order? Is he right to say that the universe might have been chaotic?

5 Can we conclude that there is order in the world from the fact that the world appears to us to be orderly? If so, why? If not, why not?

6 Design arguments are arguments from analogy. They are arguments from like effects to like causes. Hume says that they cannot, therefore, justify belief in the existence of what God is commonly taken to be. Is Hume right here? If so, why? If not, why not?

7 Is there a strong likeness between human artefacts and non-animate things in nature? How strong would the likeness have to be to justify the claim

that non-animate things in nature derive from something like human intelligence?

8 Did Darwin refute design arguments?

9 Can you make sense of the notion of personal explanation which does not itself depend on the regular behaviour of inanimate things?

10 'Design arguments do not establish the existence of God. At best, they show that it is reasonable to believe in the existence of one or many clever non-material agents active in our world.' Do you agree? If so, why? If not, why not?

5

ONTOLOGICAL ARGUMENTS

....

We can explain the significance of a word without supposing that any-thing corresponds to it. According to the *Oxford English Dictionary*, one meaning of 'goblin' is 'a mischievous and ugly demon'. But that defin-ition does not imply that there really are any goblins. Knowing what 'goblin' means does not involve knowing that goblins exist. Yet some philosophers have argued that a proper understanding of what 'God' means ought to lead us to conclude that God exists, that the meaning of 'God' entails God's existence. Defenders of this exercise in natural the-ology agree that definitions and the like do not, in general, have con-sequences when it comes to what there is. But, they suggest, a grasp of what the word 'God' means proves to be an exception to the rule. Kant has a famous discussion of this approach to God in his *Critique of Pure Reason*.[1] He refers to it as 'the Ontological Argument'—a phrase much used by philosophers since Kant's day. In truth, however, there is no such thing as *the* Ontological Argument. In what follows, therefore, I shall speak of 'ontological arguments'. All of them are 'ontological' since they turn on what seems to be involved in what God is supposed *to be*.[2]

Ontological Arguments

(a) Anselm

The most famous ontological argument is to be found in St Anselm's *Proslogion*, chapters 2 and 3, where Anselm offers a *reductio ad absurdum* argument (i.e. an argument whose aim is to show that a proposition is true because its denial entails a contradiction or some other absurdity).[3]

To begin with, says Anselm, we need to consider what God is. The answer Anselm comes up with is that God is 'something than which nothing greater can be conceived' (*aliquid quo nihil maius cogitari possit*). This, he observes, is what 'we believe' God to be.[4]

But suppose someone says that there is no God. That person, says Anselm, 'understands what he hears, and what he understands is in his intellect (*in intellectu*)'. From this Anselm concludes that God exists even in the intellect of one denying his existence. 'Even the Fool [in Psalms 14 and 53], then, is forced to agree that something than which nothing greater can be conceived exists in the intellect, since he understands this when he hears it, and whatever is understood is in the intellect.'

But does God exist in any other sense? According to Anselm, the answer must be 'Yes'. God, he argues, must exist not only in the intellect but in reality (*in re*). Why? Because, says Anselm: '*Et certe id quo maius cogitari nequit non potest esse in solo intellectu. Si enim vel in solo intellectu est potest cogitari esse et in re quod maius est.*'

What does Anselm mean here? The text can be translated in two ways (people rarely see that there are two possibilities here):

1. And for sure that than which a greater cannot be conceived cannot exist only in the intellect. For if it is only in the intellect it can be thought to be in reality as well, which is greater.

2. And for sure that than which a greater cannot be conceived cannot exist only in the intellect. For if it is only in the intellect, what is greater can be thought to be in reality as well.

Either way, however, it is clear that Anselm is arguing that something than which nothing greater can be conceived does not exist just in the intellect.

That is as far as Anselm gets in *Proslogion* 2. But the argument continues in *Proslogion* 3. I can acknowledge the existence of someone while agreeing that the person does not *have* to exist. By the same token, Anselm assumes, even if we know that God exists both in the intellect and outside it, it does not follow that there is no possibility of God not existing.[5] If we think that God exists of necessity, we need to know more of him than that he exists both in the intellect and outside it. *Proslogion* 3, however, claims that we do know this of him.[6]

How? Because, says Anselm, it can be thought that there is something which cannot be thought not to exist, and because God must be such a being if he is something than which nothing greater can be conceived. Why? Because something that *cannot* be thought not to exist would be greater than something which *can* be thought not to exist.

> Something can be thought to exist that cannot be thought not to exist, and this is greater than that which can be thought not to exist. Hence, if something than which a greater cannot be conceived can be thought not to exist, then something than which a greater cannot be conceived is not that than which a greater cannot be conceived, which is absurd.[7]

(b) Descartes, Malcolm, and Plantinga

So much, then, for Anselm's ontological argument. But there are other notable ontological arguments. In particular, there are ones defended by Descartes, Norman Malcolm, and Alvin Plantinga.

Descartes's argument comes in the fifth of his *Meditations*. Here Descartes says that by the word 'God' we mean 'a supremely perfect being'. And this definition of 'God', he continues, allows us to conclude that God really exists. Why? Because, Descartes argues, existence is 'a certain perfection'. If God is by definition something supremely perfect, and if existence is a perfection, it follows that God exists and that to deny that this is so is to contradict oneself. Or, in Descartes's words:

> Existence can no more be separated from the essence of God than the fact that its three angles equal two right angles can be separated from the essence of a triangle, or than the idea of a mountain can be separated from the idea of a valley. Hence it is just as much a contradiction to think of God (that is, a supremely perfect being) lacking existence (that is, lacking a perfection), as it is to think of a mountain without a valley . . . I am not free to think of God without existence (that is, a supremely perfect being without a supreme perfection) as I am free to imagine a horse with or without wings.[8]

Malcolm's ontological argument begins by trying to remove certain difficulties.[9] Philosophers often object to ontological arguments by saying that they wrongly treat existence as a perfection. Malcolm agrees with this criticism (more of which below). But he also thinks that in *Proslogion* 3 Anselm has an ontological argument which does not assume that existence is a perfection. According to Malcolm, in *Proslogion* 3

Anselm is saying not that God must exist because existence is a perfection, but that God must exist because the concept of God is the concept of a being *whose existence is necessary.* As Malcolm sees it, Anselm's *Proslogion* 3 considers God as a being who, if he exists, has the property of *necessary existence.* But since a being who has this property cannot fail to exist, it follows that God actually exists.

> If God, a being a greater than which cannot be conceived, does not exist then He cannot *come* into existence. For if He did He would either have been *caused* to come into existence or have *happened* to come into existence, and in either case He would be a limited being, which by our conception of Him He is not. Since He cannot come into existence, if He does not exist His existence is impossible. If He does exist He cannot have come into existence . . . nor can He cease to exist, for nothing could cause him to cease to exist nor could it just happen that He ceased to exist. So if God exists His existence is necessary. Thus God's existence is either impossible or necessary. It can be the former only if the concept of such a being is self-contradictory or in some way logically absurd. Assuming that this is not so, it follows that He necessarily exists.[10]

This argument is criticized by Plantinga. But Plantinga also suggests that it can be salvaged if restated with the help of the notion of possible worlds, a notion much invoked by modal logicians.[11] Roughly speaking, a possible world is a complete way things could be. For Plantinga, our world is a possible world. So too is a world exactly like ours but where, for example, Alvin Plantinga is a farmer instead of a philosopher. Working with this notion of possible worlds, therefore, Plantinga first reformulates Malcolm's argument in the two following propositions:

1. There is a possible world, W, in which there exists a being with maximal greatness.

2. A being has maximal greatness in a world only if it exists in every world.[12]

According to Plantinga, this argument establishes that in every world there is a being with maximal greatness. But unfortunately, says Plantinga, the argument does not establish that there is a God in the actual world. It establishes that there is something with maximal greatness. But being maximally great only means existing in every possible world. It does not mean having the attributes traditionally ascribed to God.

As I have said, however, Plantinga thinks that ontological arguments can be defended. And at this point he begins his defence. If he is right in his assessment of Malcolm's argument, it follows that there is a possible world where a being has maximal greatness, which entails that the being exists in every world. But it does not entail that in every world the being is greater or more perfect than other inhabitants of those worlds. Plantinga therefore introduces the notion of 'maximal excellence', which he thinks of as a possible property connected with maximal greatness.

> The property *has maximal greatness* entails the property *has maximal excellence in every possible world*.

> Maximal excellence entails *omniscience, omnipotence*, and *moral perfection*.[13]

Now, says Plantinga, there is a possible world in which there is a maximally great being. In that case, however (and in view of the understanding of maximal greatness just introduced), in any possible world this being has maximal excellence. And, says Plantinga, it follows from this that in our world there is a being who has maximal excellence, which is to say that there is actually a God whose existence follows from his essence and who can thus be thought to exist in reality by reasoning that counts as a form of ontological argument.

How Successful are Ontological Arguments?

(a) Anselm's argument

Anselm's argument (however we interpret it) appears to come with a weakness at the outset. For it seems to suppose that something can exist in two different ways: 'in the intellect' and 'in reality'. But this, of course, is not so. A thing which exists only in thought (in the intellect) just does not exist and is in no way comparable to, or distinguishable from, something which actually does exist. My imagined wealth is in no way similar to or different from the wealth that I actually have. And, we might say, it is therefore wrong to argue for God's existence with reference to the notion of something in the intellect which is less great (for whatever reason) than something in reality. Anselm might reply that

God must exist in reality since the concept of God is the concept of something than which nothing greater can be conceived. Yet, if that is so, could we not rightly deduce the existence of things which it seems silly to think of as existing? Suppose I say that I can conceive of a student than which none greater can be conceived. Does it therefore follow that there is a student than which none greater can be conceived? Surely not.

After the appearance of the *Proslogion*, Gaunilo, a monk from Marmoutiers, criticized Anselm's argument somewhat along these lines.[14] According to Gaunilo, if Anselm is right, then it is not only God's existence that can be established.

> For example: they say that there is in the ocean somewhere an island which, because of the difficulty (or rather the impossibility) of finding that which does not exist, some have called the 'Lost Island'. And the story goes that it is blessed with all manner of priceless riches and delights in abundance, much more even than the Happy Isles, and having no owner or inhabitant, it is superior everywhere in abundance of riches to all those islands that men inhabit. Now, if anyone tell me that it is like this, I shall easily understand what is said, since nothing is difficult about it. But if he should then go on to say, as though it were a logical consequence of this: You cannot any more doubt that this island that is more excellent than all other lands exists somewhere in reality than you can doubt that it is in your mind; and since it is more excellent to exist not only in the mind alone but also in reality, therefore that it must needs be that it exists. For if it did not exist, any other land existing in reality would be more excellent than it, and so this island, already thought by you to be more excellent than others, will not be more excellent. If, I say, someone wishes thus to persuade me that this island really exists beyond all doubt, I should either think that he was joking, or I should find it hard to decide which of us I ought to judge the bigger fool.[15]

Should we agree with Gaunilo here? There is one reply that Anselm could offer to him.[16] He could say that he never talks about something that is in fact greater than anything else of the same kind. Gaunilo concentrates on the notion of an island which is better than all other islands. But, Anselm might observe, his concern is with God considered as something that cannot be surpassed in any respect.

A defender of Gaunilo might, however, accept this point and still try to preserve the thrust of his argument. For what if we take it as urging that, if Anselm is right, then it is possible to establish the existence, not of the island which is better than all others, but of the island than which no more perfect island can be conceived?

In response to this question some have said that there is little sense in the notion of an island than which no island more perfect can be conceived. No matter what description of an island is provided, it has been suggested, it is always possible that something could be added to it so as to give an account of a better island. Hence, for example, Plantinga writes:

> No matter how great an island is, no matter how many Nubian maidens and dancing girls adorn it, there could always be a greater—one with twice as many, for example. The qualities that make for greatness in islands—number of palm trees, amount and quality of coconuts, for example—most of these qualities have no *intrinsic maximum*. That is, there is no degree of productivity or number of palm trees (or of dancing girls) such that it is impossible that an island display more of that quality. So the idea of a greatest possible island is an inconsistent or incoherent idea; it's not possible that there be such a thing.[17]

Plantinga is here suggesting that Gaunilo's argument works only if we suppose that something inconceivable is conceivable. But does this line of thinking really refute Gaunilo? Arguably not.

One reason for saying that it does not is that perfection in things is not always something to which addition can be made. Perhaps we can always put another coconut or dancing girl on an island, and maybe the island will thereby be improved (though it is not obvious that this is so). But what, say, of orchids? It makes sense to speak of a perfect orchid. And it makes equal sense to say that a perfect orchid cannot be improved on in any specifiable way. A perfect orchid is just a perfect orchid, and adding things to it would probably spoil it. So, why should we not conclude that the existence of a perfect orchid follows from the notion of a perfect orchid?

It is a question like this that Gaunilo seems to have in mind in his criticism of Anselm. And it is not a silly question. Plantinga's critique of Gaunilo holds (a) that the existence of something does not follow from the concept of something finite, something which can always be added to in principle, and (b) that Anselm's claim to have shown that there is something than which nothing greater can be conceived is not undermined by our ability to conceive of perfect islands, and the like. Yet, if

Anselm is saying that 'that than which nothing greater can be conceived' exists since it is better (or more perfect) to exist than not to exist, the difference (if there is one) between islands (or whatever) and that than which nothing greater can be conceived does not matter too much. Why? Because Anselm's argument, if cogent, would now be something we could invoke with reference to the concept of any perfect thing regardless of whether it is finite or infinite. For, as Morris and Alice Lazerowitz observe:

> If we can have the idea of an unlimited perfect being we can unquestionably have the idea of a limited perfect being, that is to say, a perfect thing of its kind. We can have the concept of a perfect orchid, than which a more perfect is inconceivable, a perfect detective, one who can solve every conceivable crime. Given this, the ontological form of reasoning applies to the concept of perfect finite things with the same force precisely that it applies to an unlimited perfect being.[18]

If Anselm is right to say that an X which exists is better than an X which does not exist, then a non-existing orchid or detective will be less perfect than an existing one. So it would seem to follow by Anselm's reasoning that perfect orchids and perfect detectives exist. But is it not implausible to suggest that this is, indeed, the case?

(b) Kant and ontological arguments

It was Kant who invented the phrase 'the Ontological Argument'. And he has two main objections to what he takes it to signify. He expresses the first of these as follows:

> If, in an identical proposition, I reject the predicate while retaining the subject, contradiction results; and I therefore say that the former belongs necessarily to the latter. But if we reject the subject and predicate alike, there is no contradiction; for nothing is then left that can be contradicted. To posit a triangle, and yet to reject its three angles, is self-contradictory; but there is no contradiction in rejecting the triangle together with its three angles. The same holds true of the concept of an absolutely necessary being. If its existence is rejected, we reject the thing itself with all its predicates; and no question of contradiction can then arise. There is nothing outside it that would be contradicted, since the necessity of the thing is not supposed to be derived from anything external; nor is there anything internal that would be contradicted, since in rejecting the thing itself we have at the same time

rejected all its internal properties . . . I cannot form the least concept of a thing which, should it be rejected with all its predicates, leaves behind a contradiction.[19]

Is this reasoning acceptable? We may wonder exactly what Kant is driving at. But his main point seems clear. Kant is saying that, 'God does not exist' is not self-contradictory. Whereas Descartes would say that to deny God's existence is like denying that triangles have three sides, Kant is arguing that 'God does not exist' could be true even if it is, in fact, false. On Kant's view, to define something is to say that, if anything matches the definition, then it will be as the definition states. But whether anything does match a given definition is a further question.

Is that right? Considered as a response to Descartes's ontological argument, the answer is surely 'Yes'. Descartes supposes that the concept of God is the concept of something having the perfection of existence. But even if we accept that this is so, it does not follow that there actually is any such thing as Descartes takes God to be. From a given perfection's being part of the concept of a thing, it does not follow that the thing actually exists. We may define a thing however we like, but definitions by themselves do not guarantee that there is anything corresponding to them.

But we may wonder whether Kant's argument really engages with what Anselm writes. For, is it true that Anselm proposes to define God into existence? Most people writing on Anselm assume that he does. But we may challenge this assumption. Early in the argument of *Proslogion* 2, Anselm introduces a premise asserting existence ('Something than which nothing greater can be conceived exists in the intellect'). And his question in *Proslogion* 2 is not whether we can move from a definition of God to the reality of God, but whether we can reasonably suppose that something than which nothing greater can be conceived exists *only in the intellect*.

What of Kant's second objection, however? This is stated by him in the following (famous) passage.

'*Being*' is obviously not a real predicate; that is, it is not a concept of something which could be added to the concept of a thing. It is merely the positing of a thing, or of certain determinations, as existing in themselves. Logically, it is merely the copula of a judgement . . . If, now, we take the subject (God) with all its predicates (among which is omnipotence), and say 'God is' or 'There is God', we attach no new predicate to the concept of God, but only posit the subject in itself with all its predicates, and indeed posit it as being an *object* that stands in relation to my *concept*. The content of both must be one and the same ... Otherwise stated, the real contains no more than the merely possible. A hundred real thalers do not contain the least coin more than a hundred possible thalers.[20]

Kant is saying here that, although ontological arguments take 'existing' to be a quality, attribute, or characteristic which God must have, when we say that something exists we are *not* ascribing to it any quality, attribute, or characteristic. And, although this suggestion is often rejected, it seems to me to be correct. Or, to put it another way, '——exist(s)' can never serve to tell us anything about any object or individual. By 'object' or 'individual' I mean something that can be named. On my account, then, Brian Davies (the writer of the book you are reading) is an object or individual; and to say that existence (or being) is not a predicate is to say that, while there are predicates which do give us information about Brian Davies (predicates truly ascribing properties to him) '——exist(s)' is not one of them. If 'Brian Davies snores' is true, someone who comes to know this learns something about Brian Davies. 'Brian Davies snores' says something about Brian Davies. This is not the case, however, with 'Brian Davies exists'.

One reason for thinking so lies in the fact that the contrary supposition leads to paradox. If '——exists' ascribes a property to Brian Davies in 'Brian Davies exists', then it looks as though 'Brian Davies does not exist' denies that he has this property. If Brian Davies does not exist, however, how can it be true of him that he lacks a property? Hence the paradox.[21] On the assumption that '——exists' signifies a genuine property of individuals, affirmative existential statements (e.g. 'Brian Davies exists') would seem to be necessarily true, and negative existential ones (e.g. 'Brian Davies does not exist') would seem to be necessarily false.

We may feel, however, that this can hardly show that '——exists' does not signify a property of individuals. At this point, therefore, let us note that the work done by 'exist' in sentences of the form 'A's exist' can be equally well done by the word 'Someone'. 'Faithful husbands exist' can just as well be rendered by 'Someone is a faithful husband'. Nothing is thereby lost.[22] But 'Someone is a faithful husband' can hardly be taken to be *about* any particular individual. We may assent to it because we know of certain faithful husbands; but the falsity of the proposition would not follow even if all husbands known to us become unfaithful.[23] Given that 'Someone' in 'Someone is a faithful husband' is doing the work of 'exist' in 'Faithful husbands exist', it would therefore seem that the work of '——exists' is not to tell us anything about any individual.

That appearances here are not deceptive, however, is best brought out by noting the way in which statements of existence can be viewed as statements of number. The way forward at this point is, I think, indicated by Gottlob Frege in *The Foundations of Arithmetic*, where he attacks the suggestion that numbers are properties of objects.

To begin with, Frege draws attention to the difference between propositions like 'The King's carriage is drawn by four horses' and 'The King's carriage is drawn by thoroughbred horses'. Going by surface appearances, we might suppose that 'four' in the first proposition qualifies 'horses' as 'thoroughbred' does in the second. But that, of course, is false. Each horse which draws the King's carriage may be thoroughbred, but each is not four. 'Four' in 'The King's carriage is drawn by four horses' cannot be telling us anything about any individual horse. It tells us how many horses draw the King's carriage.

So, Frege argues, statements of number are primarily answers to questions of the form 'How many A's are there?'; and when we make them, we assert something not of an object (e.g. some particular horse) but of a concept. 'While looking at one and the same external phenomenon', Frege writes, 'I can say with equal truth both "It is a (one) copse" and "It is five trees", or both "Here are four companies" and "Here are 500 men".' He continues:

> Now what changes here from one judgement to the other is neither any individual object, nor the whole, the agglomeration of them, but rather my terminology. But that itself is only a sign that one concept has been substituted for another. This suggests . . . that the content of a statement of number is an assertion about a concept.[24]

Frege then reinforces his point by means of the example 'Venus has 0 moons'. If number statements are statements about objects, about which object(s) is 'Venus has 0 moons'? Presumably, none. If I say 'Venus has 0 moons', says Frege, there 'simply does not exist any moon or agglomeration of moons for anything to be asserted of; but what happens is that a property is assigned to the concept "moon of Venus", namely that of including nothing under it.' That is, if 'one' is a property of an object, and if numbers greater than one are properties of groups of objects, 'nought' must be ascribable to non-existent objects. But to ascribe a property to a non-existent object is not to ascribe it to anything.

Now, says Frege, 'In this respect, existence is analogous to number. Affirmation of existence is in fact nothing but denial of the number nought.'[25] And if Frege is right about number, that is correct. Indeed, we can strengthen the claim. For statements of existence are more than *analogous* to statements of number; they *are* statements of number. As C. J. F. Williams puts it:

> Statements of number are possible answers to questions of the form 'How many A's are there?' and answers to such questions are no less answers for being relatively vague. Nor do they fail to be answers because they are negative. In answering the question 'How many A's are there?' I need not produce one of the Natural Numbers. I may just say 'A lot', which is tantamount to saying 'The number of A's is not small', or 'A few', which is tantamount to saying 'The number of A's is not large'. If I say 'There are some A's', this is tantamount to saying 'The number of A's is not 0'. Instead of saying 'There are a lot of A's' I may say 'A's are numerous', and instead of saying 'There are some A's' I may say 'A's exist'. All these may be regarded as statements of number.[26]

Statements of existence, then, are statements of number. They are answers to the question 'How many?' and, considered as such, they do not ascribe properties to objects. And if that is correct, Kant is right to resist the suggestion that we can argue for God's existence on the assumption that existence is a quality, attribute, or characteristic which God must have. The question, however, is 'Does this criticism successfully demolish ontological arguments?' The answer, I think, is 'Yes and no'.

It clearly does damage to Descartes's argument. Descartes is manifestly passing from a definition of God to the conclusion that God exists by means of the premise that existence is a perfection which God must possess. He even invokes the analogy of a triangle, as Kant does. Contrary to what is often suggested, however, we are not obliged to say that Anselm argues in this way. Everything here hinges on the proper translation of his words: '*Et certe id quo maius cogitari nequit non potest esse in solo intellectu. Si enim vel in solo intellectu est potest cogitari esse et in re quod maius est.'*

As I noted above, we can translate this passage thus: 'And for sure that than which a greater cannot be conceived cannot exist only in the intellect. For if it is only in the intellect it can be thought to be in reality as well, which is greater.' And if that is the right translation, then Kant's point about existence or being holds against Anselm, who would, on this way of translating him, be treating 'being in reality' as a perfection or great-making quality, as Descartes does.[27] But Anselm is not making this move if the proper translation of our Latin text is 'And for sure that than which a greater cannot be conceived cannot exist only in the intellect. For if it is only in the intellect, what is greater can be thought to be in reality as well.' If that is what Anselm is saying, his argument is as follows:

1. On the assumption that that than which nothing greater can be conceived is only in a mind, something greater can be conceived.

2. For something greater can be thought to exist in reality as well.

3. The assumption is therefore contradictory. Either there is no such thing even in the intellect, or it exists also in reality.

4. But it does exist in the mind of the fool.

5. Therefore, that than which nothing greater can be conceived exists in reality as well as in a mind.

If we want to contest this argument, we should not worry about the premise 'Existing in reality as well as in the understanding is greater than existing in the understanding alone, i.e. than not existing'. Rather, we should concern ourselves with asking whether it is true that we can conceive of something than which nothing greater can be conceived, and whether, if that than which nothing greater can be conceived exists only in the mind, something which is greater can be conceived to exist also in reality.

(c) Malcolm and Plantinga

Thus we come to the ontological arguments defended by Malcolm and Plantinga. And the first thing to say is that Malcolm is right to think of necessary existence as a possible perfection. In speaking of a thing having 'necessary existence', Malcolm is thinking of something which does not depend for its existence on anything apart from itself, something, furthermore, which cannot pass out of existence. It is plausible to hold that such a thing would clearly differ from things (e.g. human beings) which do depend on other things for their existence. It would also differ from things the existence of which can be threatened by what happens. And it makes sense to say that a thing of this kind would consequently enjoy a certain privilege or perfection.

Yet, what of Malcolm's claim that God's existence follows from the fact that God, if he exists, enjoys necessary existence? That, too, is reasonable. For could something which necessarily exists fail to exist? Obviously not. If something exists by nature, then that thing's non-existence is strictly inconceivable. And if something which exists by nature is omnipotent, omniscient, and whatever else God is said to be, then it makes sense to add that God exists by nature, as Plantinga argues. One might object to this conclusion on the ground that Plantinga is merely trying to define God into existence. But is he?

Plantinga's argument starts with a kind of definition and might, therefore, strike us as initially suspicious. But the definition is unique. For Plantinga, 'God' signifies something with divine attributes, something, furthermore, that exists of necessity. He is supposing that, if God exists, then God is essentially thus and so (omnipotent, omniscient, and so on) and also essentially existent. But on that understanding of God, it is absurd to deny that God exists. If it is possible that anything corresponds to Plantinga's understanding of God, then it is necessary that something corresponds to it. Or, at any rate, it is necessary that something corresponds to it if we assume that, if it is possible that a given proposition is necessarily true, then the proposition is necessarily true. Yet that is not an unreasonable assumption.[28] If it is possible that I am necessarily embodied, then I am necessarily embodied. If it is possible that triangles are necessarily three-sided, then triangles are necessarily three-sided. So, why should we not hold that, if it is possible that God necessarily exists (and if it is possible that God is essentially omnipotent, omniscient, and so on), then God necessarily exists?

That we should hold this is, I think, nicely brought out by Peter Van Inwagen. He suggests that we take the expression 'a perfect being' to mean 'something which possesses all of its perfections essentially'. Like

Norman Malcolm, he also suggests that we take necessary existence to be a perfection. He then argues as follows:

If a perfect being is possible, then a perfect being exists in some possible world (that is, at least some among the intrinsically possible ways for reality to be include the existence of a perfect being). If a perfect being exists in some possible world, then in that world it is not only existent but necessarily existent . . . Necessary existence, however, is the same thing as existence in all possible worlds: a necessarily existent being is just a being whose non-existence is impossible, and the impossible is just that which is not included in any of the possible ways for reality to be (which is not included in any possible world). A being that exists necessarily in some possible world *w*, however, must exist in *this* world, our world, the actual world—for if that being did not exist in the actual world, it would not be *necessarily* existent in *w*; that is, it would not be true in *w* that it existed in every possible world. This being, moreover, must not only exist in this, the actual, world, but it must have all perfections in this world—for if it lacked some perfection in this world, it would not have that perfection *essentially* in *w*. If, for example, wisdom is a perfection, a being that was foolish in the actual world could not be *essentially* wise in *w*, for the inhabitants of *w* could say truly of that being that it *could have been* foolish (our world being, from their point of view, one of the ways reality could have been). If, therefore, there is a possible world *w* in which there is a necessarily existent being that has all perfections essentially—that is to say, if a perfect being is possible—there must *actually* be a being that has all perfections.[29]

Van Inwagen here is arguing cogently. And if he is right in what he says, then so is Plantinga. Some would express unease at Van Inwagen's talk about things existing in purely possible worlds. But his argument does not depend on supposing that we can make special sense of sentences like 'There is a possible world in which X exists'. Van Inwagen's basic point is that 'given only that it is not intrinsically impossible for a perfect being to exist, a perfect being actually does exist.'[30] And that is a reasonable suggestion.

Notice also that, if we accept it, we are not committing ourselves to the view that God can be defined into existence. Perhaps I can illustrate this point by saying something about how Thomas Aquinas deals with ontological arguments, which he summarizes as follows:

Once we understand the meaning of the word 'God' it follows that God exists. For the word means 'that than which nothing greater can be meant'.

Consequently, since existence in thought and fact is greater than existence in thought alone, and since, once we understand the word 'God', he exists in thought, he must also exist in fact.[31]

Aquinas goes on to reject this as a proof of God's existence. And he does so by endorsing the view that one cannot define things into existence. He says: 'Even if the word "God" were generally recognized to be "that than which nothing greater can be thought", nothing thus defined would thereby be granted existence in the world of fact, but merely as thought about.'[32] And yet, Aquinas also argues, there is an absurdity in supposing that God might not exist. Why? Because, says Aquinas, it is God's essence to exist. Or, as Aquinas puts it: 'the proposition "God exists" is self-evident in itself, for . . . its subject and predicate are identical, since God is his own existence.'[33] For Aquinas, an understanding of what God is would indeed carry with it the recognition that God cannot but exist. But he does not take this to show that God can be defined into existence. Yet Aquinas is here basically saying the same thing as Van Inwagen (and Plantinga). Without proposing to define God into existence, Aquinas thinks that *what* God is entails *that* God is (as do Van Inwagen and Plantinga).

So, if we wish to take issue with Plantinga's ontological argument (not to mention Aquinas's claim that God cannot fail to exist), perhaps what we chiefly need to consider is whether God, as conceived by Plantinga (or by Aquinas), is something that possibly exists. Unfortunately, however, such a question is not easy to settle in the abstract. A proof that God exists would decide the matter. For proof that something *is* the case is proof that it is *possibly* the case. But, in the absence of an independent proof of God's existence, the full value of Plantinga's ontological argument is hard to determine. And Plantinga actually admits as much himself. He stoutly insists that his ontological argument is logically valid. But, he adds, whether or not it serves to show that God exists depends on whether or not 'unsurpassable greatness is possibly exemplified'.[34]

Conclusion

People encountering ontological arguments for the first time often find them to have little to do with belief in God as we find it in practice. They also tend to view them as tricks or exercises in philosophical conjuring.

In this chapter I have defended some ontological arguments. I have also tried to highlight grounds for thinking that some of them fall short. Whether or not I am right in what I have said about them is something you can now go on to consider with help from the questions and reading advice appended to this chapter. At this point I would like to turn to yet another approach to the question 'Is it reasonable to believe in God?' This takes the form of suggesting that such belief is reasonable since God can somehow be directly experienced.

NOTES

1. Immanuel Kant, *Critique of Pure Reason*, A591/B619.

2. 'Ontological' is the adjectival form of 'ontology'. Ontology is discourse or teaching about being or existence as such. So 'ontological' means 'having to do with being or existence'. Kant presumably coined the expression 'the Ontological Argument' because what he has in mind by it turns on the notion of what it must be to be God.

3. For an English translation of the *Proslogion*, see Brian Davies and G. R. Evans (eds.), *Anselm of Canterbury: The Major Works* (Oxford, 1998).

4. Echoes of Anselm's definition can be found in St Augustine (cf. *De Doctrina Christiana*, I, vii). But the nearest parallel to Anselm's formula comes in Seneca (*c*.4 BC–AD 65), who says that God's 'magnitude is that than which nothing greater can be thought'. Cf. *L. Annaei Senecae Naturalium Questionum libri viii*, ed. Alfred Gercke (Stuttgart, 1907), p. 5.

5. Cf. R. W Southern, *Saint Anselm: A Portrait in a Landscape* (Cambridge, 1991), p. 130: 'If this argument [sc. *Proslogion*, ch. 2] is sound, we can go a step further. The argument has forced an intelligent listener to agree that God exists both in the mind and outside the mind. But many other things exist both in the mind and outside the mind: for instance, the pen I am holding exists both in my mind and outside my mind. It exists *in re* and *in mente*; but it does not *necessarily* exist *in re* because it exists *in mente*.'

6. That there are different purposes lying behind *Proslogion*, ch. 2 and *Proslogion*, ch. 3 is argued by D. P. Henry in *Medieval Logic and Metaphysics* (London, 1972), pp. 105 ff.

7. Anselm, *Proslogion* 3. See Davies and Evans (eds.), *Anselm of Canterbury*, p. 88.

8. René Descartes, *Meditations on First Philosophy*, trans. John Cottingham (Cambridge, 1986), pp. 46 f.

9. Norman Malcolm, 'Anselm's Ontological Arguments', *Philosophical Review* 69 (1960); reprinted in John Hick (ed.), *The Existence of God* (London and New York, 1964).

10. Hick (ed.), *The Existence of God*, p. 56.

11. See Robert C. Stalnaker, 'Possible Worlds', in Ted Honderich and Myles Burnyeat (eds.), *Philosophy As It Is* (London, 1979).

12. Alvin Plantinga, *The Nature of Necessity* (Oxford, 1974), p. 213.

13. Ibid., p. 214.

14. Gaunilo's reply to Anselm is entitled *Quid ad Haec Respondeat Quidam Pro Insipiente*. For an English translation of this work, see Davies and Evans (eds.), *Anselm of Canterbury*, pp. 105 ff.

15. Davies and Evans (eds.), *Anselm of Canterbury*, p. 109.

16. Indeed, Anselm himself offers the reply in a response to Gaunilo called *Quid Ad Haec Respondeat Editor Ipsius Libelli*.

17. Alvin Plantinga, *God, Freedom and Evil* (London, 1974), p. 91.

18. Morris and Alice Lazerowitz, *Philosophical Theories* (The Hague and Paris, 1976), pp. 120 f.

19. Immanuel Kant, *Critique of Pure Reason*, trans. Norman Kemp Smith (London, 1964), pp. 502 f.

20. Ibid., pp. 504 f.

21. W. V. O. Quine speaks, in this connection, of the 'tangled doctrine [which] might be nicknamed *Plato's Beard*'. Cf. W. V. O. Quine, 'On What There Is', in *From a Logical Point of View* (Cambridge, MA, and London, 2nd edn., 1961), p. 2.

22. 'Faithful husbands exist' might be thought to state that there are several faithful husbands, while 'Someone is a faithful husband' does not. To avoid this difficulty we can say that 'A faithful husband exists' is equivalent to 'Someone is a faithful husband', or that 'Faithful husbands exist' is equivalent to 'Some people are faithful husbands'. My point is just that the work done by 'exist' in 'Faithful husbands exist' is the work done by 'some' in either 'Someone is a faithful husband' or 'Some persons are faithful husbands'.

23. Cf. Bertrand Russell, *Logic and Knowledge* (London and New York, 1956), p. 234: 'You sometimes know the truth of an existence-proposition without knowing any instance of it. You know that there are people in Timbuctoo, but I doubt if any of you could give me an instance of one. Therefore you clearly can know existence-propositions without knowing any individual that makes them true. Existence-propositions do not say anything about the actual individual but only about the class or function.'

24. Gottlob Frege, *The Foundations of Arithmetic*, trans. J. L. Austin (Oxford, 1980), p. 59.

25. Ibid., p. 65.

26. C. J. F. Williams, *What Is Existence?* (Oxford, 1981), pp. 54 f.

27. Notice that my above defence of Gaunilo against Anselm operates on the supposition that Anselm is thinking that existence is a perfection.

28. That 'Possibly necessarily-P' entails 'Necessarily P' is a theorem of the modal logic system commonly known as S5. For an introduction to it, see G. E. Hughes and M. J. Cresswell, *An Introduction to Modal Logic* (London, 1968), ch. 3.

29. Peter Van Inwagen, 'Ontological Arguments', in Brian Davies (ed.), *Philosophy of Religion: A Guide to the Subject* (London, 1998), p. 57.

30. Ibid.

31. Thomas Aquinas, *Summa Theologiae*, Ia, 2, 1. Here, and in the next two notes, I quote from volume 2 of the Blackfriars Edition of the *Summa Theologiae* (London and New York, 1964).

32. Ibid.

33. Ibid.

34. Plantinga, *The Nature of Necessity*, p. 216. Cf. also Van Inwagen, 'Ontological Arguments', pp. 57 f.

FURTHER READING

For a short treatment of ontological arguments, see Jonathan Barnes, *The Ontological Argument* (London, 1972). For a comprehensive analysis and discussion of a large range of ontological arguments (from Anselm to the present), a basic reference work is Graham Oppy, *Ontological Arguments and Belief in God* (Cambridge, 1995). For helpful essays introducing the topic of ontological arguments, see Clement Dore, 'Ontological Arguments', in Philip Quinn and Charles Taliaferro (eds.), *A Companion to Philosophy of Religion* (Oxford, 1997), and Peter Van Inwagen, 'Ontological Arguments', *Nous* 11 (1977). For a Reader on ontological arguments, see John Hick and Arthur McGill (eds.), *The Many Faced Argument* (London, 1967).

For an introduction to interpretations of Anselm on ontological arguments, see Jasper Hopkins, *A Companion to the Study of St. Anselm* (Minneapolis, MN, 1972), ch. 3 and Jasper Hopkins, *A New, Interpretative Translation of St. Anselm's Monologion and Proslogion* (Minneapolis, MN, 1986), pp. 3–42. For an interesting article defending one reading of *Proslogion*, ch. 2, see G. E. M. Anscombe, 'Why

Anselm's Proof in the *Proslogion* Is Not an Ontological Argument', *The Thoreau Quarterly* 17 (1985) For a critique of Anselm as interpreted by Anscombe, see C. J. F. Williams, 'Russelm', *The Philosophical Quarterly* 43 (1993). This edition of *The Philosophical Quarterly* also contains a response from Anscombe to Williams. For a helpful discussion of Gaunilo's criticism of Anselm, see Nicholas Wolterstorff, 'In Defense of Gaunilo's Defense of the Fool', in C. Stephen Evans and Merold Westphal (eds.), *Christian Perspectives on Religious Knowledge* (Grand Rapids, MI, 1993).

There is a certain amount of disagreement when it comes to interpreting Descartes's defence of ontological arguments. For introductions to Descartes's defence, see Anthony Kenny, *Descartes* (New York, 1968), ch. 7, and Bernard Williams, *Descartes: The Project of Pure Enquiry* (Harmondsworth, 1978), ch. 5. For a commentary on Kant's discussion of the Ontological Argument, see Norman Kemp Smith, *A Commentary to Kant's 'Critique of Pure Reason'* (2nd edn., London and Basingstoke, 1979), pp. 527–31. See also James Van Cleve, *Problems from Kant* (New York and Oxford, 1999), ch. 12, and S. Morris Engel, 'Kant's "Refutation" of the Ontological Argument', in Robert Paul Wolff (ed.), *Kant: A Collection of Critical Essays* (London and Melbourne, 1968).

Kant's claim about existence and predication has generated a lot of literature. An impressive introduction to the topic of existence and predication (which ends up defending Kant via Frege) is C. J. F. Williams, *What is Existence?* (Oxford, 1981). See also C. J. F. Williams, *Being, Identity and Truth* (Oxford, 1992). For a very different approach to the topic of existence, see William F. Valicella, *A Paradigm Theory of Existence: Onto-Theology Vindicated* (Dordrecht, Boston, MA, and London, 2002).

Ontological arguments all seem to conclude that God's existence is necessary (that God exists of necessity). The notion of 'necessary existence' has been subject to a lot of philosophical debate which is worth pursuing with an eye on ontological arguments. Good, introductory discussions include: Robert M. Adams, 'Has It Been Proved That All Real Existence Is Contingent?' and 'Divine Necessity', in id., *The Virtue of Faith* (Oxford, 1987), and Anthony Kenny, 'God and Necessity' and 'Necessary Being', in id., *Reason and Religion* (Oxford, 1987).

QUESTIONS FOR DISCUSSION

1 'You cannot define things into existence.' Is that really so? If so, why exactly?

2 Can things in the mind be compared or contrasted with things 'outside' the mind?

3 Can we think of something which is greater than something existing 'in the mind'?

4 Did Gaunilo refute Anselm?

5 Kant says: 'I cannot form the least concept of a thing which, should it be rejected with all its predicates, leaves behind a contradiction.' What does Kant mean? Do you agree with him?

6 Do we learn anything about something by being told that it exists? If so, what?

7 'Existence is a perfection.' Do you agree?

8 Does 'God necessarily exists' add anything to 'God exists'? If so, what?

9 'If it is possible that God exists, then God exists of necessity.' Is that a sound inference?

10 Is it possible for there to be something which is both necessarily existent and perfect in ways that God is said to be?

6

EXPERIENCE AND GOD

How do we attempt to justify our beliefs? We often simply appeal to what people have told us. We meet someone, for instance, and believe that his name is Tommy just because he says that this is his name. But we also tend to defend our beliefs in other ways. Sometimes we offer an abstract process of inference of a logical or mathematical kind. And sometimes we argue inferentially with an eye on empirical data, as detectives do when urging the conviction of people whom they take to be criminals.

Frequently, however, we defend ourselves by referring to what we have directly encountered. Suppose we have all been informed that Fred is dead. And suppose I then meet him. 'He's alive!', I tell everyone. 'How do you know?', they ask. 'I've seen him', I reply. Here I am not relying on anyone's testimony. Nor am I offering logical inference or inference based on empirical facts. I am reporting how things seem to me. I am drawing on personal experience. And this is something which people do continually. Ask Londoners how they know that their city is crowded. They will probably tell you about the people they see there daily. Ask people from Moscow how they know that it gets cold there in the winter. They will probably tell you to try spending a winter in Moscow.

Defenders of cosmological, design, and ontological arguments evidently believe that we have inferential reason for supposing that God exists. But might not the belief that God exists be solidly grounded in personal experience? Is it reasonable to suppose that God exists because people have seen, perceived, or met him?

Experience of God: What is the Idea?

The author of the Gospel of John roundly declares: 'No one has ever seen God.'[1] But there is a lot of talk about seeing God in the Old Testament. For instance, we are told that Jacob said: 'I have seen God face to face.'[2] In the book of Exodus we read that 'the Lord used to speak to Moses face to face, as a man speaks to his friend'.[3] In the book of Deuteronomy, the children of Israel cry out: 'Behold the Lord our God has shown us his glory and greatness, and we have heard his voice . . . we have this day seen God speak with man and man still live.'[4] And the prophet Isaiah writes: 'In the year that King Uzziah died I saw the Lord sitting upon a throne, high and lifted up.'[5]

Interpreting such texts is, doubtless, a difficult matter. On the surface, however, they appear to suppose that God can be directly encountered (as opposed to inferred). And this supposition has been employed by some philosophers arguing that belief in God has rational support. Hence, for example, according to John Baillie (d. 1960): 'There is no reality by which we are more directly confronted than we are by the Living God.'[6] Baillie opposes the notion that knowledge of God is arrived at by inference. We must, he says, acknowledge God to be 'of all realities, that by which we are most directly and immediately confronted'.[7] According to Baillie, human beings have four 'subjects' of knowledge: 'ourselves, our fellows, the corporeal world, and God'.[8] Baillie is saying that God can be directly experienced. And other philosophers have suggested that we could have reason to believe in God on the basis of direct experience. Two notable recent examples include Richard Swinburne and William Alston.

Swinburne takes his stand on what he calls 'the principle of credulity'. Am I justified in supposing that something is present just because it seems to me that the thing is there? Yes, says Swinburne. It is, he suggests, 'a principle of rationality that (in the absence of special considerations) if it seems (epistemically) to a subject that x is present, then probably x is present; what one seems to perceive is probably so'.[9] And, Swinburne suggests, this principle allows one reasonably to hold that God exists on the basis of experience. 'If it seems to me that I have a glimpse of Heaven, or a vision of God', he asserts, 'that is grounds for me and others to suppose that I do.'[10]

And this is basically what Alston maintains. In *Perceiving God* he suggests that 'people sometimes do perceive God and thereby acquire justified beliefs about God'.[11] Alston draws attention to people reporting an awareness of God which is experiential (as opposed to inferential), direct, lacking in sensory content, and focal (as strongly attracting attention). Alston then appeals to what looks very similar to Swinburne's principle of credulity. He says:

> Any supposition that one perceives something to be the case—that there is a zebra in front of one or that God is strengthening one—is *prima facie* justified. That is, one is justified in supposing this unless there are strong enough reasons to the contrary. In the zebra case these would include reasons for thinking that there is no zebra in the vicinity and reasons for supposing oneself to be subject to hallucinations because of some drug. According to this position, beliefs formed on the basis of experience possess an initial credibility by virtue of their origins. They are innocent until proved guilty.[12]

Alston concedes that claims to experience God are different from claims based on sense experience. He also notes that some seek to account for purported experiences of God in naturalistic terms and that not everyone agrees about ways in which reports of an awareness of God can be checked for accuracy. But Alston does not think that these admissions show that there cannot be knowledge of God from experience. He asks, for example, why experience of God should not give one knowledge of God even though it is not sensory experience. He also asks why God cannot be the cause of an experience of God even though other causal factors enter into the having of the experience. One may think that claims to be aware of God should be discounted since their accuracy cannot be verified as are claims based on sense perception. Yet why, asks Alston, should methods of verification for one set of experience claims be taken as determining what can be truly experienced and known? To suppose that they must be so taken is, says Alston, to exhibit 'epistemic chauvinism'.[13] One might think that someone's claim to have perceived God should be discounted since it fares badly when set beside people's claim to have perceived things physically. But, says Alston, the claim that sense perception gives us access to things fares no better than the claim that there is genuine experience of God.[14] Why not? Because, says Alston, there is no non-circular defence of sense perception considered as a source of knowledge. If we take sense perception to lead us to truth, we must, says Alston, start by trusting it. And, he asks, why should people not similarly trust what seems to them to be an encounter with (a perception of) God?

Objections to the Above Views

A number of reasons have been given for rejecting the view that God can reasonably be said to exist since there is direct awareness or experience of him. Those most often advanced can be summarized as follows:

1. Experience is frequently deceptive. We often say that we are aware of X or that we experience Y when argument or further experience forces us to revise our position. And we often identify things wrongly, misinterpret evidence, and hallucinate. Any claim based on experience is therefore suspect.

2. People who claim an experience of God are only influenced by psychological or social pressures leading them to believe that there is a God.

3. Any proclaimed experience of God must be rejected at the outset (a) because there are no agreed tests for verifying that there has in fact been an experience of God, (b) because some people report an experience of the absence of God, and (c) because there is no uniformity of testimony on the part of those who claim to experience God.

But do these objections show that it cannot be reasonable to believe in God on the basis of experience?

Comments on the Objections

The main argument against the first objection is that we have no general reason to reject a claim that something is so just because it is based on experience. For experience is a source of knowledge. Claims based on experience may be withdrawn by the people who make them, but this does not mean that they can never be correct. And, even if it is possible to be mistaken in a claim based on experience, not all such claims need be mistaken. A general argument from illusion, or from the possibility of mistaken identification or misinterpretation of evidence, cannot always be rationally used in assessing the correctness of assertions based on experience that something is the case.

Context is very important here. It would be reasonable to challenge someone's claim to have met an elf. But if I am assured by doctors to be in good health, with normal eyesight, of average sanity and intelligence, it would be unreasonable for me to doubt that, when I seem to see a train bearing down upon me, there really is such a thing. We need to remember the implications involved in our notions of mistaken identity, misinterpretation of evidence, and hallucination. Mistakenly to identify X is to have an experience of X and erroneously to believe that X is something other than X (e.g. to take Jones for Smith). It must therefore be possible to have an experience of X and correctly to believe that it is X (it must be possible to come across Jones and to identify him correctly). To misinterpret evidence is to be aware of something and to draw mistaken conclusions about it. It must therefore be possible to be aware of something and to draw correct conclusions about it. To have an hallucination is mistakenly to believe that something is present to one. It must therefore be possible to believe correctly that something is present to one.

In short, there is good reason to say that some claims can be reasonably upheld on the basis of experience. At a theoretical level, we can argue about the existence of Martians until we are blue in the face. But meeting them when they land will settle the matter once and for all. Sometimes one may just have to say that one sees that something is the case. And, of course, if one could not reasonably do this, then one could not even reasonably say that the objections made against claims based on experience are worth taking seriously. For how does one know that there are any such objections? Only by supposing that at least some things that seem directly given to one in one's experience are there in reality. We certainly make mistakes about reality because we fail to interpret our experience correctly. But if we do not work on the assumption that what seems to be so is sometimes so, then it is hard to see how we could establish anything at all and how we could correct beliefs that are in some way mistaken. As Swinburne says, rational enquiry presupposes that it is generally reasonable to say that what directly seems to be so is so. People who claim an experience of God may be mistakenly identifying the object of their experience. Since some people sometimes hallucinate and are insane, and since our beliefs might be determined by psychological or social pressures, one must, presumably, also allow that a particular claim to experience of God might spring only from hallucination, insanity, or the effects of psychological or social pressures. But several points need to be added.

From 'It is usually or often or sometimes the case that-P' we cannot deduce that it is always the case that-P. So Fred may be as mad as a hatter and as drunk as a lord, and it may still be true that on some particular occasion Fred got it right and was reasonable in believing something on the basis of experience. From 'It is usually or often or sometimes the case that-P', we cannot even infer that it might possibly always be the case. It might be that most men are below some average height. But all men cannot possibly be below average height. Furthermore, the truth of a belief is not affected by the factors that bring the belief about. Suppose that Fred says he believes in God on the basis of experience, and suppose that some psychologist or sociologist produces a plausible account of how Fred came to believe in God. It still does not follow that Fred is wrong or that his experience can never give him grounds for asserting that something is the case.

If, then, we point to possibilities of hallucination and so forth, the most we can demand is a bias in favour of disregarding particular claims to experience God. Given clear evidence that Fred normally misinterprets the objects of his experience, that he regularly hallucinates, that he is insane or largely influenced by psychological or social pressures, it might be reasonable to conclude that he is probably mistaken on some given occasion. If people regularly hallucinate, they regularly believe that things exist when they do not. One might therefore argue that it is possible that, in any further claim of theirs that something is the case, they are mistaken. But one should not argue that, therefore, nobody can reasonably believe in God on the basis of experience. The fact that some people are prone to get things wrong is not a sufficient reason for others to suppose that they always get things wrong.

It may be said, however, that there are no agreed tests for distinguishing experience of God from illusion or mistaken identification. And it is often urged that, if something is said to be the case, it must be possible to state tests which can be conducted by several people as a means of its confirmation. Some philosophers would add that these tests must be empirical. And they would argue that, since God is not an empirical entity, it follows that experience of God should never be claimed to have occurred. But these points are not enough to discredit the view that one can reasonably believe in God on the basis of experience. A claim to the effect that such and such is the case might be true even though there are no agreed tests to which one can appeal in order to corroborate it. And something could be the case even though its being so cannot be empirically verified (see Chapter 2 above).

In addition to these points there is something further that needs to be said about the question of agreed tests and experience of God. For are there really no agreed tests for picking out a genuine experience of God? Those who believe that there actually is experience of God frequently say something about its effects on the experient, the content of the experience, and the results to be expected in the behaviour of the experiment. They say, for example, that an experience of God is accompanied by a unique sense of humility, of creatureliness, of fear and awe mingled with a strong sense of passivity and dependence. They often say that the object of the experience is holy and awe-inspiring. They frequently tell us that an experience of God leads people to a conversion or to a change of attitude. One may not think that any of these facts shows that people experience God. But they seem to suggest that there are agreed tests when it comes to experience of God.

We come, then, to the following objections: that people sometimes report an experience of the absence of God, and that those who claim an experience of God give no uniform testimony concerning the nature and object of their experience. But these objections do not get us very far either.

Indeed there are people who say that they are struck by the absence of God in their experience. And there are people who never give the notion of God a second thought. But the fact that some people's account of their experience does not square with other people's account of theirs does not, by itself, establish that one of the accounts is wrong, unreasonable, or in some way unwarranted. A number of people may have good evidence that a certain animal is to be found in the jungle because they have seen it. Let us suppose that a second group of people goes to the jungle to look for the animal in question. They search for a very long time, but they do not find it. Can we conclude from this that the first group of people did not have reasonable grounds for affirming that the animal was actually there? Obviously not.

And if 'uniformity of testimony' means 'absolute agreement', then there is no reason to believe that a claim to have experienced God is irrational because those who claim experience of God do not provide uniformity of testimony concerning the nature and object of their experience. Two astronomers can agree about the existence of a star and be reasonable in holding that it exists even though they see it from different locations and with different instruments. And two doctors can be presented with a virus and be reasonable in believing in its existence without agreeing about its nature. If A and B claim on the basis of experience that something is the case, but if they also disagree about the nature of the experience and the nature of what is experienced, it does not follow that one of them is not right. Nor does it follow that both of them are not somehow right.

Recognizing God

With all of that said, however, there still remains a problem with the claim that God can be directly known by experience. For suppose we think that we are experiencing, encountering, or perceiving God. How are we to know that it is God that we are experiencing, encountering, or perceiving?

If I know by experience that such and such exists, then I must be able to identify it correctly when I come across it. If, for instance, my experience can tell me that there is a spider in the bath, then I must first be able to recognize a spider when I see one. And I must be able to distinguish it from other things (I must know the difference between spiders and cats, for example). By the same token, if anyone is in a position to know by experience that God exists, then he or she must be able to recognize God and distinguish what is encountered from other possible objects of experience.

Now, can anyone be in such a position? All theists agree that in some sense one can, since the end for human beings is union with

God. Hence, for example, Aquinas explains that, even though our knowledge of God is indirect in this life, if 'the created mind were never able to see the essence of God, either it would never attain happiness or its happiness would consist in something other than God'.[15] But Aquinas does not think of seeing God's essence on the model of encountering an object, as defenders of the notion of experience of God seem to do. Nor does he think of it as the basis of a case for the reasonableness of belief in God. And that is just as well if we bear in mind some of the things that have been said about God.

Consider, for instance, the assertion that God is the Creator, the Maker of heaven and earth. What recognizable property of an object is being the Creator? God has also been said to be omnipresent, infinite, omnipotent, and eternal. But how, simply by virtue of an awareness of an object of experience, can anything be recognized to have all those attributes? God has also been said to be omniscient. But how can anybody recognize omniscience simply by encountering something omniscient? To recognize omniscience in an object which one comes across surely presupposes that one is omniscient oneself. One can recognize that X is P without actually being P (I can see that you are drunk without being drunk myself). But if I 'notice' that Fred is omniscient, must not my knowledge be equal to his? Maybe one can infer that something or other is omniscient; but we are not now concerned with matters of inference. At present we are concerned with recognizing a property as something belonging to what one encounters and knows by experience.

With respect to the problem of how anyone can identify God as an object of experience, some have noted that it is possible to identify objects of experience without them appearing to be what they uniquely are. Hence, for example, Alston observes:

> To perceptually recognize your house, it is not necessary that the object even display features that are *in fact* only possessed by your house, much less features that only your house *could* possess. It is enough that the object present to my experience display features that, in this situation or in situations in which I generally find myself, are sufficiently indicative of (are a reliable guide to) the object's being your house.[16]

And, Alston adds, this is how it stands with experience of God. For me to recognize what I am aware of (X) as God, he says, 'all that is necessary is that X present to me features that are in fact a reliable indication of their possessor's being God'.[17]

What sort of features? According to Alston, one could recognize that one was experiencing God if the object of one's experience presented itself as being or doing 'what it would be natural or reasonable to expect God to be or to do'. But this is a very puzzling suggestion. God is often said to be all-knowing, all-powerful, and unchangeable. But how could an object of one's experience present itself so as to be recognizable as such? The object might act and talk in ways that give us reason to suppose that it has knowledge, power, and some degree of stability. But that is not reason for us to suppose that it is all-knowing, all-powerful, and immutable. It supports only the conclusion that the object of our experience is somehow like what God is said to be. And that conclusion is, of course, quite different from 'the object of our experience is, and is recognizable by us to be, God'.

What if an object of our experience told us that it was God? Would we have reason to suppose that it was? Suppose that you and I meet for the first time. I say, 'Hello, I'm Brian Davies'. Would it be unreasonable for you then to tell people that you have met Brian Davies? We could imagine circumstances that might make it unreasonable for you to do so (e.g. your having evidence of my death a year ago). In general, though, you would have reason to believe that you have met Brian Davies if that person says he is Brian Davies. But what are we to think of when it comes to the notion of God telling people that it is God who is talking to them? Perhaps we are to think that people hear a voice which says 'I am God'. Or perhaps we are to think that they see a bright light, or a lot of smoke, and that they hear a voice saying 'It is God you are looking at now'. But people subject to experiences like this have no special reason to suppose that they have had an experience of God. To suggest that hearing the sound 'I am God' coming out of the blue is reason to suppose that one is directly aware of God is absurd. And one cannot be looking at God if one is looking at a light, or a lot of smoke (or anything comparable). For God is not supposed to be corporeal.[18]

It is, of course, true that there are biblical texts which seem to be talking about direct encounters with God which take the form of a sensory looking at (apparently) physical phenomena accompanied by talk purporting to come from God. A classic example is the account of Moses and the burning bush (Exodus 3). Here we are told that Moses saw a burning bush which was not consumed by flame. Moses said, 'I will turn aside and see this great sight, why the bush is not burned.' Then God 'called to him out of the bush' and said, 'I am the God of your fathers, the God of Abraham, the God of Isaac, and the God of Jacob.' But do accounts such as these, even if we take them to be historically accurate, give credence to the suggestion that God can be recognized as an object of experience as, for example, Alston suggests?

Maybe they do. But notice that the Exodus account never suggests that Moses encountered God directly or that he had what philosophers such as Alston have in mind when they speak of direct experience of God. According to Exodus, Moses heard a voice and acted on what it said. Exodus says nothing about Moses experiencing what God might be expected to be or do. And biblical texts never speak about encounters with God which can be known to be such on any such basis as this. When 'encounters' with God are reported in the Bible, questions about identifying God by experience are never raised. Biblical authors typically content themselves with reporting that God spoke to someone or that so and so saw God. In the Gospel of John, the apostle Thomas looks at Jesus of Nazareth and touches his resurrected body. Then he says, 'My Lord and my God'. But Thomas's words are not presented as a report of a direct experience of God. Rather, they are presented as being a confession of faith—one which is certainly not grounded in what Jewish theology at the time of Thomas would have expected with respect to God. For that matter, it is not based on what contemporary Jewish theologians would expect.

In this connection, it is also worth noting that biblical texts sometimes suggest that God is not recognizable as an object of experience (and not to be expected to be so). Hence, for example, while Exodus 33: 11 tells us that 'the Lord used to speak to Moses face to face as a man speaks to his friend', Exodus 33: 20 has God telling Moses 'You cannot see my face, for man shall not see me and live'. Then again, according to St Paul, God 'alone has immortality and dwells in unapproachable light, whom no man has ever seen or can see' (1 Timothy 6: 16). That we can experience God directly, and identify him as such on the basis of what we might expect of him, is not a biblical teaching. This, of course, is not to say that we cannot identify God as an object of direct experience. But how can we do this? And on what basis?

Some would reply by saying that some things must be discovered for the first time and that God is such a thing. But to be in a position to know that one has met something for the first time is to be able to recognize it for what it is. Yet, as we have seen, there are problems with the notion of recognizing God. In response to these problems, some philosophers have said that knowledge that one has come across God comprises a self-guaranteeing experience of certainty. On their account, one can know that one has encountered God simply by virtue of the experience of having encountered him. But this line of thinking wrongly presupposes that knowledge is a special state of mind to be recognized in the having of it. It ignores the fact that whether or not I know something depends on how things stand in relation to how I take them to be.

Here we need to distinguish between feeling sure and being right. Those who speak about a self-guaranteeing experience of certainty usually mean that we can introspectively distinguish between knowledge and mere belief. With knowledge we are certain, and that is an end to the matter. With belief we are somewhat unsure. But my feelings of certainty cannot be the arbiter of what I really know. For feelings of certainty can occur when one is wrong about that of which one feels certain. One may be convinced that-P and it may well be that-P. But one's knowing that-P cannot be deduced from the conviction alone.

In any case, 'I just know' is not a proper answer to 'How do you know?' That question is looking for reasons apart from one's convictions—reasons which entitle one to say that one knows. If I am asked how I know that my pen is on the desk, it is no good for me simply to refer to my conviction that I just know it. I will need to be able to say something like 'I can see it', 'It looks like what I've been taught to call a pen', 'The light is good', 'I'm not drunk', 'You can pick it up', 'I put it there', and so on. It is considerations like these that make sense of my claim to know about the pen. Some may reply that 'knowledge' is hard to define, and they would be right. 'Knowledge' is notoriously hard to define. But our not being able to define X does not prevent us from reasonably maintaining that X is not such and such. And we have excellent grounds for denying (a) that knowledge is a special state of mind recognizable in the having of it and (b) that experience of God occurs just because people are convinced that this is what they have had.

Other People, the Dependent, the Ineffable, and the Mystical

At this point, I have said enough to indicate some of the difficulties with the notion of experience of God. But there still remain four considerations frequently advanced in its defence, and I ought, at least briefly, to say something about each before concluding this chapter.

According to the first, experience of God is an intelligible notion once we reflect on our knowledge of each other. The basic idea here is that direct experience of God can be compared to our experience of other people. According, for instance, to H. P. Owen: 'Our direct knowledge of God takes the form of an intellectual intuition which is analogous to our intuition of other human persons in so far as, firstly, it is mediated by signs, and, secondly, it terminates in a spiritual reality.'[19] According to Owen, we cannot physically see the minds, selves, or egos of other people because these, strictly speaking, are spiritual or immaterial. What happens, thinks Owen, is that other minds, selves, or egos are perceived via their bodies. And, so he suggests, God can be thought of as similarly perceived via the world. This, thinks Owen, constitutes a complex set of 'signs' through which we can 'intuit' God's existence.[20]

According to the second, there is such a thing as a non-inferential recognition that everything apart from God is absolutely and intrinsically dependent, from which it follows that experience of God can be taken as a fact since directly to apprehend the dependence of everything on God is a way of directly apprehending God.

According to the third, the fact that it is hard to characterize experience of God does nothing to show that there is no such experience, since the experience now in question is ineffable, or since its object is ineffable.

According to the fourth, 'the experience of the mystics' constitutes impressive evidence that God is an object of some people's experience.

Comments

(a) Experience of people and experience of God

A major problem with the analogy between our knowledge of people and a possible, experiential knowledge of God lies in the fact that there are reasons for denying that people are not essentially creatures of flesh and blood. The analogy now at issue trades on views about persons such as those associated with Descartes, according to whom I am essentially an incorporeal substance contingently connected to my body and able to survive without it. As I have promised, we shall return to such views in Chapter 13, but, for the moment, we can note that they have been seriously challenged. So perhaps we should hesitate to grant the premise that the people of whom we are aware in day-to-day life are analogous to God since they are essentially incorporeal. In any case, the God/people analogy has other drawbacks which make it unhelpful as a means of understanding what experience of God is and how claims that it occurs should be evaluated.

First, even if people are not essentially corporeal, they always come with their bodies. And knowing that they are there involves knowing that their bodies exist. God, on the other hand, is supposed to be incorporeal. He has no body at all. So we might wonder how our encounter with people could possibly throw light on what an encounter with God could be.

Second, our dealings with people allow us to count them. We can speak of meeting ten people in a room or five on a bus. But what entitles us to say that we have met one person rather than ten or five? An obvious answer is that in coming across one person we come across a physical unit distinguishable in some way from others. In other words, our ability to count the people we meet involves reference to material factors. But, while God is nothing material, he is also said to be one. Those who speak of experience of God do not suppose that they are talking about an encounter with five, ten, or twenty deities. If, however, the analogy between coming across people and coming across God is stressed, that is surely a possibility for which they ought to allow. Insofar as they do not, then the usefulness of the God/person analogy is hard to fathom.

(b) Dependence and experience of God

With respect to the notion of absolute dependence, there are two things to say. The first is that a conviction that everything apart from God is dependent does not by itself warrant the conclusion that it is dependent. Once again, we must distinguish between being sure and being right. Secondly, however, one may doubt that dependence can be identified as an intrinsic property of things. People in an aeroplane depend absolutely for their survival on the machine which bears them along. But they lose no intrinsic property when they leave it and enter an airport. They undergo no real change, since dependence is a matter of relation between things, not a matter of what things are like in themselves.

Whether or not there are creatures who depend on God would not, therefore, seem to be decidable by a direct perception of them as dependent (as one might directly perceive them to be green, bulky, or less than five foot tall). Rather, it would seem able to be settled only by knowledge that there actually are things which depend on God, knowledge which will be derivable only from something other than direct perception of them as dependent.

(c) Ineffability and 'Mysticism'

The last two considerations mentioned above raise issues which I cannot adequately deal with in the space available here. Briefly, however, there are two points worth making about them. First, if God and the experience of him are strictly ineffable, the obvious thing to do is to stop talking about them. And second, if mystics are evidence for experience of God, they are also evidence against it, since classic instances of them often deny that God is in any intelligible sense an object of human experience.

The drift of the first point here should be obvious: we can hardly make a case for the occurrence of experience of God if this, and indeed God himself, cannot be put into words. If 'we do not know what' is an experience of 'we do not know what', then we do not know what we are talking about.

With respect to the second point, I can only suggest that to read what has been said by the supposedly standard examples of mystical authors is to find oneself confronted not only by a wealth of divergent reports and judgements, but also by a repeated insistence that, since God is not a creature, he is just not accessible in the way suggested by defenders of the notion of experience of God. Consider, for example, St John of the Cross (1542–91)—a text-book 'mystic' if ever there was one.[21] According to him, union with God is a matter of faith, and 'no supernatural apprehension or knowledge in this mortal life can serve as a proximate means to the high union of love with God'.[22] 'The Soul', says St John, 'must be voided of all such things as can enter its capacity, so that, however many supernatural things it may have it will ever remain as it were detached from them and in darkness. It must be like to a blind man, leaning upon dark faith, taking it for guide and light, and leaning upon none of the things that he understands, experiences, feels and imagines.'[23] The language that St John uses here seems far removed from what we find in the writings of authors such as Swinburne and Alston.

Other readers of mystical texts, however, may have different things to impart concerning their content. And some may thereby be convinced that there is such a thing as 'the experience of the mystics' and that it is good evidence of there being direct experience of God. But if their conviction is to warrant agreement, it will need not only to be justified by extensive documentation and research, but also to answer the problems outlined above concerning the question of recognizing God.

Conclusion

Where, then, does all this leave us on the topic of experience and God? Claims to have directly experienced God are often quickly dismissed. As we have seen, however, scepticism concerning such claims is not as easily defensible as we might at first think. And those who are sceptical need to explain why they should not be sceptical of less unusual claims based on experience. We might think it obvious that people can have no good reason to think that they know of God by direct experience. But it is not obvious that this is the case.

And yet, as I have suggested, the claim to experience God is problematic. In this chapter I have tried to defend that suggestion by focusing on the notion of recognizing God.[24] Some philosophers would say that I would have done better just to observe that there can be no experience of God since talk about God makes little sense in general. I touched on this view in Chapter 2. But it deserves a more extended treatment, one which I reserve for the next chapter.

NOTES

1. John 1: 18.

2. Genesis 32: 30.

3. Exodus 33: 11.

4. Deuteronomy 5: 24.

5. Isaiah 6: 1.

6. John Baillie, *Our Knowledge of God* (New York, 1959), p. 166.

7. Ibid., p. 175.

8. Ibid., p. 178.

9. Richard Swinburne, *The Existence of God* (rev. edn., Oxford, 1991), p. 254.

10. Ibid., p. 260.

11. William Alston, *Perceiving God* (Ithaca, NY, and London, 1991), p. 3.

12. William Alston, 'God and Religious Experience', in Brian Davies (ed.), *Philosophy of Religion: A Guide to the Subject* (London, 1998), p. 67.

13. Ibid., p. 69.

14. Cf. Alston, *Perceiving God*, ch. 3.

15. Thomas Aquinas, *Summa Theologiae*, Ia, 12, 1. I quote from volume 3 of the Blackfriars edition of the *Summa Theologiae* (London and New York, 1964).

16. Alston, *Perceiving God*, pp. 96 f.

17. p. 97.

18. For criticism of Alston along lines I offer here, see Richard Gale, 'Why Alston's Mystical Doxastic Practice Is Subjective', *Philosophy and Phenomenological Research* LIV (1994).

19. H. P. Owen, *The Christian Knowledge of God* (London, 1969), p. 307.

20. Ibid., pp. 130–6.

21. Others include Meister Eckhart (c.1260–1327), Jan Van Ruysbroeck (1293–1381), St Catherine of Siena (1347–80), and St Teresa of Avila (1512–82).

22. A. E. Peers (ed.), *The Complete Works of Saint John of the Cross* (London, 1943), p. 96.

23. Ibid., p. 74.

24. Christians often speak of 'the beatific vision'—the 'seeing' of God on the part of those who have died and are united to God. Does the notion of the beatific vision compel us to suppose that we can know by experience that God exists? It does, if the notion is a coherent one and if we can know that there are those who enjoy the beatific vision. But, for obvious reasons, those who appeal to experience as a way of knowing that there is a God never appeal to the notion of the beatific vision. That is why I do not discuss it here.

FURTHER READING

The notion of experience of God is frequently discussed by philosophers under the heading 'Religious Experience'. For a classic treatment, see William James, *The Varieties of Religious Experience*. Originally published in 1901–2, the best edition of this text is now volume 15 of the Harvard series *The Works of William James* (Cambridge, MA, and London, 1985). For a recent attempt to categorize and comment on 'religious experiences', see Caroline Franks Davis, *The Evidential Force of Religious Experience* (Oxford, 1989). For a general, philosophical discussion of the notion of 'religious experience', see T. R. Miles, *Religious Experience* (London, 1972). For an unusually sophisticated and sustained treatment of the notion, see Simon Tugwell, 'Faith and Experience I–XII', *New Blackfriars* (August 1978–February 1980). For a collection of essays, see S. Hook, *Religious Experience and Truth* (New York, 1961). A very influential and much quoted text on the notion of religious experience is Rudolf Otto, *The Idea of the Holy*, trans. John W. Harvey (2nd edn., London, Oxford, and New York, 1950).

With respect to experience of God, you should certainly consult Richard Swinburne's *The Existence of God* (rev. edn., Oxford, 1991) and William Alston's *Perceiving God* (Ithaca, NY, and London, 1991). You should also look at what Alvin Plantinga has said about properly basic belief (see the Further Reading for Chapter 2 above) since he can be taken as defending the notion of something like a direct awareness of God. For another book-length treatment which complements that of Alston, see Keith E. Yandell, *The Epistemology of Religious Experience* (Cambridge, 1995). For some other notable discussions with a bearing on the topic of experience of God, see John Bowker, *The Sense of God* (Oxford, 1973); Antony Flew, *God and Philosophy* (London, 1966), ch. 6; Richard M. Gale, *On the Nature and Existence of God* (Cambridge, 1991), ch. 8; N. Horsburgh, 'The Claims of Religious Experience', *Australasian Journal of Philosophy* 35 (1957); Anthony Kenny, 'Mystical Experience: St John of the Cross', in id., *Reason and Religion* (Oxford, 1987); H. D. Lewis, *Our Experience of God* (London, 1959); and Wayne Proudfoot, *Religious Experience* (Los Angeles, CA, 1985).

The question of whether there is or can be experience of God is one which you need to think about with an eye on what philosophers have said about human knowledge in general. For good recent introductions to this area of philosophical enquiry, see Robert Audi, *Epistemology* (London and New York, 1998) and John Greco and Ernest Sosa (eds.), *The Blackwell Guide to Epistemology* (Oxford, 1999). For a useful Reader on the subject, see Kenneth G. Lucey (ed.), *On Knowing and the Known* (Amherst, NY, 1996).

For attempts to explain what mysticism is, see Cuthbert Butler, *Western Mysticism* (3rd edn., London, 1967); W. T. Stace, *Mysticism and Philosophy* (London, 1960); Evelyn Underhill, *Mysticism* (London, 1977); William Wainwright, *Mysticism* (Brighton, 1981); and R. C. Zaehner, *Mysticism, Sacred and Profane* (London, 1957). For a useful selection of philosophical essays on mysticism, see Steven T. Katz, *Mysticism and Philosophical Analysis* (London, 1978).

QUESTIONS FOR DISCUSSION

1 Can we sensibly distinguish between inference and experience? If so, how? If not, why not? Consider the bearing of your answer when it comes to the suggestion that God can be known directly and non-inferentially.

2 If it seems to me that I am seeing a 50-foot penguin, should I conclude that there is a 50-foot penguin before me? If not, why not? If it seems to you that you have a book in your hand, should you conclude that there is a book in your hand? If not, why not? If it seems to Fred that he is in pain, should he conclude that he is in pain? If not, why not? Are the examples involved in these questions different in significant ways?

3 To what extent might one's understanding of the word 'God' affect one's evaluation of claims to have experienced God directly?

4 If someone offers me what purports to be a proof that there could be no God, should I suppose that what I take to be my experience of God has to be nothing of the kind?

5 'Experience can be a source of knowledge.' What might this assertion mean? Is it a believable assertion? What might its bearing be on the claim that God is directly experienced by some people?

6 Can one know what God is *only* by virtue of an 'experience' of God?

7 Is there such a thing as 'what an experience of God is like'? If so, what

might that be? And might it give me reason to think that I know what an experience of God is? If your answer to these questions is 'No', explain the relevance of your answer to the suggestion that I can know that I am directly aware of God.

8 If Mary and John claim to have experienced God, is there any way for them or for others to determine that what they have experienced is the same?

9 Is it correct to suppose that God is such that expectations can be formed by us concerning what is or what is not likely to be him insofar as he enters into our experience?

10 To what extent do biblical texts support the suggestion that God can be recognized on the basis of experience? To what extent do they seem not to support this suggestion?

7

TALKING ABOUT GOD

....

'I love you', says Mary. 'Do you really mean that?' asks John. 'Yes', Mary replies. And the ensuing conversation goes like this:

JOHN.   Then you want to be with me?

MARY.   No.

JOHN.   But you do want to talk to me?

MARY.   No.

JOHN.   Surely you want to share things with me?

MARY.   No.

JOHN.   And you don't want us to make love together?

MARY.   That's right.

At the end of this discussion John is speechless, and not without reason. Mary's 'I love you' seems to say nothing significant. What she gives with one hand, she takes back with the other. She claims to love John, but she then appears to deny this.

Some people have felt that those who believe in God are rather like Mary. And, in their view, this means that belief in God raises an insurmountable problem, one which derives from two facts. The first is that people who speak of God do so by attributing to him certain properties (usually ones implying perfection or excellence) which are normally attributed to things in the world (especially people). The second is that God is also often said to be very different from anything else. On the one hand, God is said to be, for example, good or wise. On the other, it is said that God is unique and that our talk of him fails to do him justice—that God is not, for instance, good or wise as people are good or wise.[1]

Here, then, is the problem. If we say that God is very different from anything else, can we really talk significantly about him? How, for example, can we say that God is good or wise but not in the sense that ordinary things are? Is there not a real dilemma here for those who believe in God?

Threads of Connection

Some philosophers have answered this question with a resounding 'Yes'. As they see it, and given certain claims that theists often make about God, the words typically used in talking about God really convey nothing.

Take, for example, the assertion (common among theistic personalists) that God is a person. Does this mean that God is just like you and me? Not according to those who accept the assertion. They would usually say that God is, for example, incorporeal. But can we make sense of the notion of an incorporeal person? Some philosophers would say that we cannot, that our understanding of 'person' is too closely tied to the notion of people being bodily for it to make sense when applied to what is supposed to be incorporeal.

Or again, consider the sentence 'God is a wise, willing agent'. Can we make sense of this if we also have to believe that God has no human body? Not, for example, according to Antony Flew. In his view (as in that of many others):

> Being an agent, showing willpower, displaying wisdom are so much prerogatives of people, they refer so entirely and particularly to human transactions and human experience, that it becomes more and more forced and unnatural to apply the relevant expressions the further you go down the evolutionary scale. To try to apply them to something which is not an animal at all cannot but result in a complete cutting of the lines of communication.[2]

Flew surely has a point here. We give words a sense by getting into a way of using them. And our way of using words like 'person', 'wise', 'willing', and 'agent' are very much bound up with our talk of what is bodily. There are strong links between talk about persons who are wise, willing agents and talk about people as we meet them (as bodily individuals) in day-to-day life. And we might therefore wonder whether sense can be made of our talk if these links are broken.

Some would say that sense can be made of talk about non-bodily persons since the connecting links just mentioned are not as strong as people like Flew suppose. According to Richard Swinburne, for example, there could be a bodiless person since it is possible to conceive of oneself continuing to think and be aware independently of one's body.[3] Swinburne also argues that 'personal identity is not constituted by such things as bodily continuity and continuity of memory and character'.[4] But is Swinburne right here? And even if he is not, does it follow that talk about God cannot be thought of as intelligible. Are there not other ways of trying to make sense of it?

Meaning the Same

One answer given to this question denies that there is any particular problem when it comes to talk about God. Why? Because, so the argument goes, the words we use to talk of God have much the same sense as they do when we use them to speak about what is not divine. The idea here is that, although God is very different from anything else, the nouns, verbs, and adjectives used to talk about him mean basically what they do when describing and reporting on other (mundane) things.

Take, for example, the sentence 'God is all-powerful'. Just because 'powerful' is prefaced by 'all' and predicated of God, should its meaning in 'God is all-powerful' be thought to be different from the meaning of 'powerful' in, say, 'The US President is powerful'? Defenders of our present view answer: 'Why should it be? We know what power is, even though the powerful things we know are still somewhat limited in the power they wield. To call God all-powerful is just to say that he has power, in the ordinary sense, without limit.'

Or consider the sentence 'God is wise'. Should 'wise' be thought to signify something different when applied to God from, say, to Socrates? Not according to proponents of our present view. On their account, we know what it means to say that Socrates is wise. And that is what 'wise' means when God is said to be wise. We might, of course, presume that God is a whole lot wiser than Socrates. But that, so our present view holds, does not mean that to call God wise is to say anything seriously different from what is being said when Socrates is described as wise. The difference between God and Socrates is merely a matter of degree. Or as the medieval philosopher Duns Scotus (*c.*1266–1308) puts it:

> Take, for example, the formal notion of 'wisdom' or 'intellect' or 'will'. Such a notion is considered first of all simply in itself and absolutely. Because this notion [sc. as applied to God] includes formally no imperfection nor limitation, the imperfections associated with it in creatures are removed. Retaining this same notion of 'wisdom' and 'will', we attribute these to God—but in a most perfect degree.[5]

But can words applied when we speak of God really mean the same as they do when we talk about what is not divine? How we answer this question will greatly depend on how we conceive of God in the first place.

The theistic personalist might have little difficulty in supposing that a great deal said about God means the same as what it does when asserted of what is not divine. Hence, for example, Swinburne (a paradigm theistic personalist) suggests that, 'unless there is reason to suppose otherwise, clearly we ought to assume that theists are using words in their ordinary mundane senses'.[6]

Yet, what if we are classical theists? In that case, we might think that there is, indeed, what Swinburne calls 'reason to suppose otherwise'. Take, for example, Aquinas. Focusing on the notion of wisdom, and presupposing that God is entirely simple (that there is no real difference between the 'individual' God is and the 'properties' God has),[7] Aquinas observes that 'wisdom' means 'a quality when used of creatures, but not when applied to God. So then it must have a different meaning . . . the same applies to other words.'[8]

> When wise is used of a man, it, so to speak, contains and delimits the aspect of man that it signifies. But this is not so when it is used of God. What it signifies in God is not confined by the meaning of our word but goes beyond it. Hence it is clear that the word 'wise' is not used in the same sense of God and man. And the same is true of all other words.[9]

In the tradition of classical theism, the gulf or distance between God and other things points strongly away from an attempt to make sense of 'God-talk' by taking it to use words in the sense that they have when used to talk about what is not divine.[10]

Causation and Talk about God

Another approach to God-talk suggests that it is perfectly intelligible since it is grounded in God's activity. The idea here is that God can be said to be thus and so just because he has brought it about that there are things which are thus and so (that 'God is X, Y, or Z' means 'God produces things that are X, Y, or Z'). We sometimes describe causes in the way that we describe their effects. We say, for example, that a hot oven is the cause of its contents being hot. And in the light of this fact, some have suggested that we can meaningfully talk about God simply by noting his effects and by then describing him as we describe them. Thus, for example, it has been argued that we can say that God is good merely because he is the cause of things that are good, or that God is wise because he is the cause of wisdom as we encounter it in people.

Yet, although it is easy to see the logic of the reasoning present in this line of thinking, there are at least two problems with it. For, is it true that causes always literally resemble their effects? And even if it is, will we not soon be reduced to absurdity if we try to make sense of talk about God by describing him as we describe his effects?

The answer to these questions is 'No' and 'Yes' respectively. Causes do not always literally resemble their effects. People responsible for a state of justice might be just. And the parents of a human baby are themselves human. But criminals can give birth to saints. And makers of ice-cream are not made of ice-cream. As for the view that positive discourse about God can be grounded on the fact that God is like what he causes, what about the fact that, if God exists, he has presumably caused a material world containing coloured objects? Are we to say that, since God has done this, he is material and coloured? Few who believe in God would be happy with that conclusion.[11]

Another problem with the 'God is X just because God causes what is X' line of thinking springs from what those who believe in God often say about his relation to the world as its Creator. Does God *have* to create? A traditional theistic response says that God does not have to create since his act of creating is *free*. In terms of this way of thinking, there might have been nothing but God. But if that is the case, talk of God cannot be grounded in the 'God is X just because God causes what is X' principle.

For this would make God being what he is dependent on there being something to which he stands as cause—which conflicts with the notion that God might never have created (caused to be) anything at all. God cannot be the cause of all things other than himself unless he has brought into existence things other than himself. But those who believe in God normally think that his being, for example, good and wise, does not depend on the fact that he has brought good and wise things into existence. They would say that God is wise in and of himself and regardless of what he has produced. And they would typically say the same when it comes to various other terms used to describe God (e.g. living, loving, merciful, omnipotent, and eternal).

Metaphor and Talk about God

Yet another approach to the sense involved in talk about God focuses on the notion of metaphor. We may summarize it as follows. When we form positive statements about God, we must somehow mean what we say. But God is very different from anything in the universe. We need, then, to speak positively about him without denying the difference between God and creatures. But we can do this if we think of our talk about God as metaphorical. When we use metaphors, we refer to things by means of words which we can also use when alluding to something very different. We can speak, for example, of the 'ship of state' without implying that the government floats on water. Or we can call people 'donkeys' without supposing that they have four legs and a tail. By the same token, then, we can also refer to God using words which name or describe things in the universe. We can do so metaphorically and without being committed to absurd consequences concerning the similarity between God and his creatures.

Or so the argument goes. And we can defend it to some extent. Very different things can be given the same title or described in the same way. Poetry flourishes because of this. But can we say that *all* talk of God is metaphorical? The answer is surely 'No'. For, with metaphorical language, we can always raise a question about literal truth. We can ask, for example, whether the state is really a ship, or whether our friends really are donkeys. And if we say that all talk of God is metaphorical, then we should have to deny that God is really what many would say that he really is.

This may not seem obvious at first. Someone might say 'God is a mighty fortress'. We then ask: 'Is that really true? Is God made of stone, for example?' The answer will probably be: 'Of course not. I am speaking metaphorically.' Here it would seem that nothing anyone could wish to affirm of God is being denied. And we might well see some reason to assert that God is a mighty fortress.

But suppose someone now says 'God is alive' or 'God is good'. Again we ask: 'Is that really true? Is he really alive and good? Or are we now using a figure of speech?' If the statements are metaphorical, we ought to be able to reply 'No'. But can we do that? Not if we profess anything recognizable as a traditional belief in God, for that holds that God is literally alive and good and that it is not just a figure of speech to call him such. Those who believe in the living and good God (whether classical theists or theistic personalists) would not say 'It is not really the case that God is alive and good', although they might be happy to concede 'It is not really the case that God is a mighty fortress'.

God and Negation

With thoughts such as these in mind, some theists have tried to explain how we can speak significantly about God by appealing to the importance of negation. They have argued that we can do so by saying what God is *not*. A notable advocate of this view is Maimonides, according to whom:

> There is no necessity at all for you to use positive attributes of God with the view of magnifying Him in your thoughts . . . I will give you . . . some illustrations, in order that you may better understand the propriety of forming as many negative attributes as possible, and the impropriety of ascribing to God any positive attributes. A person may know for certain that a 'ship' is in existence, but he may not know to what object that name is applied, whether to a substance or to an accident; a second person then learns that a ship is not an accident; a third, that it is not a mineral; a fourth, that it is not a plant growing in the earth; a fifth, that it is not a body whose parts are joined together by nature; a sixth, that it is not a flat object like boards or doors; a

seventh, that it is not a sphere; an eighth, that it is not pointed; a ninth, that it is not round shaped; nor equilateral; a tenth, that it is not solid. It is clear that this tenth person has almost arrived at the correct notion of a 'ship' by the foregoing negative attributes . . . In the same manner you will come nearer to the knowledge and comprehension of God by the negative attributes . . . I do not merely declare that he who affirms attributes of God has not sufficient knowledge concerning the Creator . . . but I say that he unconsciously loses his belief in God.[12]

But is Maimonides correct here? In his defence, we could say that talking of God by means of negation is justified given the way in which God has been understood within the Judaeo-Christian tradition. As we have seen, God has regularly been thought of as the Creator, as the source of all things other than himself. And if that is how we think of God, it looks right to say that we can speak truly in saying what God is *not*. It will be true, for example, to say that God is not anything bodily (i.e. physical or material). If God is the source of the universe, he cannot be something bodily since anything bodily is part of the universe and cannot therefore account for there being a universe. Only something which is not a body could account for there being a universe of physical objects.[13]

Then again, if God is the source of everything other than himself, it would seem to follow that his existence cannot derive from anything else and that God cannot be limited in his activity as things in the world are. So there is a case for calling God *un*derived, *un*created, and *un*limited, all of which expressions express negations. We might also argue that God is *un*changeable and *non*-temporal. For, if we take God to account for all change (as some theists do), and if we take being changeable to imply being temporal (as some do), it would seem that God cannot be changeable without being himself an effect of himself; and it would also seem that God cannot be temporal without being part of his own created (changeable) order.

Yet the position that we can talk significantly about God *only* by means of negation is still difficult to defend. Here there are at least two points to note.

The first concerns the claim that we can come to an understanding of God simply by recognizing what God is not. Maimonides evidently thinks that this claim is true. But only saying what something is not gives no indication of what it actually is. And if we can only know what God is not, we cannot understand him at all. We can come to make true statements about things by means of negation. It is, for example, true to say 'The moon is not a piece of cheese'. And sometimes we can guess what something is when we know only one thing that it is not. If a mother who has just given birth is told 'It's not a boy', she will know at once that her baby is a girl. Yet it still remains that, except in rather special cases, if we know only what something is not, we do not know what it is. Suppose I say that there is something in my room, and suppose I reject every suggestion you make as to what is actually there. In that case, you will end up with no idea at all as to what is in my room. And, returning to the above quotation from Maimonides, it is simply wrong to say that someone who has all the negations there mentioned 'has almost arrived at the correct notion of a "ship" '. Such a person could equally well be thinking of a wardrobe (a stand-up closet) or a coffin.

The second point is that people who talk about God do not normally speak about him only in negations. They usually want to say that some things are positively true of him. They make positive affirmations about God. They say, for example, 'God is alive', 'God is powerful', 'God has knowledge', 'God is everywhere', 'God is eternal', and 'God is good'. Sometimes, indeed, what looks like a positive assertion about something may be no such thing. In certain circumstances 'You are a great help' may mean 'You are no help at all'. But all the assertions just mentioned not only *look* to be positive; they would normally be understood *to be* such by those who subscribe to them. As Aquinas puts it: 'When people speak of "the living God" they do not simply want to say . . . that he differs from a lifeless body.'[14]

God and Analogy

Historically speaking, however (and forgetting about authors such as Scotus), it is the notion of analogy that has most interested those who agree that even a unique God can be spoken about significantly. In this connection, it is even possible to speak about 'the theory of analogy'.

Suppose I say that Fido and Rover are dogs. And suppose that what I am talking about are indeed canine animals. I am therefore saying that

Fido and Rover have something definite in common, so that 'dog' means the same when applied to each of them. To say that Fido is a dog and that Rover is a dog is to say exactly the same thing of each of them.

But suppose I say that A is a bat and that B is also a bat. Must 'bat' mean exactly the same in 'A is a bat' and 'B is a bat'? Not at all. For A may be an object with which cricketers hit balls. And B may be a mammal with wings. The word 'bat' can be applied to two things without meaning the same thing at all.

In more technical language, the difference we have just noted between 'dog' and 'bat' can be expressed by saying that the word 'dog' in 'Fido is a dog' and 'Rover is a dog' is being used *univocally*, while 'bat' in 'A is a bat' and 'B is a bat' is being used *equivocally*. To apply a word univocally to two things is to say that they are exactly the same in some respect, that the word means the same in both its applications. To apply words equivocally, however, is to use the same words in completely different senses.

Now, according to the theory of analogy, there is a third way of applying the same word to different things, a way which it is important to keep in mind when thinking about how we may sensibly talk about God. The idea is that we can use words analogically. The analogical use of words is supposed to lie somewhere between the univocal and the equivocal.

We can see the notion of analogy classically applied to God in the work of Aquinas, who explicitly asks: 'Are words used univocally or equivocally of God and creatures?' His answer comes in three stages.

First, says Aquinas, God is infinite, incomprehensible, and entirely simple. Aquinas takes this to suggest that the same term cannot be applied to God and to creatures univocally:

> It is impossible to predicate anything univocally of God and of creatures. Every effect that falls short of what is typical of the power of its cause represents it inadequately, for it is not the same kind of thing as the cause. Thus what exists simply and in a unified way in the cause will be divided up and take various different forms in such effects—as the simple power of the sun produces many different kinds of lesser things. In the same way ... the perfections which in creatures are many and various pre-exist in God as one.[5]

On the other hand, however, Aquinas also argues that words applied to God and creatures cannot always be used equivocally:

> Although we never use words in exactly the same sense of creatures and God, we are not merely equivocating when we use the same words, as some have said, for if this were so we could never argue from statements about creatures to statements about God—any such argument would be invalidated by the Fallacy of Equivocation. That this does not happen we know not merely from the teachings of the philosophers who prove many things about God but also from the teaching of St Paul, for he says, 'The invisible things of God are made known by those things that are made'.[16]

Aquinas goes on to conclude that 'words are used of God and creatures in an analogical way'. What does he mean by this? He distinguishes between different kinds of analogy, but his main point is that certain terms can be applied both to God and to creatures, neither univocally nor equivocally, but because of some relation between God and creatures. And the relation which Aquinas has in mind is causal. According to Aquinas, we can say, for example, both that God is good and that some creature is good because creaturely goodness exists in God inasmuch as creatures and their properties derive from God as their first cause.

> Some words are used neither univocally nor purely equivocally of God and creatures, but analogically, for we cannot speak of God at all except in the language we use of creatures, and so whatever is said both of God and creatures is said in virtue of the order that creatures have to God as to their source and cause in which all the perfections of things pre-exist transcendently.[17]

It is important to note that Aquinas does not mean by this that, for example, 'God is good' is simply equivalent to 'God causes goodness in creatures'. Aquinas does not subscribe to the 'God is X just because God causes what is X' theory. In fact, he explicitly rejects it on the ground that it entails that 'everything we said of God would be true only in a secondary sense'.[18] He does, however, think that we can sometimes use the same words in speaking of God and creatures because of certain similarities between God and creatures. And he thinks that we can do so because creatures derive from or are caused to exist by God.

For Aquinas, causes and their effects are intimately connected.[19]

Effects, he thinks, flow from their actual causes (rather than from other things) because these causes belong to certain kinds and, as such, have definite ways of being or working.[20] Aquinas therefore concludes that, because creatures come from or are brought about by God, they reveal or reflect something of what he is. And on this basis, says Aquinas, God can (in principle) be named from his creatures, i.e. spoken of by means of words which we use in describing them.[21] For Aquinas, causes can be thought of as exerting themselves or as imposing their character on things. This leads him to think of the world as something in which we can see something of what God is like. You cannot give what you have not got, and even though what you give may not look like you, it will still reflect what you are. By the same token, so Aquinas reasons, God's world reflects what he is, and we may well suppose that he can sometimes be spoken of in ways in which we speak about some of his creatures.

But is the notion of analogy helpful when it comes to making sense of talk about God? Some philosophers have found it unhelpful, but there is a lot to be said for the view that the same word can be literally applied to different things neither univocally nor equivocally. This point can be illustrated by quoting a passage at the beginning of Wittgenstein's *Philosophical Investigations*:

> Consider for example the proceedings that we call 'games'. I mean board-games, card-games, ball-games, Olympic games, and so on. What is common to them all?—Don't say: 'There *must* be something common, or they would not be called "games" '—but *look and see* whether there is anything common to them all.—For if you look at them you will not see something that is common to *all*, but similarities, relationships, and a whole series of them at that. To repeat: don't think, but look!—Look for example at board-games, with their multifarious relationships. Now pass to card-games; here you find many correspondences with the first group, but many common features drop out, and others appear. When we pass next to ball-games, much that is common is retained, but much is lost.—Are they all 'amusing'? Compare chess with noughts and crosses. Or is there always winning and losing, or competition between players? Think of patience . . . And we can go through the many, many other groups of games in the same way; can see how similarities crop up and disappear.[22]

Here Wittgenstein helpfully indicates that at least one word can significantly be used in different but related senses without it being true that the word is being used figuratively. And, following the clue offered by his example, we can quickly come to see that many words can significantly be used in this way. Take, for instance, 'good'. You can have good food and good books, not to mention good people, good wine, and a good night's sleep. It makes sense to say that food, books, people, wine, and sleep can all be literally good. But we are surely not saying exactly the same of them all when we call them good. Or consider the word 'love' in 'I love my wife', 'I love my job', and 'I love a rare steak'. 'Love' in each of these sentences can be understood literally without it being thought that it means exactly the same in each case.

So it is wrong to hold that the same words literally applied must always bear exactly the same meaning. And it is wrong to insist that nobody can talk significantly about God just because words applied to him do not mean exactly what they do when applied to other things. To put it another way, the problem raised at the beginning of this chapter is not obviously insurmountable. Just because people do not apply words to God and to creatures either univocally or equivocally, it does not follow that they cannot talk about God significantly and literally. That is what the theory of analogy is basically saying, and in this it is surely right. As James Ross observes: 'Analogy is a general feature of words depending upon their verbal context and larger environment of use. It comes about by semantic contagion . . . Analogy of meaning is a general linguistic phenomenon.'[23]

But we are still left with a difficulty. Even if we grant that the uni-vocal/equivocal distinction can be supplemented, we can still ask why particular words are used in talking about God and whether they are capable of being used significantly and literally. We may accept that the word 'game' can be used literally to describe things which lack a common feature, but we would also agree that not just anything can be called a game. Rescuing a drowning child is not a game; nor is performing a surgical operation. So there is still a general problem for talk about God. Some reason must be given for choosing the terms which are actually applied to him. This point is nicely made by Patrick Sherry, who suggests that:

> It is not just a matter of saying that there must be some grounds for ascribing perfections to God. We must also insist that if we ascribe the same terms to

God and creatures, then there must be a connection between the relevant criteria of evidence and truth. Thus the grounds for ascribing terms like 'love', 'father', 'exist' and 'life' must bear some relationship to the grounds used for our normal everyday application of these terms. Similarly, even if 'God created the world' expresses a unique relationship, its truth conditions must bear some resemblance to our familiar uses of terms like 'make' or 'depends on'.[24]

In other words, it looks as though the terms used in talking about God must be justified in some way if they are not to appear arbitrary and empty of meaning. And the question is, can they be? Aquinas, for example, thought that they can. He held that we can come to a knowledge of God and significantly apply to God words which also apply to creatures because there is reason for doing so. But is Aquinas right in adopting this position? Could anybody be right in adopting it?

Talk of God and Reasons for It

In previous chapters we have seen how some have argued that God may be thought of as literally being the Creator or Designer of the world. We have also seen how some have thought that God is truly that than which nothing greater can be conceived, or that he is truly an object of human experience. So, when trying to reflect on the questions raised at the end of the last paragraph, you might start by considering what you make of the arguments offered in defence of these claims. In the next two chapters we shall turn to some other things that have been said of God, and to reasons which have been given for saying such things. In concluding this chapter, however, perhaps I might make two final observations.

The first concerns what we may call 'the incomprehensibility of God'. Even from what we have seen already, it should be clear enough that people who believe in God (whether classical theists or theistic personalists) are committed to thinking of him as being decidedly out of the ordinary. Some would say that God is essentially mysterious or incomprehensible. But does this mean that he could not exist? And does it mean that there could never be reasons for belief in God or belief that God can truly be said to be X, Y, or Z?

Affirmative answers have been offered to both these questions. It has been suggested that, if God is really mysterious, then we cannot understand what is being said when he is talked about, in which case it is nonsense to affirm his existence. It has also been said that if God is really mysterious, then it is pointless to seek reasons for holding that he exists and pointless to try to describe him. But these views are not very plausible. We do not have to know exactly what a word means in order to have some understanding of it or to use it intelligibly. I may not know what a volcano is exactly, but I can still talk sensibly, knowingly, and truly about volcanoes. And I can reasonably and truly say that Jones has malaria without being clear as to what exactly I am saying. As Peter Geach puts it, 'I certainly could not define either "oak-tree" or "elephant"; but this does not destroy my right to assert that no oak-tree is an elephant.'[25] This point does nothing to show that there is a God. But it does suggest that, in order to speak meaningfully and truly about God, we do not have to understand what God exactly is. It may not be possible to define God; we may not be able to comprehend him. But this does not mean that we cannot talk sense about God; nor need it prevent us from asking whether he is there in the first place.

My second point is one about meaning and truth. Can questions about the sense or meaningfulness of what people claim always be settled just by attending to the words they use? Sometimes, of course, they clearly can be, as when we recognize, straight off, that Fred is talking nonsense when he tells us about the square circle that he captured and locked in his room. For the most part, however, whether or not it makes sense to say such and such needs to be settled with respect to reasons for saying that such and such is true.

As I noted at the end of Chapter 5, proof (or good reason to think) that-P (where P is a purportedly true proposition) is proof (or good reason to think) that P is possibly true. As we saw in Chapter 2, some philosophers have asserted that talk about God is evidently meaningless because of what 'meaningful' means. And in this chapter we have been looking in a general way at the meaningfulness of talk about God. But can we not suggest that questions about the sense or meaningfulness of talk about God (not to mention the sense or meaningfulness of talk about other things) can only be settled in the light of reasons for thinking that talk such as this is actually true?

My own view is that the answer to this question is 'Yes', from which I conclude that the intelligibility of talk about God largely depends on (1) the reasons people have for saying what they do about God, and (2) whether these reasons stand up to serious intellectual scrutiny. As you will realize on the basis of Chapter 2, it is not only thinkers such as A. J. Ayer who would disagree with this line of thinking. It would also be considered highly suspect by philosophers such as D. Z. Phillips, though not, perhaps, by philosophers in sympathy with what Alvin Plantinga says about properly basic beliefs. At this point, however, I leave it to you to decide who, if anyone, is right on this matter. My intention now is to turn to some specific claims that have been made about God.

NOTES

1. Cf. Antony Flew's comments on the parable of the gardener in Chapter 2 above.

2. Antony Flew, *God and Philosophy* (London, 1966), p. 37. Flew famously applies this line of thinking in 'Can a Man Witness his own Funeral?' in which he suggests that 'If it is really I who witness, then it is not my funeral but only "my funeral" (in inverted commas). If it is really my funeral, then I cannot be a witness; since I shall be dead and in the coffin' (*The Presumption of Atheism and Other Essays*, (London, 1976) p. 126).

3. Richard Swinburne, *The Coherence of Theism* (rev. ed., Oxford, 1993), pp. 106 f.

4. Ibid., p. 127.

5. I quote from Duns Scotus, *Philosophical Writings*, trans. Allan Wolter (Indianapolis, IN, and Cambridge, 1987), p. 25. Scotus, sometimes referred to as 'the Subtle Doctor' (*Doctor Subtilis*) was Scottish. He taught in Oxford, Paris, and Cologne. He is generally regarded as one of the greatest of medieval philosophers.

6. Swinburne, *The Coherence of Theism*, p. 72.

7. Cf. Chapters 1 and 8.

8. Thomas Aquinas, *Summa Theologiae*, Ia, 13, 5. I quote from volume 3 of the Blackfriars edition of the *Summa Theologiae* (London and New York, 1964).

9. Ibid.

10. I derive the convenient expression 'God-talk' from John Macquarrie. See

his *God-Talk: An Examination of the Language and Logic of Theology* (New York, 1967).

11. Cf. Aquinas, *Summa Theologiae*, Ia, 13, 2.

12. Moses Maimonides, *The Guide for the Perplexed*, trans. M. Friedlander (London, 1936), pp. 86 ff.

13. Cf. Chapter 3 above.

14. Aquinas, *Summa Theologiae*, Ia, 13, 2.

15. Ibid., Ia, 13, 5.

16. Ibid. In citing St Paul, Aquinas is quoting from Romans 1: 20.

17. Ibid.

18. Ibid., Ia, 13, 2.

19. Aquinas (following Aristotle) distinguishes between different kinds of cause (efficient, formal, final, and material). As I am reporting him here, he is thinking in terms of efficient causation. For Aquinas (as for Aristotle) an efficient cause is an active agent that brings about or produces an effect (as, for example, one who kicks a ball is an efficient cause of its moving, or as a chef is an efficient cause of a meal). For Aquinas, God, as Creator, is an (albeit unique) efficient cause of there being any universe at all.

20. For more on this, see Chapter 12.

21. Notice that Aquinas's distinction between univocal, equivocal, and analogical is a distinction among *literal* modes of discourse.

22. Ludwig Wittgenstein, *Philosophical Investigations*, trans. G. E. M. Anscombe (Oxford, 1968), §66.

23. James Ross, 'Religious Language', in Brian Davies (ed.), *Philosophy of Religion: A Guide to the Subject* (London, 1998), p. 122.

24. Patrick Sherry, 'Analogy Today', *Philosophy* 51 (1976), p. 445.

25. P. T. Geach, *Reason and Argument* (Oxford, 1976), p. 39.

FURTHER READING

For detailed discussions of the issues touched on in this chapter, the following books can all be recommended (though the positions they defend vary): William P. Alston, *Divine Nature and Human Language* (Ithaca, NY, and London, 1989); Frederick Ferré, *Language, Logic and God* (London and Glasgow, 1970); R. S. Heimbeck, *Theology and Meaning* (London, 1969); John McQuarrie, *God-Talk* (London, 1967); Kai Nielsen, *Scepticism* (London, 1973); Kai Nielsen, *An Introduction to the Philosophy of Religion* (London, 1982); I. T. Ramsey, *Religious*

Language (New York, 1963); Patrick Sherry, *Religion, Truth and Language-Games* (London, 1977); Janet Martin Soskice, *Metaphor and Religious Language* (Oxford, 1985); and David Tracy, *The Analogical Imagination* (London, 1981).

The claim that God should often, or even primarily, be spoken about by means of negation deserves much more space than I have been able to give it here. For it has played a very prominent part in the writings of many theologians and philosophers, especially those between the second and thirteenth centuries. In this connection, two figures are especially worth mentioning: John Scotus Eriugena (*c.*810–*c.*877) and the (anonymous) writer commonly referred to as Pseudo-Dionysius (*c.*500), both of whom firmly champion what is usually called 'negative theology' (theology which proceeds by stressing what God is *not*). For an introduction to Eriugena, see Deirdre Carabine, *John Scotus Eriugena* (Oxford, 2000). The writings of Dionysius are conveniently available in *Pseudo-Dionysius: The Complete Works*, trans. Colm Luibheid (New York and Mahwah, NJ, 1987). For a commentary on Dionysius, see Paul Rorem, *Pseudo-Dionysius: A Commentary on the Texts and an Introduction to their Influence* (New York and Oxford, 1993). For a contemporary defence of negative theology, see Denys Turner, 'How to be an Atheist', *New Blackfriars* 83 (2002). For a recent discussion of negative theology coming from an especially famous contemporary philosopher, see Hilary Putnam, 'On Negative Theology', *Faith and Philosophy* 14 (1997).

For more on Aquinas on God and analogy, see Brian Davies, *The Thought of Thomas Aquinas* (Oxford, 1992), chs. 3 and 4. Also see id., *Aquinas* (London and New York, 2002), ch. 8, and 'Aquinas on What God is Not', *Revue Internationale de Philosophie* 52 (1998), reprinted in Brian Davies (ed.), *Thomas Aquinas: Contemporary Philosophical Perspectives* (New York and Oxford, 2002). For a study of Aquinas on God-Talk which relates it to the teaching of Maimonides, see David B. Burrell, *Knowing the Unknowable God* (Notre Dame, IN, 1986). In *Aquinas: God and Action* (London and Henley, 1979) Burrell also offers a focused treatment of Aquinas on talk about God which sets it in the context of Aquinas's overall thinking. For a recent book-length study of Aquinas on talk about God, see Ralph McInerny, *Aquinas and Analogy* (Washington, DC, 1996). For more general (and strongly contrasting) discussions of analogy and talk about God, see E. L. Mascall, *Existence and Analogy* (London, 1966) and Humphrey Palmer, *Analogy* (London, 1973).

For a detailed and sophisticated study of analogy in language as a whole, the definitive work is James F. Ross, *Portraying Analogy* (Cambridge, 1981). Here Ross argues that analogy is all-pervasive in our discourse. The book contains a section on talk about God. For a discussion by Ross of religious discourse and analogy, one explicitly aimed at students, see Brian Davies (ed.), *Philosophy of Religion: A Guide to the Subject* (London, 1998), ch. 4.

QUESTIONS FOR DISCUSSION

1 'God is very different from everything else.' Comment on this assertion. What can be said both for and against it?

2 Is talk about God more puzzling than other kinds of talk? If so, why? If not, why not?

3 We can often deduce the nature of a cause from its effects. But can we deduce God's nature from his effects? If so, can we thereby show that talk about God makes sense?

4 Is there some way of distinguishing between talk of God that is metaphorical and talk of God which is literally true?

5 Supposing that God exists, which of the following statements would you regard as metaphorical and which as literally true: 'God is our father'; 'God creates'; 'God knows'; 'God is present'; 'God loves'; 'God thinks'; 'God is good'; 'God acts'; 'God remembers'; 'God is a cause'; 'God is mighty'; 'God is a just judge'; 'God is our king'; 'God is angry'; 'God never forgets'; 'God is alive'; 'God sees all that we do'; 'God is a spirit'; 'God can be seen'?

6 Suppose that God exists. What might he be said *not* to be? Does your answer to this question leave you with any understanding of what God is? If not, to what extent does this pose a problem for those who say that God exists?

7 Is Aquinas right in what he says about our ability to speak of God by using words which signify analogically?

8 To what extent is the analogical use of words a feature of human language? In answering this question, be sure to give examples.

9 'God is incomprehensible.' Is that statement true? If so, why? If not, why not?

10 Let 'P' be what seems to be an assertion made by someone. How can one determine whether or not 'P' states anything that is possibly true?

8

DIVINE SIMPLICITY

....

Theists never just claim that God exists. They also seek to describe him. So it now seems appropriate to turn directly to the question 'What is God?' It is hard to know where to begin or end when writing about this question for the purposes of a book like the present one. I have chosen to deal with it here and in the next chapter by turning to three assertions: (1) God is simple; (2) God is omnipotent; and (3) God is omniscient. I shall address the first assertion in this chapter and turn to the others in Chapter 9. And in Chapters 10 and 12 I shall consider the statement that God is good.

Why Divine Simplicity?

Why am I devoting a whole chapter to the topic of divine simplicity? One answer is that the claim that God is simple has featured in a lot of theistic literature. Contemporary authors sometimes refer to 'God is simple' as if it were an unusual or peculiar teaching about God. Yet although 'God is simple' is, by some standards, peculiar, it is not unusual given what theists have said over the centuries. The teaching that God is simple is embraced by patristic authors such as St Athanasius (*c.*296–373) and St Augustine of Hippo.[1] It is defended by later writers such as Anselm of Canterbury, Thomas Aquinas, Moses Maimonides, and the Islamic thinkers Avicenna and Averroes (1126–98). There are echoes of it in the works of Descartes (who seems to be in favour of it) and of Hume (who seems to be against it). It is endorsed by the teachings of Catholic Church councils such as Lateran IV (1215) and Vatican I (1869–70). And it is currently defended by a number of contemporary writers. For these reasons alone, I assume that the teaching that God is simple is worthy of attention in an introduction to the philosophy of religion.

But the teaching is also worth turning to since it provides an interesting way of indicating and reflecting on the differences between classical theism and theistic personalism. As I said in Chapter 1, belief in God's simplicity is characteristic of classical theism and is usually rejected by theistic personalists. And many of the differences between classical theists and theistic personalists spring directly from their reactions to the notion that God is simple. In turning to this notion, therefore, we shall be looking at a major bone of contention among theists.

The Meaning of 'God is Simple'

What does it mean to say that God is simple? Here is St Augustine's answer:

> The reason why a nature is called simple is that it cannot lose any attribute it possesses, that there is no difference between what it *is* and what it *has*, as there is, for example, between a vessel and the liquid it contains, a body and its colour, the atmosphere and its light or heat, the soul and its wisdom. None of these *is* what it contains; the vessel is not the liquid, nor the body the colour, nor the atmosphere the light or heat; nor is the soul the same as its wisdom.[2]

God, Augustine holds, is simple because he is unchangeable.[3] But Augustine also thinks that God is simple in the sense of not possessing different properties or attributes. According to Augustine, expressions like 'the knowledge of God' and 'the goodness of God' do not name different things. Or, as St Anselm puts it, echoing Augustine:

> You [God] are therefore the very life by which You live, the wisdom by which You are wise, the very goodness by which You are good . . . There are no parts in You, Lord; neither are You many, but You are so much one and the same with Yourself that in nothing are You dissimilar with Yourself. Indeed, You are unity itself not divisible by any mind. Life and wisdom and the other [attributes], then, are not parts of You, but all are one and each of them is wholly what You are and what all the others are.[4]

Anselm acknowledges that theists use different statements to speak of God's nature. They say, for example, 'God is good', 'God is just', and

'God is wise'. But, Anselm argues, we should not think of God as having really distinct attributes. According to Anselm, there is no difference between God and anything we might call 'the attributes of God'. For Anselm, the attributes we ascribe to God in sentences of the form 'God is X', 'God is Y', and so on, are not discrete realities in God. They *are* God.

But some defenders of divine simplicity have wanted to say even more than this. For they have added that God is simple because there is no difference between God's nature (or essence) and his existence. On their account, God is also simple since it is God's nature to exist. According to them, God is simple because he is Being or Existence without qualification. Having asked whether *Qui Est* ('*The One Who Is*') is the most appropriate name for God, Aquinas replies that it is, since, among other reasons, it signifies 'Existence Itself'. 'Since the existence of God is his essence', says Aquinas, 'and since this is true of nothing else . . . it is clear that this name (sc. 'The One Who Is') is especially appropriate to God.'[5]

Why Call God Simple?

So, we can summarize the doctrine of divine simplicity as follows:

1. God is unchangeable.[6]
2. There is no distinction between God and his attributes.
3. God's nature and his existence amount to the same thing.

But why should anyone subscribe to these theses?

With respect to (1), some have argued that God must be perfect and that perfection implies immutability. Anselm, for instance, suggests that 'God is whatever it is better to be than not to be', from which he concludes that God is not 'enclosed' by place or time and is, therefore, not subject to change.[7] The reasoning here runs: if perfect, then timeless; and if timeless, then immutable.

More commonly, however, the suggestion that God is unchangeable has been defended with respect to the view that God is the Creator of everything other than himself. The argument here goes like this: (a) the 'everything' which God accounts for as Creator clearly includes a world in which things undergo change; (b) only something immutable could account for there being a world in which change occurs; (c) so God must be immutable. Why say that only something immutable could account for there being a world in which change occurs? Defenders of the present argument would reply: 'If something changeable accounted for there being a world in which change occurs, it would be *part* of such a world and could not, therefore, *account for* it.'[8]

With respect to thesis (2), some have also argued with an eye on the notion that God is perfect. Once again, we may take Anselm as an example. Given that God is perfect, he reasons, God must be wholly indivisible. Why? Because something divisible 'is not absolutely one, but in a sense many and other than itself'.[9] By 'parts' here, Anselm includes attributes considered as things which can be distinguished from the one who has them. So his conclusion is that God, strictly speaking, has no attributes to be distinguished from himself.

As with thesis (1), however, thesis (2) has also been defended without reference to the notion of perfection. Take, for example, the way in which Aquinas argues for it. He suggests that, if God is immaterial, then he cannot be thought of as an instance of a kind (as you and I are, since we are both examples of what is meant by 'human being'). Why does Aquinas think this? Because he believes that we can make sense of there being instances of kinds only because we can distinguish between the instances at a material level. For Aquinas, two people, or two dogs, are two (not one) since they are distinct physical units. Accordingly, an immaterial human being (or dog) would not be an instance of a kind. It would be, so to speak, the kind itself. It would be humanity itself (or caninity itself). And hence, so Aquinas concludes, if God is wholly immaterial, then God must be nothing but the divine nature. In Aquinas's view, God and God's nature amount to the same thing, which is what (2) above says.[10] Or, in Aquinas's own words: 'God is identical with his own godhead, with his own life, and with whatever else is similarly said of him.'[11]

But what, now, of thesis (3)? It amounts to the claim that the answer to 'What is God?' is 'Something whose nature it is to exist'. The idea here is that God's existence cannot derive from anything else. We have already seen Anselm arguing that God cannot but exist, given a certain understanding of God (cf. Chapter 5 above). In Aquinas, (3) takes a causal form. He observes:

If the existence of a thing is to be other than its nature, that existence must either derive from the nature or have an external cause. Now it cannot derive merely from the nature, for nothing with derived existence suffices to bring itself into being. It follows then that, if a thing's existence differs from its nature, that existence must be externally caused. But we cannot say this about God [who is] the first cause.[12]

Objections to the Claim that God is Simple

(a) Divine immutability

But should God be thought to be simple? Many would say that he should not, since, for a start, there are problems with the view that God is immutable. What sort of problems? Mostly, as those who raise them tend to say, ones deriving from the 'fact' that God is a person.

If God is a person, the argument goes, then how can he be immutable? Persons are acting agents who think and plan and choose. And they go through various changes. So, how can God be immutable if God is a person? As Grace Jantzen puts it:

A living God cannot be static: life implies change . . . This means that the doctrine of immutability cannot be interpreted as absolute changelessness, which would preclude divine responsiveness and must rather be taken as steadfastness of character.[13]

Or, in the words of Richard E. Creel:

An absolutely perfect being will have the power of agency, i.e., be able intentionally to cause things to happen. But for an agent intentionally to cause something to happen which was not happening requires that he was not willing it and then began to will it—but to change from not willing something to willing it is to change. Therefore, in order to have this power of agency, an individual must be able to change . . . Therefore, God must be able to change. Therefore God must be mutable.[14]

Another attack on divine immutability comes from those who focus on the traditional claim that God loves (at least some of) his creatures. Hence, for example, the contemporary Latin American theologian Jon Sobrino writes:

We must insist that love has to be credible to human beings in an unredeemed world. That forces us to ask ourselves whether God can really describe himself as love if historical suffering does not affect him ... We must say ... 'We find suffering that is not wished, suffering that is accepted, and the suffering of love. If God were incapable of suffering in all those ways, and hence in an absolute sense, then God would be incapable of loving.'[15]

Sobrino, like many others, thinks that to call God immutable is to commit oneself to the conclusion that God cannot be affected by anything and, hence, cannot suffer. For Sobrino, however, if God is truly loving, being affected and suffering have to form part of his life. The same thought has often been expressed by authors commonly referred to as 'process theologians'—authors such as Charles Hartshorne.[16]

Yet another common criticism of the claim that God is unchangeable comes from those who think that 'God is unchangeable' entails that God has no freedom. Theists have always held that God freely chooses to do whatever he does. But can he do so if he is immutable? Not according to some thinkers. If God is immutable, they reason, then he can only (unchangeably) will what he does will. For example, it has been argued, if God is immutable, then he is immutably the Creator of the universe and had no choice but to create it.

Belief in divine immutability has also been held to be incompatible with belief in divine omniscience. Roughly speaking, to call God omniscient is to claim that God knows all that is the case.[17] But can God know this without undergoing change? Some have argued that he cannot, since what is the case comes to be the case over time and can only be known completely by one who, as time passes, comes to acquire knowledge of what is going on as it comes to be the case. As time goes on, my knowledge increases (and I therefore change) as I learn what is happening from one moment to the next. By the same token, so it has been suggested, God must change as he comes to know what is going on as time passes.

Finally, it has been argued that to call God immutable is flatly to reject the picture of God provided in the Bible. According, for example, to John Lucas, 'the whole thrust of the biblical record' implies that God changes. The Bible, says Lucas:

is an account of God both caring and knowing about the world, even the five sparrows, which at one time had not yet been, and later had been, sold for two farthings, and intervening in the world, doing things, saying things, hearing prayers, and sometimes changing his mind.[18]

'The changelessness of God', says Lucas, 'is not to be naturally read out of the Bible.'[19]

(b) God, properties, and existence

Critics of the doctrine of divine simplicity have not only rejected its claim that God is immutable. As I should now point out, some have also denied that God is simple by contesting (2) and (3) above. Why? Because, they think, both of these teachings lead to absurdities.

Take, to start with thesis (2)—the suggestion that there is no distinction between God and God's attributes. Is that even possibly true? Not, for example, according to Alvin Plantinga. 'If God is identical with each of his properties', says Plantinga, 'then each of his properties is identical with each of his properties, so that God has but one property.'[20] And, Plantinga adds, 'if God is identical with each of his properties, then since each of his properties is a property, he is a property', which is false since, 'if God is a property, then he isn't a person but a mere abstract object; he has no knowledge, awareness, power, love or life.'[21]

Then again, consider thesis (3)—the conclusion that God's nature and God's existence amount to the same thing. Aquinas expresses this conclusion by saying that God is 'Subsisting Existence Itself' (*Ipsum Esse Subsistence*). But does talk like this make sense? Some have suggested that it does not because of what philosophers such as Kant and Frege say about 'being' and 'existence'. As we saw in Chapter 5, such thinkers hold that being or existence is not a property or quality of anything. If they are right, however, it would seem to follow that we cannot truly characterize God's nature by saying that it amounts to existence (or being). Hence, for example, C. J. F. Williams, endorsing Frege's claim that statements of existence are statements of number (implying that 'X's exist' means 'The number of X's is not nought'), observes: 'What God is can hardly be indicated by saying that the number of gods is not nought.'[22] Williams is saying that to hold that God's nature is existence is to try to tell us what God is by using a term which could never tell us what anything is. And in this he is supported by other philosophers. According to Terence Penelhum, for example:

The distinctive character of the concept of existence precludes our saying that there can be a being whose existence follows from his essence; and also precludes the even stronger logical move of *identifying* the existence of anything with its essence ... It is not our ignorance that is the obstacle to explaining God's existence by his nature, but the logical character of the concept of existence.[23]

Like Williams, Penelhum is arguing (a) that 'exists' cannot enter into an account of what something is, and (b) that it, therefore, cannot be identified with anything's nature.

Are the Objections Decisive?

We may summarize the above objections to 'God is simple' as follows:

1. If God lives and acts, then God changes.
2. If God loves, then God changes.
3. If God is immutable, then God is not free.
4. If God knows, then God is changeable.
5. The Bible says that God changes.
6. If God is simple, then God is a property, not a person, and God's distinct properties are really one property (which cannot be true).
7. God's nature cannot be to exist since existence cannot constitute the nature of anything.

But are these objections irrefutable? Let us take them in order.

(a) Life, action, and change

What do we mean by 'living'? Grace Jantzen contrasts 'living' with 'static'. And the contrast is fair enough. Stones, for instance, are static. And stones are good examples of non-living things. Animals are examples of living things. And animals are anything but static.

But 'not being static' is surely not what we chiefly have in mind when we say that something is alive. Rather, we mean that it is a genuine *automobile*. To call something living is to say that it is *self-moving*, that it has a principle of operation within itself, that its history is not just a record of the impact of other things on it, that it can act of itself, that it can bring about effects which proceed from itself and not from the work of other things in or on it. Yet, if that is so, it is far from clear that life cannot be attributed to God even on the supposition that God is changeless.

To begin with, we might argue, life can be attributed to God since God acts and since nothing else makes him do so. If God's actions are not the effect in him of other things that impinge on him, then there is clearly a case for saying that God is alive. But can God be alive (can he be a self-acting agent) if he is also unchangeable? Authors like Jantzen and Creel obviously think that the answer to this question is 'No'. And they would seem to be right if we think about living animals and what goes on when they act of themselves. Take people, for example. They are continually changing. They breath, walk, learn, and so on. Notice, however, that they also get things done. They act in the sense of bringing it about that changes occur in other things. They close doors, clean clothes, cook meals, and so on. And they do so by undergoing change themselves. But is it part of the notion of bringing about a change that the changer must itself undergo change?

Suppose we ask how people manage to teach. It is natural to say that they do so by uttering words or by writing on blackboards (and therefore by undergoing various changes). But teaching cannot be *defined* as the going through of particular motions. I can utter true statements until I am blue in the face. I can fill a thousand blackboards with letters and diagrams. But none of these processes will amount to teaching unless somebody actually *learns* something. When interested in whether or not I have taught somebody, we are interested, not in changes occurring in me, but in changes occurring in somebody else. I cannot teach you except by undergoing change of some kind. But my undergoing these changes does not constitute my teaching you. Unless you actually learn something, they are simply fruitless bits of behaviour on my part. Teaching occurs when learning occurs, when someone passes from ignorance to knowledge.

What follows from this? That agency (in the sense of bringing about an effect) is more about changes in things other than the agent than it is about changes in the agent. And if that is so, then it is not absurd to suggest that a living God might be changeless. For, if there is reason to suppose that there are effects brought about by God (and not by something working in or through God), then life can intelligibly be ascribed to God as long as the effects can be ascribed to him and even if he is himself unchangeable.

(b) Love and change

But can an unchangeable God be loving? The answer is clearly 'No' if 'love' is what Sobrino and Hartshorne take it to be. They think that love always comprises passion or emotion—being affected by something external. And love, understood in this sense, is obviously not ascribable to something unchangeable. But is this the only way in which love can be understood? And can love be ascribed to God only if thought of in this way?

When people love, they are moved by what is outside them, and they often suffer as a consequence. Love can even lead people to their deaths, since one way of loving is to sacrifice yourself for those whom you love. But why should we suppose that divine love must be costly for God in any similar way? God, after all, is commonly held to be perfect. Yet suffering is a limitation, a restriction on one's freedom. To say that God suffers can therefore be taken to imply that he is vulnerable, defective, and thwarted. One might reply that love and limitation always go together. But is that always so? We may display our love by limiting ourselves, but that is not to say that love and limitation are inseparable. Indeed, we might argue, love is capable of its fullest development only if the lover is not limited by anything.

We might also observe that a subject may be said to love if the subject in question can be thought of as willing the good of others. And we might add that even an unchangeable God can do that if he is also the Creator and sustainer of the universe. For, if God is this, must it not be true that he is thereby the source of all that is good in creatures? According to Aquinas:

> God loves all existing things. For in so far as it is real each is good; the very existence of each single thing is good, and so also is whatever it rises to . . . God's will is the cause of things, and . . . in so far as it has reality or any goodness at all each thing must needs be willed by God. God therefore wills some good to each existing thing, and since loving is no other than willing good to someone, it is clear that God loves everything.[24]

Is that a bad argument? We might worry about its attempt to equate 'being real' and 'being good'. But can a theist seriously deny that God wills the goodness of his creatures? And if not, does a theist not have grounds for ascribing love to God on this count alone and regardless of whether or not God is changeable or unchangeable?

(c) Changelessness and freedom

But perhaps an unchangeable God cannot freely choose to will as he does when it comes to creatures, which brings us to the argument that an immutable God cannot act freely. And, up to a point, the argument has merit. For if God is immutable, then God is changelessly the Creator of whatever it is that he creates or wills to come about. Given that God has willed to create, creation is somehow inevitable (assuming, of course, that God's will cannot be thwarted). But, given that God is also free (as our present objection to divine immutability supposes), all that now follows is that God has freely willed to create what, by virtue of his changeless will, comes about by virtue of his freely willing to create. Or, as Aquinas puts it: 'Granted that God wills whatever he does from eternity, the inference is not that he has to except on the supposition that he does.'[25] In other words, from the fact that God is immutable, it does not follow that he is bound to create. Given that God wills to create, it follows only that he changelessly wills to create. Nothing whatever follows about God's freedom to create. In order to show that God is immutably coerced, to show that God cannot immutably and freely will to produce whatever he brings about, we would need to show that something in God's nature compels him to do what he does, or that something other than God achieves this result.

(d) Changelessness and knowledge

On the other hand, however, our knowledge changes over time. We undergo change as knowers. And since what is there to be known is not always there to be known, we might suggest that, if X knows all (is omniscient), then X changes as X comes to know what appears on the scene to be known and as X comes to know that what was once there to be known is no longer on the scene.

In this connection we might also focus on certain tensed statements.

Suppose I know that it is now 7 July. Should we not suppose that an omniscient God would also know this? But what about 8 July? On that day I might know that it is now 8 July. But if an omniscient God knows this, does it not follow that he has changed with respect to his state of knowledge as between 7 July and 8 July? And should we not conclude that an omniscient God must, therefore, be something changeable?

Well, we should evidently conclude that an unchangeable, omniscient God's knowledge cannot take the form of him being able to utter or think such thoughts as 'I know that such and such is the case now and I shall soon know that such and such will be the case' or 'I know that it is now 7 July and tomorrow I shall know that it is 8 July'. Yet uttering or thinking such thoughts is open only to creatures in space and time. And why should we suppose that divine omniscience is to be understood only with reference to knowledge as it exists in spatio-temporal creatures?

We shall be returning to omniscience in the next chapter. For the moment, however, ask yourself whether or not it makes sense to say that God, without changing, can know his own nature and the nature of temporal creatures (together with the relations in which these creatures stand to each other).

You might say that God can know his own nature just because he must know himself. And you might add that, if God is unchangeable, then he can know himself (know what he is) unchangeably.

But if God's knowledge is irreducibly subject to change, then God cannot know himself to be unchangeable. So 'God can know what God is' does not obviously entail 'God unchangeably knows what God is'.

On the other hand, if God is indeed unchangeable, and if God knows himself, then he unchangeably knows himself to be unchangeable.

But what about God's knowledge of the nature of and relationships among all things in time other than God? Perhaps this has to imply that God exists as a changeable individual learning as time goes on. But is that really so?

It would be, if all knowledge results from taking a look at something present to one at some particular time. But knowledge is not just a matter of looking at things. We can, after all, look at something and have no idea as to what it is that we are looking at. Knowledge is essentially a matter of understanding—of realizing what things are and how they fit together with other things. And a question to ask about it is: 'Does it, by definition, have to involve change in a knower?'

It normally does in the case of human beings. Yet is it absurd to suppose that there could be simple and complete understanding which has not come to be? With respect to the notion of God's knowledge of what is not divine, is it absurd to suggest that God, without having *come* to do so, understands what all things not divine are and how they relate to each other?

Perhaps it is not absurd to say this. For the notion of understanding does not seem irrevocably tied to the notion of coming to understand. In a simple glance I can take in a lot of what is around me. So, might we not suggest that an unchanging God in (so to speak) a glance can 'take in' all that he creates and all that links its parts together? Such a God would not be someone taking a look, since those who learn by looking gain their knowledge as modified by something outside themselves. But what is to stop such a God from knowing his creation simply by being its Creator?

Let us suppose that God knows himself. And let us suppose that God accounts for the existence of all that is not God—that all that is not God is somehow God's *doing*. In that case, it would seem that God knows himself as the doer of what he does, which would seem to imply that he knows the done of which he is the doer. In that case, too, it would not seem to be evidently true that God's knowledge of his creation has to be that of something capable of change. For why cannot God unchangeably know ('in a glance', so to speak) all that he is and all that he is about?

(e) Change, God, and the Bible

Yet the God of the Bible does not seem to be unchangeable. The biblical God is depicted as going through all sorts of changes. He is frequently described as being like any number of changeable things with which we are familiar—e.g. a father, a judge, a king, a lord, an eagle, a builder, a husband whose wife has been unfaithful, a woman in childbirth, and even a case of dry rot. And biblical authors use tenses when speaking of God: they say that he *has* done such and such, that he *is* doing such and such, and that he *will* do such and such. As the biblical scholar James Barr puts it: 'In the Bible God is presented above all as active and personal: he can change his mind, he can regret what he has done, he can be argued out of positions he has already taken up, he operates in a narrative sequence.'[26]

But should these points lead us to dismiss the teaching that God is simple? Some would reply that what we believe about God should not be determined only by biblical teaching. They would argue that, if reason suggests God is unchangeable, then we should believe in divine immutability regardless of the Bible. John Locke once said: 'Whatever God has revealed is certainly true; no doubt can be made of it. This is the proper object of faith. But whether it be a divine revelation or no, reason must judge.'[27] If we side with Locke here, we would probably be tempted to conclude that it does not matter what the Bible says about God's changeableness. Authors such as John Lucas may insist that 'the changelessness of God is not to be naturally read out of the Bible'. But is that fact (if it is a fact) relevant when it comes to what we should say about God?

Yet suppose that we think that what we say about God should indeed be strongly influenced by what we find in the Bible. Must we therefore conclude that God is essentially changeable? Perhaps not, and for three main reasons.

To begin with, although Scripture speaks of God as changing, it also teaches that God is unchanging. In Malachi 3: 6, for instance, we read: 'I the Lord do not change.' In the New Testament letter of James (1: 17), we find: 'Every good endowment and every perfect gift is from above, coming down from the Father of lights with whom there is no variation or shadow due to alteration.'

Second, there is a case to be made for treating biblical talk of God's changing as merely metaphorical. Some would say that all biblical statements about God should be interpreted literally. But that view is untenable. If God is the Creator of the universe, then he cannot walk in a garden, as he is said to do in Genesis 3: 8.[28] And if God is the Creator of the universe, he cannot have a nose (as he is said to have in Psalm 11), nor can he literally breathe, as he is said to do in many places in Scripture (e.g. Job 4: 9). In both the Old and New Testaments all sorts of images are used with respect to God. And not all of them can be taken literally. So why should we suppose that biblical talk about God's changing should be taken literally? To some extent we can appeal to the Bible itself. For this also tells us that God is the maker of the universe. And if God is that, then biblical texts depicting God as a changeable individual can reasonably be taken as metaphorical. For, can we sensibly think of the maker of the universe as undergoing change in the way that things in the universe itself do? At any rate, if we do think of God as changing in the same way that things in the world do, some awkward questions arise.

For example, what accounts for the changes which God undergoes? Is there a cause of these changes beyond God himself? If there is such a cause, then how does this square with the common notion that God is the unoriginated source of everything other than himself? And if there is no need for a cause of any changes which God undergoes, then why should it be thought (as it commonly is by theists) that God is needed to account for changes in the universe?

Then again, if God undergoes change, what has happened to his previous states? Have they lapsed into nothingness? If God undergoes change, then what God used to be at one time is not still there. But can we make sense of there no longer being what God once was? And if we think that we can make sense of this, are we not dangerously assimilating God to items in the world which lose what once they were? God is said to be perfect. But can he be so if he is constantly losing what once he was? Something may continue to be wonderful even though it changes. Yet there is a connection between change and limitation. Something changing is always becoming deprived of what it once possessed. And, we might argue, 'deprivation' and 'God' are not harmonious concepts.

Finally, and returning to the thought expressed by Locke in the quotation above, we might ask about reasons for thinking that God is unchangeable. Are there such reasons? As we have seen, some have held that there are. And if the reasons are cogent, then we have grounds for interpreting biblical talk of God's change as metaphor rather than literal truth. We might reply that nobody should stand as judge over the exact words of Scripture. But who really believes that? Even the most strident biblical fundamentalist (i.e. someone holding that every sentence in Scripture is literally true) is likely to deny that, for example, God really sits on a throne holding a sceptre (cf. Psalm 45: 6).

(f) God and God's properties

But can God be identical with his properties? Here we come to Plantinga's attack on the notion of divine simplicity. And there is much to be said in its favour. As Plantinga says, if God's properties are identical with each other, and if they are all identical with God, then God is just a single property, which hardly fits with ways in which theists typically speak about him. Then again, what of the fact that theists offer a range of descriptions when talking about God. They say, for example, that God is good, knowing, and powerful. If all God's attributes are identical, however, then statements like this seem unwarranted. They appear to be telling us different things about God. Yet if all God's attributes are identical, then God's goodness, knowledge, power, and so on, would seem to be just one and the same reality.

But cannot the different terms theists use to describe God latch on to one and the same reality? We might think not. We might suppose that the contrary view amounts to saying: (a) properties which are different are not different in God, which sounds contradictory; and (b) God is really just one property. But may not defenders of divine simplicity distinguish between meaning and reality? Might they not, for instance, agree that statements like 'God is good', 'God is knowing', and 'God is powerful' certainly differ in meaning. But might they not then add that the reality in God which makes these statements true is something simple and undivided? The expressions 'the square of——' and 'the double of——' have different functions. But the square and the double of 2 are both 4. With this sort of example in mind, might not defenders of divine simplicity reasonably suggest that our different statements characterizing God differ in meaning without it being the case that what we thereby say is true because God really possesses a range of distinct properties?

For what it is worth, that is Aquinas's line as he turns to divine simplicity and to the different things said about God by theists. In his view, statements like 'God is good', 'God is knowing', and 'God is powerful' are not synonymous. And all of them can be defended philosophically. Yet, Aquinas adds, the reality which makes them true (i.e. God) is not an individual with different properties. According to Aquinas, we cannot 'know what God is, but only what he is not'.[29] Yet we can, Aquinas thinks, still talk positively about God. We can say, for example, that God is good, knowing, and powerful. And according to Aquinas, we can suppose that God is *not* really an individual with distinct attributes. Hence, for instance, he suggests that statements like 'God is Goodness itself', 'God is Knowledge itself', and 'God is Power itself' are as justifiable as 'God is good', 'God is knowing', and 'God is powerful'.[30] Notice that Aquinas is not saying here that different properties are somehow not different in God. Nor is he saying that God is a property. Rather, he is presenting a negative doctrine, an account of what God *cannot* be. His view is that we have reason on our side as we try to do justice to the divine reality by saying such things as 'God is good', 'God is knowing', and 'God is powerful'. But Aquinas also thinks that we have reason on our side as we qualify such statements so as to indicate that they cannot be picking out different ways of being in God.

Is Aquinas right here? Arguably, his way of talking about divine simplicity (which is not very different from the way in which other defenders of it have spoken) does not leave him subject to the worries about it expressed by Plantinga. But whether or not his account is ultimately successful depends on the cogency of his reasons for saying that God is not distinct from his nature. And, of course, whether or not Aquinas's account of divine simplicity succeeds also depends on whether or not it is grounded in good reasons for saying such things as that God is good, knowing, just, and so on.

(g) Simplicity and existence

But when it comes to the suggestion that God's nature is to exist (or the suggestion that God is 'Subsisting Existence Itself') other considerations become relevant—ones having to do with the view that words such as 'being' and 'existing' cannot tell us what something is like (cannot be thought to signify properties or qualities of things). I discussed and defended this view in Chapter 5, and you will now realize that I sympathize with those (such as C. J. F. Williams and Terence Penelhum) who are sceptical of the conclusion that God's nature is to be. Roughly put, my view is that we cannot sensibly say that God's nature is what is meant by 'is' or 'are' in statements like 'There is a city called New York' or 'There are elephants in India'. I find it hard to believe that, if we ask whether God exists, and if we ask what God is, the true answer to the second question could be the same as an affirmative answer to the first.

Yet a number of philosophers reject the understanding of existence represented by authors like Williams and Penelhum.[31] These have argued that we can indeed assert a truth about an individual just by saying that it exists. And, even if they are wrong to argue in this way, defenders of the claim that God's nature is to be might yet be able to defend themselves. For, does someone who thinks that God's nature is to be have to claim that existence (or being) is a property or quality with which God can be identified?

Here, once again, we can consider the position of Aquinas. When he claims that God's simplicity means that God is 'Existence Itself' (he sometimes puts this by saying that God's 'essence' is 'to be' [*esse*]), he does not suggest that there is a property or quality of existence with which God should be identified. Rather, he says that God is 'Existence Itself' since 'God exists' is true and since there is nothing which caused or causes it to be true. In other words, Aquinas's teaching that God's nature is to be amounts to the conclusion that God is not *created* by anything. And that conclusion is not obviously absurd. It can be expressed by saying that God is a 'necessary being'. Some philosophers would observe that there are no necessary beings since necessity is a feature of propositions, not of real, self-contained, concrete individuals (like people or cats). On their account, necessity is always a matter of logical necessity, as when we say that it is logically necessary that if p implies q, and if p, then q. Yet, as Peter Geach observes: 'Since what is "necessary" is what "cannot" not be, to say that "necessary" can only refer to logical necessity is equivalent to saying that whatever cannot be so, *logically* cannot be so—e.g. that since I cannot speak Russian, my speaking Russian is logically impossible: which is absurd.'[32] 'Necessary' can be predicated of more than logical truths, and it is far from obvious that it cannot be predicated of God considered as something which depends on nothing whatsoever for being all that it is (the idea involved in the teaching that God is the Creator of everything other than himself).

Conclusion

The teaching that God is simple has both defenders and detractors. Are the arguments of the defenders decisive? Are the arguments of the detractors definitive? In this chapter I have tried to present some of the major arguments for and against divine simplicity in a (forgive the pun) simple way. From what I have said, you might fairly conclude that belief in God's simplicity (very much a feature of classical theism) can be reasonably defended (as many theistic personalists deny). But you might also reach a different conclusion, as many philosophers and theologians would suggest that you should. One thing, at any rate, is certain. The topic of divine simplicity is complex and difficult. And it is something which you can now go on to brood on for yourself as I pass to other, though related, matters.

NOTES

1. The adjective 'patristic' is commonly applied to Christian writers from the end of the first century AD to the close of the eighth. They are commonly referred to as 'the early church fathers', and the study of their works is sometimes called 'patristics'.

2. Augustine of Hippo, *The City of God*, XI, 10. I quote from the translation by Henry Bettenson (Harmondsworth, 1984). Cf. also Augustine *Confessions*, I, vi, 10 and *Confessions*, XIII, iii, 4.

3. Augustine of Hippo, *The City of God*, XI, 10.

4. Anselm, *Proslogion*, chs. 12 and 18. Here and below I quote from Brian Davies and G. R. Evans (eds.), *Anselm of Canterbury: The Major Works* (Oxford, 1998).

5. Thomas Aquinas, *Summa Theologiae*, Ia, 13, 11. I quote from volume 3 of the Blackfriars edition of the *Summa Theologiae* (London and New York, 1964). For other texts in which Aquinas argues in defence of God's simplicity, see *Compendium Theologiae*, chs. 8–17, *De Potentia*, VII, and *Summa Contra Gentiles*, I, 14–18.

6. We need to distinguish between 'unchanging' and 'unchangeable'. Something unchanging might yet be thought capable of change even if it does not, in fact, change. Something unchangeable is incapable of change.

7. Cf. Anselm, *Proslogion*, chs. 5 and 13.

8. This is basically the argument of Aquinas in *Summa Theologiae*, Ia, 9,1.

9. Anselm, *Proslogion*, ch. 18.

10. Note that I am here assuming, as defenders of divine simplicity do, that all God's 'attributes' are essential, or belong to him by nature.

11. Aquinas, *Summa Theologiae*, Ia, 3, 3. I quote from volume 2 of the Black-friars edition of the *Summa Theologiae* (London and New York, 1964). By 'whatever else is said of him', Aquinas is thinking only of what is said of God so as to describe or report what God is in himself ('essentially', as Aquinas would say). Aquinas is not here thinking of statements like 'God delivered the Israelites from Egypt', which he regards as a report of an historical event, not a report on what God is by nature. You might say that I wrote the present book. You might also say that I am a human being. For Aquinas, it is 'Davies is a human being' that says what I am by nature, not 'Davies wrote the present book'.

12. Aquinas, *Summa Theologiae*, Ia, 3, 4.

13. Grace Jantzen, in Alan Richardson and John Bowden (eds.), *A New Dictionary of Christian Theology* (London, 1983), p. 573.

14. Richard E. Creel, 'Immutability and Impassibility', in Philip L. Quinn and Charles Taliaferro (eds.), *A Companion to Philosophy of Religion* (Oxford, 1997), p. 314.

15. Jon Sobrino, *Christology at the Crossroads* (London, 1978), p. 197. Sobrino is quoting from Jürgen Moltmann, *The Crucified God* (London, 1974).

16. Cf. Charles Hartshorne, *A Natural Theology For Our Time* (La Salle, IL, 1967), p. 75. Cf. also Chapter 1 above.

17. We shall be turning more directly to divine omniscience in the next chapter.

18. John Lucas, *The Future* (Oxford, 1989), p. 214.

19. Ibid., p. 215.

20. Alvin Plantinga, *Does God Have A Nature?* (Milwaukee, WI, 1980), p. 47.

21. Ibid.

22. C. J. F. Williams, 'Being', in Quinn and Taliaferro (eds.), *A Companion to Philosophy of Religion*, p. 226.

23. Terence Penelhum, 'Divine Necessity', *Mind* 69 (1960), reprinted in Basil Mitchell (ed.), *The Philosophy of Religion* (Oxford, 1971). I quote from Mitchell's volume, p. 184 f.

24. Aquinas, *Summa Theologiae*, Ia, 20, 2.

25. Ibid., Ia, 19, 3 ad. 1.

26. James Barr, *Fundamentalism* (London, 1977), p. 277.

27. John Locke, *An Essay Concerning Human Understanding*, ed. Peter H. Nidditch (Oxford, 1975), Book IV, ch. XVII.

28. In the light of the doctrine of the Incarnation, Christians believe that God indeed walked in a garden. At this point, however, I am concerned only with what might be said about divinity as such, not about divinity as incarnate.

29. Aquinas, *Summa Theologiae*, introduction to Ia, 3.

30. Cf. *Summa Theologiae*, Ia, 13, 2.

31. See, for example, Barry Miller, *A Most Unlikely God* (Notre Dame, IN, and London, 1996), and *The Fullness of Being: A New Paradigm for Existence* (Notre Dame, IN, and London, 2002).

32. P. T. Geach, in G. E. M. Anscombe and P. T. Geach, *Three Philosophers* (Oxford, 1961), p. 114.

FURTHER READING

For an account of some classical statements of the teaching that God is simple, and for some philosophical evaluation of them, see David Burrell, *Aquinas: God and Action* (London, 1979); *Knowing the Unknowable God: Ibn-Sina, Maimonides, Aquinas* (Notre Dame, IN, 1986); and *Freedom and Creation in Three Traditions* (Notre Dame, IN, 1993). See also Vivian Boland, *Ideas in God According to Saint Thomas Aquinas: Sources and Synthesis* (Leiden, 1996).

For a book-length defence of the notion of divine simplicity, see Barry Miller, *A Most Unlikely God* (Notre Dame, IN, and London, 1996). For a full-scale attack on the notion, see Christopher Hughes, *On a Complex Theory of a Simple God* (Ithaca, NY, 1980).

For some article-length defences of the teaching that God is simple (or aspects of that teaching), see David B. Burrell, 'Distinguishing God from the World', in Brian Davies (ed.), *Language, Meaning and God* (London, 1987); Brian Davies, 'Aquinas, God and Being', *Philosophical Quarterly* 80 (1997); Brian Davies, 'Classical Theism and the Doctrine of Divine Simplicity', reprinted in Brian Davies (ed.), *Philosophy of Religion: A Guide and Anthology* (Oxford, 2000); John King Farlow, 'Simplicity, Analogy and Plain Religious Lives', *Faith and Philosophy* 1 (1984); William Mann, 'Divine Simplicity', *Religious Studies* 18 (1982); William Mann, 'Simplicity and Immutability in God', *International Philosophical Quarterly* 23 (1983); Timothy O'Connor, 'Simplicity and Creation', *Faith and Philosophy* 16 (1999); Eleonore Stump and Norman Kretzmann, 'Absolute Simplicity', *Faith and Philosophy* 2 (1985); Katherine A. Rogers, *Perfect Being Theology*

(Edinburgh, 2000), ch. 3; James Ross, 'Comments on "Absolute Simplicity" ', *Faith and Philosophy* 2 (1985); and Eleonore Stump and Norman Kretzmann, 'Simplicity Made Plainer: A Reply to Ross', *Faith and Philosophy* 4 (1987).

For some article-length attacks on the teaching that God is simple (or aspects of that teaching), see William Hasker, 'Simplicity and Freedom: A Response to Stump and Kretzmann', *Faith and Philosophy* 3 (1986); Thomas V. Morris, 'On God and Mann: A View of Divine Simplicity', *Religious Studies* 21 (1985); William J. Wainwright, 'Augustine on God's Simplicity: A Reply', *The New Scholasticism* 53 (1979); and C. J. F. Williams, 'Being', in Philip L. Quinn and Charles Taliaferro (eds.), *A Companion to Philosophy of Religion* (Oxford, 1997). For a Fregean critique of Aquinas's teaching on being and God, see Anthony Kenny, *Aquinas on Being* (Oxford, 2002).

As we have seen, the teaching that God is simple is bound up with the view that God is immutable. Books to recommend with a bearing on God's unchangeableness include: F. H. Brabant, *Time and Eternity in Christian Thought* (London, 1937); Michael J. Dodds, *The Unchanging God of Love: A Study of the Teaching of St. Thomas Aquinas on Divine Immutability in View of Certain Contemporary Criticism of this Doctrine* (Fribourg, 1986); Paul Helm, *Eternal God* (Oxford, 1988); Brian Leftow, *Time and Eternity* (Ithaca, NY, 1991); Alan G. Padgett, *God, Eternity and the Nature of Time* (London, 1992); Nelson Pike, *God and Timelessness* (London, 1970); Richard Sorabji, *Time, Creation and the Continuum* (London, 1983); and Thomas G. Weinandy, *Does God Change?* (Still River, MA, 1985). For more on what process theologians have said about God, a good book to start with is Santiago Sia, *God in Process Thought* (Dordrecht, Boston, and Lancaster, 1985). For a critical survey of process theologians, see Illtyd Trethowan, *Process Theology and the Christian Tradition* (Still River, MA, 1985). For a lively attack on classical theism coming from a process thinker, see Charles Hartshorne, *Omnipotence and Other Theological Mistakes* (Albany, NY, 1984).

QUESTIONS FOR DISCUSSION

1 Is changelessness a perfection?

2 'Only an unchanging and unchangeable God could account for there being a world of changing and changeable things.' Is that true? If so, why? If not, why not?

3 Let X be a wholly immaterial being. Can X be thought of as belonging to a class of things of which there might be many members?

4 Must everything living undergo change?

5 'God is love.' What might this statement be taken to mean?

6 Can there be knowledge which does not depend on learning or coming to know?

7 In the Old Testament book of Genesis, we are told that God needed to 'go down' to Sodom and Gomorrah to 'see' what exactly was going on there (Genesis 18: 21). Should we therefore conclude that God is a learner? If not, why not? If so, what are we to make of biblical texts implying that nothing that happens is unknown to God?

8 On the supposition that the Bible teaches truly, is there a way of determining which biblical texts should be read as literally true and which should not?

9 Can different descriptive statements succeed in saying what is true of something which is not, in itself, composed of different properties or qualities?

10 Is there reason to suppose that anything exists by virtue of its nature? If so, why? If not, why not?

9

OMNIPOTENCE AND OMNISCIENCE

In Psalm 68 we read: 'Ascribe power to God whose majesty is over Israel, and his power is in the skies.' In his letter to the Romans, we find St Paul exclaiming: 'O the depth of the riches and wisdom and knowledge of God!' So the notion that God has power and knowledge has clear biblical warrant. The Bible takes it for granted that God's power and knowledge are unsurpassed. And, although the Bible does not use such words, many theists have said that God is 'omnipotent' and 'omniscient'—meaning that God is somehow unlimited when it comes to power and knowledge. But what could it mean to call God omnipotent and omniscient? And is there any reason to think that God is either of these things?

The Meaning of 'God is Omnipotent'

'Omnipotent' means 'all-powerful'. But how should we understand 'God is all-powerful'? Theists have offered three main answers. According to the first, 'God is omnipotent' means that God can do anything. According to the second, it means that God can do anything, including what is logically impossible. And according to the third, it means that God can produce any conceivable thing or arrangement of things. So let us now consider each of these understandings.

(a) 'God can do anything'

What could we mean by saying that God can do anything? An obvious reply would be: 'You name something that can be done, and God can do it.' But how can that be so? People can get married. Getting married is something that can be done. So should we conclude that God can get married? Not if he is incorporeal. If God is incorporeal, then God, considered as such, can never turn up to be linked to a bride anywhere.[1] He cannot, for instance, walk up an aisle and say 'I do'. Then again, I can turn over in bed. But can God do this? If we think of God as incorporeal, the answer, again, is 'No'. And this answer is appropriate when it comes to a whole range of comparable questions, such as: 'Can God run a mile in 30 seconds?', 'Can God gargle?', and 'Can God swim the Atlantic Ocean?'

So 'You name something that can be done, and God can do it' is not plausible as a way of explaining what divine omnipotence amounts to. If we say that God can do anything, it looks as though we could truly assert 'God can——' where the blank is filled in with a description of any logically possible feat. Yet there must be some logically possible feats that are beyond God's power. As Peter Geach puts it:

> One good example suffices: making a thing which its maker cannot afterwards destroy. This is certainly a possible feat, a feat which some human beings have performed. Can God perform that feat or not? If he cannot, there is already some logically possible feat which God cannot perform. If he can perform the feat, then let us suppose that he does . . . Then we are supposing God to have brought about a situation in which he *has* made something he cannot destroy, and in that situation destroying this thing is a *logically* possible feat that God cannot accomplish, for we surely cannot admit of the idea of a creature whose destruction is logically impossible.[2]

As Geach adds, even the Bible admits that there are things God cannot do, e.g. swear by anything greater than himself or break his word.[3]

(b) 'God can do anything, including what is logically impossible'

Descartes is a famous example of someone who seems to endorse the conclusion that God can do anything, including what is logically impossible. He alludes to 'eternal truths', by which he means truths of logic and mathematics. Many philosophers would say that these are logically necessary, that to deny them is to contradict oneself. And yet, Descartes asserts, they owe their existence to God just like anything else which God has created. Writing to Marin Mersenne (1588–1648), he says:

The mathematical truths which you call eternal have been laid down by God and depend on him entirely no less than the rest of his creatures . . . In general we can assert that God can do everything that is within our grasp but not that he cannot do what is beyond our grasp . . . Even those truths which are called eternal—as that 'the whole is greater than its part'—would not be truths if God had not so established.[4]

On this view, 'God is omnipotent' appears to mean that God can bring it about that contradictions are true.

But is such a conclusion tenable? In a sense it is irrefutable. For, as J. L. Mackie says:

[Descartes] need never be disturbed by any reasoning or any evidence, for if his omnipotent being could do what is logically impossible, he could certainly exist, and have any desired attributes, in defiance of every sort of contrary consideration. The view that there is an absolutely omnipotent being in this sense stands, therefore, right outside the realm of rational enquiry and discussion.[5]

But, Descartes's position is highly questionable. It is sometimes hard to know whether or not we are dealing with what is logically impossible. But expressions like 'a part which is greater than a whole', 'square circle', and 'a proposition which is both true and false' are clearly contradictory. And for this reason it makes sense to say that an omnipotent God cannot bring it about that they refer to anything. As Mackie again observes: 'A logical contradiction is not a state of affairs which it is supremely difficult to produce, but only a form of words which fails to describe any state of affairs.'[6]

(c) 'God can produce any conceivable thing or arrangement of things'

The third view of divine omnipotence (c) is the one most commonly defended by classical theists, and it goes with the notion of God as Creator. If God creatively brings it about that things exist, why suppose that there are limits to what he can create? According to this view, there are no such limits except those of logic. It states that, if we can consistently speak of X as existing, then God can produce X.

A notable advocate of this view is Aquinas. As he puts it:

God's power, considered in itself, extends to all such objects as do not imply a contradiction . . . And as regards things that imply a contradiction, they are impossible to God as being impossible in themselves. Consequently, God's power extends to things that are possible in themselves: and such are the things that do not involve a contradiction.[7]

At first glace it might seem that Aquinas is here saying that God can do whatever is logically possible. But Aquinas thought that there were many logically possible feats barred to God (e.g. feats involving their doers being bodily). His basic point in the above quotation is that God can make (create) whatever can genuinely be. 'Something is judged to be possible or impossible', he argues, 'from the implication of the terms: possible when the predicate is compatible with the subject, for instance, that Socrates is seated; impossible when it is not compatible, for instance, that a human being is a donkey.'[8] And Aquinas's conclusion is that God can bring about anything that is possible absolutely speaking:

The divine being, on which the notion of divine power is founded, is infinite existence, not limited to any kind of being, but holding within itself and anticipating the perfection of the whole of existence. Whatever can have the nature of being falls within the range of things that are absolutely possible, and it is with respect to these that God is called all-powerful.[9]

But is this view cogent? Some philosophers reject it because, so they argue, we can mention possible things which God cannot create or produce. Examples which have been suggested include 'a stone too heavy for God to lift' and 'something its maker cannot destroy'. Yet these examples hardly serve to undermine the present account of omnipotence. There are stones which are too heavy for people to lift. But why should anyone suppose that God can create stones that he cannot lift or cause to rise? We might say that, if God cannot create such things, then he is not omnipotent since there is something he cannot do (i.e. make a stone which is too heavy for him to lift). But (c) is not saying that there is nothing God cannot do. It is only saying that God can *make to be* anything which can be thought of as *able to be*. And a stone which God cannot lift is not obviously capable of being. The same is true when it comes to 'something its maker cannot destroy'. As Geach says, making something one cannot destroy is a logically possible feat. People can construct what they cannot then obliterate. But could there be anything the existence of which God cannot terminate at will? If the existence of everything other than God is wholly derived from God, the answer is 'No'. If creatures are willed to be by God, then God can surely will that they cease to be. And even if he cannot (e.g. because he has sworn not to destroy some creature or other), we still do not have a counterexample to what (c) is claiming about omnipotence. For that is couched in terms of what God can make to be, not in terms of what God can make *not* to be.

But perhaps there are other things which can be but which God cannot make to be. What, for example, of an England in which Richard III won the battle of Bosworth and survived as King of England until 1500? Can God bring it about that Richard III lived beyond 1485? If Richard had lived until 1500, English history might have been very different. But he died in 1485. So should we conclude that God cannot bring it about that Richard III won the battle of Bosworth? And should we not therefore conclude that God cannot be omnipotent?

Then again, what about 'John is freely choosing to get married'? Can God bring this about? If you are not a determinist (if you do not believe that nobody acts freely), you will presumably say that 'John is freely choosing to get married' could be true with respect to some John or other. But can God bring it about that it is true? Some philosophers would say that he cannot, since what a person does freely cannot be brought about by something else, including God.

Yet these examples also fail to count against Aquinas's view of divine omnipotence. If we deny that everything that happens comes about of necessity, we might concede that the past could have been different. But it is no objection to Aquinas that God cannot now make the past not to have been. For that would require that God produce what is logically contradictory (a world in which such and such both *has* and *has not* happened), while (c) is only claiming that God can bring about what, in itself, can be thought to exist without contradiction. And when it comes to 'John is freely choosing to get married' and similar examples, defenders of (c) can again appeal to the notion of what can be thought to be without contradiction. Suppose that there cannot be a freely chosen action which is brought about by God. Then, according to (c), God cannot bring it about that there is such an action. As it happens, and as we shall see in Chapter 10, Aquinas believes that 'a human free action brought about by God' is no contradiction in terms. But even if he came to admit that he was wrong on that score, he could still stick by his account of omnipotence. All he would need to do is abandon his claim that 'a human free action brought about by God' is not a contradiction in terms.

Can God Sin?

So perhaps it is indeed possible to formulate a tenable account of divine omnipotence. For the third view discussed above (c) seems to be a reasonable way of trying to say what it might mean to call God omnipotent (given that God is the maker of everything other than himself). But before we move on to the notion of omniscience, it is worth touching briefly on a question which some philosophers have found vexing with regard to omnipotence: can God sin?

You and I can sin. Or, if you take that statement to imply a belief in God, let us put the point by saying that you and I can do what is wrong. Sinning, or wrongdoing, is all too common.[10] So, can God sin? If he cannot, then some would say that he is not all-powerful. But if he can, then it would seem that he is not essentially good (as theists commonly take him to be). Or, as St Anselm writes: 'How are You [God] omnipotent if You cannot do all things? But how can You do all things if You cannot be corrupted, or tell lies?'[11] Anselm is raising a dilemma. On the one hand, theists typically say that God is all-good. On the other hand, they also say that God is all-powerful. But if God is all-powerful, then he can surely do wrong. If he is all-good, however, it would also seem that he cannot.

Can we escape from the dilemma by denying one of the premises which seem to give rise to it? Obviously we can. We might, for instance, deny that God can do no wrong. And, we might argue, to do so need not commit us to denying that God is essentially good. '*Can* God do wrong?' is a different question from '*Does* God do wrong?' So, might we not say that God, although he never does wrong, *could* do so?

Some philosophers have suggested that we might indeed say this.[12] But can we do so if we take God to be essentially good (i.e. good by nature)? Perhaps we can. Perhaps something essentially good might be such even though able to do wrong. Yet to call something essentially good might also be thought of as saying that doing wrong is just not something of which it is capable. I might say that Fred is essentially good even though he sometimes misbehaves. But what if 'essentially' means 'of its very essence'? Cats are essentially mammalian. There just cannot be a non-mammalian cat. And, one might argue, there cannot be an essentially good God who is able to do wrong. For, might not such a God be reasonably thought of as unable even to countenance wrongdoing? Might not such a God be reasonably thought of as being unable to do wrong as cats are unable to be non-mammalian?

Well, suppose that we think that the answer to these questions is 'Yes'. Can we continue to hold that God is omnipotent or all-powerful?

We can obviously do so if we adopt the first understanding of omnipotence noted above (a), namely, 'You name something that can be done and God can do it'. But, as we have seen, that understanding is open to question.

We might claim that God, though able to do wrong, can still be essentially good if we think that God can bring about what is logically contradictory—the second view of omnipotence discussed above (b). For, even if there is a logical impossibility in the notion of an essentially good God who is able to do wrong, a God who can override logic can, presumably, deal with the problem. As we have also seen, however, (b) is pretty untenable.

View (c) of omnipotence (that defended by Aquinas) might be thought to be able to cope with the suggestion that God can do wrong even though he is essentially good since (c) might be thought to entail that God can make something to be, though doing so would be wrong. Yet, if 'God is essentially good' means that the notion of God doing wrong is logically suspicious, then (c) is incompatible with the suggestion that an essentially good God might wrongly bring it about that something or other exists. For (c) depends heavily on the idea that accounts of omnipotence must respect the principle that what is contradictory cannot be the case. And if there is something logically fishy about 'God can do wrong', then defenders of (c) would seem to be committed to fighting shy of it.

Yet, would doing so commit one to anything that might be thought of as a serious denial of the claim that God is omnipotent? Arguably not. As we have seen, it seems reasonable to suppose that one can give sense to the notion that God is omnipotent even though there are some things that God cannot do (e.g. get married). So, why should one not say that God can be omnipotent even though his nature prevents him from doing wrong? And why might not one also add that the ability to do wrong is more a sign of weakness than of power? In an obvious sense, of course, it is not. If I can commit genocide, then I must clearly be pretty powerful. But might not my ability to engage in genocide also be thought of as the sign of a flawed character? Might it not be thought of as showing that I am a failure rather than a success? And might it not, in this sense, be taken as a matter of weakness, not of power? If you think that the mere ability to impose one's will (whatever that happens to be) is an indication of power, then you will reply that the capacity to do what is wrong (or the capacity to do what most people take to be wrong) is not a sign of weakness. But other views are possible.

Take, for example, the way in which Anselm answers the question we saw him raising above. He concedes that God cannot 'be corrupted or tell lies'. But he denies that this means that God is somehow weak. On the contrary, he suggests:

> He who can do these things can do what is not good for himself and what he ought not to do. And the more he can do these things, the more power adversity and perversity have over him and the less he has against them. He, therefore, who can do these things can do them not by power but by impotence . . . When someone is said to have the 'power' of doing or suffering something which is not to his advantage or which he ought not to do, then by 'power' here we mean 'impotence'.[13]

Here, of course, Anselm is thinking that wrongdoing always somehow harms the one who does wrong. And if that view is untenable (as many would say that it is), then the back of Anselm's argument is broken. But if to do wrong is somehow to fall short, then there is a case to be made on the other side, as Aquinas observes in a discussion of the question 'Can God be omnipotent if God cannot sin?' To sin, says Aquinas, 'is to fall short of full activity'. And that, he concludes, has to mean that omnipotence positively requires that God cannot sin. Or in Aquinas's own words: 'To be able to sin is to be able to fail in doing, which cannot be reconciled with omnipotence. It is because God is omnipotent that he cannot sin.'[14]

Is there Knowledge in God?

Turning now to divine omniscience, we need to ask, as we did with omnipotence, what people have meant when invoking the notion. Before doing so, however, there is surely an even more basic question to ask: why suppose that God has any knowledge?

Apart from relying on texts like the Bible, those who believe that knowledge can be ascribed to God tend to do so for one or more of the following reasons:

1 God has knowledge because God is perfect.

2 God has knowledge because he acts freely and intelligently.

3 God has knowledge because he is wholly immaterial.

Reason (1), of course, assumes that God is perfect. But, supposing that God is perfect, why should we suppose that he has knowledge? The usual answer given is that, since it is better to know than not to know, God must therefore know if he is perfect. Hence, for example, having argued that God exists as something than which nothing greater can be conceived (cf. Chapter 5), St Anselm argues that God must have knowledge since 'God is whatever it is better to be than not to be' and since it is better to know than not to know.

But is that really true? We sometimes say that ignorance is bliss. Yet people like Anselm are thinking of God as perfect without qualification. Ignorance may be bliss, but only because people are sometimes spared pain by not knowing that something or other is the case. But would a wholly perfect being need to be spared in this way? Would a wholly perfect being ever run the risk of knowing anything that could diminish it in any way? Whether rightly or wrongly, we commonly do link knowledge and perfection. A perfection is something valuable. And, rightly or wrongly, we typically value that which knows, or is capable of knowing, more than we value that which is ignorant or incapable of knowing.

But should knowledge be ascribed to God because he acts freely and intelligently? Is reason (2) believable? The obvious answer, of course, is that (2) is eminently believable if there is a God who acts freely and intelligently. For if 'freedom' means freedom to choose between

alternatives, and if 'intelligently' means something like 'with understanding', then freedom and intelligence imply knowledge. The question, of course, is: 'Is there a God who acts freely and intelligently?'

Defenders of some of the arguments considered in Chapters 3–6
would say that there is. Supporters of ontological arguments ascribe
freedom and intelligence to God considered as perfect or as that than
which nothing greater can be conceived. Those who endorse a cosmological argument for God's existence commonly suppose that God's
making the world cannot be the result of coercion and is, therefore,
something that God does freely and with knowledge of what he is doing.
And defenders of design arguments are clearly committed to including
the notion of intelligence in their understanding of God. So (2) may be
defensible in the light of theistic arguments such as those outlined
above. If the arguments lack cogency, however, defenders of 'God has
knowledge' will have to seek other means to defend their conclusion
philosophically. Or they will have to resort to a hypothetical way of
reasoning. They will have to say something like 'If God is free and
intelligent, then God has knowledge'.

Yet what about (3), the suggestion that God knows because God is
wholly immaterial? Let us suppose that there is a wholly immaterial
God. Must we therefore conclude that he has knowledge? Some philosophers have argued that we should, because of what is true of knowing
in general. For, they argue, knowing just *is* existence unrestricted by
matter. On their account, anything immaterial is, by nature, knowing.
Take, for example, Aquinas again. Like Aristotle, he is struck by the fact
that there seems to be a profound difference between what happens in
particular bodies and what happens when we achieve understanding.
Bodily processes, he thinks, are confined to the bodies in which they
occur. But what about the knowledge that water is composed of
hydrogen and oxygen? Is this something confined to me? Aquinas (and
Aristotle) think that it is not. Many people know that water is composed
of hydrogen and oxygen. That knowledge is shareable and shared. But
how can it be so if knowledge (or understanding) is something merely
physical? How can it be so if, for example, 'John knows that water is
composed of hydrogen and oxygen' is simply a report on John's physical
state? Aquinas suggests that, since (in the case of people) what happens
when knowledge occurs cannot be captured by describing what an

individual is physically like, knowledge in us must be what comes about as material things transcend their physical individuality. In his view, reality is either material or non-material. If it is material, then it can be exhaustively described in physical terms. Yet, Aquinas reasons, what happens when human knowledge occurs cannot be so described since it is not a physical state or process trapped in the body of any physical thing. So he concludes that knowledge and immateriality go together. On his account, knowledge is nothing but liberation from materiality, and liberation from materiality is nothing but knowledge. And for this reason Aquinas endorses (3). Knowledge, he says, must be ascribed to God since God is wholly immaterial.[15]

But is Aquinas right? Not if 'X knows that-P' is true only if X is in some physiological state. Yet, for example, to ascribe to John the knowledge that cats are mammals is different from ascribing to him a physiological state. When we say 'Cats are mammals', we are using our bodies to speak, and we speak by means of physical symbols (words spoken or written). But we are not expressing our personal bodily processes. It would not make sense to say, 'For me cats are mammals, but for you they are reptiles'. 'For me' and 'for you' just do not come into play in this context. Cats are either mammalian or not regardless of what is going on in my body or in yours. And, in that case, it makes sense to suppose that knowledge is, indeed, something that occurs as knowers transcend their physical particularity. It is, we may suggest, what immateriality means insofar as we can understand it. And if that is indeed so, then the move from 'immaterial' to 'knowing' is a natural one to make, as is the inference from 'God is immaterial' to 'there is knowledge in God'. Since our coming to know depends on material things (e.g. our senses and the objects around us), it could not be that a wholly immaterial God has knowledge just as we do. If there is an immaterial God, however, then it is not absurd to suppose that knowledge can be attributed to him just because of his immateriality.

The Meaning of 'God Is Omniscient'

(a) What does God know?

But we can clearly have knowledge without being all-knowing or omniscient. So now we need to ask what 'God is omniscient' could mean.

The answer, you might reply, is perfectly obvious, since 'omniscient' means 'all-knowing'. You might say that, in thinking of God's omniscience, there is a simple rule of thumb to follow: 'Take a string of words reporting something known or knowable and ascribe this knowledge to God.' But that does not really help us when it comes to thinking about divine omniscience? If you say to me 'Tell me something you know', I might reply 'Well I know that it's raining here'. And 'It's raining here' certainly seems to express what someone could know. But one who knows that can do so only by actually being physically located in a particular place, a 'here'. You can know that it is raining where I live without being where I live. And you can know that it rained where I lived even though you acquired your knowledge long after my death. But to know that it is raining *here* is possible only for one who is physically present at some precise location. And it is hard to see how an immaterial God can physically be anywhere that rain falls.[16]

But what if we say that God is omniscient since he knows all that was, is, and will be the case? Does that way of putting things serve to answer the question 'What might it mean to call God omniscient?'? We might think not since there are problems with assertions like 'God knows that it's raining here'. But even if one is not located in a particular place, one can surely still know what makes someone right in saying 'It's raining here'. If I am right to say 'It's raining here', I am so because rain is falling where I am speaking. But this can be known even by one who is not where I am when I say 'It's raining here'. So, why not suppose that an all-knowing God can know that rain is falling where I am speaking? For that matter, why not suppose that an all-knowing God can know not only that rain was falling when I was speaking but also that rain will be falling when I will be speaking?

But can there be knowledge of what will be the case? Let us suppose that there could be a knower who has somehow registered all that was and is the case. Such a knower would know all that has happened and all that is happening now. Such a knower would also know the natures of everything past and present as well as the relationships in which these things stood or stand to each other. Let us put this by saying that to know all that is and has been the case is to know all that is and has been real or actual. But the future is not real or actual. So it cannot be thought of as an object of knowledge as can the past and the present. What was the case was once real enough. And what is the case is equally real. The future, however, is what is not and never has been the case. So, how can there can be knowledge of that? And how can an omniscient God know all that will be the case as well as all that has been and is the case?

One answer to this question holds that, even though the future is unreal or non-actual, it can still be captured by means of the phrase 'is the case that'. Suppose it comes to pass that Martians invade the earth in 3000 AD. Would it not now be true to say 'It is the case that Martians will invade the earth in 3000 AD'? And might an omniscient God not know that this is so? Or suppose that it does not come to pass that Martians invade the earth in 3000 AD. Would it not now be true to say 'It is not the case that Martians will invade the earth in 3000 AD'? And might an omniscient God know that this is so? Yet many philosophers would reply that statements like 'It is the case that Martians will invade the earth in 3000 AD' falsely presuppose that the future is fixed or determined. According to these philosophers, statements like 'God knows that it is the case that Martians will invade the earth in 3000 AD' entail what is simply unbelievable—that the earth *cannot but* be invaded by Martians in 3000 AD.

So what should we say? Should we take 'God is omniscient' to mean that God knows all that was, is, and will be the case? Or should we not? Since space here is limited, I must now leave you to consider this question on your own. But notice that, even if the right answer is 'Yes', it might still need some modification. For what about all that *could have* been the case even though it was not the case? And what about all that *could be the case now* even though it is not the case now? And what about what *could come to be the case* even though it will never become the case? Should divine omniscience be thought of as encompassing knowledge of all this as well as of what all that was, is, and will be the case? Those who believe that there is an omniscient God typically suppose that the answer to this question is 'Yes'. So perhaps we should include knowledge of possibilities as contained in what should be meant by 'divine omniscience'. At any rate, it would seem odd to say that God is omniscient if he is ignorant of what was possibly the case, of what is possibly the case now, and of what could be the case in the future.

(b) How does God know?

But if God is omniscient, how does he come by his omniscience? You might reply that God knows because he knows and that there is nothing more to be said. Yet it is reasonable to ask how, for example, I have come to acquire the knowledge that I have. So, why not ask how God acquires his knowledge?

Could he do so in just the way that we acquire our knowledge? Well, hardly. If God is unchangeable, his knowledge cannot be something *acquired*, since the notion of acquiring is bound up with the notion of undergoing change. And if God is simple, then God's knowledge cannot be distinguished from God, as our knowledge can be distinguished from ourselves. I would still be me even if I lost all the knowledge that I have. But God, as simple, would no longer be God if he lost his knowledge. To lose his knowledge would be to lose himself.

But even if God is changeable and non-simple, the manner of his knowing must be very different from what it is in us. Our knowledge greatly depends on what we take in by means of our senses. We learn as we encounter the world at a physical level. This is so even where our knowledge derives from what we are taught. We are bodily knowers. Yet God is supposed to be wholly immaterial, which means that divine knowledge cannot be the result of any physical process.

Some philosophers have suggested that God's knowledge, while that of a wholly immaterial being, can still be compared to ours, since knowledge in people is not a physical object or process. But even if human knowing is somehow immaterial, its coming about crucially derives from what happens in and to our bodies. We are not born with knowledge or understanding. We come to know. And our bodies play a crucial role in our doing so. We might say that knowledge arises in God just as it does in us, since God, like us, perceives, looks, or observes. But we perceive, look, and observe as embodied things in particular physical contexts. Our perceiving, looking, and observing are inseparably connected with our bodily constitution and our physical location. God, however, is not supposed to have a bodily constitution or a physical location.

Yet there is human knowledge which does not derive from physical observation. What about knowledge of logical or mathematical truths, for example? We do not come to know these by taking a look or listening very hard. So we might suggest that God can arrive at such knowledge without being corporeal. But do we attain knowledge of logical and mathematical truths independently of the fact that we are parts of a physical world? Arguably not. We come to understand such truths only because we are users of language. And the use of language involves being bodily because (a) it arises from (and is) an interpretation of bodily experience and (b) it is expressed in the use of bodily symbols.

So, how might knowledge be thought of as coming to be in God? Surprisingly, the question has not been much addressed by philosophers. Most of those who have written about God's knowledge (those favourable to theism, at any rate) have tended to start from the supposition that God indeed knows. They have not been much concerned with how God arrives at his knowledge (whether as one who undergoes change or as one who is immutable). But there have been exceptions. Take, for example, Aquinas, who spends a lot of time asking how God knows and who has one basic answer: God has knowledge in something like the way that we have knowledge of ourselves.

We have not always had self-knowledge or self-awareness. We were not born with it, nor is it always with us. But we do have it sometimes. We can know what we are doing or thinking. We can also know how we feel. And knowing what we are doing or thinking, and knowing how we feel, might reasonably be thought of as amounting to self-knowledge or self-awareness. And this knowledge has content. If I know what I am doing or thinking, then I know what is the case. The same goes for knowing how I feel, for this involves knowing that something or other is true of me. I might, for example, feel nauseous. And to feel nauseous is not to know anything. But I can know that I feel nauseous.

Does human self-knowledge or self-awareness depend on physical factors? Yes, if only because human beings rely on their brains in order to know at all. For the sake of argument, however, let us suppose that there could be an incorporeal knower. Such a knower, not being part of a physical world, could not know objects other than itself, or processes other than its own, by perceiving, looking, or observing as we do. But might not this knower know or be aware of itself? Even human self-knowledge does not involve a physical perceiving, looking, or observing. Its object or objects are not physically distinct from those who have it. Many philosophers have insisted that meanings are not in anyone's head. And that view seems right if only because understanding cannot be a purely private process (more on this in Chapter 13). Yet human self-knowledge or awareness arises 'from within' rather than 'from without'. So, could not a wholly immaterial knower have something akin to human self-knowledge?

Aquinas suggests that it could. On his account, and as we have seen, God knows because he is immaterial. And, Aquinas argues, knowledge in God must therefore be essentially a matter of self-knowledge or self-understanding. As a defender of belief in divine simplicity, Aquinas does not think that God's self-knowledge is distinguishable from himself. Nor does he think of it as subject to change. So he is not suggesting that God's self-knowledge is just like ours. He does, however, think that the notion of God knowing himself is not incoherent. And on this basis he goes on to argue that God can be thought of as knowing things other than himself.

For, says Aquinas, everything other than God owes its existence to God and is, therefore, what God is bringing about. And, Aquinas adds, it follows from this that everything other than God can be known to God insofar as he knows himself as the one who brings about the existence of everything other than himself. If God knows himself, then God, suggests Aquinas, must know what he is doing. And, Aquinas reasons, if God's doing is the making to be of all that is not divine, then God must know everything other than himself, though not as an observer looking at something external which causes knowledge of it in the observer.

Does this way of thinking shed light on what it might plausibly mean to say that there is knowledge in God or that God is omniscient? Not if there can be no such thing as an immaterial knower. If such a knower is possible, however, then Aquinas's approach to God's knowledge is fruitful. It does not require us to think of God's knowing as dependent on his physical constitution and location. So it does not demand that we think of God as knowing by taking a look at an external object or by something akin to this (e.g. hearing a noise or feeling a body). Instead, it basically says that God knows all just by knowing himself, and it trades off the (surely not implausible) idea that one can know what one brings about simply by knowing oneself as its source.

Yet, if God knows what is other than himself insofar as he knows himself as the cause of its existing, does it not follow that all that is other than God has to be just what it is simply because God makes it to be what it is? Does not Aquinas's account of divine understanding lead to the conclusion that everything other than God cannot be other than it is? And even if we forget about Aquinas on God's knowledge, does it not follow that, if God is omniscient, then nothing other than God can be different from what it is? Many philosophers have thought that the answer to this question is 'Yes'. According to them, divine omniscience entails universal determinism. In particular, they have argued that belief in divine omniscience is incompatible with belief in human freedom.

Divine Omniscience and Human Freedom

(a) The problem

Why should omniscience be thought to conflict with human freedom? Those who think that it does usually hold that the problem derives from two facts: (a) that omniscience includes foreknowledge, and (b) that 'God foreknows that X will do such and such' means that X cannot but do such and such and cannot, therefore, be acting freely. The idea here is that, if God is omniscient, then his knowledge of all human actions must be something he had even before people were there to act. To this idea is added the thought that human action, being future to God's knowledge of it, has to accord with this knowledge of necessity.

Suppose that I go for a walk today. And suppose that God knew that I would do so as long ago as the time that our planet was forming. Since 'X knows that-P' entails that-P (since, if I know that such and such is the case, then such and such is, indeed, the case), should we not now conclude that, even when our planet was forming, it was certain that I would take a walk today? Those who hold that omniscience conflicts with human freedom tend to suppose that the answer to this question is 'Yes'. The past, they suggest, cannot be altered. And if the past includes knowledge on God's part of what people would do in the future, then people can only act in accordance with how God knew that they would act—meaning that people can act only in one (pre-known) way. Or as Richard Sorabji (echoing many other philosophers) puts it:

> If God were not *infallible* in his judgement of what we would do, then we might be able so to act that his prediction turned out *wrong*. But this is not even a possibility, for to call him infallible is to say not merely that he *is* not, but that he *cannot* be wrong, and correspondingly we *cannot* make him wrong ... The restriction on freedom arises not from God's infallibility alone, but from that coupled with the *irrevocability* of the past. If God's infallible knowledge of our doing exists *in advance*, then we are *too late* so to act that God will have had a different judgement about what we are going to do. His judgement exists *already*, and the past *cannot* be affected.[17]

By 'infallible in his judgement' Sorabji clearly means 'knowing'. And, he suggests, if God knows what people will do in the future, then their doing so is guaranteed even before they come on the scene.[18]

(b) Some attempts to deal with the problem

How might we deal with the problem just introduced? We might deny that people ever do act freely. Yet few theists have done this. Some of them have been happy (even anxious) to concede that God is ignorant of what we will do in the future.[19] And if they are right, then arguments like that of Sorabji cannot even get started. With an eye on the notion of omniscience, however, many theists have felt uncomfortable about denying that God knows what people will do. Instead, these theists have suggested that there are ways of responding to Sorabji-type arguments, ways which allow us consistently to believe both in God's knowledge of the future and in human freedom.

One popular argument rejects the inference from 'God foreknows that X will do such and such freely' to 'X cannot but do such and such'. Defenders of this argument agree that the past cannot be changed. But they also hold that the past can sometimes depend on what is future. And, they add, this is the case when it comes to our present actions and

God's previous knowledge of them. In their view, God can only foreknow that such and such will be the case if such and such really will be
the case. But what if what will be the case is that I act freely on some
occasion? Then, it has been suggested, God can foreknow this only if I
act freely on the occasion in question. As William Lane Craig makes the
point:

> The reason God foreknows that Jones will mow his lawn is the simple fact
> that Jones will mow his lawn. Jones is free to refrain, and were he to do so,
> God would have foreknown that he would refrain. Jones is free to do what-
> ever he wants, and God's foreknowledge logically follows Jones's action like
> a shadow, even if chronologically the shadow precedes the coming of the
> event itself.[20]

Sorabji's argument treats the past as in no way constituted by what is
future. For authors like Craig, however, the past may be what it is
precisely because of what follows it.[21]

But do the notions of past and future have any proper place when it
comes to the topic of God's knowledge and human action? This question
brings us to yet another popular way of responding to arguments like
that of Sorabji. For arguments like these depend on supposing that God's
knowledge of what we do is *fore*knowledge, knowledge whose occurrence in God is temporally prior to that of which it is knowledge. Yet,
should we suppose that divine omniscience includes foreknowledge?
Without wishing to deny that God knows what is future to us or to
anything else in time, many theists have suggested that we should not
suppose this. They have also suggested that we should not, therefore,
worry about omniscience being in conflict with human freedom.

Why? Because, they argue, God is not in time and, therefore, has no
foreknowledge. This line is famously defended by the classical theist
Boethius (c.475/77–c.524/26). In his *The Consolation of Philosophy*, he
summarizes a Sorabji-type argument to indicate a possible incompatibility between God's omniscience and human freedom. But he then argues
that there is no incompatibility if God's knowledge exists outside time
and is a grasp of history by a mind that knows all without undergoing
change. Boethius does not claim fully to understand the knowledge of a
timeless God. But, he thinks, it certainly cannot be thought of as foreknowledge. It is, he suggests, knowledge pure and simple. And, he adds,

if we think of it only in those terms, then we need not suppose that it prevents people from acting freely. Although 'I know that-P' entails that P is true, 'I know that Mary is reading a book' does not entail that Mary cannot but be reading a book. And, says Boethius, the same holds when it comes to what God knows. God might (timelessly) know that I am reading a book. But, says Boethius, this does not mean that I cannot but be reading a book. It does not mean that I might not be freely reading a book.

Yet, suppose we choose not to focus on the notion that God's knowledge is timeless. Is there another way of defending the view that God can know what I will freely do? Yes, thought the sixteenth-century Jesuit Louis De Molina (1536–1600), whose views on God and human freedom have been much applauded by a number of contemporary philosophers.

Molina argues that God has something called 'middle knowledge' (*scientia media*). In Molina's view, as well as knowing what is actually the case and what might, in some absolute sense, be the case, God also knows what *would be the case if*. According to Molina, God has knowledge of what uncreated people would do if they were to find themselves in certain circumstances. This, says Molina, is not knowledge of what is actually the case. But it is knowledge with a bearing on what would actually be the case if the uncreated people in question were, in fact, created.

In Molina's view, by virtue of his middle knowledge, God knows how uncreated, possible people would freely act if created. Then he creates some of them, and they act as he knows them to act by virtue of his middle knowledge. And yet, Molina argues, what they do as created is not determined by God's knowledge since, as created, they are merely living out what they freely chose to do as items in God's middle knowledge. For Molina, God's middle knowledge encompasses how I would freely act if created by God. And, thinks Molina, the fact that God creates me and knows me as his creature cannot interfere with my freedom if my freedom is something that God brings about by creating me as a freely acting object of his middle knowledge.

(c) Some comments on the above attempts

But is Molina's solution to our problem convincing? As I have said, it is currently favoured by some thinkers. Yet its assertion that God has middle knowledge is also very curious. At first glance it appears to involve a straightforward and believable claim: that God knows the difference between what is the case and what could be the case. Actually, however, it requires us to believe more than this. For Molina's concept of middle knowledge includes the idea that among the objects of God's knowledge are people who act otherwise than they actually do—unreal people somehow 'there' to be translated into reality by God with all their unreal choices intact. And we might well wonder whether sense can be made of this supposition.

Is there really any such thing to know as, for example, what you would have done if you had not died as a child? If Molina is right, the answer is clearly 'Yes'. But the notion of there being any such thing to know is surely very questionable. Are people who lived for years, though they actually died as children, objects of knowledge in any sense? Given their actual circumstances, people might make different choices. And their lives might go different ways depending on the contexts in which they find themselves. But does it make sense to suppose that among the things to be known (whether by God or anything else) are the choices and careers of non-actual people capable of being brought into reality and different from their actual *alter egos* only by being non-existent?

So the Molinist response to the Sorabji-type argument is, perhaps, questionable. But do the other ways of countering it noted above fare any better? Many would reply that they do not. Take, to begin with, the line of thought defended by Craig. This, you might say, is plausible since we can know that-P only if P is indeed the case and since knowing that people will act freely depends on them acting freely. 'God foreknows that Brian will freely take a walk' *entails*, we might naturally think, that Brian will freely take a walk and cannot, therefore, threaten his ability to do so. If God can foreknow that Brian will freely take a walk, then Brian will walk freely. But can God indeed do this?

Then again, can we seriously suppose that God is outside time, as Boethius's approach to omniscience and human freedom requires us to do? Theistic personalists often hold that it does not, since, so they argue, (a) God is a person and (b) there cannot be a timeless person.[22] Others have maintained that a timeless God cannot live or act.[23] And yet other thinkers have suggested that to say that God is timeless commits us to the absurd position that different temporal events are not temporally different since they are all 'present' to God if God is timeless.[24] And even supposing that God and his knowledge are timeless, is there any less of a problem when it comes to omniscience and human freedom than is supposed by those who think that human freedom is incompatible with divine foreknowledge? According to some philosophers, the answer to this question is 'No'. For instance, Linda Zagzebski says:

> Surely the timeless realm is as ontologically determinate and fixed as the past. Perhaps it is inappropriate to say that timeless events are *now* necessary. Even so, we have no more reason to think that we can do anything about God's timeless knowledge than about God's past knowledge. If there is no use crying over spilt milk, there is no use crying over timelessly spilt milk either.[25]

Yet the question, of course, is: does God's knowledge (whether considered as foreknowledge or as timeless knowledge) prevent human beings from acting freely? We might reply that it does and therefore take authors like Craig and Boethius to be supposing what is impossible (that God foreknows, or timelessly knows, a human act as free). But 'X knows that-P' does not entail that P is a necessary truth. 'If someone knows something, it follows of necessity that what they know is the case. [But] it does not follow that it was *unavoidably* the case, any more than my seeing that you are sitting implies that you could not have avoided sitting down.'[26] So we might therefore wonder why it should be thought that 'X foreknows that-P' or 'X timelessly knows that-P' should entail that P is a necessary truth.

Craig certainly supposes that God can foreknow what I will freely do. But why should he not if it could not be true both that God foreknows that I will do such and such freely and if I do not do such and such freely? And why should Boethius have to concede that God's timeless knowledge cannot encompass people's free actions at various times? If God knows timelessly, then we can report his knowledge of what people do only by saying that God just knows them as acting as they do. But our knowing that people are acting as they do does not compel them when it comes to what they actually do. So, why should it be different if God is the knower?

Some would say that the right answer to this question is: 'God's knowledge differs from ours. Our knowledge that such and such is the case follows from the such and such being the case to start with. But God, unlike us, does not know by, so to speak, taking a look. God knows what is other than himself by making it to exist. Yet, if God makes acting people to exist, they cannot be really free. Their actions will be nothing but God's doing.' But this response clearly depends on assuming that something like Aquinas's approach to God's knowledge is correct. It depends on supposing that God knows what is other than himself by being its cause. And, so some would say, there can be no human freedom if that supposition is true and if God is indeed omniscient.

But is belief in human freedom truly incompatible with the belief that God is the cause of the existence of everything other than himself? This question brings us to a topic which naturally arises from the subject matter of Chapter 11, so for now I introduce it simply as something you might care to think about as you reflect on what the present chapter has been about. My purpose has been to help you to see something of how philosophers have tried to find their way when it comes to two claims commonly made about God. You can now consider whether any of their ways lead anywhere significant.

NOTES

1. Here, as earlier, I am abstracting from the implications of the Christian doctrine of the Incarnation, according to which God, as incarnate, can do a number of things possible only for human beings. Note, however, that this doctrine does not claim that God can do them *as God*.

2. P. T. Geach, *Providence and Evil* (Cambridge, 1977), pp. 15 f.

3. Hebrews 6: 13 and 6: 18.

4. I quote from John Cottingham, Robert Stoothoff, Dugald Murdoch, and Anthony Kenny (eds.), *The Philosophical Writings of Descartes*, vol. III (Cambridge, 1991), pp 23 and 103.

5. J. L. Mackie, 'Omnipotence', *Sophia* 1 (1962), p. 16.

6. Ibid.

7. Aquinas, *De Potentia*, I, 1, 7. I quote from the translation of the English Dominican Fathers (London, 1932).

8. Thomas Aquinas, *Summa Theologiae*, Ia, 25, 3.

9. Ibid.

10. Some would say that there is no 'right' and 'wrong' apart from human conventions or tastes. On their account, 'P acts wrongly' does not state anything that might be called a truth or a fact (see Chapter 12 below). At this point, however, for the sake of argument, I am working on the opposite assumption.

11. Anselm, *Proslogion*, ch. 7. I quote from Brian Davies and G. R. Evans (eds.), *Anselm of Canterbury: The Major Works* (Oxford, 1998), p. 90.

12. Cf. Nelson Pike, 'Omnipotence and God's Ability to Sin', *American Philosophical Quarterly* 6 (1969).

13. Anselm, *Proslogion*, ch. 7.

14. Aquinas, *Summa Theologiae*, Ia, 25, 3 ad., 2.

15. Cf. *Summa Theologiae*, Ia, 14, 1.

16. Again, I am abstracting from what Christians say in the light of the doctrine of the Incarnation. In terms of that, (a) Jesus of Nazareth could have known that it was raining where he was, and (b) it would follow that God knew what Jesus knew. In terms of the orthodox understanding of the Incarnation, however, it would not follow that Jesus, as God, knew something expressible by a sentence like 'It's raining here'.

17. Richard Sorabji, *Time, Creation and the Continuum* (London, 1983), p. 255.

18. A similar line of argument can be found in, for example Jonathan Edwards, *Freedom of the Will* (1754), Section 12. For a more recent version of the same line of thinking, see Nelson Pike, 'Divine Omniscience and Voluntary Action', *The Philosophical Review* 74 (1965). An edited extract of Pike's article appears in Brian Davies (ed.), *Philosophy of Religion: A Guide and Anthology* (Oxford, 2000).

19. For recent examples, see Clark Pinnock, Richard Rice, John Sanders, William Hasker, and David Basinger, *The Openness of God: A Biblical Challenge to the Traditional Understanding of God* (Downers Grove, IL, 1994).

20. William Lane Craig, *The Only Wise God* (Grand Rapids, MI, 1987), p. 74.

21. For earlier writers offering arguments akin to Craig's, see St Augustine, *De Libero Arbitrio*, III, 3, and St Anselm, *De Concordia*, 1–3.

22. Cf. J. R. Lucas, *A Treatise on Time and Space* (London, 1973), p. 200. Cf. also Nelson Pike, *God and Timelessness* (London, 1970), ch. 7.

23. Cf. Pike, *God and Timelessness*, pp. 106 ff.

24. Cf. Anthony Kenny, *The God of the Philosophers* (Oxford, 1979), pp. 38 ff.

25. Linda Zagzebski, 'Recent Work on Divine Foreknowledge and Free Will', in Robert Kane (ed.), *The Oxford Handbook of Free Will* (Oxford, 2002), p. 52.

26. Gerard J. Hughes, 'Omniscience', in Brian Davies (ed.), *Philosophy of Religion: A Guide to the Subject* (London, 1998), p. 89.

FURTHER READING

Discussions of divine omnipotence can be found in a number of books devoted to the nature of God in general. Ones especially worth turning to are: Stephen T. David, *Logic and the Nature of God* (London and Basingstoke, 1983); Richard Gale, *On the Nature and Existence of God* (New York and Cambridge, 1991); Gerard J. Hughes, *The Nature of God* (London and New York, 1995); Anthony Kenny, *The God of the Philosophers* (Oxford, 1979); Thomas V. Morris, *Our Idea of God* (Notre Dame, IN, and London, 1991); Ronald H. Nash, *The Concept of God* (Grand Rapids, MI, 1983); Katherin A. Rogers, *Perfect Being Theology* (Edinburgh, 2000); Richard Swinburne, *The Coherence of Theism* (rev. edn., Oxford, 1993); and Edward R. Wierenga, *The Nature of God* (Ithaca, NY, and London, 1989).

A full-scale study of medieval views on omnipotence is Lawrence Moonan, *Divine Power* (Oxford, 1994). For Aquinas on omnipotence, see *Summa Theologiae*, Ia, 25. For a helpful book-length treatment of omnipotence with an eye on contemporary authors, see G. van den Brink, *Almighty God: A Study of the Doctrine of Divine Omnipotence* (Kampen, 1993).

Significant articles on divine omnipotence include: Harry H. Frankfurt, 'The Logic of Omnipotence', *The Philosophical Review* 74 (1964); Peter Geach, 'Omnipotence', *Philosophy* 48 (1973); J. L. Mackie, 'Omnipotence', *Sophia* 1 (1962); George I. Mavrodes, 'Some Puzzles Concerning Omnipotence', *Philosophical Review* 72 (1963); and Thomas P. Flint and Alfred J. Freddoso, 'Maximal Power', in Alfred J. Freddoso (ed.), *The Existence and Nature of God* (Notre Dame, IN, 1983).

Material relevant to the topic of divine omniscience can be found in all the volumes listed in the first paragraph above. Also see George J. Mavrodes, 'Omniscience', in Philip L. Quinn and Charles Taliaferro (eds.), *A Companion to the Philosophy of Religion* (Oxford, 1997). For a discussion of God's knowledge which pays special attention to the notion of the future, see P. T. Geach, *Providence and Evil* (Cambridge, 1977).

Linda Zagzebski provides a brief overview of contemporary treatments of omniscience and human freedom in 'Recent Work on Divine Foreknowledge and Free Will', in Robert Kane (ed.), *The Oxford Handbook of Free Will* (Oxford, 2002). For solid book-length studies, see William Lane Craig, *The Only Wise God* (Grand Rapids, MI, 1987); Jonathan L. Kvanig, *The Possibility of an All-Knowing God* (London, 1986); John C. Moskop, *Divine Omniscience and Human Freedom* (Macon, GA, 1984); Robert Young, *Freedom, Responsibility and God* (London, 1975); and Linda Zagzebski, *The Dilemma of Freedom and Foreknowledge* (New York, 1991). For a trenchant defence of Molina on God's knowledge, see Thomas P. Flint, *Divine Providence* (Ithaca, NY, 1998). For a short introduction to Molina, see Thomas P. Flint, 'Two Accounts of Providence', in Thomas V. Morris (ed.), *Divine and Human Action* (Ithaca, NY, and London, 1988).

For a brief account of Aquinas on knowledge in general and on God's knowledge in particular, see Brian Davies, *The Thought of Thomas Aquinas* (Oxford, 1992), ch. 7. See also Scott MacDonald, 'Theory of Knowledge', in Norman Kretzmann and Eleonore Stump (eds.), *The Cambridge Companion to Aquinas* (Cambridge, 1993). For a detailed exposition of Aquinas on God's knowledge, see Vivian Boland, *Ideas in God According to Saint Thomas Aquinas* (Leiden, New York, and Koln, 1996). For an introduction to Boethius which includes discussion of Boethius on divine knowledge, see Edmund Reiss, *Boethius* (Boston, 1982). For more detailed treatments, see Henry Chadwick, *Boethius: The Consolations of Music, Logic, Theology, and Philosophy* (Oxford, 1981) and John Marenbon, *Boethius* (Oxford, 2003).

Among the many published articles on divine knowledge published in recent years, the following stand out as particularly worthy of note: Hector Neri Castaneda, 'Omniscience and Indexical Reference', *Journal of Philosophy* 64 (1967); Anthony Kenny, 'Divine Foreknowledge and Human Freedom', in Anthony Kenny (ed.), *Aquinas: A Collection of Critical Essays* (London, 1969); Norman Kretzmann, 'Omniscience and Immutability', *Journal of Philosophy* 63 (1966); Alvin Plantinga, 'On Ockham's Way Out', *Faith and Philosophy* (1986); and A. N. Prior, 'The Formalities of Omniscience', in id., *Papers on Time and Tense* (Oxford, 1968).

The topic of God's timelessness is clearly important when it comes to discussions of divine omniscience. Space prevents me from discussing it at length in this book, but for treatments of it, see Paul Helm, *Eternal God* (Oxford, 1988); Brian Leftow, *Time and Eternity* (Ithaca, NY, 1991); Alan G. Padgett, *God, Eternity and the Nature of Time* (London, 1992); Nelson Pike, *God and Timelessness* (London, 1970); and John C. Yates, *The Timelessness of God* (New York and London, 1990).

QUESTIONS FOR DISCUSSION

1 'God cannot φ.' Are there any plausible substitutes for 'φ' here which would generate a true proposition? If there are, does it make sense to call God omnipotent?

2 'God could have arranged for logical truths to have been false.' Comment on this suggestion. If you think it wrong, explain why. If you think it right, explain why.

3 'If it can be, then God can make it to be.' What might it mean to say this? And is the statement true?

4 Can God do wrong? If so, how? If not, why not? If God cannot do wrong, can he be omnipotent?

5 Is there any good philosophical reason for ascribing knowledge to God?

6 'God cannot know F'/'God cannot know that-P.' Are there any plausible substitutes for 'F' and 'P' here which would generate a true proposition? If there are, does it make sense to call God omniscient?

7 'God knows the future.' Is this statement true? If so, why? If not, why not?

8 How might God know? Could God's knowledge seriously resemble ours? If so, how? If not, does the claim that God knows make sense?

9 Suppose that I am a theistic personalist. And consider the question 'How can God have knowledge of human free actions?' Am I in a better position to answer this question than is the classical theist? If so, why? If not, why not?

10 Can people know what is going to happen? If so, how? Does your answer to this question throw any light on the topic of God's knowledge of the future?

10

GOD AND EVIL

....

In beauty competitions contestants are asked questions like 'What is your ambition?' or 'What would you most like to do?' And the answers which the contestants give are sometimes utterly ridiculous. They say things like 'My ambition is to abolish world hunger' or 'I would like to make everyone happy'. But no single person can abolish world hunger or make everyone happy. Our abilities are limited. Candidates for the title 'Miss United Kingdom' or 'Miss America' might mean well. But they are talking twaddle if they express their desires in terms like those quoted above. They need not, of course, worry about this fact since their chances of winning the titles they covet do not depend in the slightest on what they have to say.

But suppose that you were omnipotent and omniscient. How might *you* express your ambitions or desires? Unlike contestants in a beauty competition, it would not seem obviously absurd for you to say 'My ambition is to abolish world hunger' or 'I would like to make everyone happy'. If you were omnipotent, what could stop you from feeding the hungry and gratifying the miserable? 'Ignorance of their plight could thwart me', you might reply. But could it do so if you were omniscient as well as omnipotent?

With questions such as these, we come to one of the most discussed topics in philosophy of religion. God is supposed to be omnipotent and omniscient. He is also supposed to be at least as good as a decent human being. Yet, if God is all these things, what are we to make of the fact that the world seems to be full of what is bad or even evil? You might say: 'Even badness and evil have their proper place in God's world'. And theists often do say that. But are they right to do so? Should they not rather be thinking that badness and evil somehow call their belief in God into question? Many philosophers have argued that the right answer to the last question here is 'Yes'. They have suggested that theists face a 'problem of evil' which undermines their position as theists.

But what is the problem supposed to be? According to some philosophers, it consists in the fact that we cannot consistently believe in the reality of evil and the reality of God. According to others, it consists in the fact that badness or evil is strong evidence against the existence of God.

God, Evil, and Consistency

In a famous article called 'Evil and Omnipotence', J. L. Mackie argues that it is indeed inconsistent to believe both in the reality of evil and the reality of God. Mackie summarizes his position as follows:

> In its simplest form the problem is this: God is omnipotent; God is wholly good; and yet evil exists. There seems to be some contradiction between these three propositions, so that if any two of them were true the third would be false. But at the same time all three are essential parts of most theological positions: the theologian, it seems, at once *must* adhere and *cannot consistently adhere* to all three.[1]

The contradiction, says Mackie, 'does not arise immediately; to show it we need some additional premises, or perhaps some quasi-logical rules connecting the terms "good", "evil", and "omnipotent" '.[2] Yet we can, Mackie thinks, supply them: 'These additional principles are that good is opposed to evil, in such a way that a good thing always eliminates evil as far as it can, and that there are no limits to what an omnipotent thing can do.'[3] From these principles, says Mackie, 'it follows that a good omnipotent thing eliminates evil completely, and then the propositions that a good omnipotent thing exists, and that evil exists, are incompatible'.[4] In 'Evil and Omnipotence' Mackie notes ways in which theists have tried to explain how evil can be reconciled with belief in a good and omnipotent God. But he argues that these explanations are all unconvincing.[5]

God, Evil, and Evidence

After the publication of 'Evil and Omnipotence', Mackie modified his position. In *The Miracle of Theism*, he concedes that we cannot take 'the problem of evil as a conclusive disproof of traditional theism'.[6] But, he adds, the reality of evil still leaves us with 'a strong presumption that theism cannot be made coherent without a serious change in at least one of its central doctrines'.[7] Why? Because, Mackie argues, evil is strong evidence against God's existence. And this line of thinking, sometimes called 'the evidentialist argument from evil', has been much pressed by many philosophers: by William Rowe, for example, in a paper called 'The Problem of Evil and Some Varieties of Atheism'.[8]

Rowe's question here is 'Can God be justified in permitting the evil which occurs in our world?' And his answer is 'No':

> Taking human and animal suffering as a clear instance of evil which occurs with great frequency in our world, the argument for atheism based on evil can be stated as follows:
>
>
>
> 1 There exist instances of intense suffering which an omnipotent, omniscient being could have prevented without thereby losing some greater good or permitting some evil equally bad or worse.
>
> 2 An omniscient, wholly good being would prevent the occurrence of any intense suffering it could, unless it could not do so without thereby losing some greater good or permitting some evil equally bad or worse.
>
> 3 There does not exist an omnipotent, omniscient, wholly good being.[9]

Rowe presumes this argument to be logically valid. So his main concern is to argue for the truth of the first and second premises.

The second premise, says Rowe, 'seems to express a belief that accords with our basic moral principles, principles shared by both theists and non-theists'.[10] The really controversial premise for Rowe, therefore, is the first. And he admits that it could be false. Try to imagine an instance of pointless suffering. Although you may not be able to see that it serves a good which cannot be obtained without it, Rowe agrees that there might be one. And yet, he suggests, we have reason to suppose that there are instances of pointless suffering even if we cannot prove so. 'In the light of our experience and knowledge of the variety and scale of human and animal suffering in our world', says Rowe, 'the idea that none of this suffering could have been prevented by an omnipotent being without thereby losing a greater good or permitting an evil at least as bad seems an extraordinarily absurd idea, quite beyond our belief.'[11] And hence, Rowe concludes, 'it does seem that we have *rational support* for atheism, that it is reasonable to believe that the theistic God does not exist'.[12]

Theistic Responses to 'The Problem of Evil'

How have theists responded to the charge that evil is proof of, or at least good evidence for, the non-existence of God? They have mostly done so by embracing one or more of the following lines of argument.[13]

(a) The 'We Know that God Exists' argument

Suppose I know that something is the case. But suppose you suggest that it cannot be the case or that there is evidence which ought to lead me to conclude that it is not the case. Should I agree with you? Obviously not. If I know that P is true, then I am entitled to reject claims to the effect that P is impossible or that there is evidence which shows that it is unlikely to be true. If, for example, I know that it often rains in Britain, I should be right to assume that something must be wrong with attempts to show that frequent rain in Britain is impossible or unlikely in the light of some supposed evidence or other.

Yet, what if I know that both God and evil are real? Then I should be rationally justified in supposing that evil does not render God's existence impossible. I should also be justified in supposing that no evidence renders God's existence unlikely. And that is how many theists have argued. 'We know that God exists and that evil exists', they say. And, they add, 'we are therefore entitled to suppose that evil does not render God's existence either impossible or unlikely'.

(b) Means and Ends Arguments

You would probably think me bad if I cut off someone's foot just for the fun of it. But not if I were a doctor who amputated as the only way to save someone with gangrene. It is not bad to aim for something regrettable, something bad, if we are aiming for a good which we ought to aim at (or are justified in aiming at) which cannot be otherwise achieved. And this line of thinking constitutes the thrust of what I am now calling 'Means and Ends Arguments'. These suggest that evil neither disproves God's existence nor shows it to be unlikely, since evil is permitted by God with a good end in view.

The most famous of such arguments is the so-called 'Free-Will Defence', which goes as follows:

1. Much evil is the result of what people freely choose to do.

2. It is good that there should be a world with agents able to act freely.

3. Even an omnipotent God cannot ensure that free agents act well (for, if they are free, what they do is up to them).

4. So much evil is explicable in terms of God justifiably putting up with the consequences of his willing a great good.

According to the Free Will Defence, evils perpetrated by people do not count against God's existence. On the contrary, say exponents of the Defence, such evils are only the regrettable outcome of God's good will to create a world in which agents control their own behaviour.

Yet, what about that which is bad but is not the product of free human agency? Philosophers have also offered means-ends arguments in response to this question. A notable example is Richard Swinburne. According to him, it is good that people have serious moral choice to harm or to help each other (Swinburne endorses the Free Will Defence). Yet, he argues, choice like this depends on there being naturally occurring pain and suffering. He writes:

> If men are to have knowledge of the evil which will result from their actions or negligence, laws of nature must operate regularly; and that means that there will be what I may call 'victims of the system' . . . *If* men are to have the opportunity to bring about serious evils for themselves or others by actions or negligence, or to prevent their occurrence, and if all knowledge of the future is obtained by normal induction, that is by induction from patterns of similar events in the past—then there must be serious natural evils occurring to man or animals.[14]

One might say that there is too much naturally occurring evil. But Swinburne would disagree. 'The fewer natural evils a God provides', he suggests, 'the less opportunity he provides for man to exercise responsibility.'[15] To say that there is 'too much' naturally occurring evil, says Swinburne, is to suggest that 'a God should make a toy-world, a world where things matter, but not very much; where we can choose and our choices can make a small difference, but the real choices remain God's'.[16] Swinburne considers the possibility of God giving us knowledge to do good and evil by informing us of the way things are and of what we can do in the light of this (e.g. by giving us verbal information). According to Swinburne, however:

> A world in which God gave men verbal knowledge of the consequences of their actions would not be a world in which men had a significant choice of destiny, of what to make of themselves and the world. God would be far too close for them to be able to work things out for themselves. If God is to give man knowledge while at the same time allowing him a genuine choice of destiny, it must be normal inductive knowledge.[17]

A line of thinking similar to Swinburne's can be found in John Hick's book *Evil and the God of Love* (a modern classic on the topic of God and evil).[18] Hick also employs the Free Will Defence. But he elaborates on it using a line of thought derived from St Irenaeus of Lyon (*c*.140–*c*.202). He writes:

> Let us suppose that the infinite personal God creates finite persons to share in the life which He imparts to them. If He creates them in his immediate presence, so that they cannot fail to be conscious from the first of the infinite divine being and glory, goodness and love, wisdom, power and knowledge in whose presence they are, they will have no creaturely independence in relation to their Maker. They will not be able to *choose* to worship God, or to turn to Him freely as valuing spirits responding to infinite Value. In order, then, to give them the freedom to come to Him, God ... causes them to come into a situation in which He is not immediately and overwhelmingly evident to them. Accordingly they come to self-consciousness as parts of a universe which has its own autonomous structures and 'laws' ... A world without problems, difficulties, perils, and hardships would be morally static. For moral and spiritual growth comes through response to challenges; and in a paradise there would be no challenges.[19]

'No pain, no gain', say athletes. And this is basically Hick's position when it comes to God and evil. For him, much of the evil we encounter provides us with the chance to improve. Considered as such, he thinks, it does not show that God cannot, or probably does not, exist.

(c) The unreality of evil argument

But does evil exist? Another approach to the problem of evil, one to be found in, for example, the writings of Aquinas, suggests that, in a sense, evil does not exist since it is only an absence or privation of good (*privatio boni*). According to Aquinas, what makes suffering or wickedness bad is the fact that it always amounts to a *lack* of some kind. On his account, 'evil' or 'badness' is not the name of some independently existing individual, like you or me. Nor is it the name of a positive quality or attribute. Rather, it is a word we use to signify a gap between what *is actually there* and what *could and should be* there but *is not*. There can be people but not, so Aquinas thinks, 'baddities' (things whose nature is captured simply by saying that they are bad).[20] There are wooden boxes and wooden chairs. But, so Aquinas would say, while 'wooden' signifies a positive property shareable by different things, 'evil' and 'bad' do not. 'Evil', says Aquinas, 'cannot signify a certain existing being, or a real shaping or positive kind of thing. Consequently, we are left to infer that it signifies a certain absence of a good.'[21] Just as to say 'There is nothing here' is not to say of *something* that *it* is here, so, in Aquinas's view, to say that *there is* evil is not to say that there is *any real individual or any positive quality*.[22]

Aquinas regards this conclusion as significant with respect to the topic of God and evil. For he takes it to imply that God does not cause evil, considered as a substance or positive quality. Aquinas holds that God causes only the being of all that can properly be thought of as existing (i.e. actual individual things with all their positive properties). On his account, therefore, evil cannot be thought of as caused (creatively) by God. It is, he thinks, real enough (in the sense that it would be mad to say that nothing is bad or defective or sinful). But evil, Aquinas argues, is not created. Its 'reality', he says, is always a case of something missing. And it provides no positive grounds for supposing that the existence of God is impossible or improbable.

(d) The 'We Can't See All the Picture' argument

Another theistic line on God and evil focuses on the limits of human understanding. Mackie and Rowe assume that there are or have been evils that God could have no justification for permitting. But how can they be sure of this? They may say that they cannot see what the justification is. But why should that be taken to show that there is no justification. 'I can't see why' does not entail that there is no why. And that is the basic idea of what we might dub the 'We Can't See All the Picture' argument.

Shakespeare's Hamlet told Horatio that 'There are more things in heaven and earth than are dreamt of in your philosophy'. The 'We Can't See All the Picture' argument suggests that, although we may find it *hard* to see why there is evil in a world made by God, there *might* be a reason. More precisely, defenders of the argument hold, the evil we encounter could be something that God allows or brings about while aiming at a good end which cannot be reached without it (an end which justifies the means). God has his reasons, even if we cannot understand them.

A prominent contemporary defender of the 'We Can't See All the Picture' argument is William Alston. Hamlet's words to Horatio, says Alston, hit the nail on the head since 'they point to the fact that our cognitions of the world, obtained by filtering raw data through such conceptual screens as we have available for the nonce, acquaint us with only some indeterminable fraction of what there is to be known'.[23] We cannot, thinks Alston, be sure that past and present evils are not, in fact, parts of a great and good plan of God.

> The fact that we cannot see what sufficient justifying reason an omniscient, omnipotent being might have for doing something [does not provide] strong support for the supposition that no such reason is available for that being . . . Being unable to estimate the extent to which what we can discern exhausts the possibilities, we are in no position to suppose that our inability to find a justifying divine reason is a sufficient ground for supposing that there is none.[24]

(e) The 'We Cannot Judge God in Human Terms' argument

As we have seen, Mackie's case against God depends on his claim that 'a good thing always eliminates evil as far as it can'. But what can Mackie mean by this assertion? He obviously does not mean that, if X is a good thing, then X always eliminates evil. He is not, for instance, saying that a good desk or a good chair always eliminates evil. And rightly so. The notion of being a good desk, or being a good chair, carries no expectations when it comes to the elimination of evil. Mackie says that a good thing always eliminates evil *as far as it can*. So, when he refers to 'a good thing', he must be thinking of an agent with knowledge and an ability to choose between alternatives. But what sort of agent with knowledge and the ability to choose between alternatives does Mackie have in mind?

He seems to be thinking that, if God is good, then God is *morally* good (i.e., good by the standards by which we evaluate the goodness of people). And supporters of the evidentialist argument seem to be thinking along the same lines. Rowe says that a good God would not countenance the evils that exist. But what does he mean by 'good' in the phrase 'a good God'? He also appears to mean 'a God who is morally good'. But should we suppose that '——is good', when predicated of God, has to mean what it does when predicated of agents (like human beings) who can be thought to be morally good or morally bad? The 'We Cannot Judge God in Human Terms' argument says that the right answer to this question is 'No'. According to this argument, standards for evaluating things other than God cannot be applied to God. In particular, so defenders of the argument tend to say, we should not suppose that God is good or bad in accordance with the criteria we use to evaluate people morally. We might think that a morally well-behaved individual could not be responsible for the world. We might also think that the world is proof or evidence against the supposition that it comes to be from anything morally well behaved. But defenders of the 'We Cannot Judge God in Human Terms' argument suggest that we should not think of God either as a morally well-behaved individual or as a morally badly behaved individual. Or, as Anthony Kenny puts it:

> Morality presupposes a moral community: and a moral community must be of beings with a common language, roughly equal powers, and roughly similar needs, desires and interests. God can no more be part of a moral community with them than he can be part of a political community with them. As Aristotle said, we cannot attribute moral virtues to divinity: the praise would be vulgar. Equally, moral blame would be laughable.[25]

Does Evil Disprove God's Existence or Render it Unlikely?

What should we make of the various positions noted above? Should we conclude that evil shows that there *could be* no God or that there *probably* is no God? Should we seek to respond to authors like Mackie and Rowe by endorsing one or more of the views summarized above? I cannot here deal with these questions in the detail they deserve, but I can at least draw your attention to some responses to them. And to start with, perhaps I can say something about Mackie's charge of contradiction.

(a) God, evil, and contradiction

Mackie is right to say that it is not manifestly contradictory to assert that evil exists and that God is omnipotent, omniscient, and good. But is he right to suggest that a contradiction arises on the supposition that 'a good thing always eliminates evil as far as it can, and that there are no limits to what an omnipotent thing can do'? Even if we concede Mackie's rough account of omnipotence, might not something good choose not to eliminate (or choose not to prevent) an evil which it could eliminate (or prevent) because of a good which it knows (or has reason to believe) will arise from it? Suppose that a parent knows that some suffering, which she could spare her child, would in fact help the child to develop in some way. Would such a parent be necessarily bad if she allowed the child to suffer? Not obviously. In that case, however, maybe a 'good thing' does not always eliminate evil as far as it can. Mackie might say that human parents are not omnipotent and that a good, omnipotent 'thing' just could not countenance any evil that it could eliminate or prevent. It remains, however, that in the parent example we have a case of one who is able to eliminate or prevent an evil. And if we think that one (even a non-omnipotent one) who declines to exercise this ability might not be necessarily bad, then Mackie's chief reason for pressing his charge of contradiction is not good enough to sustain that charge.

But suppose that a 'good thing' does always eliminate evil as far as it can. Does this conclusion, coupled with the view that God is omnipotent and omniscient, and granted the existence of some evil, entail that there could not be a God? Here what I have called the 'We Know that God Exists' argument becomes relevant. For, if we have grounds to claim that we know that there is a good, omnipotent, God, and if we also have grounds to claim that we know there is evil, then (as far as reason goes) we are entitled to say that Mackie's case against theism (or any like it) is just mistaken. If we know that p, q, and r are true, then there has to be something wrong with arguments to the effect that they cannot all be true.

What does Mackie have to say with respect to this point? Nothing. His discussion of God and evil takes no account whatsoever of reasons people have given for supposing that God exists.[26] As such, then, it is clearly inadequate. Someone might think that they have hit on a proof that a set of propositions is inconsistent. But reason to think that each proposition in the set is true is reason to think that the set as a whole is consistent. When it comes to discussion of God and evil, this line of thinking suggests that those who hold that 'God exists and evil exists' is contradictory should look at reasons why people have come to accept this proposition and should not try to settle things without reference to these reasons.

We might also suggest that they should allow for the unknown—the basic line of thought in the 'We Can't See All the Picture' argument. In his attack on theism, Mackie is insisting that there are evils of which we cannot make sense if we also suppose that there is a good, omnipotent, and omniscient God. One way of rebutting Mackie's claim would be to point to evils of which sense can be made if we are given more information. But suppose we lack such information? We might conclude that we lack it not only (a) because it is not there but also (b) because we do not know all that there is to be known. Is it unreasonable to opt for (b) here? To say that we do not know all that there is to be known is hardly unreasonable. In that case, however, it is not unreasonable to suggest that we might not know why it is consistent to assert both that evil exists and that there is an omnipotent, omniscient, and good God.

If that is true, however, then the 'We Can't See All the Picture' argument is a decent response to those who argue along Mackie's lines. For that matter, it is a fitting response to those who claim that there is evidence sufficient to warrant the conclusion that God probably does not exist. They are suggesting that God permits more evil than a good, omnipotent, and omniscient God should permit. And they therefore conclude that there is probably no good, omnipotent, omniscient God. But what seems to us to be evidence of God's non-existence might appear in a different light given information not yet available to us. Opponents of theism have often insisted that there are evils which could never be reconciled with belief in God's existence. But how can such people know that information not presently available to us could not reasonably lead them to revise their view? 'Because', they might reply, 'there is decisive evidence to the contrary.' But such 'evidence' has to be nothing but a small part of what, if theists are right, is a very big picture indeed, one encompassing the entire history of the created order.

(b) Evil as evidence against the existence of God

In *The Miracle of Theism*, Mackie says that we cannot 'take the problem of evil as a conclusive disproof of traditional theism' since 'there is some flexibility in its doctrines, and in particular in the additional premises needed to make the problem explicit'.[27] Here Mackie is especially alluding to the suggestion that God permits some evil because of a good which could not arise without it. We might, Mackie concedes, plausibly argue that a good, omnipotent, and omniscient God could permit evil for a good reason.[28] But he also maintains that there is a difference between 'absorbed' and 'unabsorbed' evil:

> Some bit of suffering which is actually the object of kindness or sympathy whose goodness outweighs the badness of that suffering itself will be an absorbed evil, as will be miseries or injustices that are in fact progressively overcome by a struggle whose nobility is a higher good which outweighs the evils without which it could not have occurred.[29]

Can theists maintain that the only evils that occur in the world are absorbed evils? Having modified his stance in 'Evil and Omnipotence', Mackie, in *The Miracle of Theism*, suggests that the answer to this question is 'No' (which seems to be Rowe's position as outlined above).

As we have seen, however, theists have suggested that God's world contains (or might contain) what Mackie refers to as 'absorbed evils'. Exponents of the Free Will Defence seem to be doing just that, as do philosophers like Swinburne and Hick. So, could it be that their view of things successfully counters Mackie's scepticism when it comes to absorbed evils?

(c) The Free Will Defence

The Free Will Defence holds that a world of free agents is better than a world of automata. Most people would accept this premise. And it is true that we normally think well of those who allow their fellow human beings a measure of autonomy and freedom. The oppressive parent and the tyrannical lover, the dictator and the bully, tend to be regarded as less than admirable (in most western societies, anyway). So, if God is really good, can he not be expected to allow his creatures freedom? And can he not be expected to allow them to act as they choose even though they choose to act badly?

Mackie suggests that God could have made a world containing free agents who always act well and that the non-existence of God follows from the fact that actual free agents have failed to act well. He writes:

> If there is no logical impossibility in a man's freely choosing the good on one, or on several occasions, there cannot be a logical impossibility in his freely choosing the good on every occasion. God was not, then, faced with a choice between making innocent automata and making beings who, in acting freely, would sometimes go wrong: there was open to him the obviously better possibility of making beings who would act freely but always go right. Clearly, his failure to avail himself of this possibility is inconsistent with his being both omnipotent and wholly good.[30]

Yet Mackie is surely moving too quickly here. Let us agree that people might always behave well. Can God ensure that they do so? Is Mackie not requiring that God should coerce people to act freely? And is not that an impossible demand? Many theists would say that it is. An example is Alvin Plantinga:

> Of course, it is up to God whether to create free creatures at all; but if he aims to produce moral good, then he must create significantly free creatures upon whose cooperation he must depend. Thus is the power of an omnipotent God limited by the freedom he confers upon his creatures.[31]

Plantinga's position is echoed by many philosophers of religion.[32] And it is obviously correct if an action cannot be free while also being determined by God. Some philosophers (usually referred to as 'compatibilists') have argued that an action can be free even if it is also determined (even if it is the result of preceding causes which render it inevitable or necessary).[33] But to say that an action is 'determined' sounds like saying that it is not free. So we might here side with Plantinga. If Mackie is suggesting that God should have determined people's actions so that they were always good ones, then, we might think, he is making an unreasonable demand.

But is it right to say that free human actions are not caused by God? In *The Miracle of Theism*, Mackie suggests that it is wrong to say this if God is omnipotent and omniscient. If God is both omnipotent and omniscient, then, according to Mackie, God cannot fail to be responsible for what happens in the world. We might say that history includes events which God merely *allows* or *permits*. Yet, Mackie argues, this is an odd way to speak. Our everyday distinction between (a) bringing something about and (b) allowing or permitting it is an acknowledgement of the fact that one can knowingly exert a positive effort on one's environment or just refuse to do so (or just not do so). But the distinction between bringing about and allowing or permitting becomes blurred, says Mackie, the more powerful one is and the more one knows what is going on in the world. It seems, he argues, 'that as power and knowledge increase without limit', our everyday distinction between bringing something about and allowing or permitting it 'fades out, and for a being with unlimited power and unlimited vision it would not hold at all'.[34] And with this conclusion in mind, Mackie suggests (a) that 'omnipotence and omniscience together entail omnificence: God does everything', and (b) that the Free Will Defence 'cannot detach evil from God unless it assumes that the freedom conferred on men is such that God *cannot* (not merely does not) control their choosing'.[35]

Many theists would reply to Mackie here by accepting that God cannot control people's choosings. Plantinga is a case in point. But can theists deny that Mackie is right? Can they deny that, in some serious sense, God, indeed, does everything? It depends, of course, on what kind of theist one is. But what Mackie is driving at certainly squares with a lot that has been maintained by classical theists. For them, everything that exists (apart from God) owes its existence to God as the Creator *ex nihilo*. For them, God is the reason why there is a world instead of there being nothing. So classical theists have concluded that God must be the creative cause even of human free actions. Why? Simply because they exist. For classical theists, there can be no such thing as being independent of God. For them, human freedom is as creaturely a thing as Mount Everest. So it is, and in the same sense, caused to be by God. As Aquinas puts it:

> Just as God not only gave being to things when they first began, but is also—as the conserving cause of being—the cause of their being as long as they last . . . so he not only gave things their operative powers when they were first created, but is also the cause of these in things. Hence if this divine influence stopped, every operation would stop. Every operation, therefore, of anything is traced back to him as its cause.[36]

In terms of Aquinas's theism, the Free Will Defence is wholly misguided. And Aquinas has a point. If we think that God brings about the existence, and the continued existence, of everything other than himself, then, as Aquinas also observes, it must be that God 'causes everything's activity inasmuch as he gives it the power to act, maintains it in existence, applies it to its activity, and inasmuch as it is by his power that every other power acts'.[37] And if all that is so, then the Free Will Defence is a failure.

But does it follow from this that there is no such thing as human freedom? Before leaving the Free Will Defence, I should note that many classical theists would say that this conclusion does not follow at all. Why? Because, so they typically argue, God's causality is not of a kind to threaten human freedom.

Aquinas argues in this way. People, he says, sometimes choose freely. Aquinas thinks that people's actions (or refusals to act) proceed from *them* and not from other things in the world working *on* them.[38] On Aquinas's account, however, God is not something in the world, and his (creatively) making something to be does not *interfere* with it in any way. So he suggests that there is no absurdity in the conclusion that God can produce a person who acts freely in various ways. Unlike some theistic personalists, Aquinas finds it unthinkable that any created event should come to pass without God making it to be just what it actually is. But Aquinas does not therefore conclude that God is a threat to human freedom. On the contrary, he says, God is its necessary condition since

God accounts for there being free human creatures.[39] In terms of this account, God is no external agent able to interfere with human freedom by acting on it coercively from outside. Rather, God is the cause of all that is real as both free created agents and non-free created agents exist and operate. Or, in Aquinas's words:

> Free decision spells self-determination because people, by their free decisions, move themselves to action. Freedom does not require that a thing is its own first cause, just as in order to be the cause of something else a thing does not have to be its first cause. God is the first cause on which both natural and free agents depend. And, just as his initiative does not prevent natural causes from being natural, so it does not prevent voluntary action from being voluntary, but, rather, makes it be precisely this. For God works in each according to its nature.[40]

(d) Swinburne and Hick

If Aquinas is right here, then the Free Will Defence is broken-backed. But let us suppose that he is wrong and that the Free Will Defence plausibly suggests how some evil might be reconciled with belief in God's omnipotence, omniscience, and goodness. Can we now develop the defence so as to suggest that other kinds of evil cohere with the good of human freedom? Can we do so, for example, along the lines suggested by Swinburne and Hick?

Their arguments clearly have merit. Swinburne, for instance, is right to say that we come to know the good and harm we can do because of evils which naturally occur. And Hick is surely right to say that naturally occurring evils can provide us with the chance to rise above circumstances and to exhibit traditional human virtues like courage and justice. But do Swinburne and Hick show that naturally occurring evil is needed for the good exercise of human freedom which they think of as what God is aiming at in creating (or permitting) the natural evils rampant in our world?

Swinburne says that God could not give us knowledge of what we can significantly do for good or ill without the occurrence of naturally occurring evil. But is it beyond omnipotence to make people who are born with the recognition that good things can happen from doing *this* and bad things from doing *that*. As I noted in Chapter 9, we do not depend on empirical research in order to know that, for example, 2 + 2 = 4. So might not God have been able to arrange for our knowledge of our moral options to be similarly independent of empirical experience? As we have seen, Swinburne considers the possibility of God making our options clear to us by informing us about them directly. And he thinks that our freedom would be removed if God were to do this. But is Swinburne right here? He believes that people who are certain of God's existence would be thereby prevented from engaging in significant free choices. But why should being convinced of God's reality render one unable to act freely in significant ways?

In the light of what we have seen him saying, Hick might reply that human maturity is something that needs to be worked at in the face of adversity. And, he might add, God's allowing us to mature in the face of adversity 'absorbs' the adversity's evil. But there are problems with this view too. For do the character traits valued by Hick require the existence of evil? Perhaps not. As Stanley Kane observes:

> Courage and fortitude, for instance, could manifest themselves as the persistence, steadfastness, and perseverance it takes to accomplish well any difficult or demanding long-range task—the writing of a doctoral dissertation, for example, or training for and competing in the Olympic Games . . . It is hard to see why a man or a woman cannot develop just as much patience, fortitude and strength of character in helping his or her spouse complete a doctoral dissertation as in caring for a sick child through a long and serious illness. It is hard to see why people cannot learn just as much of the spirit of help and cooperation by teaming together to win an athletic championship as by coming together to rescue a town levelled by a tornado or inundated by a flood.[41]

As Kane also notes, Hick's approach to God and evil has a general absurdity built into it. Hick suggests that God is good because he allows evil for what, in the end, is a very great good. But what is this good? For Hick, it is the state in which people have become matured through tribulation. It is heaven, where there is no evil.[42] But this leaves Hick telling us that evil falls within the scheme of a good God since it leads to a state in which people have no chance to display what Hick chiefly values—virtues acquired in the face of adversity. What Hick takes to be God's aim in creating our world seems to be a state in which people are bereft of what Hick believes to be the good which justifies the world's evils. And if that is so, we might wonder whether Hick's position makes any sense at all. For, as Eleonore Stump writes:

> On Hick's view, all the evils in the world are justified as a means of developing traits of character which it will be impossible to maintain thereafter in heaven, the reward for having developed such character traits. Why should we value a process which results in a character which cannot then be manifested? And if it is the possession rather than the manifestation of these character traits which is valued, so that what is wanted is a certain disposition, which can be had in heaven even in the absence of evil, then it is not clear why God could not have imparted the disposition without the evil or why evil in the world is justified by the acquisition of such dispositions.[43]

(e) The reality of evil

As we have seen, however, some people have denied that evil is real. And, if they are right, then a major premise commonly invoked when suggesting that there is no God is false. But is it false? And if it is false, what does that truth imply when it comes to the problem of evil?

Well, what *are* we doing when we say that something is bad? Are we, for instance, attributing a distinct property to it? If we say that something is black, we are attributing a distinct property to the thing. But there is no distinct property of badness comparable to that of blackness. All black things share a property in common. But there is no property common to everything we call bad. If you know that X is black, then you know what it is for Y and Z to be black. But to know that X is bad is not necessarily to know what it is for Y and Z to be bad. As Herbert McCabe observes:

> If you know what it is like for a deckchair to be a bad deckchair you do not for that reason know what it is like for a grape to be a bad grape. A bad deckchair collapses when you sit down, but the fact that a grape collapses when you sit on it is not what would show it to be a bad grape.[44]

So, what are we doing when we call something bad? We are presumably saying that it does not come up to our expectations in some way. A bad deckchair is not what we expect a deckchair to be. And a bad grape is one which falls short of what we are looking for in grapes. In that case, however, it would seem that, in calling something bad, we are saying something *negative* about it. We are drawing attention to what it *lacks*. A bad thing may have many positive features enabling it to be bad. A successful serial killer, for instance, can be gifted in all sorts of ways. And a computer might be bad because of concrete bits and pieces clogging up its insides. But the badness of something is surely no positive reality in it. It lies in the gap between what a thing is and what it could be but is not. Yet such a gap cannot be any real thing or any distinct property of real things. And this is what Aquinas is claiming when defending his version of 'The Unreality of Evil Argument'. He is not bluntly saying that badness (or evil) is unreal. His view presupposes that we can truly describe things as bad (or evil). In his view, however, badness is not the name of a stuff (like wood) or a quality (like blackness). And that view makes sense.

But what if we accept it? Then an interesting conclusion follows when it comes to the topic of God and evil. For suppose we think of God as accounting for the existence of all individuals other than himself, together with all their positive properties. If Aquinas is right, then God produces nothing but what is good, since the good properties of bad things are made to be by God although their badness is not. And if Aquinas is right, all that is real and positive and good in a cancer victim or in a serial killer is God's doing. But the same cannot be said of the difference between what these people are and what we would like them to be. So, if Aquinas is right, God does not create evil.

(f) The morality of God

But can God be condemned for not having created more good than he has? If you agree with Aquinas, you are committed to the conclusion that God is not the cause of badness or evil, that badness (or evil) is not God's *doing*. But is it not something which God *ought* to prevent? Should an omnipotent, omniscient, and good God not have arranged for the world to be better than it is?

These are questions which defenders of the 'We Cannot Judge God in Human Terms' argument are now likely to challenge. To speak about what God ought to do or to have done is to presuppose that God is subject to moral approval or disapproval. It seems, in Kenny's phrase, to suppose that God is part of a 'moral community' together with human beings. But should we think of God in this way? Should we think of God as morally on trial?

We should if 'God is good' means that God is morally good. If 'God is good' means that, then it makes sense to wonder whether evil casts doubt on God's goodness or very existence. And this conclusion is what many discussions of God and evil simply take for granted. Mackie and Rowe are doing this. So are many authors writing in defence of God and against arguments such as theirs. Take, for example, exponents of the means and ends arguments noted earlier. They appear to be suggesting that, whatever the foes of theism say, God is morally justified in allowing certain evils. Or consider William Alston's version of the 'We Can't See All the Picture' argument. Alston seems to be suggesting that, although we cannot yet see how it is so, God might be morally entitled in allowing or causing what people often take to be bad.

But should we allow ourselves to get caught up in debates about God's moral integrity? A reason for doing so is that many people assume that 'God is good' means 'God is morally good'. Many others, however, do not assume this. Such people, I should stress, are not denying that God is good. Nor are they suggesting that God is immoral. Their position, rather, is that it is wrong to think of God as something either moral (well behaved) or immoral (badly behaved). Their idea is that, whether we are theists or non-theists, there are grounds for resisting claims like 'God is a good moral agent' or 'God is morally praiseworthy'. And there is a lot to be said for that line of thinking.[45]

One thing to be said in its favour is that it accords with what the Old and New Testaments say about God. What do the friends and foes of theism take themselves to be arguing about? The obvious answer is: 'the belief that God exists.' But how shall we decide what that belief amounts to? Reading the Bible might reasonably be thought of as a good first move. Yet, in the thinking of biblical authors, there is no suggestion that God is good because he is morally good.

Moral goodness is something we ascribe first and foremost to people. But what do we mean when we call people morally good? We often mean that they do what they are obliged to do or that they refrain from doing what they are obliged not to do. When commending people morally, we are also often saying that they display virtues of the sort listed by Aristotle in his account of the moral life—virtues such as justice, temperance, prudence, and courage.[46] Biblical authors, however, nowhere suggest that God has obligations. For them, God generates obligations by commanding people to act (or not to act) in certain ways. But they never suggest that God is himself bound by any law.[47] Nor do they think of God as Aristotle thought of the virtuous human being. Biblical authors never speak of God as being temperate, prudent, or courageous. And though they certainly call him just, they always mean that he acts in accordance with standards laid down in his commandments. According to Aristotle, just people give what they owe to others. For biblical authors, however, God owes nothing to anyone. His justice, far from conforming to a standard binding on him, sets standards for what is binding on people.

And, in general, the biblical God is not depicted as being what we would think of as a morally good human being. He favours certain people. But not because they have done anything special to deserve it. He smites certain people. But not because they are (by the canons of most moral philosophers) morally reprobate. God forms light and creates darkness. He makes weal and creates woe.[48] He is consistently portrayed as being above reproach, though not because he does his duty or is virtuous by human standards. Biblical authors sometimes complain about him. But they typically end up taking the view that God is not subject to appraisal as people are. They conclude that God is in a class of his own and is not, like people, to be judged by standards to which he is bound.[49]

Biblical authors do, of course, often speak of God as merciful, loving, and good. But they never view God's mercy as something that God is obliged to display or as something that he would be morally wrong to withhold. And this is how they commonly think of God's love. In the Old and New Testaments God is said to show love to certain select individuals. But he is not described as doing so because he ought to. For biblical authors, God's love is revealed in the light of his inscrutable choice, not in accordance with a code or law to which he is bound to conform. And it is this notion of divine love which provides the context for biblical texts saying that God is good. 'O give thanks to the Lord, for he is good', writes the psalmist.[50] But why does the psalmist say this? Because he is grateful for the blessings shown by God to the people of Israel, not because he thinks that God is a morally well-behaved individual.[51]

But suppose we forget about the biblical perspective. Are there philosophical grounds for denying that God should be thought of as a good moral agent, as one who is morally praiseworthy? If we are right to suppose that God is a person in the sense that people are persons (if we are right to think of God in ways suggested by theistic personalists), then maybe we should conclude that God is a moral agent and is therefore morally good or morally bad, morally praiseworthy or morally inexcusable. Notice, however, that this view of God's possible moral standing is not forced on us by the account of God commonly defended by classical theists. Indeed, given the classical theist's view of God, there are positive reasons for rejecting it.

For example, if classical theism is right, then God cannot possibly have what Aristotle meant by a virtue or a vice. For Aristotle, virtues are dispositions which people need in order to flourish as people (and vices are corresponding dispositions that are harmful to people). For most classical theists, however, God is simple and immutable, which means that he can have no dispositions since these belong only to things which are complex and changeable. And, so any classical theist would add, it is surely absurd to suppose that the God who creates everything from nothing depends for his well-being on anything, let alone dispositions which people need in order to thrive.

Then again, if classical theism is right, it seems odd to think of God as being subject to any duties or obligations. One has duties or obligations as part of a definite, describable context. A nurse, for example, has certain duties in the light of hospitals, drugs, sickness, doctors, death, and patients. The duties or obligations of nurses arise because of the role of nurses (something which makes no sense apart from the context in which they operate). In terms of classical theism, however, God has no context. He is the maker of all contexts and is the cause of there being situations in which people have duties and obligations. If classical theists are right, God has no role or job with standards to which he must conform. In this sense, and if classical theists are right in their view of God, we should deny that God is subject to duties or obligations.[52]

And indeed, so we find, classical theists do not generally think of God's goodness in moral terms. Hence, for example, St Anselm refers to God's goodness as 'profound' and 'hidden'.[53] It never occurs to him that it is something of which morally good people are paradigm manifestations. Brooding on what the word 'just' commonly means, Anselm wonders how God can be thought of as just, given that (as the Bible says) he is sometimes merciful to the wicked. But Anselm does not solve his problem by suggesting that God is just as people are just. Rather, he says, God is just since, even when he is merciful to the wicked, he acts in accordance with his will.[54]

We find a similar approach in the writings of Aquinas. Is God good, he asks? His answer is 'Yes'. But not because God is well behaved by human standards. God is good, says Aquinas, because all created goodness is made by him and must therefore, somehow, reflect what he is essentially.[55] According to Aquinas, 'good' chiefly signifies 'that which is desirable'. And God, says Aquinas, is supremely desirable since he must, as Creator, contain in himself all that can be thought of as desirable from a creaturely perspective. Aquinas thinks that creaturely good (in its many different forms) springs from what God essentially (and simply) is and that God, first and foremost, is good for just that reason.[56]

Theism and the Problem of Evil

If Aquinas is correct here, then there is no problem of evil if that is understood as a problem concerning God's moral integrity. But this is not to say that authors like Aquinas are not left with problems when it comes to God and evil. Nor is it to deny that the same goes for theists who think about God in ways unlike Aquinas. If God is omnipotent (or if he is just very powerful), then he could surely have made more good things than he has. So why has he not done so? And why has he not allowed some things, which clearly could have been better, to be less fulfilled than they are? These questions remain for theists in general.

In this chapter I have suggested that asking such questionss need not lead us to conclude that God could not possibly exist. I have also suggested how theists may reasonably respond to the charge that reflection on such questions forces us to conclude that the existence of God is unlikely. But they are good questions. And we might wonder whether theists can sensibly reply to them. Without worrying about God's certain or probable non-existence, can they, for instance, plausibly say how the evils in the world can be viewed as part of an order established by God?

Some have tried to do so. They have, for example, noted how suffering and adversity help to make people better human beings. They have also noted how pleasure and happiness bring dangers of their own. And they have suggested that our natural aversion to sorrow and pain should be tempered by the belief that the world we experience now is but a part of what God is making.[57] Unfortunately, space does not permit me here to document or comment on how theists have developed these ideas. But let me draw this chapter to a close by suggesting that anyone who wishes to reflect on God and evil might benefit from some detailed attention to their efforts.

NOTES

1. J. L. Mackie, 'Evil and Omnipotence', *Mind* 64 (1955). Mackie's article has been much reprinted. Here I am quoting from the edition of it to be found in Marilyn McCord Adams and Robert Merrihew Adams (eds.), *The Problem of Evil* (Oxford, 1990).

2. Ibid., p. 26.

3. Ibid.

4. Ibid. Mackie's argument is not original to him. A similar argument is cited by Thomas Aquinas in *Summa Theologiae*, Ia, 2, 3: 'It seems that there is no God. For if, of two mutually exclusive things, one were to exist without limit, the other would cease to exist. But by the word "God" is implied some limitless good. If God then existed, nobody would ever encounter evil. But evil is encountered. God therefore does not exist.' (I quote from volume 2 of the Blackfriars edition of the *Summa Theologiae* (London and New York, 1964).)

5. In Part X of his *Dialogues Concerning Natural Religion*, Hume also argues that accepting the reality of evil lands theists in self-contradiction. Other philosophers who take the same line include F. H. Bradley (*Appearance and Reality*, London, 1930, p. 174) and H. J. McCloskey ('God and Evil', *Philosophical Quarterly* X, 1960).

6. J. L. Mackie, *The Miracle of Theism* (Oxford, 1982), p. 176.

7. Ibid.

8. This article first appeared in *American Philosophical Quarterly* 16 (1979). I am quoting from the printing of it to be found in Adams and Adams (eds.), *The Problem of Evil*.

9. Ibid., pp. 127 f.

10. Ibid., p. 129.

11. Ibid., p. 131.

12. Ibid., p. 132.

13. In what follows I am concerned with theistic responses to authors like Mackie and Rowe which presuppose that God is omnipotent and omniscient. Some theists have denied that God is omnipotent and omniscient. For such theists, of course, the problem of evil as I am discussing it in this chapter does not arise.

14. Richard Swinburne, *The Existence of God* (rev. edn., Oxford, 1991), pp. 210 f.

15. Ibid., p. 219.

16. Ibid., p. 220.

17. Ibid., pp. 210 ff. By 'inductive knowledge', Swinburne means knowledge gained on the basis of past experience.

18. John Hick, *Evil and the God of Love* (2nd edn., London, 1977).

19. Ibid., pp. 372 ff.

20. Hence, for example, Aquinas holds that even Satan cannot be nothing but bad. If Satan were that, thinks Aquinas, then Satan would just not exist.

21. *Summa Theologiae*, Ia, 48, 1.

22. For Augustine's expression of the same line of thought, see *Enchiridion*, XI, and *Confessions*, III, vii, 12. For contemporary defences of evil as *privatio boni*, see Paul Helm, *The Providence of God* (Leicester, 1993), pp. 168 ff, and Herbert McCabe, *God Matters* (London, 1987), pp. 27 ff.

23. William Alston, 'The Inductive Argument from Evil and the Human Cognitive Condition', reprinted in Daniel Howard-Snyder (ed.), *The Evidential Argument from Evil* (Bloomington and Indianapolis, IN, 1996), p. 109.

24. William Alston, 'Some (Temporarily) Final Thoughts on Evidential Arguments from Evil', in Howard-Snyder (ed.), *The Evidential Argument from Evil*, pp. 317 and 321. Positions similar to Alston's can be found in M. B. Ahern, *The Problem of Evil* (London, 1971), F. J. Fitzpatrick, 'The Onus of Proof in Arguments about the Problem of Evil', *Religious Studies* 17 (1981), Bruce Reichenbach, *Evil and a Good God* (New York, 1982), and Stephen J. Wykstra, 'The Human Obstacle to Evidential Arguments from Suffering: On Avoiding the Evils of "Appearance" ', *International Journal for Philosophy of Religion* 16 (1984).

25. Anthony Kenny, *What is Faith?* (Oxford, 1992), p. 87.

26. In *The Miracle of Theism*, Mackie discusses arguments for God's existence. But his discussions of God and evil leaves such arguments entirely out of account.

27. Ibid., p. 176.

28. Ibid., pp. 154 f.

29. Ibid.

30. Mackie, 'Evil and Omnipotence', p. 33.

31. Alvin Plantinga, 'God, Evil, and the Metaphysics of Freedom', reprinted in Adams and Adams (eds.), *The Problem of Evil*, p. 106.

32. Cf., for example, William Alston: 'It is logically impossible for God to create free beings with genuine freedom of choice and also guarantee that they will always choose the right': 'The Inductive Argument from Evil', p. 112.

33. For a brief introduction to compatibilist theories, see Robert Kane (ed.), *The Oxford Handbook of Free Will* (Oxford, 2002), Part IV.

34. Mackie, *The Miracle of Theism*, p. 161.

35. Ibid., pp. 161 f.

36. Thomas Aquinas, *Summa contra Gentiles*, III, 67. I quote from Vernon J. Bourke's translation of this text (Notre Dame, IN, and London, 1975), p. 221.

37. Thomas Aquinas, *De Potentia*, III, 7. I quote from Timothy McDermott (ed.), *Aquinas: Selected Philosophical Writings* (Oxford, 1993), p. 304.

38. For a brief introduction to libertarian theories, see Kane (ed.), *The Oxford Handbook of Free Will*, Part VI.

39. Cf. Thomas Aquinas, *De Interpretatione*, I, 14.

40. Aquinas, *Summa Theologiae*, Ia, 83, 1 ad. 3. I quote from volume 11 of the Blackfriars edition of the *Summa Theologiae* (London and New York, 1970).

41. G. Stanley Kane, 'The Failure of Soul-Making Theodicy', *International Journal for the Philosophy of Religion* 6 (1975), pp. 2 f

42. Hick thinks that the goodness of God can be maintained only on the supposition that all people eventually become mature through tribulation. So he rejects the traditional Christian doctrine of Hell.

43. Eleonore Stump, 'The Problem of Evil', *Faith and Philosophy* 2 (1985), p. 397.

44. Herbert McCabe, *God Matters* (London, 1987), p. 28.

45. One might say that there is no such thing as non-moral goodness. But 'good' is a highly general term which we commonly use to describe all sorts of things, not just people we commend on moral grounds. Hence, for example, we speak of good dinners, good singers, good soldiers, good computers, good holidays, good weather, and so on.

46. Some philosophers have argued that moral evaluations of people do not

express truth claims. According to these thinkers, such evaluations are nothing but expressions of feeling. I pass over this view here since it does not seem relevant to the problem of evil as normally discussed by philosophers. Such philosophers, both theists and non-theists alike, seem to be starting from the assumption that 'God is good' says something about God and is not just an expression of how we feel.

47. Old Testament authors speak of God as binding himself to keep the terms of the covenant he established with the people of Israel. But here they only mean that God can be relied upon to act in accordance with his declared will.

48. Isaiah 45: 7.

49. This, for example, is the conclusion of the book of Job. It also seems to be what St Paul is teaching in Romans 9: 19–33.

50. Psalm 118: 1. Cf. 1 Chronicles 16: 34.

51. For more on biblical approaches to God's goodness, see pp. 752 and 756 f. of John L. McKenzie, 'Aspects of Old Testament Thought', in volume 2 of Raymond E. Brown, Joseph A. Fitzmyer, and Roland E. Murphy (eds.), *The Jerome Biblical Commentary* (Englewood Cliffs, NJ, 1968).

52. Cf. McCabe, *God Matters*, p. 37.

53. Anselm, *Proslogion*, ch. 9.

54. Ibid., ch. 11.

55. Cf. Chapter 7 above.

56. Cf. Aquinas, *Summa Theologiae*, Ia, 6.

57. For a contemporary philosopher who draws attention to these ways of approaching the topic of God and evil, see Eleonore Stump, 'Aquinas on the Sufferings of Job', in Howard-Snyder (ed.), *The Evidential Argument from Evil*.

FURTHER READING

The literature on the problem of evil is vast. But for a sense of what has been written fairly recently, see Barry L. Whitney, *Theodicy: An Annotated Bibliography on the Problem of Evil 1960–1991* (Bowling Green, OH, 1998). This volume is very comprehensive and is helpfully divided into sections listing works relevant to different ways in which people have approached the topic of God and evil. For a (now slightly outdated) survey of contemporary discussions of God and evil, also see Barry L. Whitney, *What are they saying about God and Evil?* (New York, 1989).

There are some good collections of essays on the problem of evil. Among the best are: Marilyn McCord Adams and Robert Merrihew Adams (eds.), *The Problem of Evil* (Oxford, 1990); Nelson Pike (ed.), *God and Evil: Readings on the Theological Problem of Evil* (London, 1971); and Daniel Howard-Snyder (ed.), *The Evidential Argument from Evil* (Bloomington and Indianapolis, IN, 1996). The last of these books provides an especially helpful bibliography of books and articles focusing on God and evil. For a good general reader on the problem of evil, see Mark Larrimore (ed.), *The Problem of Evil: A Reader* (Oxford, 2001).

For a short introduction to philosophical discussions concerning God and Evil, see Michael L. Peterson, *God and Evil: An Introduction to the Issues* (Boulder, CO, 1998). Significant book-length discussions of the problem of evil include: Marilyn McCord Adams, *Horrendous Evils and the Goodness of God* (Ithaca, NY, and London, 1999); M. B. Ahern, *The Problem of Evil* (London, 1971); A. Farrer, *Love Almighty and Ills Unlimited* (London, 1961); P. T. Geach, *Providence and Evil* (Cambridge, 1977); John Hick, *Evil and the God of Love* (2nd edn., London, 1975); E. Madden and P. Hare, *Evil and the Concept of God* (Springfield, MA, 1968); C. S. Lewis, *The Problem of Pain* (London, 1940); Bruce Reichenbach, *Evil and a Good God* (New York, 1982); Kenneth Surin, *Theology and the Problem of Evil* (Oxford, 1986); Richard Swinburne, *Providence and the Problem of Evil* (Oxford, 1998); and Peter Vardy, *The Puzzle of Evil* (London, 1992).

For notable recent presentations of a Free Will Defence, see Alvin Plantinga, *The Nature of Necessity* (Oxford, 1974), and Alvin Plantinga, *God, Freedom and Evil* (London, 1974). For critiques of approaches to God's goodness which see it in moral terms, see Patterson Brown, 'Religious Morality', *Mind* 72 (1963); Patterson Brown, 'Religious Morality: A Reply to Flew and Campbell', *Mind* 77 (1968); Brian Davies, 'How is God Love?', in Luke Gormally (ed.), *Moral Truth and Moral Tradition: Essays in Honour of Peter Geach and Elizabeth Anscombe* (Dublin and Portland, OR, 1994); Brian Davies, 'The Problem of Evil', in id. (ed.), *Philosophy of Religion: A Guide to the Subject* (London, 1998); Herbert McCabe, 'Evil', in id., *God Matters* (London, 1987); and Katherin A. Rogers, *Perfect Being Theology* (Edinburgh, 2000). For an introduction to biblical thinking on evil, see James L. Crenshaw (ed.), *Theodicy in the Old Testament* (London, 1983).

Augustine and Aquinas are classical Christian authors often referred to in discussions of God and evil. For an account of Augustine on evil, see G. R. Evans, *Augustine on Evil* (Cambridge, 1982). For an account of Aquinas on God and evil, see Brian Davies, *The Thought of Thomas Aquinas* (Oxford, 1992), ch. 5.

QUESTIONS FOR DISCUSSION

1 What do you mean when you say that something is good, or bad, or evil?

2 'God is good.' What should this statement be taken to mean? Explain how you arrive at your answer.

3 Are we in a position to entertain reasonable expectations concerning the kind of world that God (if he exists) is likely to make?

4 Is there any pain or suffering which God could never defend himself for permitting?

5 Can there be any created processes which are not caused to be as they are by God? If not, why not? If so, how? If not, then can theists reasonably claim that there are free, human actions? If so, where do these actions come from?

6 Some theists have said that our world is the best possible world. Can you make sense of this suggestion? If so, why? If not, why not?

7 Does it make sense to be grateful for the world in which we live? If it does, is there any conclusion to be drawn when it comes to the topic of God and evil?

8 'Badness is quite real even though it isn't the name of a stuff like milk or even the name of a quality like redness' (Herbert McCabe, *God Matters* (London, 1987), p. 29). Is that true? If so, why? If not, why not?

9 'If God is good, that can be so only because he is morally good.' Do you agree with that statement?

10 To what extent are people's approaches to the topic of God and evil a consequence of their attitudes towards issues such as the nature of human happiness and the goal of human life? Might different attitudes towards these issues reasonably lead to different approaches to the topic of God and evil?

11

MIRACLES

Religious believers often refer to miracles. They believe that these are possible. They also believe that some have occurred. Some religious believers add that miracles establish the truth of certain religious beliefs. But are miracles possible? Should we suppose that any have occurred And can miracles serve to support religious beliefs? These questions have prompted much philosophical discussion, so it is appropriate at this point to say something about them.

What is a Miracle?

What are we talking about when we speak of miracles? The answer is not all that obvious, since those who refer to miracles have offered various understandings of what it is that they are talking about.

(a) Definitions of 'miracle'

A widespread view of miracles sees them as breaks in the natural order of events in the material world. These breaks are sometimes referred to as 'violations of natural laws', often said to be brought about by God, or by some extremely powerful being who can interfere with the normal course of nature's operation. A classic definition of 'miracle' which echoes this understanding comes from David Hume, who writes about miracles in Chapter X ('Of Miracles') of his *Enquiry concerning Human Understanding*. A miracle, says Hume, 'may be accurately defined, *a transgression of a law of nature by a particular volition of the Deity, or by the interposition of some invisible agent*'.[1]

We find similar definitions in the works of other philosophers. Take, for example, Richard Swinburne and John Mackie. According to Swinburne, a miracle is 'a violation of a law of Nature by a god, that is, a very powerful rational being who is not a material object (viz., is invisible and intangible)'.[2] According to Mackie, a miracle is 'a violation of a law of nature' brought about by 'divine or supernatural intervention'. 'The laws of nature', Mackie adds, 'describe the ways in which the world—including, of course, human beings—works when left to itself, when not interfered with. A miracle occurs when the world is not left to itself, when something distinct from the natural order as a whole intrudes into it.'[3]

Here, then, is a fairly strong understanding of miracles: as events which cannot be explained in terms intelligible to natural scientists or to observers of the regular processes of nature. But it has also been suggested that a miracle need only be an extraordinary coincidence of a beneficial nature interpreted religiously.

We can find this understanding at work in a well-known article by R. F. Holland.[4] Suppose a child escapes death because a series of scientifically explicable physical events cause a train driver to hit the brakes on his vehicle, which is about to run over the child. Holland suggests that the delivery from death involved here can be thought of as miraculous from a religious point of view. In certain circumstances, he says, 'a coincidence can be taken religiously as a sign and called a miracle'. But, Holland adds, 'it cannot without confusion be taken as a sign of divine interference with the natural order'.[5]

(b) Comments on the definitions

Should we accept any of the above understandings of 'miracle'? For one reason, at any rate, the answer is 'No', because, with the possible exception of what Holland refers to, they all lack what religious people regard as an important element when it comes to what is truly miraculous. Those who believe that miracles have actually occurred normally hold that they are also events of religious significance. The idea here is that miracles always reveal something about God or teach us some religious truth. As Swinburne says: 'If a god intervened in the natural order to make a feather land here rather than there for no deep ultimate purpose, or to upset a child's box of toys just for spite, these events would not naturally be described as miracles.'[6] We may put this point by saying that those who believe in miracles would not deem as miraculous just any purported divine intervention or just any purported violation of a natural law.

But what of the notion of divine intervention? And what of the notion of a violation of a natural law? Are these not essential to the notion of a miracle? Here there are a number of points to be made, the first of which concerns the notion of God's intervening.

(i) Divine Intervention   It is very common to find people speaking of miracles as divine interventions. And Mackie, as we have seen, does speak in such terms. For him, the world has certain ways of working when left to itself, and miracles are instances of God stepping in. But should we suppose that God is literally able to intervene? Arguably not.

According to the *Oxford English Dictionary*, to intervene is to 'come in as something extraneous'. To say that something has intervened would normally be taken to imply that the thing has moved in where it was not to be found in the first place. The notion of intervention involves the idea of absence followed by presence. In this sense, I can be said to intervene in a fight when I enter the fight myself, having formerly not been part of it. But does it make sense to speak of God moving in where he has not been present before? And does it make sense to think of miracles as cases of God moving in where before he was absent?

It might make sense for us to speak and think in these ways if we take God to be an observer of the world, and if we think of the world as able to carry on independently of him. On such a view, sometimes referred to as 'Deism', there is no intrinsic problem with the notion of God intervening (although classical deists did not, in fact, believe in divine interventions).[7] But matters are different if, for example, we hold that the world is always totally dependent on God for its existence. If that is the case, then God is always present to his creatures as their sustainer and preserver. And if God is that, then it makes sense to deny that he can intervene in the world. As Alvin Plantinga puts it, commenting on Mackie's definition of 'miracle', 'on the theistic conception the world is never "left to itself" but is always (at the least) conserved in being by God'.[8]

(ii) Miracles and natural laws   On the other hand, the notion of a violation of a natural law is, surely and in some sense, part of what we may call 'the traditional view of miracles'.[9] As we have seen, R. F. Holland thinks that events with perfectly ordinary explanations can be called 'miracles'. But most people who have spoken of and debated about miracles have viewed them differently. They have commonly said that miracles are events which lack any scientific explanation. Generally speaking, the assumption has been that things in the world have properties and ways of working which cannot lead to miracles. The assumption has been that miracles are events which do not accord with what writers like Swinburne and Mackie mean by 'laws of nature', namely, theories stating how things in the world regularly or naturally operate, theories which may be used to predict how they will operate in the future. It is because miracles have been regularly understood in this sense that they have been thought of as brought about by God, or by some other agent not part of the material world.

Some writers have denied that what I am calling the traditional understanding of the miraculous is properly traditional. For, it has been argued, my 'traditional understanding of the miraculous' is not to be found in the Bible. Hence, for example, Samuel M. Thompson asserts: 'The notion of *miracle* as something which happens in nature and is contrary to the laws of nature is a curiously confused concept . . . No such conception can be found in the Biblical sources of the Hebrew-Christian tradition, for those sources did not have the conception of natural law.'[10] But, considered as an interpretation of the Bible, this view is somewhat implausible. In English translations of the Bible the word 'miracle' is sometimes used to refer only to an event which the biblical author regards as significant or as pointing beyond itself. Biblical authors never speak of 'natural laws', and some of them (e.g. the author of the fourth Gospel) do not regard the significance of miracles as exhausted by saying that they are events contrary to what modern authors mean by 'natural laws'. According to R. H. Fuller, the Bible 'knows nothing of nature as a closed system of law. Indeed the very word "nature" is unbiblical'.[11] But it is going too far to suggest that, in the sense of 'natural law' noted above, biblical authors have no notion of natural law and that they have no notion of miracles as violations of natural laws. Swinburne claims that the following events, if they occurred, would be violations of natural laws:

> Levitation, resurrection from the dead in full health of a man whose heart has not been beating for twenty four hours and who was dead also by other currently used criteria; water turning into wine without the assistance of chemical apparatus or catalysts; a man getting better from polio in a minute.[12]

Yet this is exactly the sort of event typically referred to in the Bible as miraculous. And although biblical authors do not indulge in qualifications like those presented by Swinburne, they often presuppose something like such qualifications when they speak of the miraculous. In many cases, at any rate, they presume that miracles cannot be brought about by the physical powers of objects in the world. Such a presupposition is, for example, evident in the remark ascribed to the man in St John's Gospel who declares 'Never since the world began has it been heard that any one opened the eyes of a man born blind'.[13]

Is it Reasonable to Believe in Miracles?

It should by now be apparent to you that people have disagreed about the meaning of 'miracle'.[14] But they have disagreed even more about the reasonableness of believing in the occurrence of miracles. For the most part, the disagreement has concerned the occurrence of miracles as understood by authors like Mackie and Swinburne. So let us now consider what may be said about the reasonableness, or otherwise, of believing in the occurrence of miracles in this sense. The most famous and most discussed treatment of the matter is the text of Hume mentioned above. So we can start by looking at what that has to say.[15]

Hume's Discussion of Miracles

What is Hume seeking to show in 'Of Miracles'? His readers have often been uncertain. And that is not surprising, for his remarks pull in different directions. Sometimes Hume seems to be asserting that miracles are flatly impossible. At one point, for instance, he refers to reports of miracles performed at the tomb of the Abbé Paris. Of these he observes:

> And what have we to oppose to such a cloud of witnesses, but the absolute impossibility or miraculous nature of the events, which they relate? And this surely, in the eyes of all reasonable people, will alone be regarded as a sufficient refutation.[16]

Elsewhere, however, Hume seems to go back on this (apparently) emphatic denial that miracles are possible. For example, towards the end of the second part of 'Of Miracles' he writes:

> I beg the limitations here made may be remarked, when I say, that a miracle can never be proved, so as to be the foundation of a system of religion. For I own, that otherwise, there may possibly be miracles, or violations of the usual course of nature, of such a kind as to admit of proof from human testimony.[17]

Hume here is making a much weaker claim than the one which emerges in his remarks on the Abbé Paris. He appears to be saying, not that miracles are impossible, but that they cannot show any particular religion to be true.

Yet, although he does indeed appear to say this, Hume also seems to want to press a stronger conclusion. For he also insists that we could never be justified in believing on the basis of testimony that any miracles have occurred. A key passage here occurs in Part I of 'Of Miracles', where Hume offers what he evidently regards as a fundamental principle. He writes:

> A miracle is a violation of the laws of nature; and as a firm and unalterable experience has established these laws, the proof against a miracle, from the very nature of the fact, is as entire as any argument from experience can possibly be imagined. Why is it more than probable, that all men must die; that lead cannot, of itself, remain suspended in the air; that fire consumes wood, and is extinguished by water; unless it be, that these events are found agreeable to the laws of nature, and there is required a violation of these laws, or in other words, a miracle to prevent them?[18]

Hume allows that many witnesses may testify that a miraculous event has occurred. But, he adds,

> no testimony is sufficient to establish a miracle, unless the testimony be of

such kind, that its falsehood would be more miraculous, than the fact, which it endeavours to establish; And even in that case, there is a mutual destruction of arguments, and the superior only gives us assurance suitable to that degree of force, which remains, after deducting the inferior.[19]

Here Hume is suggesting that reports of miracles are *intrinsically* such that we always have more reason to reject them than to accept them. According to Hume, 'Nothing is esteemed a miracle, if it ever happen in the common course of nature . . . There must, therefore, be a uniform experience against every miraculous event, otherwise the event would not merit that appellation.'[20] Miracles, Hume is suggesting, are 'events' which we have overwhelming reason to be sceptical about on the basis of experience.[21]

Is Hume Right About Miracles?

Which of the two conclusions noted above should actually be attributed to Hume? Perhaps both. Maybe, as R. M. Burns suggests, 'the solution [to the apparent divergences in 'Of Miracles'] lies in the recognition that . . . incompatible strains of argument lie in the text side by side'.[22] Yet evidence for attributing the above-mentioned conclusions to Hume can be found in what he writes. So let us now consider each of them in turn, starting with the conclusion that miracles are strictly impossible.

(a) Are miracles impossible?

In one sense of the word, miracles are surely not impossible. For, in saying that a miracle has occurred, one is hardly offering an assertion that is logically impossible. To say that an assertion is logically impossible is to say that it is contradictory, or that it entails what is contradictory. But although we may doubt the truth of statements like 'Jesus gave sight to a man born blind', such statements are not logically impossible. They are, for instance, hardly on a level with 'Jesus is a human being and Jesus is a fish'.

Significantly, even Hume is committed to this conclusion in spite of what he says about miracles being impossible. Why? Because of what he elsewhere says about what we can infer from a given state of affairs. In *A*

Treatise of Human Nature, Hume observes that 'there is nothing in any object, consider'd in itself, which can afford us a reason for drawing a conclusion beyond it'.[23] He means that there is no logical relation between independent matters of fact—that from one state of affairs being the case, nothing follows about what else is or could be the case. Why does Hume think this? Because he believes that we can conceive of one state of affairs being the case without also having to conceive of any other. Or, as Hume puts it in his *Enquiry concerning Human Understanding*: 'Whatever is intelligible, and can be distinctly conceived, implies no contradiction, and can never be proved false by any demonstrative argument or abstract reasoning *a priori*.'[24] Hence, Hume argues:

> It implies no contradiction that the course of nature may change, and that an object, seemingly like those which we have experienced, may be attended with different or contrary effects. May I not clearly and distinctly conceive that a body, falling from the clouds, and which, in all other respects, resembles snow, has yet the taste of salt or feeling of fire? Is there any more intelligible proposition than to affirm, that all the trees will flourish in December and January, and decay in May and June?[25]

Statements such as these, however, are plainly at odds with Hume's bald insistence that miracles are flatly impossible.

Yet, might Hume still not say that, regardless of logical possibility, miracles, as a matter of fact, just cannot happen? But why should we say this? Hume gives the following answer:

> It is no miracle that a man, seemingly in good health, should die on a sudden; because such a kind of death, though more unusual than any other, has yet been frequently observed to happen. But it is a miracle, that a dead man should come to life; because that has never been observed, in any age or country. There must, therefore, be a uniform experience against every miraculous event, otherwise that event would not merit that appellation. And as a uniform experience amounts to a proof, there is here a direct and full *proof*, from the nature of the fact, against the existence of any miracle.[26]

But is that answer acceptable?

One reason for thinking that it is not is that its conclusion seems to be assumed in the argument for it. For Hume's conclusion here depends on the supposition that no miracle has ever 'been observed in any age or country'. But how does Hume know that this supposition is true?

Unfortunately, he does not say. He does, however, clearly imply that the impossibility of miracles is shown by the fact that their occurrence would conflict with what has been regularly observed not to occur, that it would amount to the occurrence of an event which experience suggests to be impossible. But does that fact, if it is a fact, constitute a good reason for holding that miracles cannot occur? The answer is surely 'No'.

For one thing, the possibility of miracles seems to follow straightforwardly from the supposition that God exists. As William Lane Craig observes:

> If a transcendent, personal God exists, then he could cause events in the universe that could not be produced by causes within the universe. Given a God who created the universe, who conserves the world in being, and who is capable of acting freely [one is] entirely justified in maintaining that miracles are possible. Indeed, if it is even (epistemically) possible that such a transcendent, personal God exists, then it is equally possible that he has acted miraculously in the universe. Only to the extent that one has good grounds for believing atheism to be true could one be rationally justified in denying the possibility of miracles.[27]

Then again, events may come to pass which differ from what has happened in the past and which conflict with what we think possible on the basis of prior experience. On the basis of previous experience, I do not expect snakes to be crawling around my bedroom. But I would be mad peremptorily to ignore someone who warned me that I was going to find some snakes there tonight. Until someone walked on the moon, people were regularly observed not to walk on the moon. But someone *did* come to walk on the moon. And other people have come to do what earlier generations would rightly have deemed impossible on the basis of their experience.[28] Hume's reasoning concerning the impossibility of miracles has the implication that we can never revise our views concerning laws of nature in the light of observed exceptions to what we have taken to be laws. Yet, as C. D. Broad argues:

> Clearly many propositions have been accounted laws of nature because of an invariable experience in their favour, then exceptions have been observed, and finally these propositions have ceased to be regarded as laws of nature. But the first reported exception was, to anyone who had not

personally observed it, in precisely the same position as a story of a miracle, if Hume be right.[29]

We might maintain, however, that there is another reason for holding that miracles are impossible—a reason which gets its force from the idea that miracles are violations of natural laws. For, what if there are no natural laws? Then if a miracle is a violation of a natural law, there could be no miracles. Is it reasonable, however, to deny that there are natural laws? Hume thinks that there are and that they are 'established' by experience.[30] But is Hume right to think in this way?

Some philosophers have dismissed talk about laws of nature as pure mythology. And one can understand why. The notion of law has its natural home in legal or political contexts. First and foremost, a law is an ordinance issued by a ruler or governing body. And it is obeyed (or disobeyed) by those to whom it is promulgated. In that case, however, we might wonder whether it makes sense to speak of laws which nature obeys. People are part of nature, and they sometimes obey laws. But the natural world in general can hardly be thought of as obedient.

The use of the word 'law' in the phrase 'law of nature' is, however, obviously metaphorical. When people like Hume speak of laws of nature they are not implying that nature is obedient to anyone. They are focusing on the fact that we can frame statements about what nature does on a regular basis. And we can certainly do that. In fact, talk of natural laws is consonant with what scientists say. They suppose that the course of nature continues uniformly the same, and if events of type A regularly follow events of type B in one set of circumstances, then other events of type A can be expected to follow other events of type B in more or less identical circumstances, unless there is some relevant difference that can itself be understood in terms of a covering law.

We can express this point by saying that there is no obvious reason why we should rationally refuse to talk about laws of nature. To say that there are laws of nature is to say that things have natures which determine how they can and do operate. Some people (perhaps thinking about quantum physics and its talk about the random motions of fundamental particles) might observe that the behaviour of some things is irregular. Other people (perhaps thinking about how people can affect the world by means of what they choose to do freely) might suggest that no knowledge of natural laws can enable us to predict with certainty what will happen in the future. Yet those who believe in natural laws need not be taken as denying either of these points. Their main claim is that (on the macroscopic level, at any rate) things in nature have characteristic ways of working—ways which can be codified. To put the matter in simple terms, they are normally saying only that, for example, when human beings suffer massive heart attacks they can reasonably be expected to die. Normally, they are saying only that, for example, when you boil an egg for half an hour you can reasonably expect to end up with a hard-boiled egg.

(b) Miracles and testimony

So, even if only for the sake of argument, suppose we concede that Hume is right to assume that there are laws of nature. Should we also concede that he is right in what he says about the reasonableness of believing in miracles on the basis of testimony? Should we accept that we could never be warranted in believing reports of miracles?

(i) Four sceptical arguments   In addition to Hume's suggestion (to which I shall return) that the evidence against miracles having occurred must always be held to outweigh any claim to the effect that they have occurred, Hume offers four arguments designed, he says, to show that 'there never was a miraculous event established'.[31]

He argues, first, that no reported miracle comes with the testimony of enough people who can be regarded as sufficiently intelligent, learned, reputable, and so on, to justify our believing reports of miracles. Hume writes:

> There is not to be found, in all history, any miracle attested by a sufficient number of men, of such unquestioned good sense, education, and learning, as to secure us against all delusion in themselves; of such undoubted integrity, as to place them beyond all suspicion of any design to deceive others; of such credit and reputation in the eyes of mankind, as to have a great deal to lose in case of their being detected in any falsehood.[32]

Hume's second argument is that people are naturally prone to look for marvels and wonders and that this gives us grounds for being sceptical about reported miracles. 'We may', he says, observe in human nature a principle, which, if strictly examined, will be found to diminish extremely the assurance, which we might, from human testimony, have, in any kind of prodigy . . . The passion of *surprize* and *wonder*, arising from miracles, being an agreeable emotion, gives a sensible tendency towards the belief of those events, from which it is derived. And this goes so far, that even those who cannot enjoy this pleasure immediately, nor can believe those miraculous events, of which they are informed, yet love to partake of the satisfaction at second-hand or by rebound, and place a pride and delight in exciting the admiration of others.[33]

In this connection Hume adds that religious people are particularly untrustworthy. 'A religionist', he says, 'may be an enthusiast, and imagine he sees what has no reality: He may know his narrative to be false, and yet persevere in it, with the best intentions in the world, for the sake of promoting so holy a cause.'[34] Religious people, Hume says, are subject to vanity, self-interest, and impudence.[35] He also suggests that

The many instances of forged miracles, and prophecies, and supernatural events, which, in all ages, have either been detected by contrary evidence, or which detect themselves by their absurdity, prove sufficiently the strong propensity of mankind to the extraordinary and the marvellous, and ought reasonably to beget a suspicion against all relations of this kind.[36]

In his third argument Hume claims that 'It forms a strong presumption against all supernatural and miraculous relations, that they are observed chiefly to abound among ignorant and barbarous nations.'[37]

Hume's fourth and final argument is rather more complicated than the first three, which are easy enough to grasp. He says:

Let us consider, that, in matters of religion, whatever is different is contrary; and that it is impossible the religions of ancient ROME, of TURKEY, of SIAM, and of CHINA should, all of them, be established on any solid foundation. Every miracle, therefore, pretended to have been wrought in any of these religions (and all of them abound in miracles), as its direct scope is to establish the particular system to which it is attributed; so has it the same force, though more indirectly, to overthrow every other system. In destroying a rival system, it likewise destroys the credit of those miracles, on which that system was established.[38]

What is Hume driving at here? Basically, he is endorsing the following argument:

1. Adherents of different religions all report the occurrence of miracles as supporting the truth of their respective religions.

2. But religions contradict each other.

3. So, a miracle supposed to support religion A should be thought of as evidence against the truth of religion B, and vice versa.

4. Therefore, we should disbelieve reports of miracles coming from different religions. They cancel each other out.

(ii) Comments on the above arguments   Are Hume's arguments conclusive? Some have found them persuasive, but they are actually very problematic.

Hume says that history does not provide testimony to the miraculous from 'a sufficient number of men, of such unquestioned good sense, education, and learning as to secure us against all delusion in themselves'. But how many men constitute a sufficient number? And what counts as good sense, education, and learning? Hume does not explain.

Later in his discussion of miracles, Hume remarks on how people are often influenced by a fascination with the wonderful. But he does not show that people must always be so fascinated or that they must always be so fascinated in a way which would render their testimony suspect. No doubt many people are charmed by what seems to them to be extraordinary. And love of the marvellous may be the source of many reported miracles. But is it absolutely evident that everybody who has reported the occurrence of a miracle has been thus swayed in a way that casts doubt on what they report? And is there really good evidence that religious people cannot distinguish truth from error in the case of the marvellous or that they are always and exclusively governed by concern to back a religious cause?

It is exceedingly difficult to answer such questions. So much depends on taking particular cases and examining them in detail. We might reasonably think, however, that Hume is premature in supposing that his observations show that we should always disregard testimony to the effect that a miracle has occurred. And we might add that, in his consideration of testimony, there are things which Hume should have noted but does not. He appears, for example, to have forgotten about the possibility of corroborating what someone claims to have occurred. But past events sometimes leave physical traces which survive into the present.[39] A reported event of the past can be reasonably believed to have occurred because of what can be gleaned from some physical data available to us now. Even in default of such data, and unless nobody can be taken as a reliable witness, there is no reason why the existence of laws of nature should force us to conclude that somebody who reports the violation of a natural law must be misreporting. We may grant that particular instances need to be examined very carefully. But how can we rule out in advance the possibility of rationally concluding that a report of a violation of a natural law is an accurate description of what occurred?

We might reply that there still remains Hume's point about reports of miracles coming from different religions. But, here again, Hume is moving too fast. In his own day it was widely assumed that the miracles reported in the New Testament established the truth of Christianity and the absolute falsehood of all other religions. But why should we assume that, if we have reports of miracles from, for example, a Christian and a Hindu, both reports cannot relate what actually occurred? Hume assumes some such principle as: 'If a Christian miracle occurs, that is evidence against the truth of Hinduism. And if a Hindu miracle occurs, that is evidence against the truth of Christianity.' But this principle is false. For, as Richard Swinburne notes, 'evidence for a miracle "wrought in one religion" is only evidence against the occurrence of a miracle "wrought in another religion" if the two miracles, if they occurred, would be evidence for propositions of the two religious systems incompatible with each other'.[40] According to Hume, 'when two religions claim mutually exclusive revelations, it is not possible for both of them to be well evidenced by the way they report their associated miracles'.[41] And that observation is correct. But it does not entail that all reports of miracles are undermined by the fact that different religions report miracles.

(iii) Reason and the improbability of miracles   At this point, however, Hume might appeal to the argument to which I earlier promised to return. For let us suppose that those who tell us of miracles are not always disreputable, stupid, gullible, dishonest, and so on. Let us also suppose that accounts of miracles coming from people belonging to different religions do not necessarily undermine each other. Is it not still the case that, because of what a miracle is supposed to be, we have overwhelming reason to disbelieve reports of miracles? Do we not have enormous evidence for the fact that certain laws of nature hold? And must not this evidence always outweigh any claim to the effect that, on some occasion or other, something has happened which conflicts with a law of nature? Is it not evidently the case that miracles are maximally improbable on the basis of our experience?

Those who say 'Yes' to such questions might observe that experience and testimony strongly suggest that nature operates in a uniform way. They might then add that, when presented with a report of a miracle, it is reasonable for us to assess the report in the light of what we know to have regularly happened in the past. Indeed, so they might suggest, if a miracle is a violation of natural laws, then the antecedent improbability of a miracle having occurred is as high as it could be. Or, as J. L. Mackie puts it:

> Where there is some plausible testimony about the occurrence of what would appear to be a miracle, those who accept this as a miracle have the double burden of showing both that the event took place and that it violated the laws of nature. But it will be very hard to sustain this double burden. For whatever tends to show that it would have been a violation of natural law tends for that very reason to make it most unlikely that it actually happened.[42]

According to Mackie, a miracle 'must, by the miracle advocate's own admission, be contrary to a genuine, not merely a supposed law of nature, and therefore maximally improbable. It is this maximal improbability that the weight of the testimony would have to overcome.'[43]

But how do we know what has regularly happened in the past? Is it by personal observation? Obviously not. Each of us may be able to state what we have personally observed. But such a report will not encompass all that has regularly happened in the past. For the past precedes all of us. For our 'knowledge' of what has regularly happened in the past, we depend on testimony. And we are equally dependent on testimony when it comes to what is supposed to be happening in our lifetime even though we do not observe it directly. Many people think that they know that such and such is happening in, for example, the bodies of all human beings with high blood pressure. But most of them certainly do not know this by personal observation. They 'know' it because they believe what doctors say about it.

And that thought should make us wonder whether Hume ought not to be arguing in almost exactly the opposite way from the way in which he actually does argue. Hume is saying: 'Testimony should be evaluated in the light of what has regularly happened, or in the light of what regularly happens.' But what has regularly happened, or what is regularly happening, is something we come to learn about on the basis of testimony. And it follows from this that testimony is not to be judged at the bar of a notion called 'what we know to have regularly happened in the past' or 'what we know to be regularly happening in the present'. We might say that our past experience ought to lead us to conclude that a report of an event which runs contrary to this experience ought to be rejected in the name of reason. But that conclusion would be unreasonable. For one thing, it would leave us having to conclude that, for example, someone who never saw rivers freeze should automatically reject any report about Siberian rivers in winter.

Hume and his supporters might reply that we have no reason to believe that laws of nature are ever violated. They might say that a violation of a natural law is absolutely improbable on the basis of our evidence. Once again, however, we have to ask how we have arrived at what we call 'evidence' here. What are we to take as 'our evidence'? What people say is often taken as evidence, and, indeed, we believe much more on the basis of what people say than we do on the basis of what we have seen or discovered for ourselves. And how have we come to be able to recognize what counts as evidence? We were not born with this ability. Nor did we learn to distinguish between evidence and non-evidence entirely on our own. Our ability to determine what is evidence and what is not depends in great measure on what we were taught as to what, in various areas of enquiry, does and does not count as evidence.

Yet we do believe (do we not?), that miracles, if they have occurred, are rare. Let us suppose, for example, that Jesus of Nazareth was raised from the dead. It still remains that billions of other people have rotted in their graves. So, might defenders of Hume not reasonably ask us to bear this kind of fact in mind when told that a miracle has occurred? And might they not also reasonably ask us to act on the supposition that miracles are, in Mackie's phrase, 'maximally improbable'?

But is it so obvious that what we know, or what we think we know, about the regular workings of nature should always lead us to discount reports of miracles? For, might we not have good reason to believe in the general trustworthiness of people who report the occurrence of miracles? Generally speaking, we do form grounds for taking certain people to be reliable. And we act on these grounds when we believe what they tell us? So, suppose we have grounds for thinking that someone who 'informs' us about a miracle is generally reliable? Should we not now conclude that there are grounds for believing that person's report? People we have reason to trust can mislead us (whether intentionally or unintentionally), but that does not mean that we cannot reasonably believe what some of them tell us. So, again, why can we not have reason to believe someone who tells us about a miracle?

Hume would reply: 'Because they are asking us to believe what, considered abstractly, is most unlikely to have happened.' Yet, may we not retort that what is likely to have happened cannot be determined except by attending to all the available evidence, part of which could be testimony from someone we have reason to think of as reliable? We may concede that witnesses can mislead. But it does not follow that we lack good reason for believing what some of them say. Hume might observe that the strong improbability of something occurring ought always to be taken as reason for supposing that it has not occurred. But is it always reasonable to act on that imperative? Arguably not. As Keith Ward says:

> It would not, despite Hume, be reasonable to say that the improbability of my table rising into the air and the improbability of my being mistaken in claiming to see it, just cancel each other out; so that I must remain agnostic, refusing to believe my own eyes because of some probabilistic balancing-act. On the contrary, as long as I pinch myself and look especially carefully, it would be entirely reasonable to accept, without any tentativeness, that the improbable has certainly occurred, and that I have certainly seen it . . . It is true that, the more improbable an event is, the more likely it is that I have made a mistake in observing it. If a chemistry student reports that he has seen liquid helium crawling out of a glass beaker, we think it likely he has made a mistake. But it is not true, even then, that the more improbable the

event, the more probable it is that he is mistaken, whatever the conditions of observation, and however carefully he has observed. It is rather that the unusualness of the event gives us special reason to be careful in observation; it gives us a special reason for caution in making knowledge-claims. Nevertheless, in the end, if we have observed carefully, in good conditions, testimony will rationally outweigh expectation . . . The improbability of an event is one factor governing the care with which one must observe to be a credible witness. But it is not an independent variable to set against a separately weighted probability of error. Nor is it true that, the more improbable the event, the more improbable is it that I have observed it, whatever other factors might be taken into account. All we can say is that very improbable events need to be observed with special care.[44]

As Ward also argues, questions of probability cannot just be settled in a vacuum. We may view a report of a miracle as improbable because we think that nature is a closed system in which what has always happened determines what will always happen according to immutable laws. But that nature is like this is not a conclusion to be arrived at on the basis of past experience. And those who believe in miracles might reasonably do so partly because they reckon with factors in their favour. They might, for example, believe in miracles with their belief in the existence of God in mind. Given that God exists, they might say, it is not at all improbable that miracles should occur. So, and with an eye on Mackie's notion of maximal improbability, they might subsequently conclude that there is no solid factor of improbability to be appealed to as a ground for rationally dismissing accounts of miracles. Miracles may be viewed as maximally improbable relative to one set of beliefs. But they are not such when viewed against others. And, we should note, what is contrary to a law of nature may actually be *more probable than not* with respect to our evidence. For, as Alvin Plantinga observes:

Suppose (as has been the case for various groups of people at various times in the past) we knew nothing about whales except what can be garnered by rather distant visual observation. Now it might be a law of nature that whales have some property P (mammalian construction, for example) that can be detected only by close examination; but it might also be the case that we know that most things that look and behave more or less like whales do not have this property P. Then the proposition S is a whale and does not have P could very well be more probable than not with respect to our evidence, even though it is contrary to a law of nature.[45]

So perhaps we may take leave to doubt that Hume has shown that it is always unreasonable to accept a report to the effect that a miracle has occurred. Such a conclusion, does not imply that scientists are unjustified in their talk about laws of nature. Nor does it entail that what we are told should not be weighed against our common experience and against other things reported to us. It does, however, imply that Hume is wrong to claim that a reasonable person must always suppose that the evidence for a reported miracle having occurred must always be decreed to be outweighed by the evidence for its not having occurred.

And, to move beyond Hume's immediate concern with testimony, it is worth adding that people might be justified in supposing that a miracle has occurred on the basis of something other than testimony. For one thing, there is personal observation to be reckoned with. I touched on this topic briefly above. But it is one which deserves emphasis.

For, suppose that we observe an event which we have reason to think of as quite at odds with what can be brought about in terms of natural laws. Suppose, for example, that we witness one of the occurrences in Swinburne's list: 'levitation, resurrection from the dead in full health of a man whose heart has not been beating for twenty four hours and who was dead also by other currently used criteria; water turning into wine without the assistance of chemical apparatus or catalysts; a man getting better from polio in a minute'. How ought we to think in these circumstances?

We might seek to explain what we observe by bringing it under some other well-established law. We might say that what we observe accords with what we know about natural laws. But suppose that what we observe cannot be accounted for in terms of what current science takes to be the laws of nature? Suppose that what we observe seems to conflict with what science now deems to be possible? We might say that scientists do not know all there is to know when it comes to natural laws. We might say that everything we observe can be accounted for naturalistically even though we cannot, at present, provide the account. We might also note that many events occur which earlier generations would have thought of as impossible given their scientific knowledge. I can speak to someone in Australia without leaving England. So, why not take all supposed exceptions to natural laws to be nothing but conformities to hitherto unknown natural laws?

But it is conceivable that our acting on that suggestion could land us with more difficulties than we would have if we simply accepted that something had happened which nature could not accomplish on its own. Consider again the list of events given by Swinburne. Suppose that such events occur and are monitored by strict scientific methods. If we say that they can be explained in terms of some law of nature, then we will evidently have to show that they are further instances of some previously noted phenomenon and that they are understandable on that basis. But we may not be able to do this. If we want to deny that any natural law has been violated in this case, we will therefore have to revise our theories about natural laws.

The trouble now is that it could be enormously expensive (intellectually, not financially) to do so. We might have to agree, for example, that in accordance with perfectly natural laws it is conceivable that victims of polio should recover in a minute. Yet such a position would play havoc with a vast amount of scientific theory. In such circumstances it might be more economical and more reasonable to accept that a law of nature has been violated. But if this is correct, it follows that a law of nature can reasonably be said to have been violated and that it is wrong to insist that nobody can reasonably suppose that a miracle has occurred.

In response to this conclusion some writers have replied by baldly asserting that it is just not possible for us to believe in miracles today. A famous example is the German theologian Rudolf Bultmann (1884–1976). In seeking to interpret the Bible, Bultmann feels that he has to begin from some basic presuppositions. One of them is that miracles do not happen. 'It is impossible', says Bultmann, 'to use electrical light and the wireless and to avail ourselves of modern medical and surgical discoveries, and at the same time to believe in the New Testament world of spirits and miracles.'[46] But why is this impossible? It is not logically impossible. Perhaps Bultmann means that people who use electricity and the light just cannot but disbelieve in miracles. But that is clearly false. For as Plantinga again notes:

> Very many well-educated people (including even some theologians) understand science and history in a way that is entirely compatible both with the possibility and with the actuality of miracles. Many physicists and engineers, for example, understand 'electrical light and the wireless' vastly better than Bultmann or his contemporary followers, but nonetheless hold precisely

those New Testament beliefs Bultmann thinks incompatible with using electric lights and radios. There are a large number of educated contemporaries (including even some with Ph.D's!) who believe Jesus really and literally arose from the dead, that God performs miracles in the contemporary world, and even that there are both demons and spirits who are active in the contemporary world. As a matter of historical fact, there are any number of contemporaries, and contemporary intellectuals very well acquainted with science, who don't feel any problem at all in pursuing science and also in believing in miracles, angels, Christ's resurrection, the lot.[47]

In response to Plantinga, we might say that the believers of whom he speaks are believing unreasonably. And that may well be so. But his remarks seem fairly devastating as directed to people such as Bultmann, who assumes that we are all in the grip of a view of things which has to exclude the miraculous.

What Do Miracles Prove?

But does the occurrence of miracles establish anything of religious significance? For the sake of argument, let us now suppose that we can be absolutely sure that violations of natural law have occurred. What should we therefore conclude? Should we, for example, conclude that God exists? Or should we conclude that some world religion is the true religion?

As we have seen, 'miracle' has been defined so as to include the idea that miracles are brought about by God. But can they be brought about *only* by God? Swinburne suggests that there could well be circumstances that made it reasonable to say that some violation of a natural law is brought about by something like a human agent or agents. Let E be a violation of a natural law. Then, says Swinburne,

> suppose that E occurs in ways and circumstances otherwise strongly analogous to those in which occur events brought about intentionally by human agents, and that other violations occur in such circumstances. We would then be justified in claiming that E and other such violations are, like effects of human actions, brought about by agents, but agents unlike men in not being material objects. This inference would be justified because, if an analogy between effects is strong enough, we are always justified in postulating slight difference in causes to account for slight difference in effects.[48]

But would a non-material agent bringing about effects intentionally have to be divine? Plenty of people, after all, have thought that miracles can be brought about by 'demons', 'spirits', 'saints', and other agents who are not what many of those who believe in God would think of as divine.

It is often said that only God stands outside the universe as its maker and sustainer. And, if we think that a miracle is a violation of a natural law, we might, therefore, suggest that only God can bring one about. If God is not a part of the universe, he will not be subject to the constraints of natural laws (if there are such things). But could there not be agents of some kind (angels? Satan?) who, although they are not divine, can bring about violations of natural laws? We might not suppose that there are any such agents. But how are we to rule them out?

Maybe the most we can do here is appeal to a principle of economy. We might argue as follows: 'Given that there is a God, given that God can be the source of events called miracles, and given that we have no other reason to postulate non-divine agents as sources of such events, we should ascribe them to God.' Aquinas argues that only God can work miracles because: (1) a miracle is 'an event that happens outside the ordinary processes of the whole of created nature', and (2) anything other than God works according to its created nature.[49] And if we define 'miracle' as Aquinas does, his conclusion is inescapable. But not everyone (and not every theist even) has defined 'miracle' in this way. According to Pope Benedict XIV, for instance, something is a miracle if its production exceeds 'the power of visible and corporeal nature only'.[50]

What of the suggestion that miracles can prove some religion to be the true religion? That miracles do exactly this has indeed been argued.[51] A classic statement of this view can be found in the writings of Samuel Clarke (1675–1729), according to whom 'The Christian religion is positively and directly proved, to be actually and immediately sent to us from God, by the many infallible signs and miracles, which the author of it worked publicly as the evidence of his Divine Commission.'[52] We might also note Canon 4 of Vatican I's *Dogmatic Constitution on the Catholic Faith*, in which we read:

> If anyone says that all miracles are impossible, and that therefore all reports of them, even those contained in sacred Scripture, are to be set aside as fables or myths; or that miracles can never be known with certainty, nor can the

divine origin of the christian religion be proved from them: let him be anathema.[53]

But can a miracle strictly prove that some religion or other is the true one, or (to weaken the question) that some religion is true?

It is significant that the foundational documents of Christianity do not think so. In St Mark's Gospel, Jesus declares that false prophets can work miracles in order to deceive.[54] And in all the synoptic gospels he refuses to produce 'signs' in order to prove his divine mission.[55]

We might argue that miracles could support some religious tradition or some religious belief. If you ask me to show that you have my support, and if I do something in response to your request, others will have reason to think that I support you. By the same token, if, for example, people call on God to express support for their religious beliefs by effecting a miracle, and if such is effected, it would be a very thoroughgoing sceptic who would say that no miracle can lend any credence to any particular religious position.

In the end, though, we are dealing here with possibilities only. It is concrete details of particular supposed miracles that are needed for matters to be usefully taken further. At this stage, therefore, it is best to move on to next subject for discussion.

NOTES

1. David Hume, *An Enquiry concerning Human Understanding*, ed. Tom L. Beauchamp (Oxford, 2000), p. 87.

2. Richard Swinburne, 'Miracles', *Philosophical Quarterly* 18 (1968), reprinted in William L. Rowe and William J. Wainwright (eds.), *Philosophy of Religion: Selected Readings* (2nd edn., London and New York, 1973).

3. J. L. Mackie, *The Miracle of Theism* (Oxford, 1982), pp. 19 f.

4. R. F. Holland, 'The Miraculous', in D. Z. Phillips (ed.), *Religion and Understanding* (Oxford, 1967), reprinted in Richard Swinburne (ed.), *Miracles* (London and New York, 1989). I quote from this reprint.

5. Ibid., pp. 53 ff.

6. Swinburne (ed.), *Miracles*, p. 6.

7. See R. M. Burns, *The Great Debate on Miracles: From Joseph Glanville to David Hume* (London and Toronto, 1981), pp. 70 ff.

8. Alvin Plantinga, 'Is Theism Really a Miracle?', *Faith and Philosophy* 3 (1986), p. 111. We might also note that the notion of intervention is completely lacking in the account of miracles provided by Aquinas. In his thinking, God, as creator and sustainer, is always present to everything. And for this reason, he maintains, God is just as present in what is not miraculous as he is in the miraculous. Miracles, for Aquinas, do not occur because of an extra 'wonder-ingredient' (i.e. God). Rather, they occur in the *absence* of something (i.e. a created cause or a collection of created causes). Cf. Thomas Aquinas, *Summa contra Gentiles*, III, 101.

9. One might prefer to speak, in this connection, of 'exceptions' rather than violations, for to call miracles violations of natural law could be taken to imply that, when a miracle occurs, some natural law ceases to operate throughout the world. Cf. Richard L. Purtill, 'Miracles: What if they Happened?' in Swinburne (ed.), *Miracles*, pp. 194 f.

10. Samuel L. Thompson, *A Modern Philosophy of Religion* (Chicago, 1955), pp. 454 f.

11. R. H. Fuller, *Interpreting the Miracles* (London, 1966), pp. 8 f.

12. Swinburne (ed.), *Miracles*, p. 84.

13. John 9: 32 f.

14. J. C. A. Gaskin, *The Quest for Eternity* (Harmondsworth, 1984), p. 137, offers a nice definition of 'miracle' which takes account of much of the diversity to which I have referred: '*Miracle*: an event of religious significance, brought about by God or a god or by some other visible or invisible rational agent with sufficient power, *either* in violation of the laws of nature (the "violation concept") *or* as a striking coincidence within the laws of nature (the "coincidence concept").'

15. Notice, however, that all the points about miracles argued by Hume can be found in the work of writers working before the publication of 'Of Miracles'. This fact is ably demonstrated by Burns, *The Great Debate on Miracles*.

16. Hume, *An Enquiry concerning Human Understanding*, p. 94.

17. Ibid., p. 97.

18. Ibid., p. 87.

19. Ibid.

20. Ibid.

21. For an earlier statement of this argument, see Thomas Sherlock, *The Trial of the Witnesses of the Resurrection* (1st edn., 1729; 8th edn., London, 1736), p. 58.

22. Burns, *The Great Debate on Miracles*, p. 143.

23. David Hume, *A Treatise of Human Nature*, ed. L. A. Selby-Bigge, revised by P. H. Nidditch (Oxford, 1978), p. 139.

24. Hume, *An Enquiry concerning Human Understanding*, p. 31.

25. Ibid.

26. Ibid., p. 87.

27. William Lane Craig, 'Creation, Providence and Miracles', in Brian Davies (ed.), *Philosophy of Religion: A Guide to the Subject* (London, 1998), pp. 154 f.

28. Cf. J. C. A. Gaskin, *Hume's Philosophy of Religion* (2nd edn., London, 1988), pp. 163 ff.

29. C. D. Broad, 'Hume's Theory of the Credibility of Miracles', *Proceedings of the Aristotelian Society* 17 (1916–17), pp. 77–94.

30. Hume, *An Enquiry concerning Human Understanding*, p. 86.

31. Ibid., p. 88.

32. Ibid.

33. Ibid., pp. 88 f.

34. Ibid., p. 89.

35. Ibid.

36. Ibid.

37. Ibid., p. 90.

38. Ibid., p. 91.

39. Cf. Swinburne (ed.), *Miracles*, pp. 134 ff.

40. Richard Swinburne, *The Concept of Miracle* (London, 1970), p. 60.

41. Gaskin, *Hume's Philosophy of Religion*, p. 142.

42. Mackie, *The Miracle of Theism*, p. 26.

43. Ibid., p. 25.

44. Keith Ward, 'Miracles and Testimony', *Religious Studies* 21 (1985), p. 133.

45. Plantinga, 'Is Theism Really a Miracle?', pp. 112 f.

46. Rudolf Bultmann, *Kerygma and Myth* (New York, 1961), p. 5.

47. Alvin Plantinga, *Warranted Christian Belief* (New York and Oxford, 2000), p. 405.

48. Swinburne, *The Concept of Miracle*, p. 57.

49. Thomas Aquinas, *Summa Theologiae*, Ia, 110, 4. I quote from volume 15 of the Blackfriars Edition of the *Summa Theologiae* (London and New York, 1970).

50. *De Servorum Dei Beatificatione et Beatorum Canonizatione*, iv: *de Miraculis* (1738).

51. Hume is clearly targeting this argument in 'Of Miracles'. This text is obviously intended to refute the claim that a particular miracle (i.e. the resurrection of Jesus) serves to establish the truth of Christianity.

52. Samuel Clarke, *1705 Boyle Lectures* (7th edn., London, 1727), I, p. 383.

53. Norman Tanner (ed.), *Decrees of the Ecumenical Councils*, vol. 2, p. 810. I am told, however, that 'proved' in this text need mean no more than 'supported by reason'.

54. Mark 13: 22 f.

55. Matthew 4: 6; 12: 38–41; Mark 8: 11–13; 15: 31–2; Luke 4: 23.

FURTHER READING

Those who are interested in the topic of miracles ought to read something on how miracles have been understood over the centuries. In this connection, works worth consulting include: C. F. D. Moule (ed.), *Miracles* (London, 1965); R. M. Grant, *Miracle and Natural Law in Graeco-Roman and Early Christian Thought* (Amsterdam, 1952); and J. A. Hardon, 'The Concept of Miracle from St. Augustine to Modern Apologetics', *Theological Studies* 15 (1954).

For philosophical discussion of miracles, an excellent book to start with is Richard Swinburne (ed.), *Miracles* (New York and London, 1989). As well as containing some classical writings on miracles, this anthology also contains some notable recent texts dealing with them.

Two book-length treatments of miracles are C. S. Lewis, *Miracles* (rev. edn., London, 1960), and Richard Swinburne, *The Concept of Miracle* (London, 1970). Both Lewis and Swinburne write with a favourable eye on the notion of the miraculous. For discussions more hostile to the notion, see Simon Blackburn, *Think* (Oxford, 1999), pp. 176–85; Antony Flew, *God and Philosophy* (London, 1966), ch. 7; Antony Flew, 'Miracles', in Paul Edwards (ed.), *The Encyclopedia of Philosophy* (New York and London, 1967); and J. L. Mackie, *The Miracle of Theism* (Oxford, 1982), ch. 1.

To get a good sense of what Hume is saying when it comes to miracles, it helps to view his discussion of them in the context of his writings as a whole. A good book which helps one to do this is Antony Flew, *Hume's Philosophy of Belief* (London, 1961). For an excellent account of Hume's discussion of miracles, one which sets it in its historical context, the book to read is R. M. Burns, *The Great Debate on Miracles: From Joseph Granville to David Hume* (London and Toronto, 1981). Also see J. C. A. Gaskin, *Hume's Philosophy of Religion* (2nd edn., Basingstoke, 1988), ch. 8.

For some interesting articles on miracles, see C. D. Broad, 'Hume's Theory of the Credibility of Miracles', *Proceedings of the Aristotelian Society* 17 (1916–17); Paul Dietl, 'On Miracles', *American Philosophical Quarterly* 5 (1968); Patrick Nowell-Smith, 'Miracles', in Antony Flew and Alasdair MacIntyre (eds.), *New Essays in Philosophical Theology* (London, 1955); George N. Schlesinger, *New Perspectives on Old-Time Religion* (Oxford, 1988), ch. 4; and Keith Ward, 'Miracles and Testimony', *Religious Studies* 21 (1985).

The notion of natural law features in much discussion of miracles. For a good philosophical introduction to it, see Rom Harré, *Laws of Nature* (London, 1993). Also see Martin Curd and J. A. Cover (eds.), *Philosophy of Science: The Central Issues* (New York and London, 1998), sect. 7.

QUESTIONS FOR DISCUSSION

1 What do you take to be affirmed by someone who says that miracles have occurred?

2 Can there be miracles which are scientifically explicable?

3 Can one determine whether or not something that happens is religiously significant? If so, how? If not, why not?

4 'God can intervene in the world.' Consider what might be said both for and against this assertion.

5 What do biblical authors mean by 'miracle'? To what extent should their understanding of miracles influence what philosophers have to say about them?

6 Might we have reason to suppose that something has happened which cannot be accounted for naturalistically? If not, why not? If so, under what circumstances?

7 'No intelligent scientist can believe in the occurrence of miracles.' Discuss.

8 Is Hume right to say that we should always reject testimony to the effect that a miracle has occurred?

9 The Catholic Church teaches that a deceased person can be thought to be a saint if the occurrence of miracles can be ascribed to their prayers. Does this teaching make any sense?

10 Let us suppose that events occur which are scientifically inexplicable. What, if anything, might we infer from this fact?

12

MORALITY AND RELIGION

....

Why do people think that evil should lead us to conclude that there is no God? As we have seen, they often suppose that, if God exists, then God is morally good. And they believe that evil gives us grounds for concluding that there is no morally good God (or none that is also omnipotent and omniscient). In that case, however, they are effectively saying that there is a sense in which religious belief is subject to moral censure. They also seem to be suggesting that good moral thinking is somehow prior to good religious thinking.

But is that true? Might good moral thinking not actually spring from good religious thinking? Or might good moral thinking not actually imply some sort of religious belief? Is there really a serious distinction to be drawn between good ethics and good theology? With questions like these we come to the topic of morality and religion. But the topic is large. In this chapter, therefore, I shall focus on just three major questions that have been raised by philosophers with respect to it. These are: (1) Do moral considerations imply that God exists? (2) What is the relation between God and moral goodness? (3) Are religion and morality at odds with each other?

Do Moral Considerations Imply that God Exists?

Many people take themselves to be morally serious even though they have no belief in God. But should they not believe in God, given their moral seriousness? Should they not admit that morality naturally suggests, or even demands, the existence of God? The best first reply to these questions is, 'It all depends on what you mean by "morality" '.

Why? Because there are views of morality which nobody has ever claimed to have theistic implications.

Take, for example, what is commonly called the emotive theory of ethics. Associated with philosophers such as C. L. Stevenson (1908–79), and drawing on ideas to be found in the work of Hume, this theory holds that statements like 'John is a morally bad man' and 'It is your moral duty to do X' are simply (a) expressions of the likes and dislikes of the speaker and (b) encouragements to others to share and act on these likes and dislikes.[1] According to the emotive theory, moral judgements are neither true nor false. If they tell us anything, they indicate only the psychology of those who make them. For the emotive theory, moral judgements are essentially autobiographical. And they have no religious significance.

The same can be said of approaches to morality like that of Friedrich Nietzsche (1844–1900).[2] He conceived of the world as a godless place in which blind forces struggle for power and in which might is the best that can pass for right. Nietzsche described himself as having declared 'war' on morality. He was arguably wrong to do so since he clearly had certain rather traditional values even while he perceived himself as attacking such values.[3] But Nietzsche's general picture of morality is anything but what people have in mind when they argue for the existence of God with reference to morals. If your view of morality corresponds to Nietzsche's, then it has no positive religious implications and it has many anti-religious ones.

But what if you think that a statement like 'John is morally bad' truly describes John just as much as does 'John is bald'? Or suppose that you agree that 'It is your moral duty to do X' is just as fact-asserting as 'It is your ticket that won the lottery'. If that is how you think, you believe that moral judgements are not reducible to expressions of taste and that they are true regardless of how anyone feels about them. Your view is that moral goodness and badness are characteristics which we can recognize as goals to be aspired to or rejected. And if that is your view, then you agree with all who have argued that moral considerations should lead us to conclude that God exists. But how have they tried to make their case?

(a) Kant

If we are looking for a distinguished philosopher who argues that morality ought to lead us to belief in the existence of God, then Kant is an obvious person with whom to start. As we have seen, he has little time for the ontological argument for God's existence. And he rejects other arguments for theism. But he does not therefore conclude that theism is irrational. In fact, he argues that, since people ought to strive for moral perfection, and since they cannot succeed in this without divine assistance, God must exist to ensure that people can achieve that for which they should strive.

According to Kant, morality requires us to aim for the highest good: 'To bring about the highest good in the world is', he says, 'the necessary object of a will determinable by the moral law.'[4] In Kant's view, however, to will the highest good means more than willing what accords with the moral law. It also means willing a proper return of happiness to those who pursue moral goodness. For Kant, willing the highest good means willing a correlation between moral rectitude and happiness.

But now comes the snag. For, in this life, we cannot ensure what Kant takes morality to require. Or, as Kant himself writes:

> The acting rational being in the world is, after all, not also the cause of the world and of nature itself. Hence there is in the moral law not the slightest basis for a necessary connection between morality and the happiness, proportionate thereto, of a being belonging to the world as a part [thereof] and thus dependent on it, who precisely therefore cannot through his will be the cause of this nature and, as far as his happiness is concerned, cannot by his own powers make it harmonize throughout with his practical principles.[5]

We may be rational beings; but we are not omnipotent. So we have a problem on our hands. The highest good must be possible; but it also seems impossible.

How do we resolve this dilemma? Kant's answer is that we should postulate the existence of God as able to ensure that fidelity to moral requirements is properly rewarded. Why? Because, says Kant, the realization of the highest good can be guaranteed only if there is something corresponding to the concept of God, i.e. something able to ensure its realization.

We *ought* to seek to further the highest good (hence this good must, after all, be possible). Therefore the existence of a cause of nature as a whole, distinct from nature, which contains the basis . . . of the exact harmony of [one's] happiness with [one's] morality, is also *postulated* . . . The highest good in the world is possible only insofar as one assumes a supreme cause of nature that has a causality conforming to the moral attitude . . . The supreme cause of nature, insofar as it must be presupposed for the highest good, is a being that is the cause of nature through *understanding* and *will* (and hence is its originator), i.e. *God* . . . i.e., it is morally necessary to assume the existence of God.[6]

According to Kant, the fact that morality demands the realization of the Highest Good and the fact that only God can see to it that the Highest Good comes about lead to the conclusion that God exists. His argument is:

1. It is rationally and morally necessary to attain the perfect good (happiness arising out of complete virtue).

2. What we are obliged to attain must be possible for us to attain.

3. The goal of perfect good is only possible if natural order and causality are parts of an overarching moral order and causality.

4. Moral order and causality are only possible if we postulate a God as their source.

5. Therefore we are under a rational, moral necessity to postulate the existence of God.[7]

(b) Other philosophers

Kant's approach to morality and God is especially famous. But he is not the only philosopher to argue that morality furnishes grounds for belief in God. Many writers have argued that, for instance, we can infer the existence of God from the existence of moral commands or laws. These, it is said, imply the existence of a moral lawgiver or a moral commander. Take, for example, H. P. Owen (1926–96). According to him, there are moral claims which 'constitute an independent order of reality'.[8] These 'laws', as people sometimes call them, make demands on us. But can we suppose that they have no theistic reference? 'No', Owen answers. 'It is impossible', he suggests, 'to think of a command without also thinking of a commander . . . A clear choice faces us. Either we take moral claims to be self-explanatory modes of impersonal existence or we explain them in terms of a personal God.'[9] In Owen's view, the suggestion that claims can exist without a personal ground is not 'a logical contradiction'.[10] But it is not, he thinks, plausible. He agrees that the personal character of moral claims or laws could be explained in terms of demands on us made by other people. But, he adds, we are then left with the fact that moral claims or laws have 'absolute authority', which seems puzzling if they are not thought to reflect the will of one with absolute authority over us.[11]

Owen, of course, knows that many people do not think of themselves as confronted by absolute moral claims or laws. But what if you do believe in such things? Then, Owen suggests, you should conclude that they derive from a transcendent personal source (i.e. God). In his view, 'since within the human realm claims imply a claimant and laws a law-giver, the same implications must be posited within the supra-human order if we are to make morality consistent'.[12] For example, says Owen:

> [Moral] claims transcend every human person and every personal embodiment. On the other hand we value the personal more highly than the impersonal; so it is contradictory to assert that impersonal claims are entitled to the allegiance of our wills. The only solution to the paradox is to suppose that the order of [moral] claims, while it appears as impersonal from a purely moral point of view, is in fact rooted in the personality of God.[13]

And other authors have embraced this line of thinking. People often feel morally responsible, and they often feel guilty if they fail to do their moral duty. But, it has often been argued, this situation makes no sense unless moral laws have a personal explanation. Thus, for example, John Henry Newman (1801–90) writes: 'If, as is the case, we feel responsibility, are ashamed, are frightened, at transgressing the voice of conscience, this implies that there is One to whom we are responsible, before whom we are ashamed, whose claim upon us we fear.'[14]

A variation on this position has been effectively developed by Illtyd Trethowan.[15] He eschews talk about a moral *argument* for God's existence, for he thinks that we know of God, not by inference, but by awareness or experience.[16] But Trethowan also thinks that knowledge of God is mediated, that it is not, so to speak, a matter of meeting God face to face. And according to Trethowan, we are aware of God in our moral experience.

The notion of value is bound up with the notion of obligation. To say that people are worth while, that they have value in themselves, is to say that there is something about them which makes a demand upon us, that we *ought* to make them part of our own project, identify ourselves with them in some sort . . . I propose to say that an awareness of obligation is an awareness of God.[17]

In Trethowan's view, the most reasonable way of accounting for moral experience is to say that its object is absolute, unconditioned, and the source of all creaturely value, especially that of people. 'We have value', Trethowan writes, 'because we receive it from a source of value. That is what I mean, for a start, by God. We know him as giving us value. That is why the demand upon us to develop ourselves is an absolute, unconditional, demand.'[18]

(c) From morality to God?

But ought we to think of morality as leading to belief in God in the ways proposed by the authors whose ideas I have just tried to summarize? Should we, for example, agree with the way in which Kant reasons from morality to God?

(i) Kant, morality, and God   Philosophers commonly agree that 'ought' implies 'can'. If I tell people that they *ought* to do something, it must surely be true that they *can* do it. It would, for example, be absurd to tell polio victims that they ought to walk to work. We might therefore be tempted to argue that, if the highest good ought to be realized, then it can be realized. Since it cannot be realized by human agents, we might incline to conclude that morality is absurd if God does not exist.

Yet, why should we suppose that the highest good can be realized? Kant's reply would presumably be that the highest good is possible since we are obliged to aim at it. But from 'We ought to aim for the highest good' it does not follow that anything can bring about the highest good. All that follows is that we should try to aim for the highest good. If that sounds paradoxical, it is because 'P ought to——but P cannot——' sounds absurd when certain tasks are substituted for——. It is absurd to say that a polio victim ought to walk to work. But it sometimes makes sense to say that people ought to aim for what they cannot in fact achieve. It makes sense, for example, to say that children we know to be dim ought to aim at learning a foreign language.

To this, Kant could say that, if the highest good cannot be realized, we ought not to aim for it. But, then, why should we not conclude that we ought not to aim at the highest good? Kant would probably reply that we *just ought* to aim at the highest good. The trouble, however, is that his argument for God now takes on a circular character. It appears to run: 'If God does not exist, it is not the case that we ought to aim at the highest good; and we ought to aim at the highest good since God exists.' And we may well feel uneasy with that line of reasoning. Does the existence of God follow from the fact that we ought to aim for what can only come about if God exists? Why not say that we just should not aim for such a thing? In any case, why suppose that only God could ensure the realization of what Kant calls the highest good? If God exists, then perhaps he could ensure the existence of the highest good. But can only what is divine do this? Kant thinks that the realization of the highest good requires power and knowledge not found in nature. And that we may concede. But why cannot the highest good be successfully promoted by something other than people but different from what God is supposed to be? Why cannot a top-ranking angel do the job? Why not a pantheon of angels? Why not a pantheon of angels devoted to the philosophy of Kant?

(ii) Other approaches   But what about arguments such as Owen's, that moral laws imply a moral lawgiver, or Newman's, that the sense of moral responsibility and guilt implies the existence of a God to whom we are responsible and before whom we feel guilty? And what of Trethowan's view, that moral experience is an awareness of God?

We might reply to these questions by defending a view of morality in terms of which there is no room for talk about moral laws, moral responsibility, or moral truth. We might say, for example, that morality is merely a matter of human convention (that value judgements are nothing but expressions of human tastes which might differ over time and which cannot be thought of as either true or false). But what if we take a different view of morality? What if we think that there are moral claims, demands, obligations, or laws to which everyone ought to respond? In that case, we might well think that writers like Owen, Newman, and Trethowan are on to something important.

Expanding his position, Trethowan says: 'The absoluteness of moral obligation, as I see it, is so far from being self-explanatory that if it were not made intelligible by being found in a metaphysical—and in fact, a theistic—context, I should be greatly tempted to hand it over to the anthropologists and the psychologists.'[19] Trethowan is suggesting that people who believe in objective and imperious moral claims, demands, obligations, or laws are in an intellectually peculiar position if their view of reality is entirely secular. And here, we might argue, Trethowan has a point. If we believe in moral obligations or moral laws, and if we take them to be absolutely binding, is our position seriously compatible with a non-theistic view of reality? Should we not conclude, rather, that it coheres more with a theistic view of things than with a view which has no place for God?

In response to these questions, we might say, as many do, that morality is 'autonomous', that moral truth consists of a series of facts which need no support outside themselves. We might, for example, agree with the Oxford moral philosopher H. A. Prichard. In a well-known article called 'Does Moral Philosophy Rest on a Mistake?', Prichard raises the question 'Why be moral?' His answer is that there is no reason for being moral other than the fact that we *should* be. According to Prichard, if we ask 'Why should we do what we ought?', the answer has to be 'Because we *ought* to do so, and there is nothing more to be said'.[20] Yet, might we not seek to account for or to understand Prichard's 'ought' in some better way than by saying that it just 'is'? In an article as famous as Prichard's, Elizabeth Anscombe suggests that talking about morality as Prichard does once made perfectly good sense. Such talk, she notes, originated in the Judaeo-Christian belief that what we should do is what God commands us to do. But what if we employ such talk with no background notion of one from whom moral demands, obligations, claims, or laws derive? Are we not then speaking in a way which makes little sense when divorced from what gave rise to it? Anscombe suggests that we are.[21] So does H. O. Mounce:

In a society which has a purely naturalistic or secular view of the world, moral value will be in some measure anomalous . . . Anyone in such a society who is reflective will be likely to feel a tension between his moral feelings and his view of the world. It will strike him that he cannot fully account for the point or meaning of what he feels.[22]

Yet, even if demands, obligations, claims, and laws sometimes derive from (or need to be made sense of in terms of) a personal source (such as God is usually taken to be), must they always derive from such a source? Surely not. Consider, for example, the field of logic. Logicians typically say such things as 'Accepting *these* premises obliges one to accept *that* conclusion'. And they regularly speak of there being various logical laws such as the 'law' of non-contradiction, which states that a proposition cannot be both true and false. But should we therefore suppose that logical truth derives from a personal source? It is hard to see why we should. There is little plausibility in the notion of a personal source of logical laws. Yet if that is the case, why should it be thought that there has to be a personal source (e.g. God) when it comes to moral laws and the like?

And can we not develop a sensible approach to morality without introducing religious matters? Trethowan and those of like mind hold that sound moral thinking (according to which there are real moral truths) does not fit comfortably with a view which conceives of people as nothing but blips in a Godless universe. But can we not defend a non-theistic account of moral thinking which nonetheless conceives of morality as involving genuine moral truths? Some philosophers, at any rate, have thought that we can. Consider Aristotle, for example. In his view (chiefly developed in his *Nicomachean Ethics*), we need to (ought to) behave in certain ways in order to flourish as people. And the ways in which we need to behave follow from what we are by nature. People, Aristotle suggests, naturally seek to be happy. So he thinks of moral philosophy as basically boiling down to the question, 'In what does human happiness consist?' His answer is that it consists in us being virtuous. In order to be happy, says Aristotle, people need (at a minimum) to possess the virtues of prudence, justice, temperateness, and courage. But Aristotle does not suppose that a defence of this conclusion needs to invoke religious premises. He believes that we truly need (or ought) to act in certain ways. He is no ethical relativist or subjectivist.[23] Yet his ethical thinking involves no special appeal to theological positions. Rather, it is grounded in an account of what people are by nature.[24]

What Is the Relation Between God and Moral Goodness?

But suppose that we do believe in God. And suppose that we also believe that there are moral truths which everyone should acknowledge. How should we connect the one belief to the other? Should we perhaps think of moral truths as deriving exclusively from God? Should we take them to be independent of God? Or should we adopt an altogether different viewpoint?

These questions bring us to what is sometimes referred to as 'the Euthyphro dilemma'. In Plato's *Euthyphro*, Socrates asks: 'Is what is holy holy because the gods approve it, or do they approve it because it is holy?'[25] Since Plato's time, philosophers have modified this question so as to ask: 'Is X morally good because God wills it, or does God will X because it is morally good?' And they have replied in different ways.

Some have said that moral truths are nothing but expressions of God's will. According to this view, an action (or a refraining from action) is morally good (or is obligatory) simply because it is willed (or commanded) by God. On this account, whatever God wills us to do is the morally right thing to do just because God wills it. On this account, there is no moral standard apart from God's will. On this account, God's will *establishes* moral standards.[26]

Other philosophers, however, have adopted exactly the opposite position. In their opinion, moral truth in no way derives from God's will. For them, it is independent of God, something to which even he must conform. For them, our knowing that God wills us to do X might constitute a reason for us to choose X. But only on the supposition that God has perfect knowledge of what is morally right and wrong independently of him.

How should we react to these two ways of thinking? Perhaps we can start by noting that there are questions which can be pressed against both of them.

Take, to begin with, the notion that moral goodness and badness is constituted only by what God does or does not will. If that is so, then does it not follow that morality, at bottom, is arbitrary or even whimsical? Does it not also follow that morally wicked actions would be morally right if God so decreed? Yet, how can morality be grounded in nothing but a decision—even a divine decision? And how can even a divine decision make it to be true that, for example, genocide is morally good and feeding the starving is morally wrong?

On the other hand, however, can we seriously think of there being moral truths which are independent of God? If there are such truths, then, presumably, they are objects of God's knowledge distinct from God himself and in no way dependent on him. But can there be anything which does not owe its existence to God? And can we think of God as confronted by a series of commands and prohibitions which stand before him as things to which he morally ought to conform? We might think of God in this way. But, as I noted in Chapter 10, such a view does not square with how God is presented in the Bible. It is also at odds with ways in which some notable non-biblical writers have approached the topic of God and morality. Consider, for example, Søren Kierkegaard (1813–55).[27] In *Fear and Trembling* he considers the Old Testament story of Abraham being told by God to sacrifice his son Isaac.[28] He says that Abraham was bound to do what God commanded, adding that

> here there can be no question of ethics in the sense of morality . . . Ordinarily speaking, a temptation is something which tries to stop a man from doing his duty, but in this case it is ethics itself which tries to prevent him from doing God's will. But what then is duty? Duty is quite simply the expression of the will of God.[29]

In this connection, Kierkegaard talks about 'a teleological suspension of the ethical', an idea which can also be found in the work of D. Z. Phillips, who writes:

> The religious concept of duty cannot be understood if it is treated as a moral concept. When the believer talks of doing his duty, what he refers to is doing the will of God. In making a decision, what is important for the believer is that it should be in accordance with the will of God. To a Christian, to do one's duty *is* to do the will of God. There is indeed no difficulty in envisaging the 'ethical' as the obstacle to 'duty' in this context.[30]

Yet, must we suppose *either* that X is morally good just because God wills it *or* that God wills X because it is morally good independently of him? Might we not rather seek to combine these views? Might we not suggest *both* that moral goodness is somehow constituted by God's will *and* that God wills moral goodness because of its very goodness? You may think that the answer to these questions has to be 'No'. But is that really true? At least one theistic philosopher thought that it is not. Here, once again, I refer to Aquinas, whose views on goodness and God are worth noting at this point.

Aquinas insists that God is certainly good. In fact, he says, God is 'supremely good' or 'the absolutely supreme good'.[31] But why does Aquinas think that this is so? You might instinctively suppose him to believe that God is good because God always conforms to sound moral standards. But that is not Aquinas's position. For one thing, he thinks (as most people do) that not all goodness is moral goodness. More importantly, however, his view is that the primary reason for calling God good lies in the fact that God is *desirable*. In approaching the topic of goodness and God, Aquinas takes his cue from Aristotle, according to whom the good is 'that at which everything aims'.[32]

For both Aquinas and Aristotle, goodness is not a distinct, empirical property possessed by all good things, as, for example, redness is a distinct, empirical property shared by all red things.[33] But they still think that we are saying something particular when calling things good. For them, goodness is always what is somehow wanted. And, says Aquinas, this is as true when it comes to God's goodness as it is when it comes to the goodness of anything else. For him, therefore, God is good because he is *attractive*.

But why does Aquinas take God to be attractive? Because he thinks of God as the unlimited source of the existence of everything other than himself. Considered as such, says Aquinas, God is (a) the transcendent cause of all that we can recognize as creaturely good, and (b) desirable (and good) on that count alone. Why? Because, as we saw in Chapter 7, Aquinas holds that what God produces must reflect what God is by nature. So he thinks of the goodness of creatures as somehow pre-existing in God before it exists in them. In Aquinas's way of thinking, the divine mind (not to be distinguished from God himself) is a kind of blueprint reflected by all creaturely goodness. For Aquinas, aiming at creaturely goodness consists (whether we realize it or not) in desiring what is *first* in God and *only secondarily* in creatures.

Aquinas, of course, does not mean that, for example, a good surgeon or a good bicycle *looks* like God. He does not think that anything looks like God. He does believe, however, that productive causes (which he calls 'efficient causes') express (show forth) their nature in their effects even if these belong to kinds which are different from those to which their productive causes belong.[34] And for this reason Aquinas concludes that God is good. 'The perfection and form of an effect', he argues, 'is a certain likeness of the efficient cause, since every efficient cause produces an effect like itself ... [and] ... since God is the first efficient cause of everything ... the aspect of good and desirable manifestly belong to him.'[35] According to this account, then, goodness in its many created forms is a kind of image of what God, in his own way, is in himself.

And, with this thought in mind, Aquinas has an answer to the Euthyphro dilemma, one that seeks to accommodate both of its alternatives.

Is X morally good because God wills it? Aquinas thinks it is since he takes people's moral goodness to depend on their nature as moral agents created by (and therefore willed by) God.

Does God will X because it is morally good? Aquinas responds that God, as good, always wills the good. But, he thinks, in willing us to be morally good, God is not respecting a standard distinct from himself. According to Aquinas, God creates a world in which we can make true moral judgements concerning our conduct. Yet Aquinas also holds that, in creating our world, and in willing us to do what is morally good, God is willing that we act in accordance with standards he himself has established by creating standards which reflect what he essentially is.

In his approach to morality, Aquinas is basically an Aristotelian. He thinks that people need virtues such as justice, prudence, temperateness, and courage. He also believes that we can come to see that this is so even without reference to belief in God. Aquinas's overall approach to morality is essentially a religious one. But he does not claim that we have to assume theological premises in order to argue cogently that certain ways of acting are morally bad and that others are morally good. What we need to do, he believes, is to look at the way the world works, to study human nature, and to draw reasonable conclusions when it comes to how people ought to behave given that they want to flourish as people.

But where does the world come from? And what is the source of people and their nature? For Aquinas, the answer to these questions is

'God'. So he takes our moral judgements to be ultimately grounded in what God is and in what he has willed to be. In this sense, he embraces the conclusion that X is morally good because God wills it. But he is not suggesting that what God wills is arbitrary or a matter of whim. He is not asserting that God could decide tomorrow that genocide is morally good or feeding the starving morally bad and that this is how things would be.[36] He is saying that reasons we can give for arriving at true moral judgements concerning people depend on what God has created, though not with reference to standards binding on him. In this sense, Aquinas also accepts that God wills X because it is morally good.

But is Aquinas right in thinking as he does here? Not if God is a person who ought to act according to his moral duties and obligations. Aquinas can clearly make no sense of there being standards of goodness to which God must conform. For him, God is 'Goodness Itself'. And his approach to the topic of God and morality is clearly flawed if he is wrong in thinking along these lines, as many philosophers take him to be. Then again, Aquinas's view on morality and God is wrong if moral standards for evaluating people cannot be derived from a knowledge of what people are by nature. As I have said, Aquinas commends Aristotelian ways of evaluating people. And the less sympathetic we are with those, the less we will sympathize with Aquinas. We will also find fault with Aquinas on God and morality if we reject his claim that created goodness is a reflection of what God is by nature. But Aquinas's way of relating God and moral goodness is, at the least, something worth seriously considering. If nothing else, it offers an interesting approach to God and morality which, if correct, does not leave theists impaled on the horns of the Euthyphro dilemma.[37]

Are Religion and Morality at Odds with Each Other?

Many parents like their children to receive religious education in school since they think of this as likely to give them a basic grounding in ethics. But is not religion inimical to morality? Or, as I framed the question at the start of this chapter, are religion and morality at odds with each other?

(a) Some 'anti-religious' answers

Why should we suppose that they are? A popular answer holds that belief in God requires an attitude inappropriate to a truly moral person. Consider, for instance, the position of James Rachels. According to Rachels: (i) belief in God involves a total and unqualified commitment to obey God's commands, and (ii) such a commitment is not appropriate for a moral agent since 'to be a moral agent is to be an autonomous or self-directed agent . . . The virtuous man is therefore identified with the man of integrity, i.e. the man who acts according to precepts which he can, on reflection, conscientiously approve in his own heart.'[38] With this idea in mind, Rachels argues that it is even possible to disprove God's existence. He argues:

1. If any being is God, he must be a fitting object of worship.
2. No being could possibly be a fitting object of worship since worship requires the abandonment of one's role as an autonomous moral agent.
3. Therefore, there cannot be any being who is God.

Rachels thinks that God's commands cannot constitute a reason for acting in any given way. For him, such a reason must be morally compelling in its own right. And this is also the position of Kant. As we have seen, he believes that there is an argument from morality to belief in God. But he also asserts that to say that we ought to do whatever God directs 'would form the basis for a moral system which would be in direct opposition to morality'.[39]

Another line of thinking that has been defended by those who see religion and morality as being at odds notes that religious beliefs have led people to morally unacceptable ways of behaving or to morally suspect beliefs and policies. Hence, for example (and evidently on what he takes to be moral grounds), Bertrand Russell observes:

> Religion prevents our children from having a rational education; religion prevents us from removing the fundamental causes of war; religion prevents us from teaching the ethic of scientific co-operation in place of the old fierce doctrines of sin and punishment. It is possible that mankind is on the threshold of a golden age; but if so, it will be necessary first to slay the dragon that guards the door, and this dragon is religion.[40]

Russell has recently been echoed by Simon Blackburn. To begin with, Blackburn suggests that there are objections to be raised about ways in which God is depicted in texts like the Bible:

> Anyone reading the Bible might be troubled by some of its precepts. The Old Testament God is partial to some people above others, and above all jealous of his own pre-eminence, a strange moral obsession. He seems to have no problem with a slave-owning society, believes that birth control is a capital crime (Genesis 38: 9–10), is keen on child abuse (Proverbs 22: 15, 23: 13–14, 29: 15), and, for good measure, approves of fool abuse (Proverbs 26: 3) . . . Things are usually supposed to get better in the New Testament . . . Yet the overall story of 'atonement' and 'redemption' is morally dubious, suggesting as it does that justice can be satisfied by the sacrifice of an innocent for the sins of the guilty.[41]

The New Testament portrait of Jesus of Nazareth has often been admired by moralists. But Blackburn's reaction to it is ethically hostile. The persona of Jesus in the Gospels, he says,

> has his fair share of moral quirks. He can be sectarian: 'Go not into the way of the Gentiles, and into any city of the Samaritans enter ye not. But go rather to the lost sheep of the house of Israel' (Matt. 10: 5–6). In a similar vein, he refuses help to the non-Jewish woman from Canaan with the chilling racist remark 'It is not meet to take the children's bread, and cast it to dogs' (Matt. 15: 26; Mark 7: 27). He wants us to be gentle, meek, and mild, but he himself is far from it. 'Ye serpents, ye generation of vipers, how can ye escape the damnation of hell?' (Matt. 23: 33). The episode of the Gadarene swine shows him to share the then-popular belief that mental illness is caused by possession by devils. It also shows that animal lives—also anybody else's property rights in pigs—have no value (Luke 8: 27–33). The events of the fig tree in Bethany (Mark 11: 12–21) would make any environmentalist's hair stand on end.[42]

The demise of belief in God, Blackburn ends by suggesting, is 'far from being a threat to ethics'. It is 'a necessary clearing of the ground, on the way to revealing ethics for what it really is'.[43]

(b) Comments on these answers

Is Rachels right to suggest that morality provides us with a proof of God's non-existence? We might well conclude that he is were we to be powerfully struck by the conviction that we could never be morally justified in giving unqualified allegiance to anything but the truths of morality. But need even such a conviction lead to the conclusion proposed by Rachels?

Rachels supposes that, if there is a being worthy of worship, then there could not be autonomous moral agents. But there is an obvious reply to this supposition. For it is surely possible that there be a being worthy of worship who does nothing to interfere with people wishing to remain autonomous moral agents. And it is also possible that a being worthy of worship could positively require that people act as autonomous moral agents. This point is well brought out in a case against Rachels offered by Philip L. Quinn in his book *Divine Commands and Moral Requirements*. There he observes:

> An autonomous moral agent can admit the existence of God if he is prepared to deny that any putative divine command which is inconsistent with his hard-core reflective moral judgements really is a divine command. He can resolve the supposed role-conflict by allowing that genuine divine commands ought to be obeyed unconditionally but also maintaining that no directive which he does not accept on moral grounds is a genuine divine command. For the following propositions are logically compatible:
> God exists.
> God sometimes commands agents to do certain things.
> God never commands anything an autonomous and well-informed human moral agent would, on reflection, disapprove.[44]

Yet, might it not be argued that, if X is worthy of worship, then worshippers are bound to do whatever X wills? And does this not mean that worshippers cannot be autonomous moral agents? Rachels evidently supposes that the answer to these questions is 'Yes'. But is it? Cannot worshippers consistently say that they worship a being who always wills them to behave as autonomous moral agents? If a worshipper were to say this, then Rachels's case would clearly collapse. It would also collapse if someone who believes in and worships God were to say that God knows all moral truths and always directs people in accordance with them. Such a believer would be giving unqualified allegiance to God's commands. But it does not follow that the believer in question would thereby be abandoning autonomy as a moral agent.

Yet, what of the thesis that morality and religion should always be thought of as opposed to each other? If we think of certain religious beliefs, and if we think of certain moral ones, we might develop a case for their being at odds with each other (as Blackburn does). But can we defend the sweeping conclusion that morality (as such) is incompatible with religion (as such)?

One reason for saying that we cannot lies in the fact that the word 'morality' clearly has different associations for different people. What one person regards as morality another may dismiss as immorality, or as plain triviality. And it is often impossible to conclude that either party in such disputes is in some objective sense right. General statements about what morality is should be regarded with suspicion, for the boundaries dividing the moral and the non-moral are often very fuzzy.

A related reason for the same conclusion lies in the vagueness of the word 'religion'. If we insist that religion and morality are opposed to each other, we must surely be supposing that there is a fairly easily identifiable thing rightly referred to as 'religion'. But is there? Maybe not, as I indicated in Chapter 2. Many writers, in fact, would go so far as to say that 'religion' just cannot be defined. 'It is', says Ninian Smart, 'partly a matter of convention as to what is counted under the head of religion and what is not.'[45] Here Smart agrees with what William Alston writes on 'Religion' in *The Encyclopedia of Philosophy*. Alston notes various attempts to define 'religion' and suggests that none of them states necessary and sufficient conditions for something to be a religion. He concludes that the most that can be done is to note various characteristics of religion:

> When enough of these characteristics are present to a sufficient degree, we have a religion. It seems that, given the actual use of the term 'religion', this is as precise as we can be. If we tried to say something like 'for a religion to exist, there must be the first two plus any three others', or 'for a religion to exist, any four of these characteristics must be present', we would be introducing a degree of precision not to be found in the concept of religion actually in use ... The best way to explain the concept of religion is to elaborate in detail the relevant features of an ideally clear case of religion and then indicate the respects in which less clear cases can differ from this, without hoping to find any sharp line dividing religion from non-religion.[46]

The implication of such reflections, which seem reasonable ones, is that it is misleading to say that religion and morality are necessarily opposed to each other. And this means that we may challenge comments like those of Russell and Blackburn. A great deal that they consider bad may well have been perpetrated or encouraged by people in the name of religion. But many religious people would accept this conclusion while also objecting to the very things to which Russell and Blackburn object. They would, in fact, argue that many of the key values for which Russell and Blackburn stand are an essential part of religious aspiration. There are, for example, plenty of Christians who argue in favour of pluralistic and open education, for pacifism, for scientific cooperation, for non-sectarianism and anti-racism, for property rights, and for respect for the environment. And all this on theological grounds. Russell and Blackburn might reply that religion should still be seen as a source of evil which needs to be eradicated in order to make way for a kind of Utopia. But, as Mary Midgley observes, 'whatever may have been its plausibility in the eighteenth century, when it first took the centre of the stage', this view 'is just a distraction today'.[47] Moral atrocity abounds even where the influence of religion is non-existent. And, as Midgley goes on to suggest, what might be required from thinkers is 'an atrociously difficult psychological inquiry' rather than 'a ritual warfare about the existence of God' and the like.[48]

But it ought to be added that there are evidently religious believers who see their religious beliefs as entailing moral judgements sharply at odds with those accepted by many other people. And sometimes it may be quite impossible to resolve the resulting disagreement. Take, for instance, the conflict between many secular moralists and theologians who disapprove of divorce in the light of what they take to be divine instruction. These people often share a great deal of common ground when it comes to criteria for arriving at moral judgements. Yet they can evidently reach deadlock in the long run because one group thinks that some sound moral teaching has been revealed by God while the other does not. And until they can come to agree on such matters as revelation, no solution to their final disagreement seems possible.

This kind of impasse may, of course, lead us to ask whether religion is inevitably inimical to morality. But this is not a question to answer in general terms, and maybe it is none too clear to begin with. As should be evident from the diversity of views presented in this chapter, anyone concerned with the relationship between morality and religion will need to proceed slowly and with reference to various understandings of both morality and religion.

NOTES

1. For an account and discussion of the emotive theory, see J. O. Urmson, *The Emotive Theory of Ethics* (London, 1968).

2. Though largely unappreciated by philosophers in his own lifetime, Nietzsche is now ranked among the most significant of modern Continental thinkers. Famous for concluding that 'the will to power' is the most basic human drive, he was profoundly critical of religion, especially Christianity. His writings include *The Birth of Tragedy* (1872), *Beyond Good and Evil* (1886), and *Toward a Genealogy of Morals* (1887).

3. For a discussion drawing attention to traditional moral values implicit in Nietzsche's critique of morality, see R. W. Beardsmore, 'The Rebel and Moral Traditions', in id., *Moral Reasoning* (London and New York, 1969).

4. Immanuel Kant, *Critique of Practical Reason*, trans. Werner S. Pluhar (Indianapolis, IN, 2002), p. 155.

5. Ibid., p. 158.

6. Ibid., pp. 158 f.

7. Peter Byrne, *The Moral Interpretation of Religion* (Cambridge, 1998), pp. 56 f. For more from Kant on morality and God, see Immanuel Kant, *Lectures on Philosophical Theology*, ed. Allen W. Wood and Gertrude M. Clark (Ithaca, NY, and London, 1978), pp. 40 ff. and 109 ff.

8. H. P. Owen, *The Moral Argument for Christian Theism* (London, 1965), p. 49.

9. Ibid., pp. 49 f.

10. Ibid., p. 50.

11. Ibid.

12. Ibid., p. 51.

13. Ibid., p. 53.

14. J. H. Newman, *A Grammar of Assent*, ed. C. F. Harold (London and New York, 1947), p. 83. Newman's views on morality are best understood in the light of his thinking as a whole. For an excellent introduction to this, see Avery Dulles, *Newman* (London and New York, 2002).

15. See Illtyd Trethowan, *Absolute Value* (London, 1970) and *Mysticism and Theology* (London, 1974).

16. Trethowan's position in this respect bears comparison with that of authors such as William Alston, discussed in Chapter 6 above.

17. Trethowan, *Absolute Value*, pp. 84 f.

18. Ibid., p. 89.

19. Ibid., p. 117.

20. H. A. Prichard, 'Does Moral Philosophy Rest on a Mistake?', *Mind* XXI (1912).

21. Elizabeth Anscombe, 'Modern Moral Philosophy', *Philosophy* 33 (1958). Anscombe's article is reprinted in volume III of *G. E. M. Anscombe: Collected Philosophical Papers* (Oxford, 1981).

22. H. O. Mounce, 'Morality and Religion', in Brian Davies (ed.), *Philosophy of Religion: A Guide to the Subject* (London, 1998), p. 283.

23. Philosophers would normally understand an ethical relativist to be someone who holds that there are no moral truths which everyone ought to acknowledge. And they would commonly take an ethical subjectivist to be someone who thinks that moral judgements do nothing but express the feelings or tastes of the people who articulate them

24. This, presumably, is why philosophers can often sympathetically summarize Aristotle's ethical thinking without bringing in religious themes. I should note, however, that some authors argue that removing reference to religious belief seriously impairs any account of Aristotle's ethics. According to H. O. Mounce, for instance, Aristotle holds that 'value is not a projection of human feeling but an objective order, and this order is not-self-explanatory but has its source in what is transcendent and divine. The elements in this philosophy are locked together into a whole. If you remove the divine source, you undermine the order of nature; if you undermine the order of nature, you destroy all value' ('Morality and Religion', pp. 269 f.).

25. I quote from Edith Hamilton and Huntington Cairns (eds.), *Plato: The Collected Dialogues* (Princeton, 1978), p. 178.

26. William of Ockham (c.1285–1349) is commonly cited as a classical defender of this view, sometimes referred to as the 'divine command theory of ethics'. But many writers earlier and later than Ockham have endorsed it, or a position comparable to it. Cf. Janine Marie Idziak, 'Divine Command Ethics', in Philip L. Quinn and Charles Taliaferro (eds.), *A Companion to Philosophy of Religion* (Oxford, 1997). For texts endorsing a divine command theory of ethics, see Janine Marie Idziak (ed.), *Divine Command Morality: Historical and Contemporary Readings* (New York and Toronto, 1979).

27. Kierkegaard is widely admired by many contemporary theologians. His

writings include *Either-Or* (1843), *Philosophical Fragments* (1844), and *Concluding Unscientific Postscript* (1846). He is often said to be the founding father of the philosophical movement known as Existentialism. His writings had a particular influence on Martin Heidegger (1889–1976) and Jean-Paul Sartre (1905–80).

28. Genesis 22.

29. Søren Kierkegaard, *Fear and Trembling*, trans. Robert Payne (London, New York, and Toronto, 1939), pp. 84 f.

30. D. Z. Phillips, 'God and Ought', in Ian Ramsey (ed.), *Christian Ethics and Contemporary Philosophy* (London, 1966), pp. 137 f.

31. Thomas Aquinas, *Summa Theologiae*, Ia, 6, 2. I quote from volume 2 of the Blackfriars edition of the *Summa Theologiae* (London and New York, 1964).

32. Aristotle, *Nicomachean Ethics*, I, 1, 1094a. I quote from Roger Crisp (ed.), *Aristotle: Nicomachean Ethics* (Cambridge, 2000), p. 3.

33. Cf. my account of Aquinas on the meaning of 'bad' (Chapter 10 above).

34. Cf. Chapter 7 above.

35. Aquinas, *Summa Theologiae*, Ia, 6,1.

36. Aquinas thinks that God is immutable, so he would reject the notion of God first willing this and then willing something different.

37. Cf. Norman Kretzmann, 'Abraham, Isaac, and Euthyphro: God and the Basis of Morality', reprinted in Eleonore Stump and Michael J. Murray (eds.), *Philosophy of Religion: The Big Questions* (Oxford, 1999).

38. James Rachels, 'God and Human Attitudes', *Religious Studies* 7 (1971), p. 334.

39. Immanuel Kant, *Groundwork of the Metaphysic of Morals*, ed. H. J. Paton (New York, 1964), p. 111.

40. Bertrand Russell, *Why I am not a Christian* (London, 1927), p. 37.

41. Simon Blackburn, *Being Good* (Oxford, 2001), pp. 10 ff.

42. Ibid., pp. 12 f.

43. Ibid., p. 19.

44. Philip L. Quinn, *Divine Commands and Moral Requirements* (Oxford, 1978), pp. 6 f.

45. Ninian Smart, *The Phenomenon of Religion* (London and Oxford, 1978), p. 10.

46. William Alston, 'Religion', in Paul Edwards (ed.), *The Encyclopedia of Philosophy*, vol. 7 (New York and London, 1967).

47. Mary Midgley, *Wickedness* (London, 1984), p. 6.

48. Ibid.

FURTHER READING

Your reflections on morality and religion might be helped by a knowledge of the history of moral philosophy. For brief but reliable surveys of this, see Alasdair MacIntyre, *A Short History of Ethics* (2nd edn., Notre Dame, IN, 1998), Richard Norman, *The Moral Philosophers: An Introduction to Ethics* (2nd edn., Oxford, 1998), and D. D. Raphael, *Moral Philosophy* (Oxford, 1981). For a brief account of twentieth-century English-speaking moral philosophy, see W. D. Hudson, *A Century of Moral Philosophy* (London, 1980). For a survey of the history of Christian thinking on morality, see Servais Pinckaers, *The Sources of Christian Ethics* (Washington, DC, 1995). If you are approaching moral philosophy for the first time, there are some helpful anthologies currently available. These include: David E. Cooper (ed.), *Ethics: The Classic Readings* (Oxford, 1998); Louis P. Pojman (ed.), *Moral Philosophy: A Reader* (2nd edn., Indianapolis, IN, 1998); James Rachels (ed.), *Ethical Theory* (Oxford, 1998); and Peter Singer (ed.), *Ethics* (Oxford and New York, 1994).

For some notable books dealing directly with morality and religion, see Robert Merrihew Adams, *Finite and Infinite Goods: A Framework for Ethics* (New York and Oxford, 1999); William Warren Bartley III, *Morality and Religion* (London, 1971); Michael Beaty, Carlton Fisher, and Mark Nelson (eds.), *Christian Theism and Moral Philosophy* (Macon, GA, 1998); Robert Buckman, *Can We Be Good Without God?* (Amherst, NY, 2002); Peter Byrne, *The Moral Interpretation of Religion* (Grand Rapids, MI, and Cambridge, UK, 1998); Paul W. Diener, *Religion and Morality: An Introduction* (Louisville, KY, 1997); Paul Helm (ed.), *Divine Commands and Morality* (Oxford, 1981); W. G. Maclagan, *The Theological Frontier of Ethics* (London, 1961); D. Z. Phillips (ed.), *Religion and Morality* (New York, 1996); P. L. Quinn, *Divine Commands and Moral Requirements* (Oxford, 1978); I. T. Ramsey (ed.), *Christian Ethics and Contemporary Philosophy* (London, 1966); Keith Ward, *Ethics and Christianity* (London, 1970); and Michael Martin, *Atheism, Morality, and Meaning* (Amherst, NY, 2002). Most of these volumes come with good bibliographies which will help you further to pursue the questions discussed in them.

For discussions of Kant on God as a postulate of practical reason (with advice on yet further reading), see Bernard M. G. Reardon, *Kant as Philosophical Theologian* (Basingstoke and London, 1988); Keith Ward, *The Development of Kant's View of Ethics* (Oxford, 1972); Ralph C. S. Walker, *Kant* (London, 1978); Allen

W. Wood, *Kant's Moral Religion* (Ithaca, NY, 1970); and Allen W. Wood, *Rational Theology, Moral Faith, and Religion*, in Paul Guyer (ed.), *The Cambridge Companion to Kant* (Cambridge, 1992).

For more on Aquinas on morality and religion, see John Finnis, *Aquinas: Moral, Political and Legal Theory* (Oxford, 1998); Anthony Lisska, *Aquinas's Theory of Natural Law: An Analytic Reconstruction* (Oxford, 1996); and Ralph McInerny, *Ethica Thomistica* (Washington, DC, 1982). Also see Eleonore Stump and Norman Kretzmann, 'Being and Goodness', in Brian Davies (ed.), *Thomas Aquinas: Contemporary Philosophical Perspectives* (Oxford, 2002), and Brian Davies, *Aquinas* (London, 2002), ch. 14.

QUESTIONS FOR DISCUSSION

1 Do moral judgements state truths? If so, truths about what? And how can we come to know these truths? If moral judgements do not state truths, how should we understand them?

2 Is Kant right to suggest that morality ought to lead us to postulate God's existence?

3 Can I rationally sacrifice my life for the sake of my moral beliefs if I also have no religious beliefs?

4 It has been said that many cultures earlier than our own made no sharp distinction between the moral and religious. Is that view true? If it is, is there something we ought to infer when it comes to the relationship between morality and religion?

5 Must our appraisals of good and bad depend on a knowledge of God? Can any of them make sense even on the supposition that there is no God?

6 Let us suppose that there are moral laws which are binding on all people. Does this fact imply that there is a moral lawgiver before whom everyone is responsible? Let us suppose that there are moral obligations which make claims on everyone. Does this fact imply that moral obligations derive from a source with a claim on everyone?

7 'One cannot reasonably conclude that such and such ought to be done by appealing to what is, in fact, the case.' Is that true? Consider this question with special to attention to the suggestion that 'God wills that I should do X' implies 'I ought to do X'.

8 'We can think of God as good since he is the source of all that is good apart from himself.' What might this statement be taken to mean? Can it be defended?

9 'It is morally wrong to defy an omnipotent, omniscient God.' Discuss.

10 Have religious beliefs led people to do what is morally wrong? If your answer is 'Yes', then give examples and explain their significance when it comes to the topic of morality and religion.

13

LIFE AFTER DEATH

On 7 July 1776 James Boswell (1740–95) visited David Hume in Edinburgh.[1] Hume was dying. According to Boswell, he looked 'lean, ghastly, and quite of an earthy appearance'.[2] But he also appeared 'placid and even cheerful'. Boswell asked him 'if it was not possible that there might be a future state'. Hume replied 'that it was a most unreasonable fancy that he should exist forever'. When Boswell asked him if 'the thought of annihilation never gave him any uneasiness', Hume said: 'Not the least.' Boswell, who devoutly believed in a life to come, marvelled at this response. Yet he felt bound to observe: 'I could not but be assailed by momentary doubts while I had actually before me a man of such strong abilities and extensive inquiry dying in the persuasion of being annihilated.'

Was Hume right, however? Do we perish at death? Religious believers, like Boswell, normally suppose that we do not.[3] But is their position defensible? Some people would say that its truth is guaranteed by divine revelation, by, for example, Jesus's teaching that those who believe in him shall live even though they die.[4] But can belief in life after death be supported philosophically, without recourse to divine revelation? Or should we, perhaps, conclude that it is philosophically dubious for one reason or other?

Attempts to answer these questions obviously need to refer to accounts of what life after death is supposed to involve. There have been many such accounts. Two have been especially popular with religious believers and have also provoked a lot of philosophical discussion. So I shall focus on the topic of life after death by turning to them.

Two Views of Life after Death

(a) Survival as an immaterial self

The first view of life after death has a long philosophical history. It can be found, for example, in Plato's *Phaedo*. Here we read about Socrates (*c.*469–399 BC), who is about to drink poison because he has been condemned to death. His friends are grief-stricken, but Socrates is not. His friend Crito asks 'But in what fashion are we to bury you?' The text continues:

> 'However you wish,' said he; 'provided you catch me, that is, and I don't get away from you.' And with this he laughed quietly, looked towards us and said: 'Friends, I can't persuade Crito that I am Socrates here, the one who is now conversing and arranging each of the things being discussed; but he imagines I'm that dead body he'll see in a little while, so he goes and asks how he's to bury me! But ... when I drink the poison, I shall no longer remain with you, but shall go off and depart for some happy state of the blessed.[5]

Notice how Socrates here distinguishes between himself and his body which is soon to be lifeless. He evidently understands himself to be different from this body. And that is how people think who support the first of our views about life after death, according to which we survive our death in non-bodily form. Take, for example, Descartes. According to him:

> My essence consists solely in the fact that I am a thinking thing. It is true that I may have (or, to anticipate, that I certainly have) a body that is very closely joined to me. But nevertheless, on the one hand I have a clear and distinct idea of myself, in so far as I am simply a thinking, non-extended thing; and on the other hand I have a distinct idea of body, in so far as this is simply an extended, non-thinking thing. And accordingly, it is certain that I am really distinct from my body and can exist without it.[6]

On this basis, Descartes finds nothing absurd in the suggestion that people can survive the corruption of their bodies. If I am not my body, he reasons, then the demise of that mortal object need not entail my extinction. People at funerals sometimes talk of the lately deceased as observing (and sometimes even as enjoying or being entertained by) what is going on. Whether they realize it or not, such people are embracing Descartes's view of what we are. In philosophical jargon, they are 'substance dualists'. They believe that people are made up of two kinds of stuff: immaterial stuff and physical stuff. And they take the immaterial side of people (which they sometimes call their 'minds') to make them the individuals that they are.

(b) Survival and resurrection

Our second view of life after death is very different. For this teaches that people survive death in bodily form. When we die, our bodies decay or are swiftly destroyed (e.g. by cremation). According to our second view, however, we shall, after death, continue to live physically. Defenders of this view look forward to resurrection. Hence, for example, Peter Geach writes: 'Apart from the *possibility* of resurrection, it seems to me a mere illusion to have any hope for life after death . . . If there is no resurrection, it is superfluous and vain to pray for the dead.'[7] And this is the biblical approach to life after death. People sometimes assume that biblical authors think of life after death along the lines of Socrates and Descartes. But the Old Testament views people as psychosomatic unities, and it refers to human survival in bodily terms.[8] The same is true of the New Testament. Hence, for example, St Paul insists that Christians are misguided if Christ was not raised from the dead and if his followers are not likewise to be raised. For St Paul, as for other New Testament authors, we shall survive death with bodies materially continuous with those we have now.[9] He raises the questions 'How are the dead raised? With what kind of body do they come?' His answer is that the dead are raised with transformed bodies, but ones that can still be thought of as their own.[10]

Two Questions

Here, then, are two distinct views of life after death. According to the first, we shall survive as disembodied selves, or minds. According to the second, we shall live again corporeally. But what are we to make of these views? Philosophers have raised two basic questions about them. The first is conceptual. It asks whether there *could* be what our two views say that there *will* be. The second question, however, moves from possibility to actuality. It asks whether it is reasonable to believe that we can look forward to either disembodied survival or bodily life after death. Let us therefore consider each question in turn.

(a) The survival of the disembodied self

If we are different from our bodies, then, as Descartes says, we might be able to exist without them. And if we can do that, then the view that we can survive death is possibly true. We normally think of death as the end of a person's bodily life. But if people are not their bodies, then the fact that their bodies die does not entail that they perish. If X and Y are distinct, then what happens to X does not necessarily happen to Y.

But are people other than their bodies? Descartes, as we have seen, thinks that they are, and he does not lack philosophical supporters. Consider, for instance, H. D. Lewis. 'My own conclusion', he says, 'is that no recent discussions . . . have succeeded in showing that we can dispense with an absolute distinction between mind and body.'[11] 'I have little doubt', he declares, 'that there are mental processes quite distinct from observable behaviour and that each individual has an access to his own experiences in having them which is not possible for the most favoured observer.'[12] Lewis is here suggesting that I am my mind and that I am, as such, not to be identified with anything physical. Another believer in the distinction between people and their bodies is Richard Swinburne. According to him:

A person has a body if there is one particular chunk of matter through which he has to operate on and learn about the world. But suppose he finds himself able to operate on and learn about the world within some small finite region, without having to use one particular chunk of matter for this purpose. He might find himself with knowledge of the position of objects in a room (perhaps by having visual sensations, perhaps not), and able to move such objects just like that, in the ways in which we know about the positions of our limbs and can move them. But the room would not be, as it were, the person's body; for we may suppose that simply by choosing to do so he can gradually shift the focus of his knowledge and control, e.g., to the next room. The person would be in no way limited to operating and learning through one particular chunk of matter. Hence we may term him disembodied. The supposition that a person might become disembodied . . . seems coherent.[13]

With this point made, Swinburne argues that, if X can be without Y, then X and Y are different things. Since I can be without my body, it follows, says Swinburne, that I am not my body.[14]

As I have said, the theory that persons are essentially other than their bodies is usually referred to as 'substance dualism'.[15] So we may say that the notion of non-bodily survival stands or falls depending on whether or not a case can be made for substance dualism. But can such a case be made? Defenders of substance dualism often suggest that the following observations strongly favour it:

1. We often naturally talk as if our real selves were distinct from our bodies—as when we say that we *have* our bodies, and as when we agree that we can be the same persons over a number of years even though our bodies have changed in the meantime.

2. We have privileged access to our own states of mind. The knowledge we have of our own states of mind is direct and unchallengeable in a way that our knowledge of material objects is not.

Yet the fact that our language seems to imply a distinction between mind and body does not show that mind and body are distinct things. We may speak of people as *having* bodies. But we also speak of them as *having* minds. And talk about people which seems to distinguish them from their bodies shows that we are so distinct only on the assumption that talk of mind is not somehow translatable into talk of body, or on the assumption that it is talk about a non-bodily substance. Yet the truth of these assumptions is just what the substance dualist is purporting to establish. Considered as a defence of substance dualism, to say that we speak of people as *having* bodies is not to say enough. We say that a chair *has* a back, legs, and a seat. But is a chair something distinct from its back, legs, and seat?

Then again, what exactly is proved by the fact that we have privileged access to our own states of mind? Does it, for instance, follow from this fact that only I can know what I am thinking? But that is patently false. You can know what I am thinking. You can actually have the same thoughts yourself. There is not a single thought which I can have which you cannot have as well. We can sometimes keep our thoughts secret. But this does not mean that we are things which other people cannot observe or that thinking is an essentially incorporeal process.

In seeking to defend a Cartesian view of people, we might reply that we are aware of ourselves as others cannot be aware of us simply by attending to our bodies.[16] We might suggest that we can observe our own minds and comment on their contents infallibly while the minds of others are always hidden from us behind a physical veil. But are we privileged observers of the contents of our own minds? And are other people's minds really hidden from us? Some philosophers argue that the answer to these questions is 'Yes' since, while we can be wrong about the thoughts and feelings of others, we cannot be mistaken when it comes to whether or not we are thinking certain thoughts or feeling certain feelings. It makes sense to say 'I think that John is late, but I could be wrong'. But, even though we have a use for sentences like 'I do not know what I think', it would be absurd to assert 'I think that I think that John is late, but I could be wrong in thinking that I think this'. Then again, while it makes sense to say 'I think that my pain is due to gout, but I could be wrong', it makes no sense to say 'I was in pain, but I did not know this'. With these facts in mind, philosophers have often concluded that we do, indeed, have privileged access to the contents of our minds and that human minds and bodies are therefore distinct entities. But is there really such a thing as introspection considered as a private source of knowledge or an inner sense? We can, of course, say that we have a certain thought or sensation. And we cannot be mistaken here. But is that the case because we are seeing something as, for example, we see what is around us? No. Talk of introspection is metaphorical. It does not refer to a literal seeing or perceiving. It cannot be improved by getting closer or by turning on a light. We might reply that we just do know what we think or feel. But is that so?

In one sense it obviously is. In his *Philosophical Investigations*, however, Wittgenstein observes: 'I can know what someone else is thinking, not what I am thinking. It is correct to say "I know what you are thinking", and wrong to say "I know what I am thinking".'[17] And Wittgenstein here is drawing attention to something important. For one thing, if it makes sense to say that Fred knows that something is the case, it also makes sense to say that he does not know it to be the case, or that he is doubtful about the matter. But it makes no sense to say that we do not know what we are thinking, or that we are doubtful as to whether or not we think such and such. Then again, it makes sense to ascribe knowledge to people where it also makes sense to think of them as having learned, found out, or come to know. And it makes sense to ascribe knowledge to people where it also makes sense to speak of them guessing, surmising, or conjecturing with regard to what they claim to know. But it makes no sense to say that we come to learn what we think or feel, or that we discover this. Nor does it make sense to speak of our guessing, surmising, or conjecturing whether or not we think these thoughts or feel those feelings. Some people would say that we can explain how we know about our thoughts and feelings because of our ability to recognize them for what they are. But that would seem to mean that I can, for example, know that I am in pain because I feel pain. Yet is not my *feeling pain* the same as my *being in pain*? And how can it be thought of as something I may observe so as thereby to recognize that I am in pain?[18]

You might reply that there is something you know when you are in pain (or when you know that you are thinking such and such). And, to drive your point home, you might add that you lack the object of this knowledge when it comes to the pains (or thoughts) of others. But you would then be asserting that you cannot know how people think or feel, that the thoughts and feelings of people are hidden from each other. And that conclusion is exceedingly odd. People may keep their thoughts and feelings to themselves. They may even take steps to hide them from others. But such practices are secondary to the fact that people manifest how they think and feel. As Wittgenstein also says: 'Just try—in a real case—to doubt someone else's fear or pain.'[19] Wittgenstein is not here denying that people can pretend to be in pain. Nor is he identifying fear and pain with observable bodily behaviour. He is, however, implying that pain, fear, and the like are not items which are known only to those who have them. And, in doing so, Wittgenstein is surely talking sense, as ought to be clear from a telling analogy that he uses.[20]

Suppose that we all have a box with something in it. Each of us can look into our own box but not into that of anyone else. Suppose I say that what I have in my box is 'a beetle'. And suppose that everyone else says that they, too, have 'a beetle' in their boxes. What can you conclude? Not very much. You cannot see into other people's boxes, so you have no reason to suppose that what they call a beetle is not what you call a flower or a piece of silk, or even an empty space. On the scenario just envisaged, the word 'beetle' is useless for purposes of communication. In particular, it cannot name something which we might take ourselves to know. But we can talk about thoughts and feelings. And we can communicate with others while doing so. Such talk is not about what each of us knows only on our own. As Jaegwon Kim puts it: 'The apparently evident fact that such utterances can be used to transmit information from person to person and that expressions like "pain" and "the thought that it's going to rain" have intersubjective meanings, meanings that can be communicated from person to person, seems to give the lie to the Cartesian model of mind as an inner private theatre at which only a single subject can take a peek.'[21]

At this point, however, a defender of substance dualism might say that there are other arguments in its favour. What might the arguments be? How, for example, does Descartes argue in defence of his position? One of his arguments hinges on the claim that we can have a clear idea of ourselves as non-material. I can know that I exist, says Descartes. I can also come to see that I am essentially an immaterial, thinking thing. But might not appearances be deceptive here? In some cases my seeming to myself to be thus and so means that I really am thus and so. If I seem to myself to be unhappy, then I am unhappy. On the other hand, however, the fact that I seem to myself to be sober does not mean that I am sober. Nor does it follow from the fact that I seem to myself to be well that I am, in fact, well.

Another of Descartes's arguments is that, while the body is always divisible, mind is not. 'There is', he says, 'a great difference between the mind and the body, inasmuch as the body is by its very nature always divisible, while the mind is utterly indivisible.'[22] Descartes here means that someone can chop up my body without chopping me up. But how does he know that this is so? If I am essentially corporeal, then to chop up my body is to dissect me. Descartes would doubtless reply that he cannot distinguish parts in himself (his mind) to be divided. But what Descartes can or cannot distinguish is not to the point. The question is: is Descartes something divisible?

But Descartes has another argument for supposing that he is a non-bodily thing: an argument grounded in doubt. I can, he says, doubt that I have a body. But I cannot doubt that I exist. So I am not my body. As you will realize, this argument is similar to that of Richard Swinburne noted above. Descartes thinks that he can exist without his body, and that he and his body are therefore distinct. And Swinburne is of the same opinion. But Descartes's argument is invalid. Descartes says: 'I can doubt that I have a body, but I cannot doubt that I exist, therefore I am not a body.' But I might say: 'Fred can doubt that he is a professor of philosophy, but Fred cannot doubt that he exists, therefore Fred is not a professor of philosophy.' Would it follow that Fred is not a professor of philosophy? It would not. In fact, critics of Descartes can actually use his pattern of reasoning against him at this point. For, as Norman Malcolm observes:

> If it were valid to argue 'I can doubt that my body exists but not that I exist, *ergo* I am not my body,' it would be equally valid to argue 'I can doubt that there exists a being whose essential nature is to think, but I cannot doubt that I exist, *ergo* I am not a being whose essential nature is to think'. Descartes is hoist with his own petard![23]

A supporter of Descartes might say that what he is driving at in his argument from doubt can be cogently stated in the terms offered by Swinburne. But Swinburne's argument rests on the view that people can be conceived of as disembodied. Yet can they? Here we need to remember that much of our understanding of ourselves involves reference to the existence and processes of bodies. We can have a vigorous and lively 'inner' life. We can, for example, think and have emotional experiences without showing so by any bodily behaviour. In *The Concept of Mind*, Gilbert Ryle (1900–76) sometimes speaks as if our history were simply a matter of our bodily behaviour, which is false if only because people can keep certain thoughts and feelings entirely to themselves.[24] On the other hand, however, to be alive as a human person is also to be able to engage in all sorts of activities which would be impossible in the absence of a body.

Consider, for instance, thinking. We think about what we are doing. And we act thoughtfully. So a proper account of thinking requires a reference to behaviour and to physical context. The same applies to seeing. A full account of seeing will have to take notice of such sentences as 'I can't see, it's too dark', 'Let's see if he's finished', or 'I saw my friend yesterday'. As Peter Geach says:

> Well, how do we eventually use such words as 'see', 'hear', 'feel', when we have got into the way of using them? We do not exercise these concepts only

so as to pick out cases of seeing and the rest in our separate world of sense-experience; on the contrary, these concepts are used in association with a host of other concepts relating, e.g., to the physical characteristics of what is seen and the behaviour of those who do see. In saying this I am not putting forward a theory, but just reminding you of very familiar features in the everyday use of the verb 'to see' and related expressions; our ordinary talk about seeing would cease to be intelligible if there were cut out of it such expressions as 'I can't see, it's too far off', 'I caught his eye', 'Don't look round', etc. . . . I am not asking you to believe that 'to see' is itself a word for a kind of behaviour. But the concept of seeing can be maintained only because it has threads of connexion with these other non-psychological concepts; break enough threads and the concept of seeing collapses.[25]

Some writers who have insisted on the importance of the existence of bodies as far as the existence of persons is concerned have concluded that persons are nothing but bodies. I refer here both to what has been called behaviourism and to the so-called Identity Thesis, according to some versions of which thoughts, feelings, and so forth are nothing but brain processes.[26] But to point to the importance of the body in our understanding of persons is not necessarily to subscribe to forms of behaviourism or to the identity thesis.[27] It is just to say that it is extremely difficult to defend a view which allows (human) persons to be essentially distinct from their bodies.

(b) Survival as bodily

Yet what of the view that people can survive death in bodily form? Perhaps its chief virtue is that it is unaffected by any of the criticisms of substance dualism levelled above. If the argument of the preceding section is sound, we need bodies in order to exist. And if we say that there is bodily life after death, we are at least talking about something which might, if it came about, be the life of a human person.

But we might still ask whether people could live after death in bodily form. I suggested earlier that, from the logical possibility of people existing apart from their bodies, it does not follow that they are actually able to exist apart from their bodies. It may be logically possible for me to leap over tall buildings at a single bound. But that does not mean that I can actually jump over the Taj Mahal. And with that truth in mind, I might wonder whether I can survive death in bodily form.

It might be said that my worries can be dispelled by my recognizing that people can live after death because replicas of their bodies can be present, and because they can therefore be said to survive even if they have died. We can find this suggestion in the work of John Hick, who asks us to imagine certain extraordinary states of affairs:

> We begin with the idea of someone suddenly ceasing to exist at a certain place in this world and the next instant coming into existence at another place which is not contiguous with the first. He has not moved from A to B by making a path through the intervening space but has disappeared at A and reappeared at B. For example, at some learned gathering in London one of the company suddenly and inexplicably disappears and the next moment an exact 'replica' of him suddenly and inexplicably appears at some comparable meeting in New York. The person who appears in New York is exactly similar, as to both bodily and mental characteristics, to the person who disappears in London. There is continuity of memory, complete similarity of bodily features, including fingerprints, hair and eye coloration and stomach contents, and also of beliefs, habits and mental propensities. In fact there is everything that would lead us to identify the one who appeared with the one who disappeared, except continuous occupancy of space.[28]

Hick thinks that this is a logically possible sequence of events. He also thinks that the person who appears in New York could be thought of as the same as the one who disappeared in London. The person in America, says Hick, may act and behave just as we expect the person in London to. He may be as baffled by appearing in New York as anybody else. Yet his friends and relations may stoutly and reasonably declare that he is the person who went to the meeting in London.

But, Hick continues, suppose now that the sequence of events is slightly different.

> Let us suppose that the event in London is not a sudden and inexplicable disappearance, and indeed not a disappearance at all, but a sudden death. Only, at the moment when the individual dies a 'replica' of him as he was at the moment before his death, and complete with memory up to that instant, comes into existence in New York.[29]

Faced with the first sequence of events, it is reasonable, Hick says, to extend our concept of 'the same person' to cover the strange new case. Faced with this second sequence, could we not be justified in doing so again? Hick argues that we could:

Even with the corpse on our hands it would still, I suggest, be an extension of 'same person' required and warranted by the postulated facts to say that the one who died has been miraculously re-created in New York. The case would, to be sure, be even odder than the previous one because of the existence of the dead body in London contemporaneously with the living person in New York. And yet, striking though the oddness undoubtedly is, it does not amount to a logical impossibility. Once again we must imagine some of the deceased's colleagues going to New York to interview the person who has suddenly appeared there. He would perfectly remember them and their meeting, be interested in what had happened, and be as amazed and dumbfounded about it as anyone else; and he would perhaps be worried about the possible legal complications if he should return to London to claim his property and so on. Once again, I believe, they would soon find them- selves thinking of him and treating him as the same person as the dead Londoner. Once again the factors inclining us to say that the one who died and the one who appeared are the same person would far outweigh the factors inclining us to say that they are different people. Once again we should have to extend our usage of 'same person' to cover the new case.[30]

But suppose we now consider another story. Suppose you give me a lethal dose of poison. This, of course, does not make me very happy. But, you say: 'Don't worry. I've arranged for a replica of you to appear. The replica will seem to have all your memories. He will be convinced that he is you. And he will look exactly like you. He will even have your fingerprints.' Should I be relieved? Speaking for myself, I would not be in the slightest bit relieved. Knowing that a *replica* of myself will be enjoying himself somewhere is not to know that *I* shall be doing so. For the continued existence of a person, more is required than replication. More is required than replication even when it comes to the continued existence of unambiguously physical objects. You will not get much money from art dealers if you offer them copies of paintings by Turner or Rembrandt. They want the original paintings. They want objects which are physically continuous with what Turner or Rembrandt worked on in their studios.

It might be said, however, that I can survive the death of my body simply by coming to inhabit a different body. As I noted in Chapter 1, something like this possibility is entertained by John Locke as he dis- tinguishes between 'same man' and 'same person'. A person, says Locke, is not the same as a man. A man, for Locke, is a living organism.

Men are biological entities. But persons, says Locke, are not. On Locke's account, persons might move from body to body. As Locke puts it:

> Should the soul of a prince, carrying with it the consciousness of the prince's past life, enter and inform the body of a cobbler, as soon as deserted by his own soul, everyone sees he would be the same person with the prince, accountable only for the prince's actions . . . Had I the same consciousness that I saw the ark and Noah's flood, as that I saw an overflowing of the Thames last winter, I could no more doubt that I who write this now, that saw the Thames overflowed last winter, and that viewed the flood at the general deluge, was the same self . . . than that I who write this am the same myself now whilst I write . . . that I was yesterday.[31]

As many have pointed out, however, this position fairly bristles with difficulties. For one thing, it supposes that personal identity over time is constituted by psychological matters such as the fact that I seem to remember certain things. But, as Joseph Butler (1692–1752) observed against Locke, memory *presupposes* personal identity and cannot, by itself, constitute it.[32] Another problem with what Locke says is that it leads to an impossible conclusion. As Thomas Reid notes, on Locke's view we get the curious result that

> a man may be, and at the same time not be, the person that did a particular action. Suppose a brave officer to have been flogged when a boy at school for robbing an orchard, to have taken a standard from the enemy in his first campaign, and to have been made a general in advanced life; suppose, also, which must be admitted to be possible, that, when he took the standard, he was conscious of his having been flogged at school, and that, when made a general, he was conscious of his taking the standard, but had absolutely lost the consciousness of his flogging. These things being supposed, it follows . . . that he who was flogged at school is the same person who took the standard, and that he who took the standard is the same person who was made a general. Whence it follows, if there be any truth in logic, that the general is the same person with him who was flogged at school. But the general's consciousness does not reach so far back as his flogging; therefore . . . he is not the person who was flogged. Therefore the general is, and at the same time is not, the same person with him who was flogged at school.[33]

So perhaps we may suggest that, if I am a bodily individual, I will survive my death only by being physically continuous with what I am now. When it comes to life after death, the key question is 'Can what we are now be physically continuous with what is there after our death?' In an obvious sense, of course, it can. The corpses that people bury are physically continuous with the bodies of living things that have died. But can these corpses become living human beings again?

An obvious answer to this question is 'No. Human beings are not naturally capable of rising from their graves as living people.' People are naturally capable of walking, running, singing, and shouting. But they cannot rise from their graves of their own accord. Indeed, we might argue, people who die cease to be human beings. A human corpse is not a *kind* of human being, as caucasian or oriental people are human beings of particular kinds. A human corpse, we may say, is what *used to be* a human being and is now something else.[34] Yet it does not therefore follow that people cannot be raised from their graves. For what if there exists an omnipotent God? Can such a God not bring the dead back to life as materially continuous with the individuals that they were before death? You might say that God cannot do this since the bodies of the dead are transformed into other things over time and since, for many people, at least, there is nothing physical left for God to raise. But physical transformation is compatible with material continuity.

This point is well made by Peter Geach. He believes that we cannot rightly identify someone living 'again' with someone who died unless material conditions of identity are fulfilled. There must, says Geach, 'be some one–one relation of material continuity between the old body and the new'.[35] But need there be material identity? Must a human being's body at time 6 be exactly the same body as the person possessed at time 1? Geach's answer is 'No'. An old man's body, he says, need not contain a single atom of the body he had at birth. But, Geach adds, this does not mean that the man's identity over time is not constituted by physical continuity.

> If it is a difference of matter that makes two bodies different, it may seem to follow that a body can maintain its identity over time only if at least some identifiable matter remains in it all the time; otherwise it is no more the same body than the wine in a cask that is continuously emptied and refilled is the same wine. But . . . it does not follow, if difference in a certain respect at a certain time suffices to show non-identity, that sameness in that respect over a period of time is necessary to identity.[36]

Imagine a pair of socks which start as made of silk and which end as made of wool because of many mendings. The socks are the same socks at the end of the day. They have not turned into two distinct pairs of socks. And, so Geach implies, my body over time might be the same body even though it is made up of what it never contained at some earlier time.[37]

If Geach is right, then the physical transformation of people's bodies (or corpses) need not imply that they cannot continue to exist and be sufficient to secure personal identity at some point. And we might wonder whether an omnipotent God could not arrange for people who have died to be raised again as physically continuous with what they were throughout their lives. This train of thought, however, is useless if there are no grounds for supposing that anything is omnipotent. It does not constitute a reason for believing in life after death. So I should now say something about reasons that philosophers have given for thinking that we actually do survive death.

Reasons for Believing in Life after Death

Two famous reasons appear in Plato's *Phaedo*. The others basically boil down to the following: (1) people must survive death since they are incorporeal; (2) moral considerations support belief in life after death; and (3) there is empirical evidence for human life after death.

(a) Plato's arguments

The discussion of life after death in the *Phaedo* starts with the question 'Does a man's soul exist when he has died?' Socrates argues that opposites come from opposites in the case of things which have an opposite. Thus: the beautiful and the ugly, the just and the unjust, the larger and the smaller, the stronger and the weaker, the faster and the slower, the better and the worse. So, says Socrates, a thing comes to be alive from being dead. For the opposite of living is being dead.

> 'You say, don't you, that being dead is opposite to living?'
> 'I do.'
> 'And that they come to be from each other?'
> 'Yes.'

'Then what is it that comes to be from that which is living?'
'That which is dead.'
'And what comes to be from that which is dead?'
'I must admit that it's that which is living.'
'Then it's from those that are dead . . . that living things and living
people are born.'
'Apparently.'
'Then our souls do exist in Hades.'[38]

To this argument, Plato adds a second. He suggests that, if everything which came to be dead remained dead, then everything would end up dead. If everyone who went to sleep did not awake, then all would be asleep. If everyone who died did not come to life from death, all would be dead. So 'there really is such a thing as coming to life again, living people *are* born from the dead, and the souls of the dead exist'.[39]

Ingenious though these arguments may seem, however, they are surely misguided. Things may have opposites, but it does not follow that, if something comes to be, there is something which is its opposite from which it comes. Nor does it follow that, if something ceases to be, something comes to be which is opposite to something existing earlier. As one commentator on Plato puts it:

> Life and existence, it may be reasonably be held, both begin for a living thing at birth or conception. Yet [Plato's first argument for survival after death] treats the predicate 'alive' as if it stood for an attribute capable of being acquired by an antecedently existing subject, and 'birth' as if it were something undergone by such a subject, rather than the coming into being of something that did not previously exist . . . If 'death' consists in a living thing's ceasing to exist, then when someone passes from being alive to being dead, he will not, in the latter state, enjoy discarnate existence, but will have ceased to exist altogether.[40]

As for Plato's second argument, it does not work because it mistakenly assumes that, if all who have lived come to be dead, it follows that everyone has come to be dead. It is true that, if everyone who has gone to sleep has not awoken, then everyone who has gone to sleep has not awoken. But it does not follow that nobody is awake. And although it is true that all who have died have died and (maybe) do not exist, it does not follow that everyone has died and is dead or non-existent. Those who have died may constitute a given number which is added to as people come to be born and die. But there need be no limit to the number.

(b) From 'I am incorporeal' to 'I survive death'?

The argument that people must survive death since they are incorporeal is straightforward and can be simply stated as follows:

> How is it that things pass out of existence? By means of a dissolution of parts which usually comes about because of the action of some exterior force. Thus, for example, a human body perishes because something harms it, thereby causing it to break up in some way. The human person, on the other hand, is not to be identified with a body. The human self is really a non-material and unextended entity. But if this is the case, then it cannot pass out of existence by means of a dissolution of parts. And since it is not a material thing, it is hard to see how something can exert any force on it so as to bring about its destruction.[41]

But this argument is very weak. For one thing, it presupposes that people are disembodied selves, and we have now seen reason for questioning that view. But even allowing that the view is correct, the argument is flimsy. For it assumes that something can only cease to exist because it undergoes physical deterioration or because something else acts on it physically. Yet why should we suppose that something can cease to exist only because it has parts to be broken up? And why should we believe that something can cease to exist only because something physical has acted on it? Insofar as the argument from incorporeality to survival is cogent, its strength lies in the fact that its defenders, given their view of human persons, need not conclude that familiar physical processes prove that people perish at (physical) death. But the argument does not show that incorporeal things cannot cease to exist. It might be thought to show that incorporeal people are naturally incorruptible. But it does not show that they cannot but live forever.[42]

(c) From morality to life after death?

A famous moral argument for life after death comes from Kant. In the last chapter we saw how he moves from moral obligation to the existence of God. But he also holds that moral obligation has implications for life after death. For, in his view:

To bring about the highest good in the world is the necessary object of a will determinable by the moral law. In such a will, however, the *complete adequacy* of attitudes to the moral law is the supreme condition of the highest good. This adequacy must therefore be just as possible as its object, because it is contained in the same command to further this object. Complete adequacy of the will to the moral law, however, is *holiness*, a perfection of which no rational being in the world of sense is capable at any point of time in his existence. Since this adequacy is nonetheless demanded as practically necessary, it can be encountered only in a progression proceeding *ad infinitum* toward that complete adequacy; and according to principles of pure practical reason it is necessary to assume such a practical advance as the real object of our will.

This infinite progression, however, is possible only on the presupposition of an *existence* and personality—of the same rational being—continuing *ad infinitum* (which is called the immortality of the soul). Therefore the highest good is practically possible only on the presupposition of the immortality of the soul, and hence this immortality, as linked inseparably with the moral law, is a *postulate* of pure practical reason.[43]

But this line of argument also fails to provide good reason for believing in life after death. I may say that I ought to do certain things, and I may regret that I cannot do them this side of the grave. But if I really cannot do them, then it is wrong to say that I ought to do them. Kant, of course, will reply that I can actually do what I ought even though I cannot do so in this life. According to Kant, the existence of God guarantees that the highest good will finally be realized. As I argued in Chapter 12, however, Kant's argument for God as ensuring the realization of the highest good is a poor one. If we could rely on there being a God to ensure that the highest good is realized, then we might reasonably hold that human beings will survive their deaths as part of the grand realization. But Kant's case for saying that there is such a God is not convincing.

Can it be restated so as to appear convincing? Some would argue that it can, suggesting that morality is pointless if there is no life after death. In the words of Joseph Prabhu:

The seriousness of our endeavour to shape our lives according to ideals of truth, wisdom, love and compassion, and all that they entail in terms of the development of virtue, together with the sense of inadequacy in our actual achievement, warrant the presumption that a single life cannot be all that we are destined to have. To grant that would make a mockery of our moral experience.[44]

But if there is any point in being moral in this life, then morality *ipso facto* has a point without reference to life after death. And for many people, of course, morality makes perfectly good sense in thoroughly worldly terms. Think back to Geach's position touched on in the previous chapter.

(d) Empirical reasons for life after death

Yet should we not at least concede that some ordinary, human experience suggests that life after death is a reality? You might say that we certainly should not since experience firmly shows that death is the end of people. Our graveyards, you might note, are filled with empirical evidence proving this fact. But some have suggested that this evidence is not enough to warrant the conclusion that physical death is our end. And some have held that there is empirical evidence which shows that it is not. Here I am thinking of two lines of argument. According to the first, psychical research gives us reason for thinking that people survive death. According to the second, there is at least one instance of someone having been raised from the dead.

(i) Psychical research   People often regard psychical research as a hobby for cranks. But some well-known philosophers have taken it seriously, especially when considering cases of 'mediums' claiming to convey 'messages' from the dead.[45] Yet, does such testimony give us good reason to think that people survive their death? Psychical researchers have assembled a vast amount of data which I cannot note and discuss in this book. But I can briefly offer some comments for you to reflect on should you choose to look in detail at what they have to offer.

Let us suppose that a medium conveys a 'message' purportedly coming from Fred, who died and was buried a year ago. Let us also suppose (a) that the 'message' squares with what Fred might be expected to say and (b) that its content contains information which could not be independently known to the medium. Should we therefore conclude that Fred is alive and communicating with us? There are reasons for supposing that we should not.

For one thing, 'what Fred might be expected to say' is not an expression which serves to identify what is said as the words of any particular person. You might expect Fred to say such and such; but the saying of such and such does not guarantee that the speaker is Fred.

Then again, the fact that words uttered by mediums include information that they are not independently likely to know does not imply that they are conveying the knowledge of a dead person seeking to share what he or she knows. If we can identify the words as expressing what is true, then we must have knowledge with respect to what they are expressing. And we can have such knowledge without being dead. Conveying what someone else knows does not imply that the someone else in question is deceased.

More importantly, however, what would we be supposing if we thought that the words of a medium were evidence for Fred's continued existence? Given Fred's funeral, we would presumably be supposing that Fred exists disembodied. But can something disembodied be Fred? If it can, then maybe Fred can communicate with us via a medium. But what if Fred cannot be disembodied? In that case, the 'evidence' of mediums, whatever it amounts to, cannot be evidence that those who have died are still alive. It cannot be evidence for the continued existence of people.

In other words, psychical research, whatever its merits, cannot reasonably be viewed as empirical evidence for life after death unless we suppose that people are non-material objects. Those who appeal to such research as empirical evidence for life after death never suppose that it is evidence for people existing as creatures of flesh and blood. They always take it to be evidence for the existence of people considered as immaterial or 'spiritual'. But can we intelligibly think about people in these terms? Earlier in this chapter I suggested why we cannot. And if my arguments are cogent, then psychical research provides no evidence for life after death.[46]

(ii) The dead who have been raised   Yet, what about the claim that someone has been raised from the dead? Might we think of that as providing empirical grounds for belief in life after death? If we are right to suppose that at least one person has been raised from the dead, we would at least have reason for thinking that death is not necessarily the end for us. If one human being has been raised from the dead, then, perhaps, others can be as well. But do we have reason for thinking that anyone has been raised from the dead?

Those who think that we do chiefly appeal to New Testament accounts of the resurrection of Jesus, which, they suggest, is a reason to hope for our own.[47] But are the biblical accounts reliable here? Do they rationally warrant the belief that someone has been raised from the dead? Many people would say that they do not, since one or all of the following arguments are sound:

1. If New Testament accounts of Jesus's resurrection are true, then miracles occur. But it is not reasonable to believe that miracles occur.

2. The New Testament accounts of Jesus's resurrection do not present a single, clear picture of this and should, therefore, be discounted as evidence concerning it.

3. To believe that Jesus was raised from the dead on the basis of biblical accounts would mean believing that he was raised only on the basis of what people have reported. But we should not hold beliefs simply on the say so of others.

But these are not decisive arguments. As I suggested in Chapter 11, it need not be unreasonable to suppose that miracles have occurred. And, as I argued in Chapter 2, testimony is not to be discarded as no good basis for reasonable beliefs. Nor is it obvious that the New Testament fails to present an intelligible and coherent testimony to Jesus's resurrection.[48] Its accounts of this doubtless raise many difficult questions. But, unless we have prior reason for discounting these accounts, we need not view them as essentially ambiguous or lacking in content.

Notice, however, that even if all that is so (and many would deny that it is), nothing strictly follows about the fate of anyone other than Jesus. New Testament writers argue from belief in his resurrection to belief in the resurrection of others.[49] But not on purely philosophical grounds. Or, if that is not quite the right way to put it, they proceed with reference to a set of beliefs concerning Jesus and his teaching, beliefs which they take on trust. They do not argue: 'Jesus was raised from the dead, so it follows that all people will be raised from the dead.' And it is just as well that they do not argue in this way since that argument clearly does not work.[50]

The Desirability of Life after Death

I have so far suggested that life after death is possible. I have also suggested that certain arguments in favour of it are open to question. In conclusion, I would like to say something about a problem concerning belief in life after death which is rarely considered but which evidently interests some people. For, suppose it could be shown that there is reason to believe in life after death. Would that be good news? Should it cause us to rejoice? And would it mean that human beings have something to look forward to?

It may seem strange to wonder whether the knowledge that we shall survive death would count as good news. Is life not intrinsically desirable? Who would choose to pass out of existence? Is not the prospect of extinction terrible? But lots of people wish for death while also believing that this will be the end of them. My first Philosophy teacher committed suicide, though he strongly disbelieved in life after death. And it is far from obvious that continued existence is necessarily desirable. Suppose I am frozen and that I continue to exist forever in unconscious suspended animation. Would that be an attractive end for me?

Some writers have held that any kind of existence is better than extinction. A good example is Miguel de Unamuno (1864–1936). 'For myself', he confesses, 'I can say that as a youth, and even as a child, I remained unmoved when shown the most moving pictures of hell, for even then nothing appeared to me quite so horrible as nothingness itself.'[51] Elsewhere he declares: 'I do not want to die—no; I neither want to die nor do I want to want to die; I want to live for ever and ever and ever. I want this "I" to live—this poor "I" that I am and that I feel myself to be here and now, and therefore the problem of the duration of my soul, of my own soul, tortures me.'[52] But not everyone would speak in such terms. They would say that survival after death is cause for rejoicing only if it brings with it a life worth living. People who believe in life after death have, of course, rarely spoken about it as nothing but the alternative to extinction. They have referred to it as something to look forward to. But is it really worth having?

Not, perhaps, on the view that people survive death as non-bodily things. This point is well made by Bernard Williams in dialogue with

H. D. Lewis. According to Lewis, we can believe in a non-bodily life after death if we think of it either as involving experiences like those we have when dreaming or as a state of living in 'a world of thoughts alone'.[53] Referring to Lewis's first alternative, Williams replies:

> [This] makes the whole of future life into a kind of delusion. It is very like perceiving . . . but it obviously is not perceiving, in just the same way that dreaming is not perceiving and it seems to me that one thing I do not want to do is to spend the rest of eternity in a delusive simulacrum of perceptual activity. That just seems to me a rather lowering prospect. Why should a future of error be of interest to me?

And referring to Lewis's 'world of thoughts alone', Williams continues:

> The alternative was the slightly higher-minded alternative, that [life after death] might consist of purely intellectual activity, which of course many philosophers have seen as the ideal future. I can see why *they* might be particularly interested in it; others might be less so . . . I mean, suppose that the prospects of Heaven or the future life are those of intellectual contemplation, and I am a jolly, good hearted fun-loving sensual character from the seaside.[54]

So, if life after death is something to look forward to, it might have to involve more than is possible on the picture of it provided by a theory of a disembodied future. But it would also have to involve more than bodily resurrection, if that is understood as nothing but the continuation of our present mode of life. For some people's lives are not all that desirable. Some people are beautiful, healthy, intelligent, and happy. But others are ugly, sick, stupid, and suffering.

Yet this does not mean that people whose lives are now a burden cannot become transformed. Suppose we continue with the notion of life after death as conceived in terms of resurrection. That would mean continuing with the model of life after death as a continued physical life for the people who have died. Now, many people suffer from various disadvantages in this life. But it is surely possible that these disadvantages could be removed without the people who suffer from them ceasing to be human beings. For, as long as we are dealing with a human being, we are dealing with something that could, logically speaking, be relieved of its disadvantages without ceasing to be human. Take, for example, the extreme disadvantage which follows from severe brain damage. Let us suppose that people suffer such damage but continue to live. We might say that their lives are not worth living. We might call them 'human vegetables'. But we might hesitate to say that they are no longer human beings. To become a 'human vegetable' is not to become a real vegetable. And if 'human vegetables' were relieved of their disadvantages, then it would make sense to say that they would be restored to full human life.

Reflecting along these lines, we might reasonably hold that life after death, conceived of in terms of resurrection, could be attractive. We might also argue that life after death (whether bodily or not) could be desirable insofar as it unites us to God. Theologians often tell us that some of the dead share in the life of God. And, if these theologians are right, then life after death might be thought of as positively agreeable. But I cannot now pursue matters further when it comes to theology and what this might be thought of as contributing to our thinking with respect to a life to come. That task would oblige me to turn to topics which do not belong in a short introduction to philosophy of religion. Such topics are full of interest, even for philosophers. But they are matters for a different book than this one.

NOTES

1. Boswell is most famous for his association with Samuel Johnson (1709–84), whose biography he wrote.

2. James Boswell, 'An Account of my Last Interview with David Hume, Esq.'. This text is reprinted in Norman Kemp Smith (ed.), *David Hume: Dialogues Concerning Natural Religion* (Indianapolis, IN, 1947).

3. Note, however, that belief in life after death is absent in many Old Testament texts. It appears only to have arisen fairly late on in the history of Jewish thinking. Hence, for example, John L. McKenzie reports: 'It is generally held by scholars that no hope of individual survival after death is expressed in the OT before some of its latest passages, which were probably written in the 2nd cent. BC.' See Raymond E. Brown, Joseph A. Fitzmyer, and Roland E. Murphy, *The Jerome Biblical Commentary* (Englewood Cliffs, NJ, 1968), vol. 2, p. 765.

4. John 11: 25.

5. David Gallop (ed.), *Plato's Phaedo* (Oxford, 1975), pp. 69 f.

6. René Descartes, *Meditation* VI. I quote from John Cottingham (trans. and ed.), *René Descartes: Meditations on First Philosophy* (Cambridge, 1986), p. 54.

7. Peter Geach, *God and the Soul* (London, 1969), p. 29.

8. See Brown, *et al.*, *The Jerome Biblical Commentary*, vol. 2, pp. 746 f. and 765 f.; Walter Eichrodt, *Theology of the Old Testament* (London, 1967), vol. II, ch. 16 and 19; Edmond Jacob, *Theology of the Old Testament* (New York, 1958), Part II, ch. 3; and Hans Walter Wolff, *Anthropology of the Old Testament* (Philadelphia, PA, 1974). In the Old Testament itself, see Daniel 12: 2 and Isaiah 27: 19.

9. Cf. 1 Corinthians 15. Note, however, that there are a few New Testament passages which can be read as teaching that there is non-bodily human survival. See John W. Cooper, *Body and Soul and Life Everlasting: Biblical Anthropology and the Monism-Dualism Debate* (Grand Rapids, MI, 1989), pp. 119 ff.

10. 1 Corinthians 15: 35–44. At one point in his discussion, St Paul refers to the resurrected body as 'spiritual' rather than 'physical'. But he is not here denying that it is material. He is insisting that it is full of God's living power and not subject to constraints which affect our lives in the present. Cf. C. K. Barrett, *A Commentary on the First Epistle to the Corinthians* (New York, 1968), p. 379; Jerome Murphy O'Connor, *1 Corinthians* (Wilmington, DE, 1979), pp. 146 ff.; William F. Orr and James Arthur Walther, *1 Corinthians* (New York, 1976), pp. 346 f.; and Herman Ridderbos, *Paul: An Outline of His Theology* (Grand Rapids, MI, 1975), pp. 539 ff.

11. H. D. Lewis, *Philosophy of Religion* (London, 1965), p. 286.

12. Ibid., p. 282. Cf. id., *The Self and Immortality* (London, 1973), pp. 62 and 68.

13. Sydney Shoemaker and Richard Swinburne, *Personal Identity* (Oxford, 1984), pp. 23 f.

14. Swinburne has defended this argument in a number of places, including 'Dualism Intact', *Faith and Philosophy* 13 (1996).

15. We might understand the expression 'Substance dualism' to refer to a view of people (such as that of Aquinas) which takes them to consist of distinct elements (soul and body) without also taking them to be distinct from their bodies. But the expression is most commonly used to refer to what I have just described Descartes, Lewis, and Swinburne as endorsing. And, to simplify matters, that is how I understand it here.

16. 'Cartesian' is the adjectival form of the name 'Descartes'.

17. Ludwig Wittgenstein, *Philosophical Investigations*, trans. G. E. M. Anscombe (Oxford, 1968), p. 222.

18. Some philosophers have suggested that there are conscious experiences which we can identify introspectively as being what it is like to have such

experiences. For an excellent demolition of this position, see P. M. S. Hacker, 'Is There Anything it is Like to be a Bat?' *Philosophy* 77 (2002).

19. Wittgenstein, *Philosophical Investigations*, §303.

20. See ibid., §293.

21. Jaegwon Kim, *Philosophy of Mind* (Boulder, CO, 1996), p. 27.

22. *Meditation* VI (trans. Cottingham) p. 59.

23. Norman Malcolm, 'Descartes's Proof that his Essence is Thinking', in Willis Doney (ed.), *Descartes* (London, 1968), p. 329.

24. Gilbert Ryle, *The Concept of Mind* (London, 1949). This book is generally regarded as a milestone in twentieth-century philosophy of mind.

25. Geach, *God and the Soul*.

26. Cf. C. V. Borst (ed.), *The Mind/Brain Identity Thesis* (London, 1970).

27. Hence, for example, Aquinas is no supporter of Behaviourism or the Identity Thesis; but he does not think of people as essentially incorporeal. See below.

28. John Hick, *Death and Eternal Life* (London, 1979), p. 280.

29. Ibid., p. 284.

30. Ibid.

31. John Locke, *An Essay Concerning Human Understanding*, ed. Peter H. Nidditch (Oxford, 1975), Book II, ch. 27.

32. Joseph Butler, 'Of Personal Identity', in Joseph Butler, *The Analogy of Religion* (Oxford, 1897).

33. Thomas Reid, *Essays on the Intellectual Powers of Man* (Edinburgh, 1785), Essay VI, ch. 5.

34. We do, in fact, work on this assumption. You would (presumably) worry about my burying people alive. But you do not (presumably) have comparable worries when it comes to undertakers burying the dead.

35. Geach, *God and the Soul*, p. 26. Geach, therefore, has no time for Hick-type replica theories of human survival.

36. Ibid., pp. 26 f.

37. You might say that if a sock you held in your hands a year ago (call it X) was made of silk, and if one you hold now (call it Y) is made of wool, then X cannot be the same sock as Y. But it could be. Given material continuity between X and Y, there is no reason to speak of a new individual thing having come into existence even though X drastically changes to become what we call Y.

38. Gallop (ed.), *Plato's Phaedo*, pp. 17 ff.

39. Ibid., p. 19.

40. Ibid., pp. 105 f.

41. For an argument along these lines, see J. M. E. McTaggart, *Some Dogmas of Religion* (London, 1906), pp. 108 f.

42. Aquinas argues that the human soul, being immaterial, is naturally incorruptible. But he does not therefore think that it cannot be reduced to non-existence by God. Cf. *Summa Theologiae*, Ia, 75, 6.

43. Immanuel Kant, *Critique of Practical Reason*, ed. Werner S. Pluhar (Indianapolis, IN, 2002), p. 155.

44. Joseph Prabhu, 'The Idea of Reincarnation', in Steven T. Davis (ed.), *Death and Afterlife* (London, 1989), p. 66.

45. Cf. C. D. Broad, *Lectures on Psychical Research* (London, 1962).

46. If my arguments are not cogent, then, of course, my present conclusion does not follow. Is it, however, true that psychical research provides evidence for life after death even on the view that people can exist immaterially? For discussions of this question allowing for the possibility of a negative answer, see John Hick, *Philosophy of Religion* (4th edn., Englewood Cliffs, NJ, 1990), pp. 125 ff., and William L. Rowe, *Philosophy of Religion: An Introduction* (3rd edn., Belmont, CA, 2001), pp. 140 ff.

47. Cf. St Paul in 1 Corinthians 15: 1–12.

48. Cf. William Lane Craig, *Assessing the New Testament Evidence for the Historicity of the Resurrection of Jesus* (Lewiston, ME, 1989). See also Brian Davies, 'The Resurrection and Christian Belief', in Paul Burns and John Cumming (eds.), *The Bible Now* (Dublin, 1981).

49. Cf. Romans 8: 11; Philippians 3: 20–1; 1 Thessalonians 4: 14.

50. To labour the obvious: from 'Such and such is true of person P', we cannot logically infer that the same such and such is true of all people.

51. Miguel de Unamuno, *The Tragic Sense of Life* (London, 1962), p. 28. A novelist, poet, and essayist, and sometimes described as an 'existentialist', Unamuno is a significant figure in the history of Spanish thinking.

52. Ibid., p. 60.

53. H. D. Lewis, *Persons and Life After Death* (London, 1978), pp. 53 f.

54. Ibid., pp. 69 and 72.

FURTHER READING

The topic of life after death quickly leads one to some basic questions in philosophy of mind—questions like 'What is the relation between mind and body?' and 'In what does personal identity consist?' In thinking about life after death, therefore, you might be helped by some good introductions to these questions. Ones especially worth recommending include: Anthony Kenny, *The Character of Mind* (Oxford, 1989); Jaegwon Kim, *Philosophy of Mind* (Boulder, CO, 1996); Colin McGinn, *The Character of Mind* (2nd edn., Oxford, 1997); John Heil, *Philosophy of Mind: A Contemporary Introduction* (London and New York, 1998); Jenny Teichman, *The Mind and the Soul: An Introduction to the Philosophy of Mind* (London and New York, 1974); and Godfrey Vesey, *Personal Identity: A Philosophical Analysis* (Ithaca, NY, 1974).

For good collections of essays (historical and contemporary) on the philosophy of mind and personal identity, see John Perry (ed.), *Personal Identity* (Berkeley, Los Angeles, and London, 1975); Amelie Rorty (ed.), *The Identities of Persons* (Berkeley, CA, 1976); David Rosenthal (ed.), *The Nature of Mind* (New York and Oxford, 1991); and Richard Warner and Tadeusz Szubka (ed.), *The Mind-Body Problem* (Oxford, and Cambridge, MA, 1994).

For trenchant defences of Cartesian dualism, see H. D. Lewis, *The Elusive Mind* (London and New York, 1969); id., *The Elusive Self* (London and Basingstoke, 1982); and Richard Swinburne, *The Evolution of the Soul* (rev. edn., Oxford, 1997). For general works on the philosophy of the human person taking a non-Cartesian line, see D. M. Armstrong, *The Mind-Body Problem: An Opinionated Introduction* (Boulder, CO, and Oxford, 1999); David Braine, *The Human Person* (London, 1993); and Gilbert Ryle, *The Concept of Mind* (Harmondsworth, 1963). In my discussion of Cartesian substance dualism I have drawn on the thinking of Wittgenstein. For clear introductions to Wittgenstein, see Robert J. Fogelin, *Wittgenstein* (2nd edn., London and New York, 1987) and Anthony Kenny, *Wittgenstein* (Harmondsworth, 1973). Much of Wittgenstein's importance to philosophy of mind derives from what he says in his *Philosophical Investigations*. An excellent introduction to this work is Marie McGinn, *Wittgenstein and the Philosophical Investigations* (London and New York, 1997). For a sympathetic introduction to Wittgenstein's philosophy of mind written with an eye on religious belief, see Fergus Kerr, *Theology After Wittgenstein* (2nd edn., Oxford, 1997).

For useful collections of essays dealing specifically with life after death, see Michael Baur (ed.), *Person, Soul, and Immortality* (Proceedings of the American Catholic Philosophical Society, vol. 75, 2001); Paul Edwards (ed.), *Immortality* (New York, 1992); Steven T. Davis (ed.), *Death and Afterlife* (London, 1989); and Antony Flew (ed.), *Body, Mind, and Death* (New York, 1964).

Some notable book-length treatments of life after death (adopting a variety of positions) are: Paul Badham and Linda Badham, *Immortality or Extinction?* (London, 1982); C. J. Ducasse, *Belief in Life After Death* (Springfield, IL, 1961); John Hick, *Death and Eternal Life* (London, 1979); Hans Küng, *Eternal Life* (New York, 1984); H. D. Lewis, *The Self and Immortality* (London and Basingstoke, 1973); H. D. Lewis, *Persons and Life After Death* (London and Basingstoke, 1978); Terence Penelhum, *Survival and Disembodied Existence* (London, 1970); Terence Penelhum, *Immortality* (Belmont, CA, 1973); John Perry, *Personal Identity and Immortality* (Indianapolis, IN, 1979); D. Z. Phillips, *Death and Immortality* (London and Basingstoke, 1970); Bruce Reichenbach, *Is Man the Phoenix? A Study of Immortality* (Grand Rapids, MI, 1978); and Simon Tugwell, *Human Immortality and the Redemption of Death* (London, 1990).

Belief in life after death has sometimes taken the form of belief in reincarnation. Considerations of space have prevented me from introducing and discussing this notion in this book. For sophisticated discussions of reincarnation, however, see Paul Edwards, *Reincarnation: A Critical Examination* (London, 1996), and Bruce Reichenbach, *The Law of Karma* (London, 1990).

For an introduction to issues and questions raised by belief in Jesus's resurrection, the text to start with is Stephen T. Davis, Daniel Kendall, and Gerald O'Collins (eds.), *The Resurrection: An Interdisciplinary Symposium on the Resurrection of Jesus* (Oxford, 1997). For a philosophical debate on the resurrection of Jesus, see Garry R. Habermas and Antony Flew, *Did Jesus Rise from the Dead?* (San Francisco, CA, 1987). For a general study on the resurrection of Jesus written with an eye on philosophy, see Peter Carnley, *The Structure of Resurrection Belief* (Oxford, 1987).

QUESTIONS FOR DISCUSSION

1 How have people tended to think about life after death? Is there general agreement among religious believers when it comes to what life after death amounts to?

2 'I am not my body.' Discuss.

3 Does it make sense to say that we might witness our own funerals?

4 Are there thoughts which only I can think?

5 To what extent do our bodies conceal us from each other?

6 What conditions must be satisfied if I am to survive my death as something having a body?

7 What makes someone to be the same person at different times?

8 'The bodily resurrection of people is impossible or unlikely.' What might be said for and against this suggestion?

9 Is there any good reason to suppose that we shall survive death?

10 It has often been said that with death comes the vision of God (the 'beatific vision'). What might be meant by this claim? Does the claim make sense? Are there reasons for supposing that it is true?

GENERAL BIBLIOGRAPHY

A very helpful book on philosophy of religion in general is Philip L. Quinn and Charles Taliaferro, *A Companion to the Philosophy of Religion* (Oxford, 1997). See also Brian Davies (ed.), *Philosophy of Religion: A Guide to the Subject* (London, 1998). Note also that in *Philosophy of Religion: The Historic Approaches* (London, 1972), M. J. Charlesworth provides a useful survey of philosophical thinking about religion. A comparable volume to that of Charlesworth is J. Collins, *The Emergence of the Philosophy of Religion* (New Haven, CT, 1967).

There are several introductions to philosophy of religion currently available. Especially to be recommended are: William Abraham, *An Introduction to the Philosophy of Religion* (Englewood Cliffs, NJ, 1985); J. C. A. Gaskin, *The Quest for Eternity* (Harmondsworth, 1984); John Hick, *Philosophy of Religion* (4th edn., Englewood Cliffs, NJ, 1990); Anthony O'Hear, *Experience, Explanation and Faith* (London, 1984); Michael Peterson, William Hasker, Bruce Reichenbach, and David Basinger, *Reason and Religious Belief: An Introduction to the Philosophy of Religion* (3rd edn., Oxford and New York, 2003); Louis Pojman, *Philosophy of Religion* (Mountain View, CA, 2001); William L. Rowe, *Philosophy of Religion* (3rd edn., Belmont, CA., 2001); Charles Taliaferro, *Contemporary Philosophy of Religion* (Oxford, 1998); William J. Wainwright, *Philosophy of Religion* (2nd edn., Belmont, CA, 1998); and Keith Yandell, *Philosophy of Religion: A Contemporary Introduction* (London and New York, 1999).

There are also a number of philosophy of religion anthologies now in print. These include: Baruch Brody (ed.), *Readings in the Philosophy of Religion* (2nd edn., Englewood Cliffs, NJ, 1992); Steven M. Cahn and David Shatz (eds.), *Contemporary Philosophy of Religion* (Oxford, 1982); Brian Davies (ed.), *Philosophy of Religion: A Guide and Anthology* (Oxford, 2000); R. Douglas Geivett and Brendan Sweetman (eds.), *Contemporary Perspectives on Religious Epistemology* (New York and Oxford, 1992); Basil Mitchell (ed.), *The Philosophy of Religion* (Oxford, 1971); William Peterson, William Hasker, Bruce Reichenbach, and David Basinger (eds.), *Philosophy of Religion: Selected Readings* (New York and Oxford, 1996); Louis P. Pojman (ed.), *Philosophy of Religion: An Anthology* (2nd edn., Belmont, CA, 1993); William L. Rowe and William J. Wainwright (eds.), *Philosophy of Religion: Selected Readings* (3rd edn., New York and London, 1997); and Eleonore Stump and Michael J. Murray (eds.), *Philosophy of Religion: The Big Questions* (Oxford, 1999).

Your thinking about philosophy of religion will be greatly helped by some knowledge of the history of philosophy as a whole. Good introductions to this include F. C. Copleston, *A History of Philosophy*, 9 vols. (London, 1946–75) and the *Routledge History of Philosophy*, 10 vols. (London and New York, 1993–8). For recent one-volume guides, see Anthony Kenny, *A Brief History of Western Philosophy* (Oxford, 1998) and id. (ed.), *The Oxford Illustrated History of Western Philosophy* (Oxford, 1994).

Dictionaries of philosophy are often worth consulting, since many of them pack a lot of information into a small space. A major reference work is Paul Edwards (ed.), *The Encyclopedia of Philosophy* (London, 1967). Others include Robert Audi (ed.), *The Cambridge Dictionary of Philosophy* (2nd, edn., Cambridge, 1997) and Ted Honderich (ed.), *The Oxford Companion to Philosophy* (Oxford, 1995). A useful, short reference work is Thomas Mautner (ed.), *Dictionary of Philosophy* (Harmondsworth, 1997). See also Julian Baggini and Peter S. Fosl, *The Philosopher's Toolkit: A Compendium of Philosophical Concepts and Methods* (Oxford, 2003).

Several contemporary journals either specialize in philosophy of religion or contain much that is relevant to the subject. These include: *Faith and Philosophy*; *International Journal for Philosophy of Religion*; *International Philosophical Quarterly*; *New Blackfriars*; *Religious Studies*; *Sophia*; and *The Thomist*

The Internet is an excellent place to get information and help on philosophy (in general) and on philosophy of religion (in particular). Good sites from which to start browsing are:

- *The Blackwell Philosophy Resource Center* at **www.blackwellpublishers.co.uk/ philos/**

- *The Internet Encyclopedia of Philosophy* at **www.utm.edu/research/iep/**

- *The American Philosophical Association* at **www.udel.edu/apa/**

For further information on the Internet and philosophy, see Andrew T. Stull, *Philosophy on the Internet 1998–1999: A Prentice Hall Guide* (Upper Saddle River, NJ, 1999).

INDEX